Michelangelo
AND BEYOND

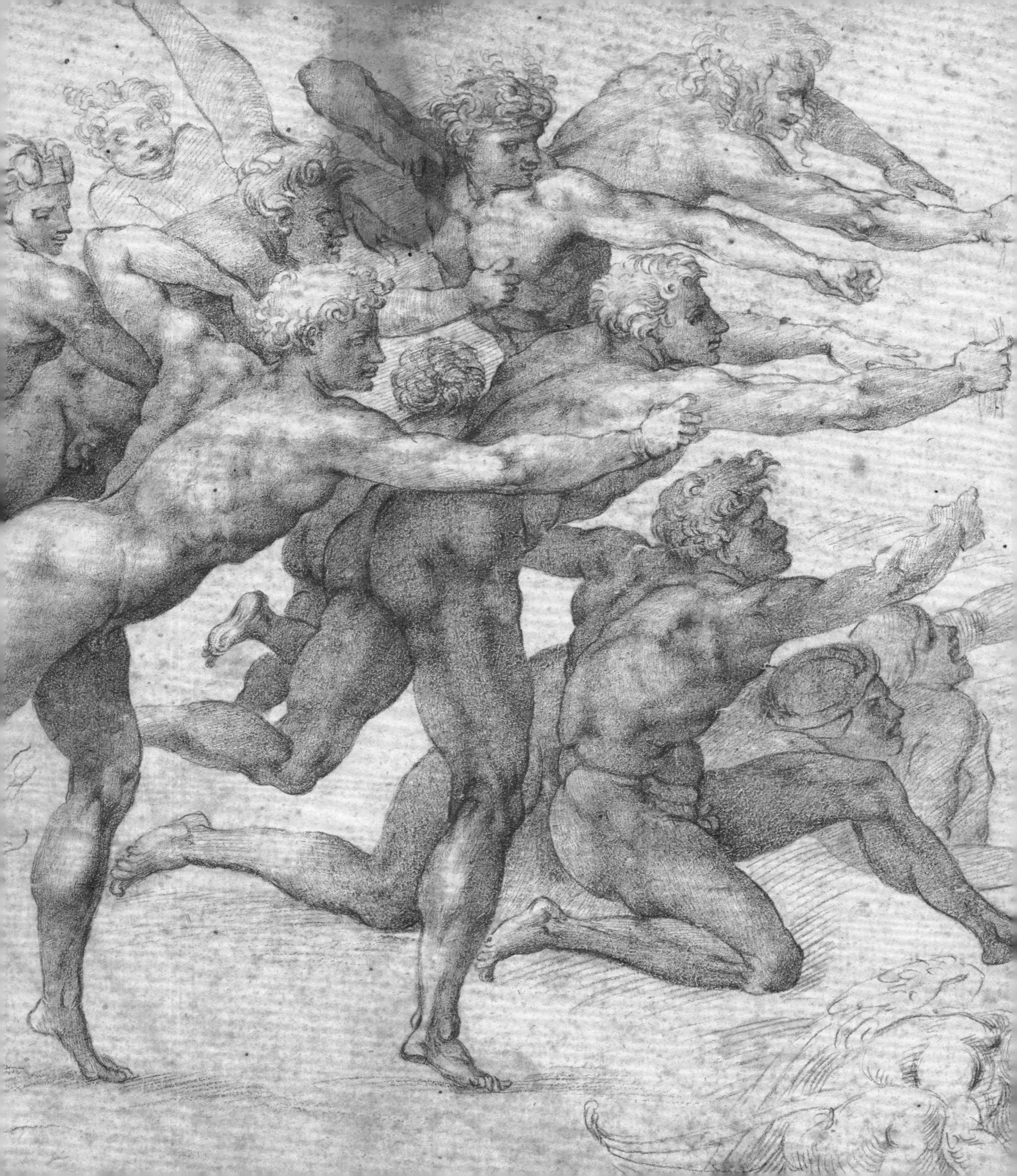

Michelangelo
AND BEYOND

Edited by
Eva Michel and Klaus Albrecht Schröder

With a Preface by Klaus Albrecht Schröder
and Texts by Elisabeth Dutz, Lydia Eder, Achim Gnann,
Constanze Johanna Malissa, Eva Michel, Martina Pippal,
and Klaus Albrecht Schröder

ALBERTINA PRESTEL Munich · London · New York

Catalogue

Preface

Doubtless, Michelangelo is one of a handful of artists whose fame has remained unbroken for centuries. His art and ideals are, to be sure, deeply rooted in the thought of his era, the High Renaissance and the advancing sixteenth century, with its Europe-wide religious conflicts and territorial disputes on the Apennine Peninsula. Nevertheless, the impact of Michelangelo's art extends well into the twentieth century, becoming newly relevant at each step. Every century experiences its own Michelangelo renaissance and, with that, a revival of the ancient masculine ideal that the great Florentine artist established as a benchmark. With such works as the cartoon for the unrealized fresco of the *Battle of Cascina*, the *ignudi* in the Sistine Chapel, and the latent stone trunks of his slaves for the tomb of Pope Julius II, Michelangelo forged a standard for representing the male nude, an unparalleled ideal that would be emulated for countless generations to come.

This canon, and what became of it, is the subject of our exhibition *Michelangelo and Beyond*. Our focus on drawing as a medium of engagement with Michelangelo's ideal owes not only to the richness of the Albertina Museum's graphic arts holdings; this emphasis also reflects the fact that drawing presents the ideal of the male nude—dynamic and powerful, strained to the limit by inner tensions—free of obfuscating narrative elements and supplementary motifs, a phenomenon only otherwise encountered in sculpture. In Michelangelo's drawings, we are faced with the canon in isolation, as if under laboratory conditions.

At the same time, the formation of this canon rooted in Michelangelo's highly individual drawings documents the emergence of the medium as an independent artistic genre. Early evidence of drawing's changing status in Italy is found in Lorenzo Ghiberti's *Commentarii*, in which *disegno* is put forward as the practical and theoretical foundation of all the arts. Undoubtedly, the notion of *disegno* during the Florentine Renaissance encompassed an aesthetic concept that went far beyond a mere technical description of the application of pen or chalk to paper.

In Michelangelo's time, paper replaced parchment as a support for drawing. In this way, the use of paper facilitated the rise of sketches and preliminary studies as alternatives to time-consuming full compositional drawings. In Michelangelo's works, a summit was reached in the Renaissance depiction of the nude. But beyond that, as Giorgio Vasari, the first historian of Western art, states in his biography of the artist, Michelangelo surpassed even the models of classical antiquity. One of the most admired works of art of the whole cinquecento was indeed Michelangelo's famous cartoon for the *Battle of Cascina*. Because the cartoon is lost, only the magnificent extant

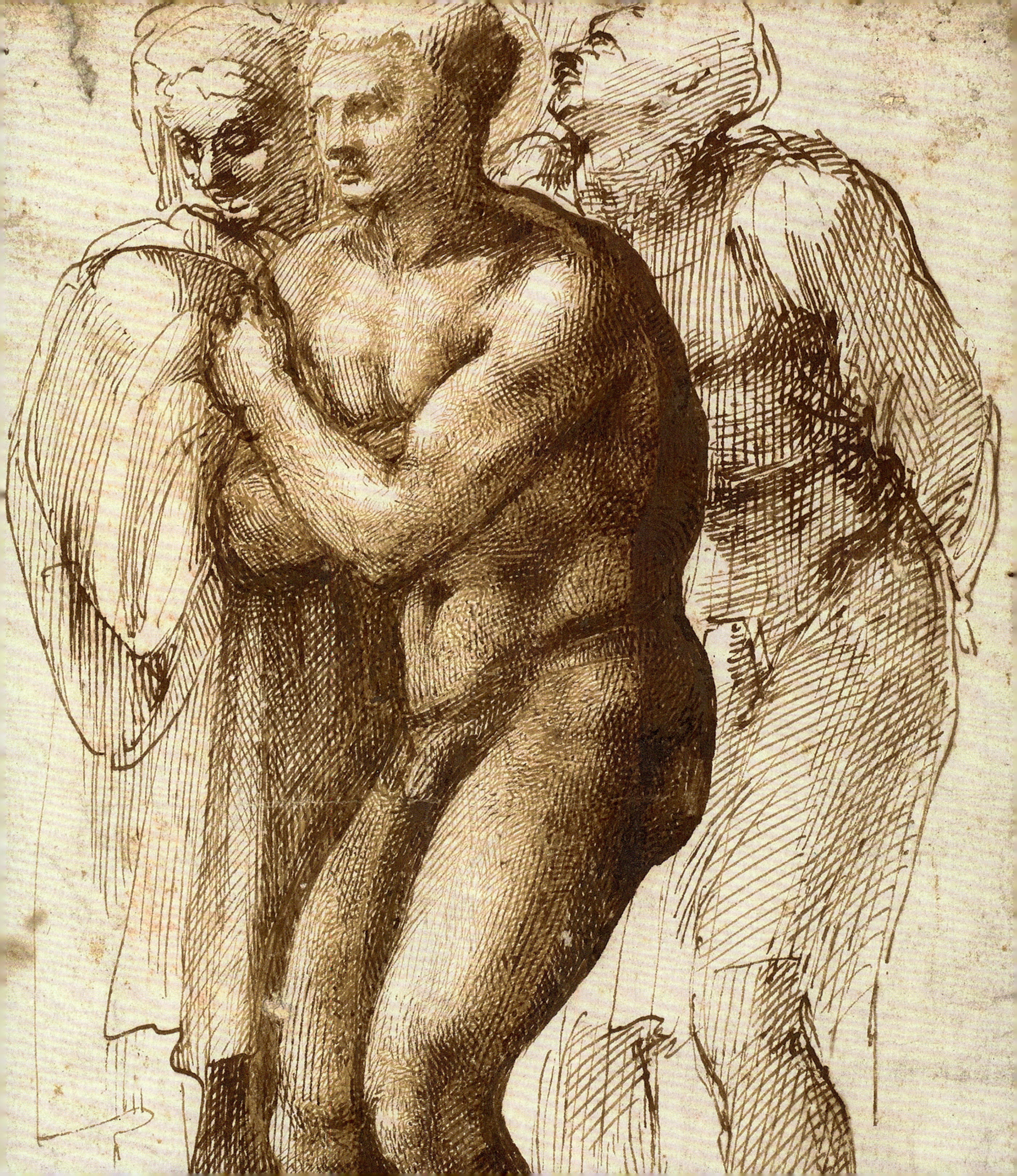

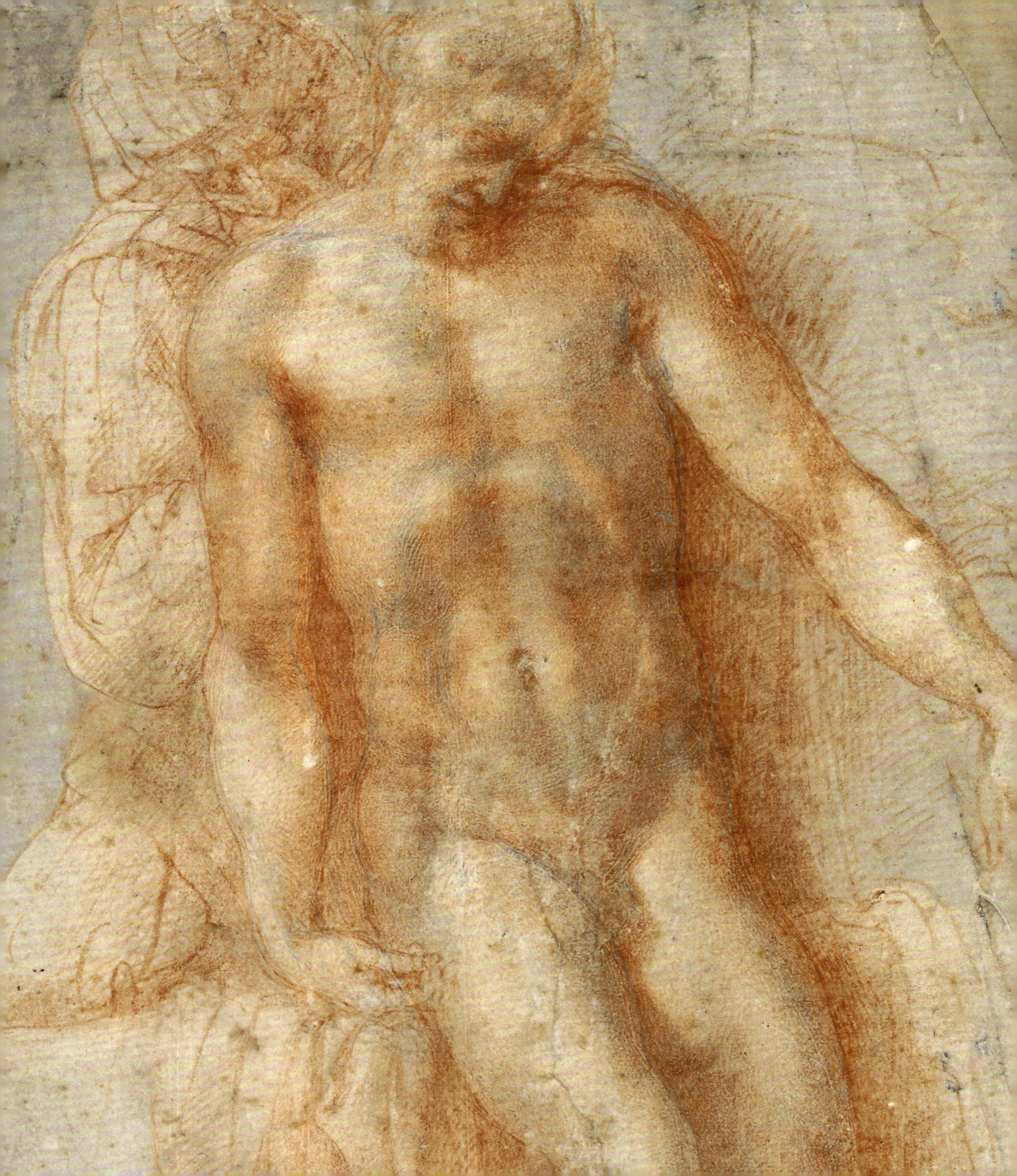

studies for it give an impression now of why the Florentine sculptor and goldsmith Benvenuto Cellini called Michelangelo's battle scene "the school of the world."

Michelangelo's drawings were in high demand among collectors of the period. Their interest reflects the new status of the drawing as an independent work of art—one that offers a distillation of an artistic idea and of the creator's temperament. Pietro Aretino assailed Michelangelo with requests for a drawing, even if just two strokes of chalk on a piece of paper. Cosimo I, Grand Duke of Tuscany, prized Michelangelo's drawings like precious gems. When the Accademia delle arti del disegno was founded in Florence, on Vasari's initiative, in 1563—the prototype of all later academies—drawing was forever elevated to the status of *the* central academic discipline, indispensable for any aspiring artist. Vasari declared drawing the father of the three major arts—architecture, sculpture, and painting. In the seventeenth century, the owner of the Michelangelo drawings now in the Albertina was none other than Peter Paul Rubens. If proof were needed that Rubens's revival of art in service of the Counter-Reformation was based on the study of nature, antiquity, and the work of Michelangelo, these sheets stand as prime evidence. The great value Rubens placed on his Michelangelo holdings attests to the importance of the Michelangesque ideal to this foremost master of the kinetic style of the High Baroque.

The nude is the main motif of our present selection and of sixteenth-century Italian drawings as a whole. Despite its dependence on an ancient ideal, the Renaissance nude was not divorced from the study of nature and real bodies—on the contrary. The classical nude that we encounter in all of its confidence in the Albertina drawings by Michelangelo, Raphael, and Domenico Beccafumi, and by such other artists as Baccio Bandinelli, Daniele da Volterra, and Francesco Salviati, always strives for a harmonious balance between general formulas and the imitation of nature. There is a synthesis: on the one hand, standardized poses, anatomical knowledge gained from antique sculptures, and formalized proportions based on Vitruvius; on the other hand, nature observed in the live model. As much as the *circumcisione*, the linear contour, may represent the formal equivalent of the ideal of the classical nude, there is great stylistic variety in how various artists implemented the ideal prescribed by Michelangelo. Yet the human body is the real focal point, the aesthetic *idée fixe* of the epoch. That is because people understood the motions of the mind to be layered throughout the visual description of the body. Only through external movement, through posture and gesture, do inner states become legible, just as facial expressions are a window onto the soul and spirit.

An exhibition of masterpieces of the nude created in the wake of Michelangelo not only offers insights into artists' interpretations of the body as a conveyor of virtue and vice, heroism and frailty. In the work of Michelangelo, as in that of his contemporary Raphael, we experience the innovative use of warm red chalk in ways that were both unprecedented and hardly to be surpassed. The softness and tonal subtlety of red chalk makes it particularly suitable for the sensual rendering of flesh tones. Over time, vivid red chalk, as used in the Albertina *ignudo* study for the Sistine ceiling, was increasingly superseded by black chalk, possibly because black chalk enabled sharper contrasts of light and dark and a wider range of tone.

Michelangelo is the key figure of this exhibition not because of the number of his drawings on display. The crucial factor is his influence, which cannot be overestimated. Laboring in Michelangelo's shadow, his contemporaries expanded the scope of possibilities for the classical nude—its interplay between ancient ideal and imitation of nature—through the appropriation of the Michelangesque figure in varying degrees of autonomy. The strong shadow that Michelangelo cast on Baccio Bandinelli in Florence and on the School of Fontainebleau in France determined our selection of major works of Mannerism and the Baroque, as well as of Neoclassicism.

Michelangelo initially made a mark on his immediate surroundings and his followers; then, for generations to come, he influenced all artists who, like Peter Paul Rubens in the seventeenth century or Pompeo Girolamo Batoni and Anton Raphael Mengs in the eighteenth century, sought a particular balance between the stony ideal of ancient sculpture and the study of nature—one that did not forgo the expression of determination, ideal beauty, and inner movement of the nude. No matter how empathetic or merely superficial the reception of Michelangelo's drawings of nudes has been over the centuries, it always proves that Michelangelo was seen as the measure of all things. He had set the standard for the grandeur and importance of the male body as the vessel and expression of both its nobility and baseness. Thereby, the perfect ideal of man—the exaltation of nature—closely related to the concept of beauty is a Neoplatonic thought.

In the first two hundred and fifty years after Michelangelo's death, artists productively engaged with his canon and explored it with all the different possibilities offered by the art of Mannerism, with its characteristic elegance, and by the art of the Counter-Reformation, with its turn to the real. In contrast, the nineteenth century and the Michelangelo reception at the turn of the twentieth century were deeply indebted to the artist without ever having understood him: Michelangelo's canon had

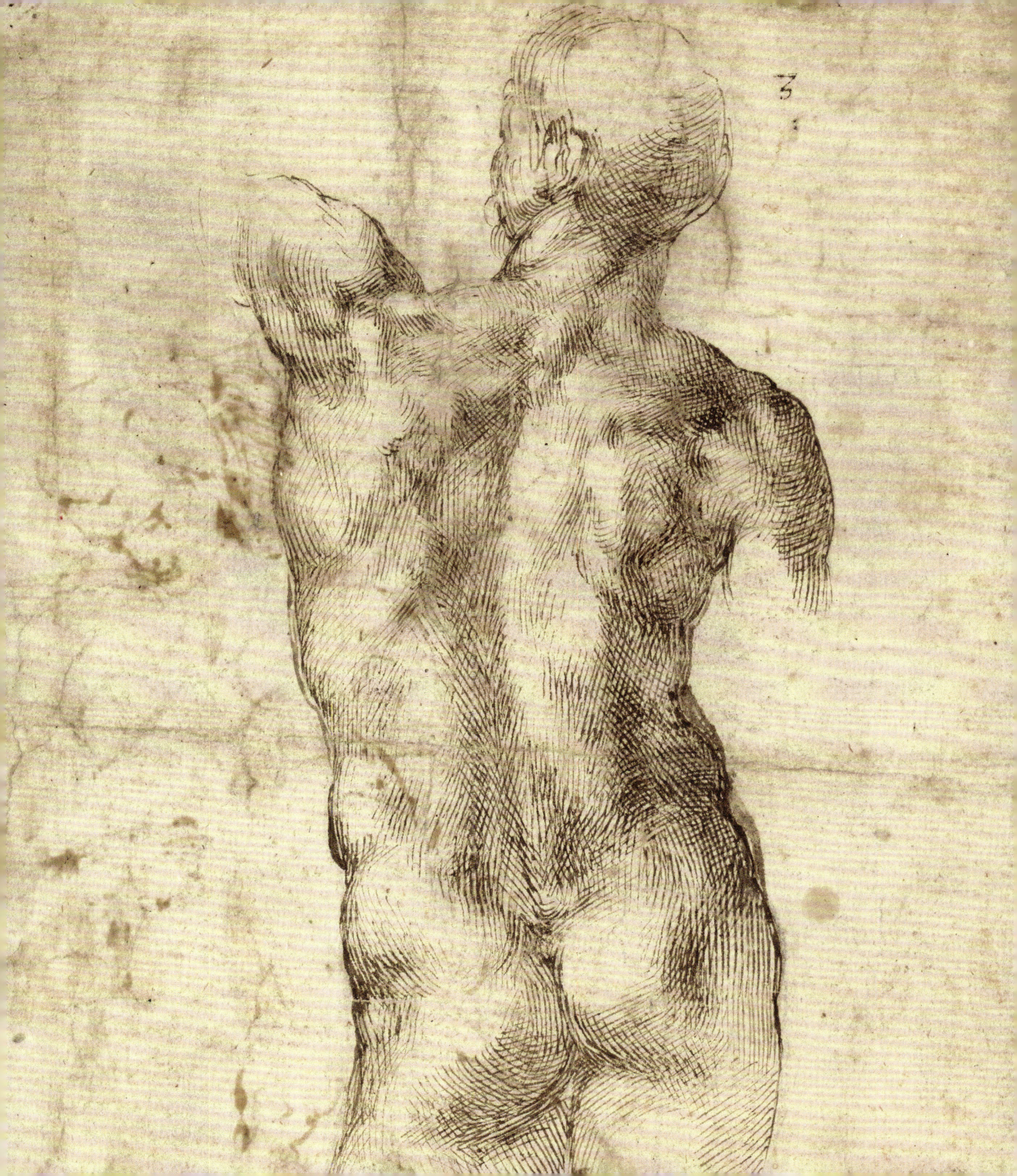

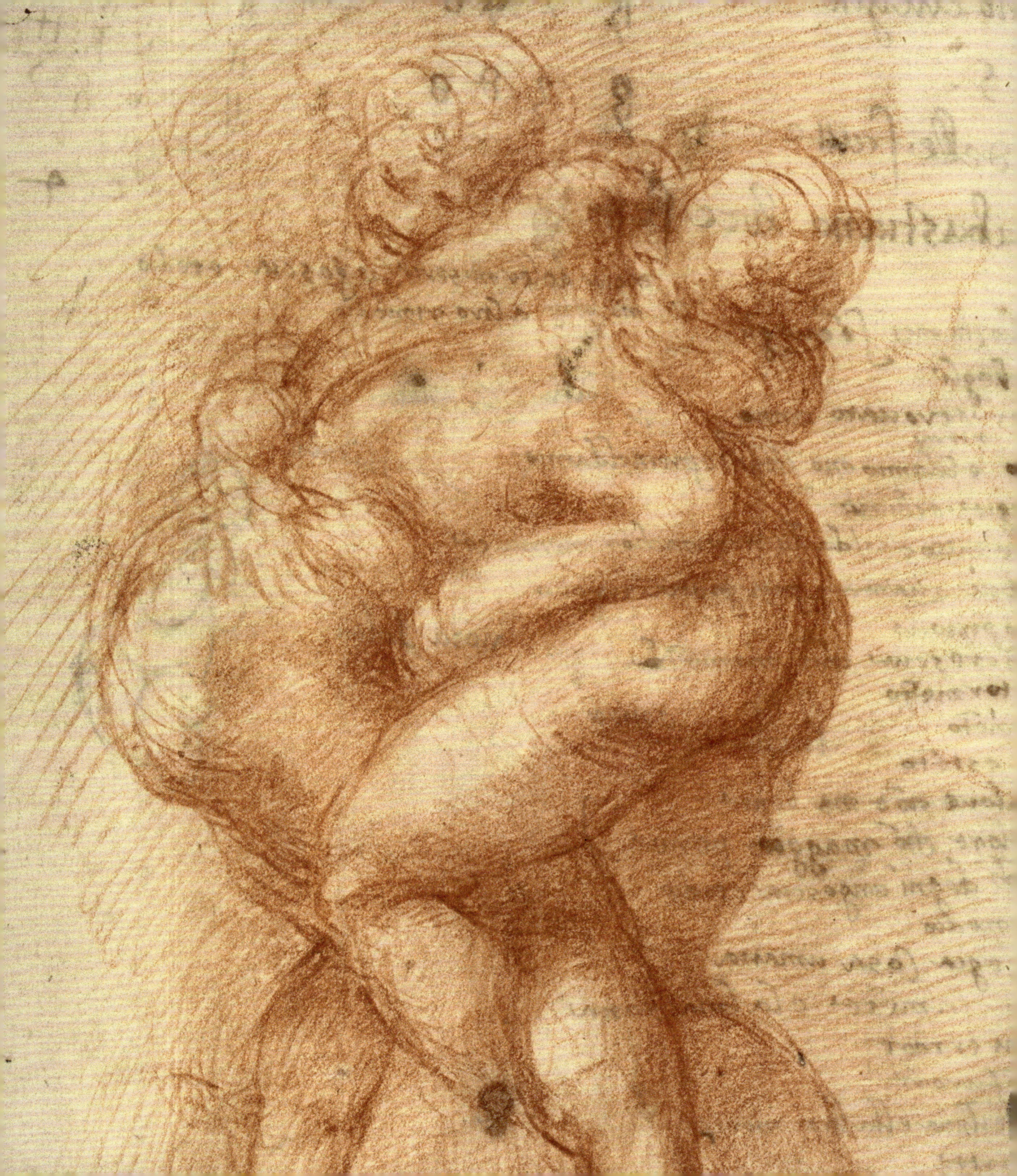

reached its zenith and was ultimately transcended. Even in the age of Gustav Klimt and Egon Schiele, the artists Alexander Rothaug and Karl Sterrer imitated the great Italian's heroic, athletic figures in a slavish and anachronistic way—externally, superficially, and lacking the spiritual depth of Michelangelo.

The rediscovery of the Greco-Roman ideal of the body revolutionized the Renaissance concept of humanity, and not just in Italy. Michelangelo's tension-filled construction of the body is the opposite of the calm, balance, and harmony that the world so admired in Raphael. Michelangelo's figures incorporate opposing movements; dynamic, violent intersections; resonant foreshortening of arms, legs, head, and shoulders; and open, almost jagged contours. Nevertheless, Michelangelo did not abandon the balance inherent in the High Renaissance between the lofty ideal and the imitation of nature.

Michelangelo's new ideal of the figure is based on the understanding of humankind, the tragedy of human existence. It did not result from superficial formalism. His power of expression, as well as his pursuit of beauty, has inspired artists across time and national borders. His conception of the solitary human figure became an ideal type, whose influence lasted for centuries. However, this image of humankind is exclusively an image of man, not woman: a limitation owing to Michelangelo's own ideal and the ideal of the era.

The exhibition traces Michelangelo's unparalleled ideal, his canon, over long stretches of time. Yet our subject is more than just variations on that ideal. In the seventeenth century's engagement with Michelangelo, two antipodes emerged that could not have been more different. On the one hand, there was Peter Paul Rubens, who in his study of the real, live model brought new vitality to the ancient nude and to Michelangelo's ideal. On the other hand, there was Rembrandt, who embraced ugliness and, in striving against the athletic concept of the human figure inherited from antiquity, created an antithesis of Michelangelo's ideal. Rembrandt pursued a naturalistic representation of the real body, of humanity in its frailty and weakness, marked by the contingencies of appearance—as then, so now. Even Rembrandt's contemporaries are known to have ascribed a base ugliness to his depictions of women, boys, and men.

Michelangelo and Beyond deals with the emergence, culmination, decline, and collapse of a canon: a canon established five centuries ago in the male nudes of Michelangelo. The exhibition reflects the historical fact that for hundreds of years only men drew men, and that women, too, were only depicted by men. Maleness, thus, defined the canon of both the male and the female nude. Michelangelo himself hardly drew the female nude; instead, he gave male bodies female attributes, which ultimately appear alien to the underlying structure. In art, woman is the dark side of the moon—known to exist, but also *terra incognita*. Using several examples from the seventeenth and eighteenth centuries, our exhibition addresses the unrealistic ideal of woman. Depicting the female nude was long disfavored and disparaged because of its association with vice, immorality, and carnal lust: the figure of Eve, informed by notions of woman's depravity, bears death and sin with her; the vice of *luxuria* appears as a naked woman, vain in demeanor. The Virtues, in contrast, are presented in flowing robes. The antithesis of the virtuously covered woman is the naked woman as an embodiment of *Weibermacht* ("the power of women"), as a witch, as a seductive Venus.

The exhibition concludes with a selection of works chosen by way of example to represent the century in which Michelangelo's canon lost its authority. This section is devoted to the contrast between the Secessionist cult of beauty, exemplified by Gustav Klimt's curvilinear ideality of the woman, and the ugliness and pathologization of nudes that are, for the first time, not deprived of their sexuality, as in the works of Egon Schiele.

I had the pleasure of developing the idea for this exhibition in collaboration with Eva Michel, the Curator of Netherlandish Drawings at the Albertina. My heartfelt thanks go to her and to all the other curators at this museum, and to external colleagues as well, who in proposing objects and writing about them contributed immeasurably to the success of this demanding project. I particularly thank the General Secretary of the Albertina, Constanze Johanna Malissa; the Italian art specialist Achim Gnann; and Martina Pippal from the University of Vienna for their courageous forays into the difficult terrain of the reception of the Michelangesque canon of the nude. My wholehearted thanks also go to Lydia Eder, who, together with Constanze Johanna Malissa, successfully and swiftly realized this exhibition as an alternative project to a different show that was postponed on short notice.

An exhibition of this scope represents an extraordinary workload, particularly for our departments of conservation and framing. I owe a very special thanks to both Eva Glück and Ines Aßmann for coordinating this project, and I thank all their departmental colleagues for the careful preparation of our priceless works. As usual, Elisabeth Wolfik provided excellent support on behalf of Exhibition Management, and Martin Kohlbauer and his team realized the exhibition's architecture with great sensitivity; Sandra Maria Rust, together with Lydia Eder, Lisa Trapp, the designer Klaus E. Göltz, and the photography studio of the Albertina under the direction of Daniel Antalfi reliably handled the production of this publication, as always. I owe a debt of gratitude to each of them.

Last but not least, I thank all the lenders who supported our exhibition with works from their collections. It was only through the generosity of the Liechtenstein Princely Collections under the former and current directors, Johann Kräftner and Stephan Koja, that we were able to complement the Albertina's master drawings and loans from the Louvre in Paris, the Metropolitan Museum of Art in New York, and private collections with some of the most beautiful examples of Michelangelo's reception in sculpture. For that, I thank Hans Kräftner and his successor, and I am grateful as well to the Bayerisches Nationalmuseum in Munich and the Kunsthistorisches Museum in Vienna for exquisite loans from their sculpture collections.

Ultimately, displaying the Albertina Museum's most beautiful and precious drawings alongside major works of sculpture once again validates the notion of the indivisibility of the arts, the guiding principle of our exhibitions and presentations over the past twenty-five years.

Klaus Albrecht Schröder
Director General
The ALBERTINA Museum, Vienna

Michelangelo, or The Birth of a Canon

Michelangelo (Caprese, March 6, 1475–Rome, February 18, 1564), Leonardo (Anchiano, near Vinci, April 15, 1452–Amboise, May 2, 1519), and Raphael (Urbino, March 28, 1483–Rome, April 6, 1520) make up the triumvirate of ingenious masters who ushered in the modern era of art. In Florence and later in Rome, beginning with Leonardo's paintings of the 1470s and continuing with the works of Michelangelo, Raphael, and Fra Bartolommeo, a new classical style emerged—the art of the High Renaissance (1500–1520/30). The period's representations of the human figure are characterized by a new awareness of the individual's personality, inner life, and self-determination. Depictions of the body acquire an extraordinary monumentality. Compositions are distinguished by their overall balance and by clear and harmonious relationships among the figures; at the same time, they give the impression of having been modeled solely on nature. Nowhere else is the new ideal of the human body as evident as in Michelangelo's nudes. The great Florentine attained his ideal through the study of live models, ancient sculpture, and human anatomy. While participating in dissections, he carefully examined the structures of the body. His anatomical knowledge helped him not only to understand organic processes of movement but also to portray the motivations and innermost feelings of the human actor. Michelangelo's nudes are by no means bodybuilders putting their gym-hardened physiques on display; rather, their muscles express unrestrained energies, violent passions, and in many cases, inner tensions and torments. In his nudes, physical strength is always accompanied by strength of mind and morals. The human body is the focal point of Michelangelo's whole painted and sculpted oeuvre. Also, because he was active much longer than Leonardo and Raphael, his legacy was broader and more varied. No artist of the sixteenth century could escape his formative influence. Artists flocked to the publicly displayed cartoon for the *Battle of Cascina* in order to make drawings after it. The expressive, twisting and broad figures of the Sistine Chapel frequently served as a point of departure for the decorative excesses of Mannerist artists, and the influence of Michelangelo's late architectural works can be seen in Baroque buildings.

One comes closest to this artist, however, through his drawings. One sees his private thoughts brought to paper with a few strokes and beholds the spontaneous emergence of a creative idea. The lines, varied in pressure and spacing, merge with one another in complex ways and lend the flat surface a sculptural tautness. Whereby,

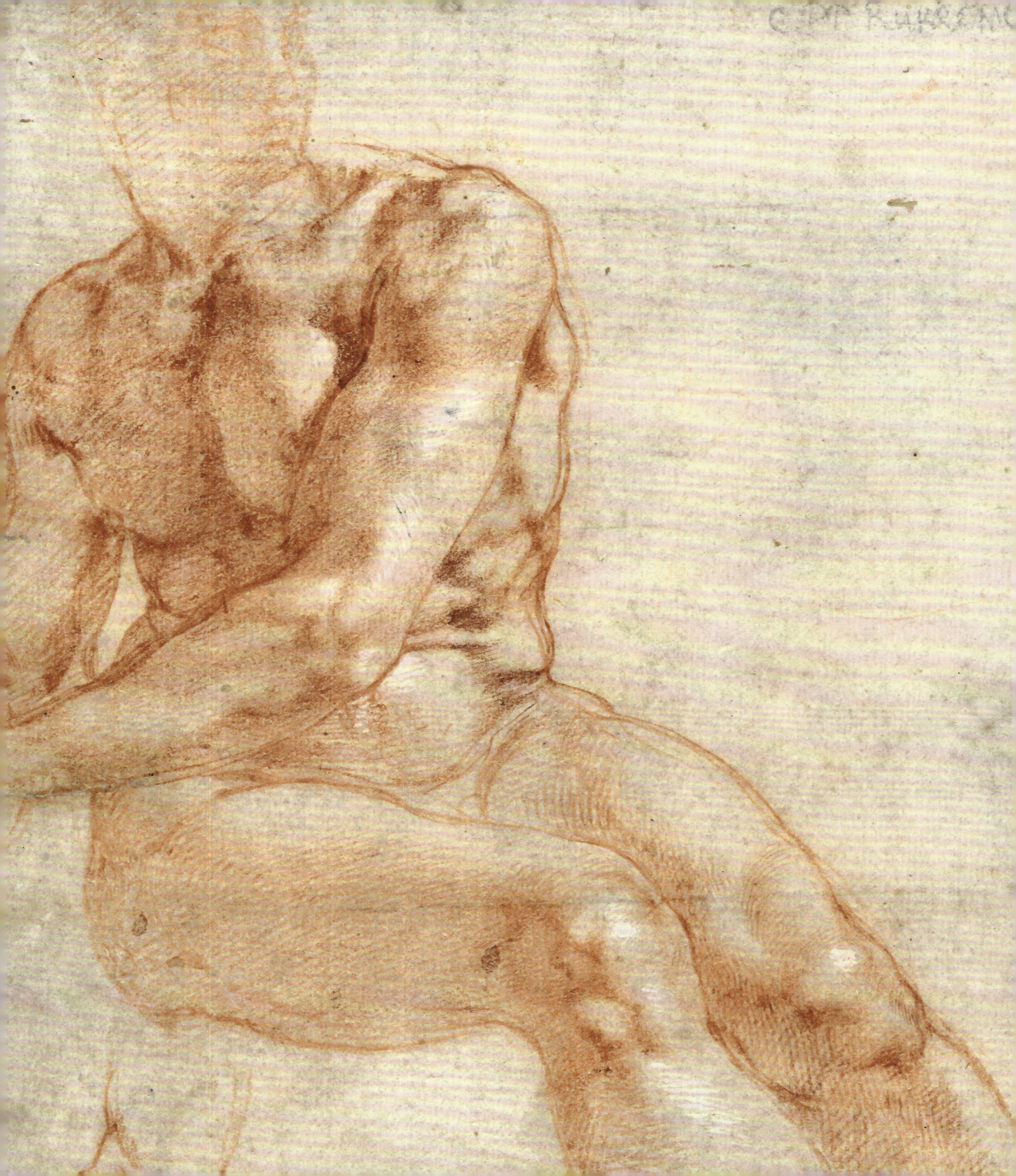

the handling of line in a composition always focuses the eye directly upon the human figure the strong contours of which clearly distinguish it from its surroundings. The drawings allow us to follow the compositional development and clarification of a motif leading up to the completed work. It is often only through his studies on paper that we know about initial ideas and modified or discarded projects. Many depictions have survived only in drawings, for example, the detailed, highly finished sheets that Michelangelo gave as gifts to the poet Vittoria Colonna, who he greatly admired, and to his friend Tommaso de' Cavalieri. Already during the artist's lifetime, his drawings were collected and guarded like jewels. Peter Paul Rubens was once the proud owner of four of the eight Michelangelo drawings now in the Albertina. In addition to his painting of *Leda and the Swan,* Michelangelo left two boxes of drawings and cartoons to his pupil Antonio Mini, who took them to France, where they aroused great admiration among artists at the royal court of Francis I. The sheets that survive today represent only a fraction of the total output of drawings by the artist, who, after all, was active for some seventy-five years. Many sheets have been lost over time, and Michelangelo himself is known to have twice destroyed entire stacks of his drawings. Apart from architectural studies and schematic drawings of blocks of marble, most of the surviving sheets are devoted to the human form. Two thirds of those are nudes.

Michelangelo's conception of the nude as a draftsman changed significantly over the course of his long career. After an initial retrospective turn to his revered forerunners Giotto and Masaccio, he developed his heroic ideal of the figure in the *Battle of Cascina* and the Sistine Chapel ceiling. In those works, conspicuously bulging muscles sculpturally express great bodily tension. The works of the 1520s and 1530s are characterized by a more unified notion of the body with figures acquiring greater overall cohesion. They appear radiant and flawless, and their movements become more supple and fluid. Then, in *The Last Judgment,* Michelangelo established his monumental figure style. In his late works, he arrived at a blocklike simplification of the body, which assumes almost colossal dimensions. At the same time, the late nudes evince a greater sense of inner life and heightened emotional expression, making even clearer than before the spiritual disposition of the deeply religious Michelangelo. The Italian artists shown in this exhibition alongside Michelangelo adopted various techniques from his drawings and took inspiration from different phases of his production, borrowing from and further developing the respective stages of Michelangelo's style.

Their drawings are fine examples of the richly varied results that engagement with the master could produce.

Michelangelo's works have left an indelible mark on our consciousness. Some of his artistic formulations are inextricably linked to our mental image of the particular event or motif depicted. Anyone who considers how God the Father brought life to the first man or how justice will be meted out on Judgment Day immediately thinks of *The Creation of Adam* on the ceiling of the Sistine Chapel and the monumental fresco on the chapel's altar wall. On this, it would seem, Michelangelo had the final word.

His artworks bear witness to an enormous creative power; to this day, they have lost none of their allure. His figures continue to fascinate us in their embodiment of deep emotional experience and their expression of tremendous energy, determination, and willpower. Armed with these qualities, the figures pursue their duties and goals, struggle against adversity, and facing setbacks, are forced to confront their own selves. Michelangelo's exploration of unexpected aspects of the human condition is one of many reasons why his works still capture our imagination.

AG

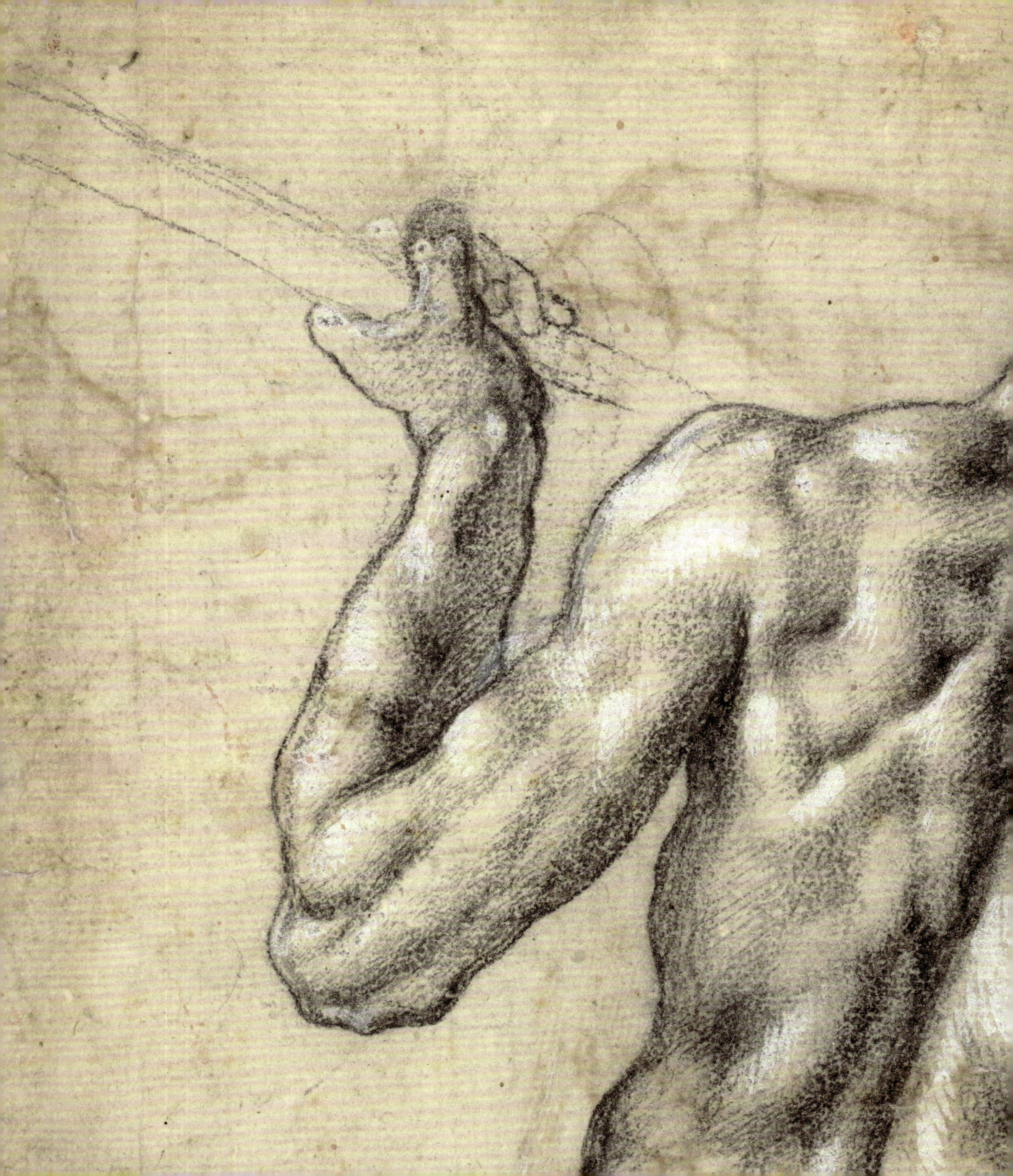

Catalogue

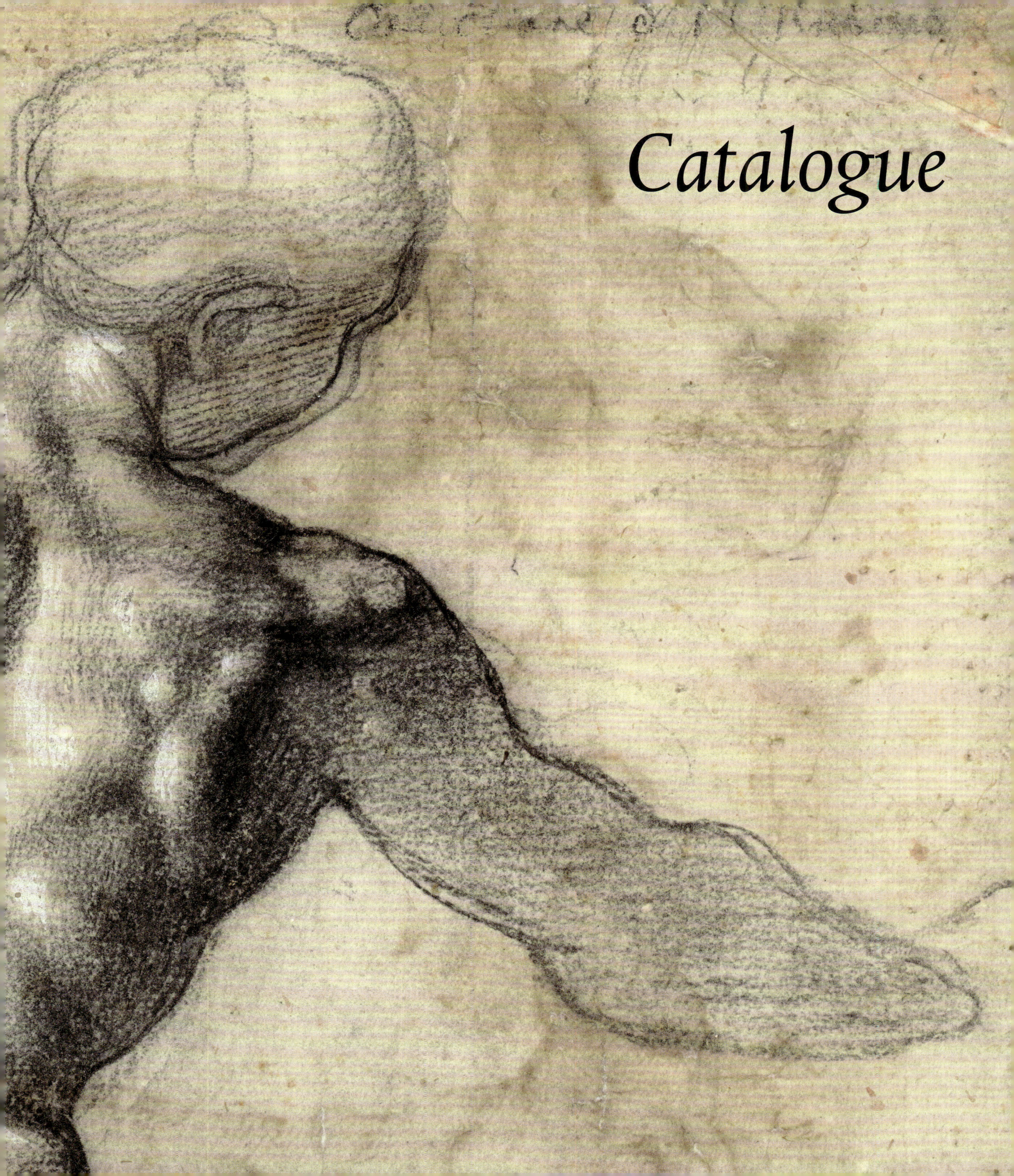

Before Michelangelo, or Nudity by Template

The goldsmith, painter, and sculptor Antonio del Pollaiuolo was an extraordinarily versatile artist, who also applied himself to printmaking. His *Battle of the Nude Men,* usually dated to about 1470 to 1475, is the largest Florentine engraving of the fifteenth century and the first such print in Italy to bear the name of its creator. It is also likely Pollaiuolo's sole engraving. This depiction of a fight taking place with unbridled vigor and sundry weapons is a bravura display of variety in pose and movement. Pollaiuolo's contemporaries admired the detailed rendering of musculature among the combatants, who are arranged in groups of two and three. In his demonstration of human anatomy in these nudes, Pollaiuolo was an important precursor of Leonardo and Michelangelo. The painter, architect, and artist biographer Vasari reports that Pollaiuolo was the first artist "to skin many human bodies" in order to study their anatomical makeup. Yet, it has been noted that his knowledge was probably rudimentary, since while some muscles are rendered correctly, others are missing, overemphasized, or vaguely indicated. Furthermore, their relationship to one another is often unclear, for example, how they cross or overlap. The evenly tensed muscles distributed over the whole body create an almost decorative effect. This is amplified by the expressive contours, the broad planar spread of the poses, and the background flora. The individual bodies lack any true center of gravity, as the dominant force throughout is vertical, and there is also no convergence of energies nor any alternation between tensed and relaxed parts. Any real buildup is lacking: the action does not develop, and the motifs seem interchangeable. Pollaiuolo was still too attached to the art of his time to develop a new ideal of the body—that would be accomplished by Michelangelo and Leonardo.

For Michelangelo, who according to contemporary reports dissected corpses on at least three different occasions, the study of anatomy had a deeper meaning. It allowed him to understand inner tensions and the organic flow of movement, both of which, in Michelangelo's hands, also reveal a person's motivations and innermost emotions. By comparison, Pollaiuolo's approach to human musculature was more superficial, concerned foremost with exterior appearances.

The engraving supposedly of Hercules battling giants is likewise based on an invention of Pollaiuolo's, but it reproduces only half of the lost original design, which, as is known from a copy, was twice as wide. Pollaiuolo did not execute the print of this uncertain scene; that was done by an anonymous engraver, as is apparent from

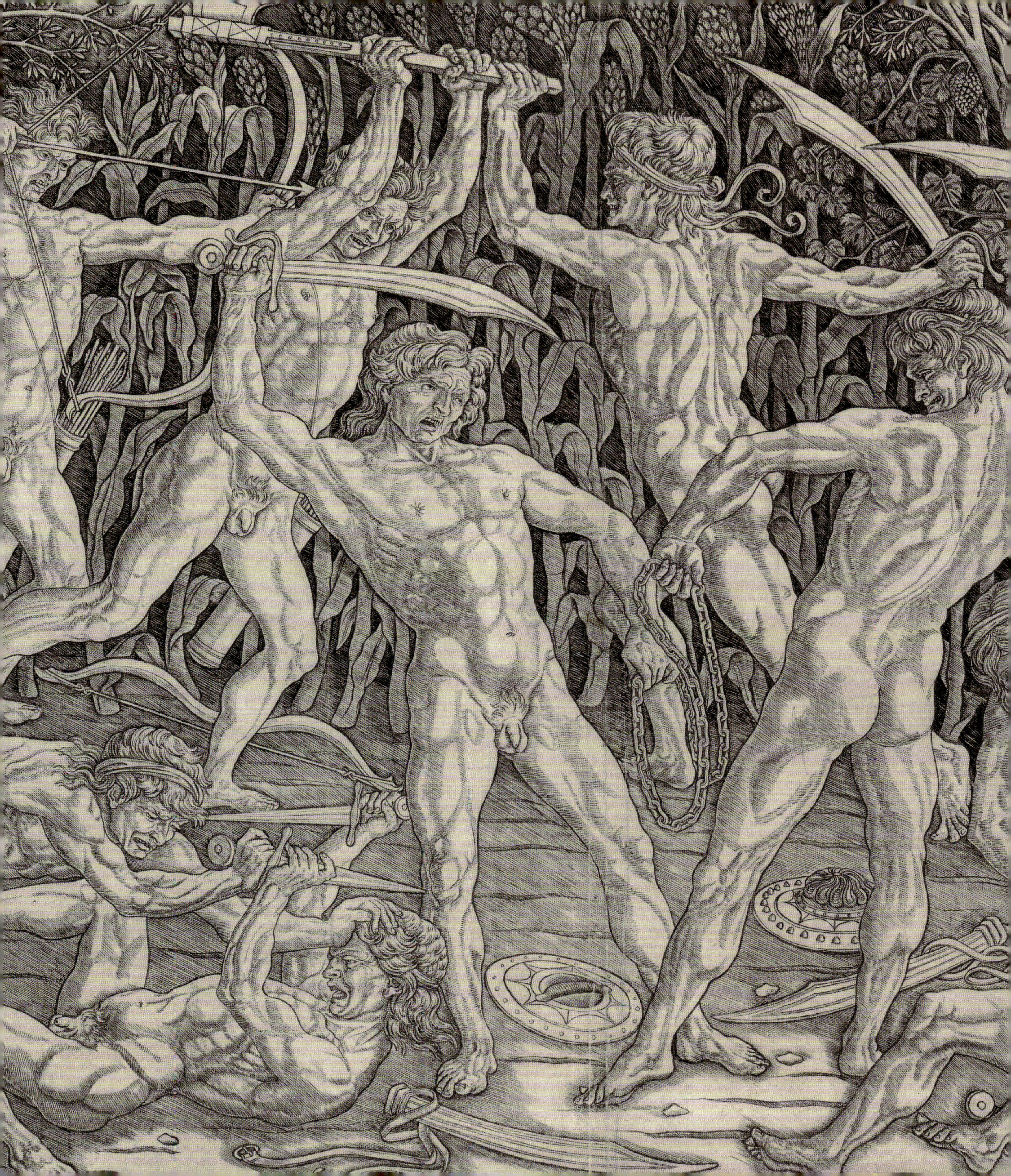

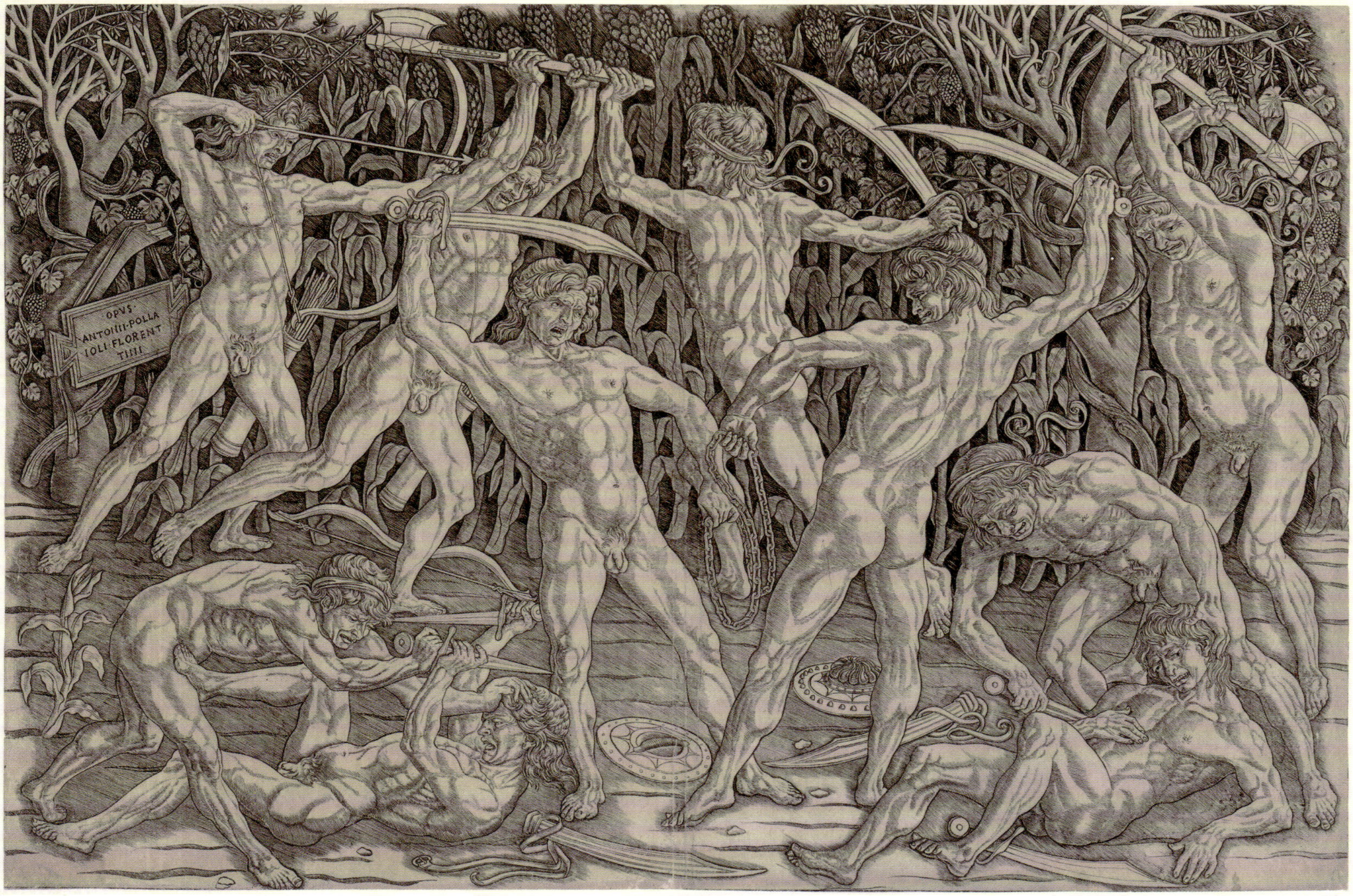

Antonio del Pollaiuolo
Battle of the Nude Men, ca. 1470–1475
The ALBERTINA Museum, Vienna

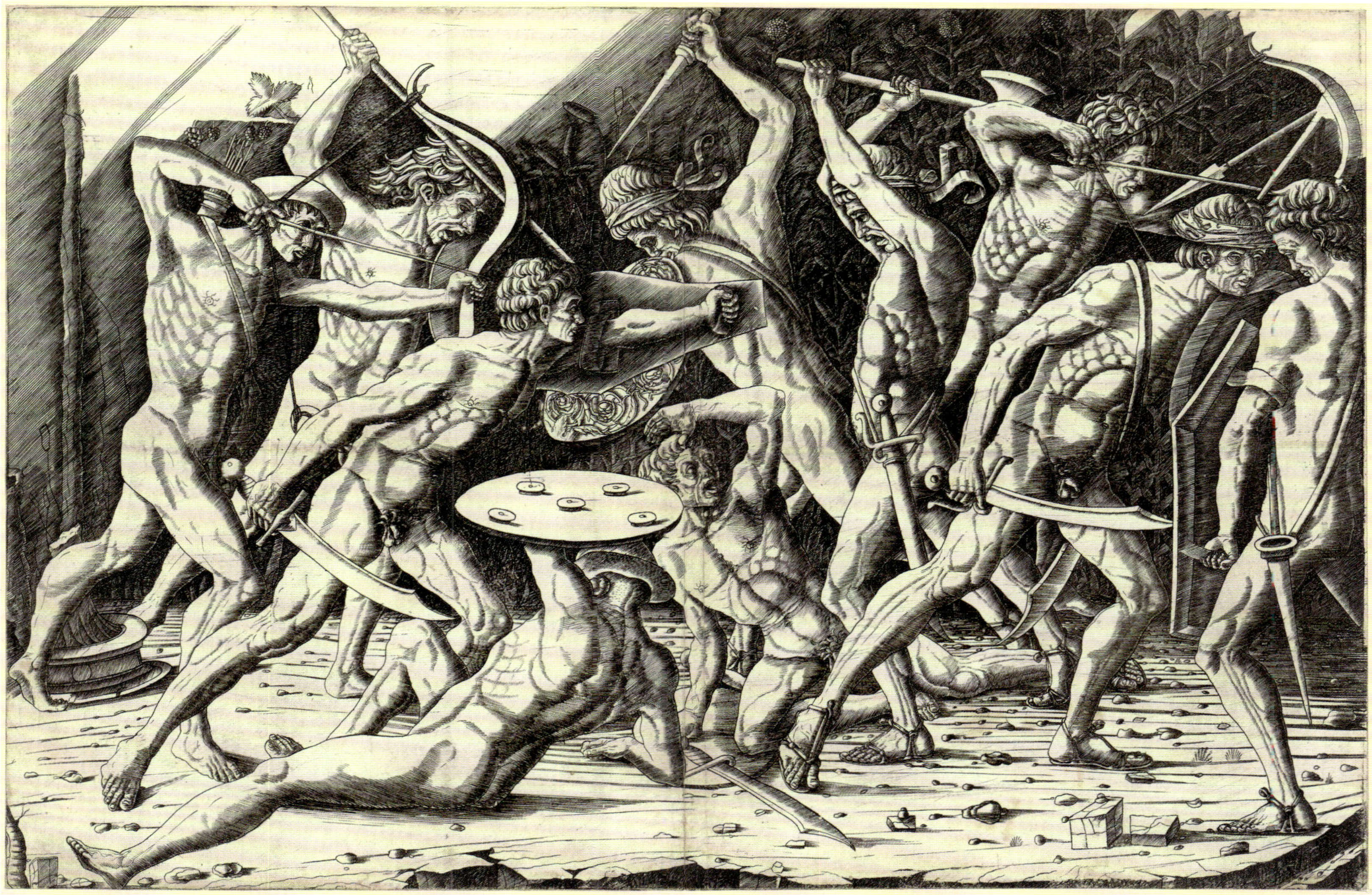

Copy after Antonio del Pollaiuolo
Hercules Combating the Giants,
ca. 1470–1475
The ALBERTINA Museum, Vienna

the more rigid poses, the more prominent contours, and the reduced modeling. The muscles are combined into schematic, sometimes mosaic-like groups. In his treatise on painting, Leonardo advised artists to accentuate musculature only in those tensed segments of the limbs, not when they are relaxed; otherwise, he noted, the artist portrays not a figure but a bag full of nuts.

Cristofano Robetta's engraving is also based, though inverted, on a composition by Pollaiuolo, this one from a now-lost series of canvases on the Labors of Hercules made for the Medici family. Pollaiuolo repeated the composition in a small painting on panel and a bronze sculpture, which are now in Florence in the Uffizi and the Bargello respectively. Vasari's admiration of the composition is apparent in his description of Antaeus screaming in pain while trying to escape Hercules' crushing grip. This striking pair of figures, marked by a heightened expressiveness of movement and an artfully sweeping outline, also left a deep impression on Leonardo and Michelangelo. It served as inspiration to Michelangelo for drawings he made about 1524/25 as designs for a marble sculpture of Hercules fighting Antaeus. That work, never carried out, was supposed to be installed as a pendant to his *David* in front of the Palazzo della Signoria. Like David, Hercules was appreciated as a brave fighter who had defeated tyrants; he therefore came politically to symbolize the righteousness of the Florentine municipal government. Whereas in Michelangelo's designs for the group, the movements are organic, the struggle unfolds in sequence, each body rotates around its own axis, and the pulsating inner forces are palpable, Pollaiuolo's figures are inscribed within a silhouette that freezes their action into a fixed state.

AG

Cristofano Robetta
Hercules and Antaeus,
ca. 1500–1520
The ALBERTINA Museum,
Vienna

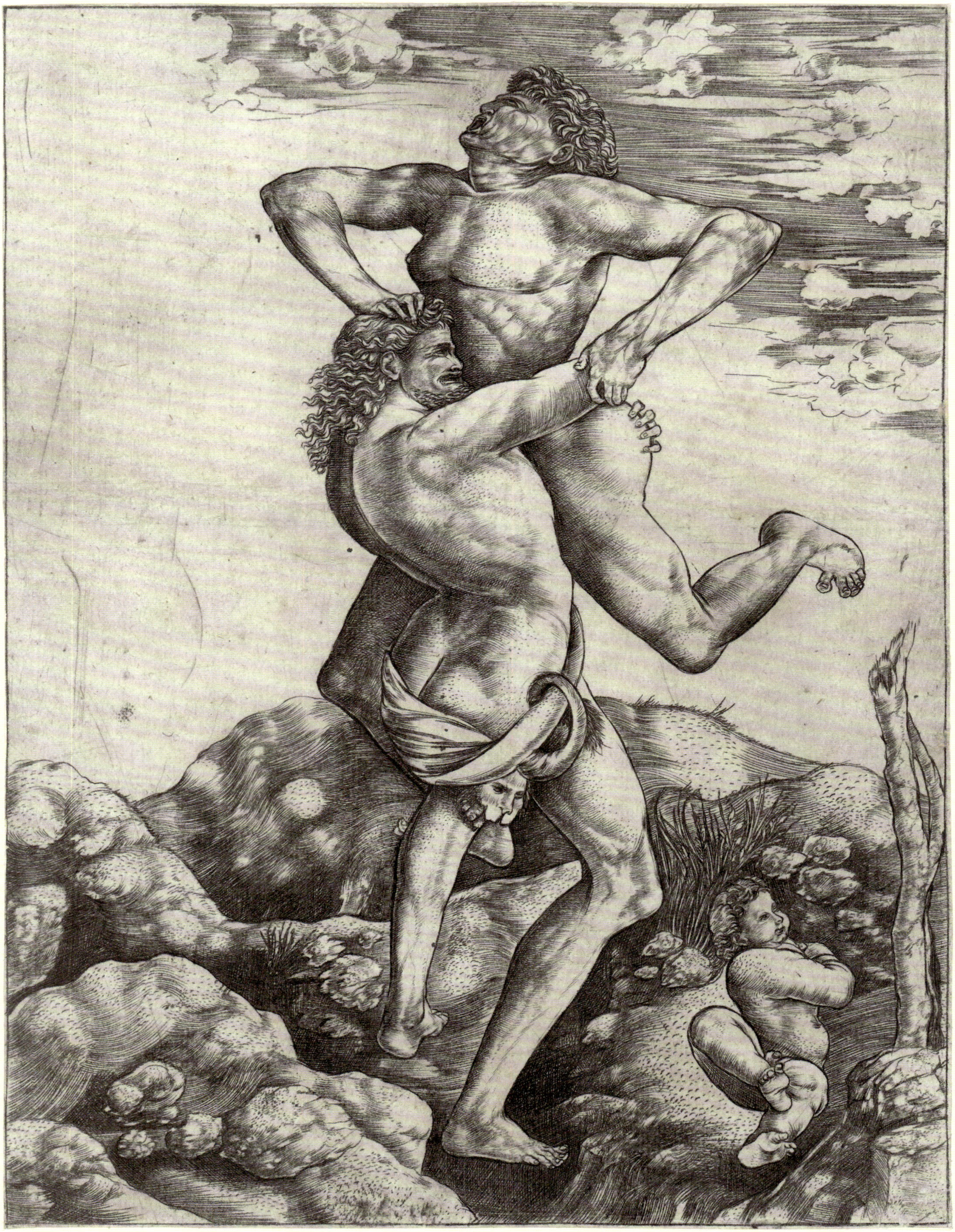

Michelangelo's Beginnings, or The Rebirth of the Body

The Albertina sheet showing three standing men is one of several fascinating youthful drawings that Michelangelo based on models by earlier Florentine masters. He admired the simplicity, dignified grandeur, and monumental unity of Giotto's and Masaccio's figural vocabulary, both of whom were closer to his ideal than the artistic styles of his contemporaries. For these large sheets of similar dimensions, he adopted single, prominent figures from the works of these admired predecessors, proportioning them to fill the dimensions of the paper. The Albertina drawing presents a detail from Masaccio's lost grisaille fresco of the consecration (*Sagra*) of Santa Maria del Carmine, which was located in the cloister of that same church and is known to us through copies. Writing about the original, Vasari praised the use of perspective and the accomplished foreshortening in the depiction of Florentine citizens, including important artists, who had taken part in the celebration, arranged in rows five and six figures deep. In the Vienna drawing, Michelangelo reproduced only one of these figures, the man in front, with a degree of faithfulness. He changed the facial expressions and gave the right rear figure wooden sandals and a belt, from which writing implements and a key are suspended—a key which, according to Vasari, was held in the hand of a porter in the original fresco. Michelangelo modeled the cloak of the voluminous man at the center using a dense network of straight, orderly strokes that branch out and overlap as cross-hatching. Even in those areas most illuminated by light, the figure loses nothing of its block-like unity. The handling of line draws attention to the tautness of the surface and its tactile qualities, aspects in which Michelangelo's primary sculptural understanding of form is apparent. The more summary rendering of the accompanying figures makes them recede in depth. The striking facial features of the porter call to mind first and foremost the influence of Leonardo's physiognomic studies.

The verso of the sheet is filled by a kneeling man, seen from behind, whose flat, round hat usually appears in depictions of Saints Cosmas and Damian, the patrons of physicians and of the Medici family. It remains unknown after which Florentine painter Michelangelo copied this rear view of a figure.

The drawing after Masaccio's *The Baptism of the Neophytes* in the Brancacci Chapel of Santa Maria del Carmine (fig. 1), recently rediscovered by Furio Rinaldi, significantly enhances our knowledge of Michelangelo's early work. Michelangelo borrowed from the fresco only the nude figure of a neophyte standing at the right edge. Vasari wrote

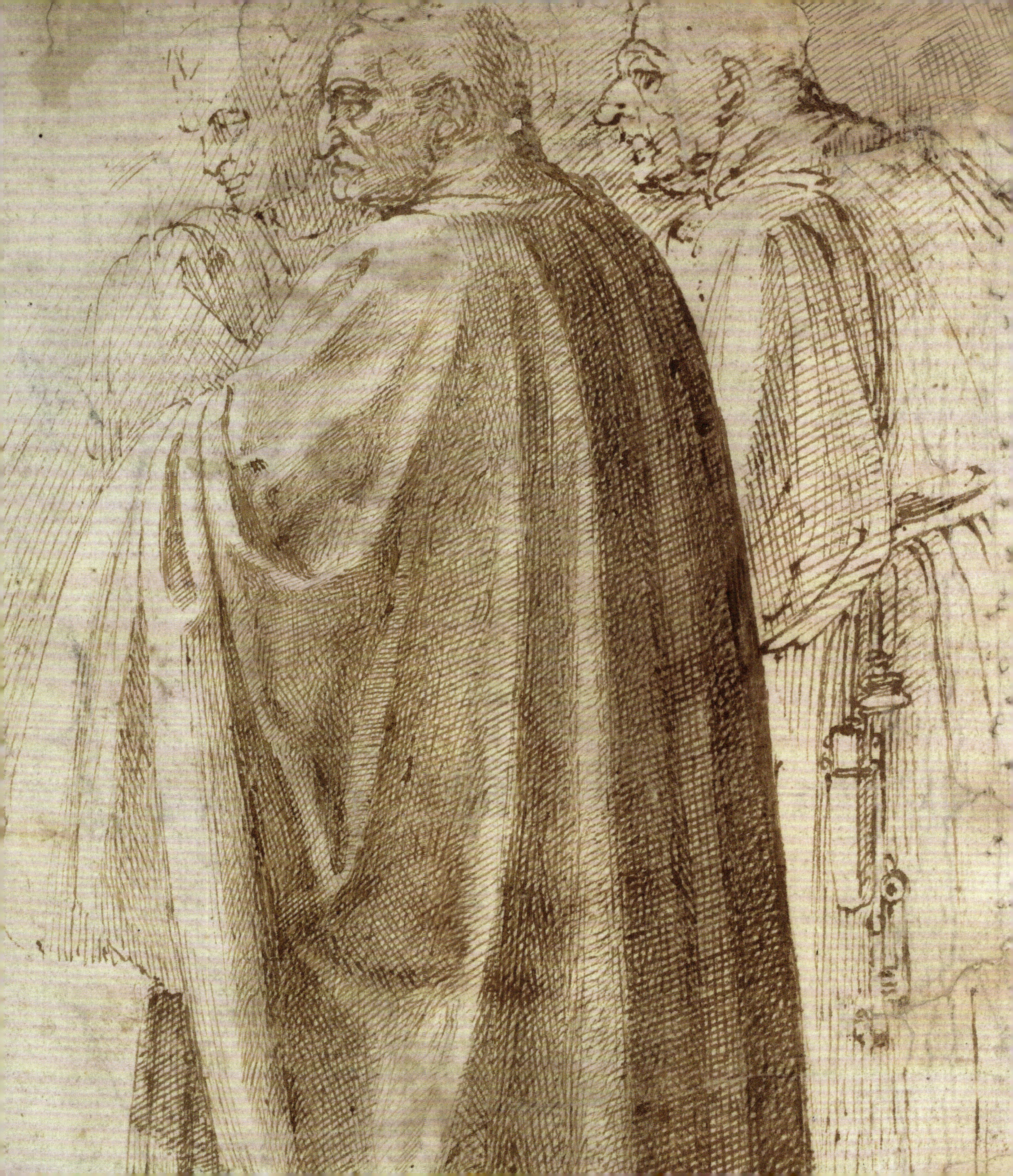

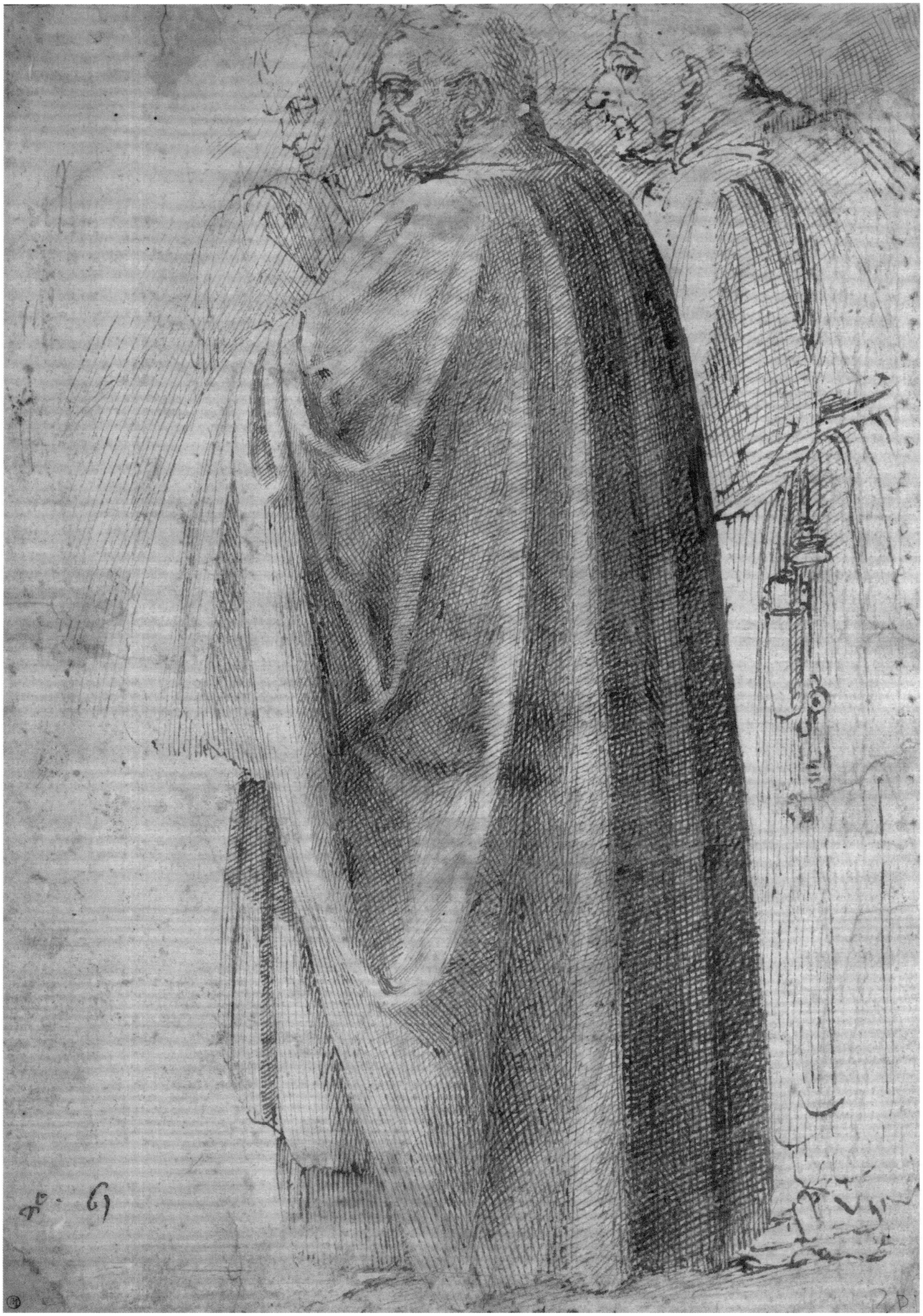

Michelangelo
Three Standing Men,
ca. 1494–1496
The ALBERTINA
Museum, Vienna

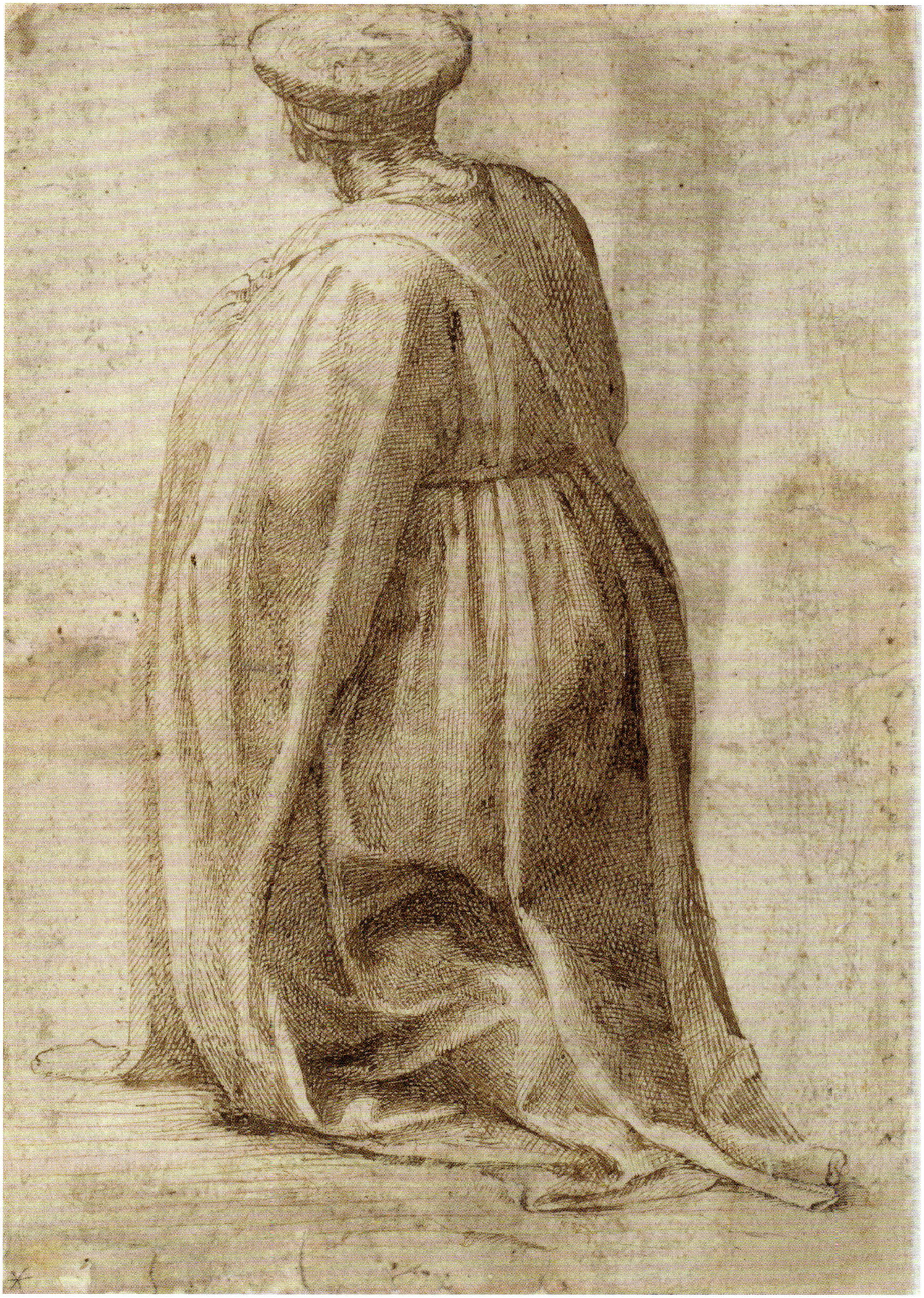

Michelangelo
Kneeling Man Seen from the Rear,
ca. 1494–1496
The ALBERTINA Museum, Vienna

approvingly of the original figure, noting that he appears to shiver from the cold and that the beautiful modeling and graceful design caused the nude to be admired by both past and contemporary artists. By extracting the single figure from its group and making it fill the center of the sheet, Michelangelo heightened its monumentality and emphasized its individuality as a human being, on whose future spiritual life and deeds the act of baptism would have a lasting impact. At first, Michelangelo positioned the right foot somewhat higher; then he shifted it to the right. As so often in his youthful drawings, he used ink in two tones. The lighter tone serves to model the body, while the darker one accentuates forms and strengthens shadows. Curved strokes lend a roundedness to the limbs. As in the Albertina drawing, the accompanying figures added by the artist are more summarily rendered. The nude in this drawing appears more powerful than the model provided by Masaccio because Michelangelo emphasizes the musculature and anatomical details and more clearly defines the joints. Whereas an upward drive seems to move through Masaccio's more delicate baptismal candidate, the central force of Michelangelo's nude is concentrated at its core. In his lean forward and intimation of a kneeling motion, the figure moves off the vertical axis. In Michelangelo's version, the figure gains a freedom to move each part of his body independently. Whereas Masaccio's nude remains confined within its outer contours, Michelangelo bestows his figure with the capacity to act autonomously.

AG

1 Masaccio, *The Baptism of the Neophytes,* ca. 1427
Fresco, 255 × 162 cm
Santa Maria del Carmine, Florence, Brancacci Chapel

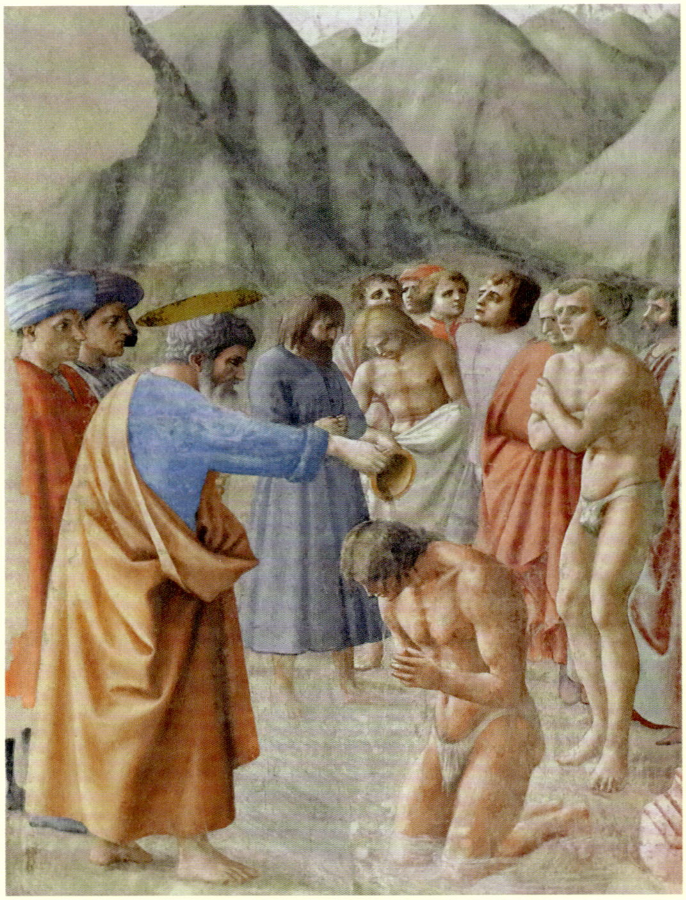

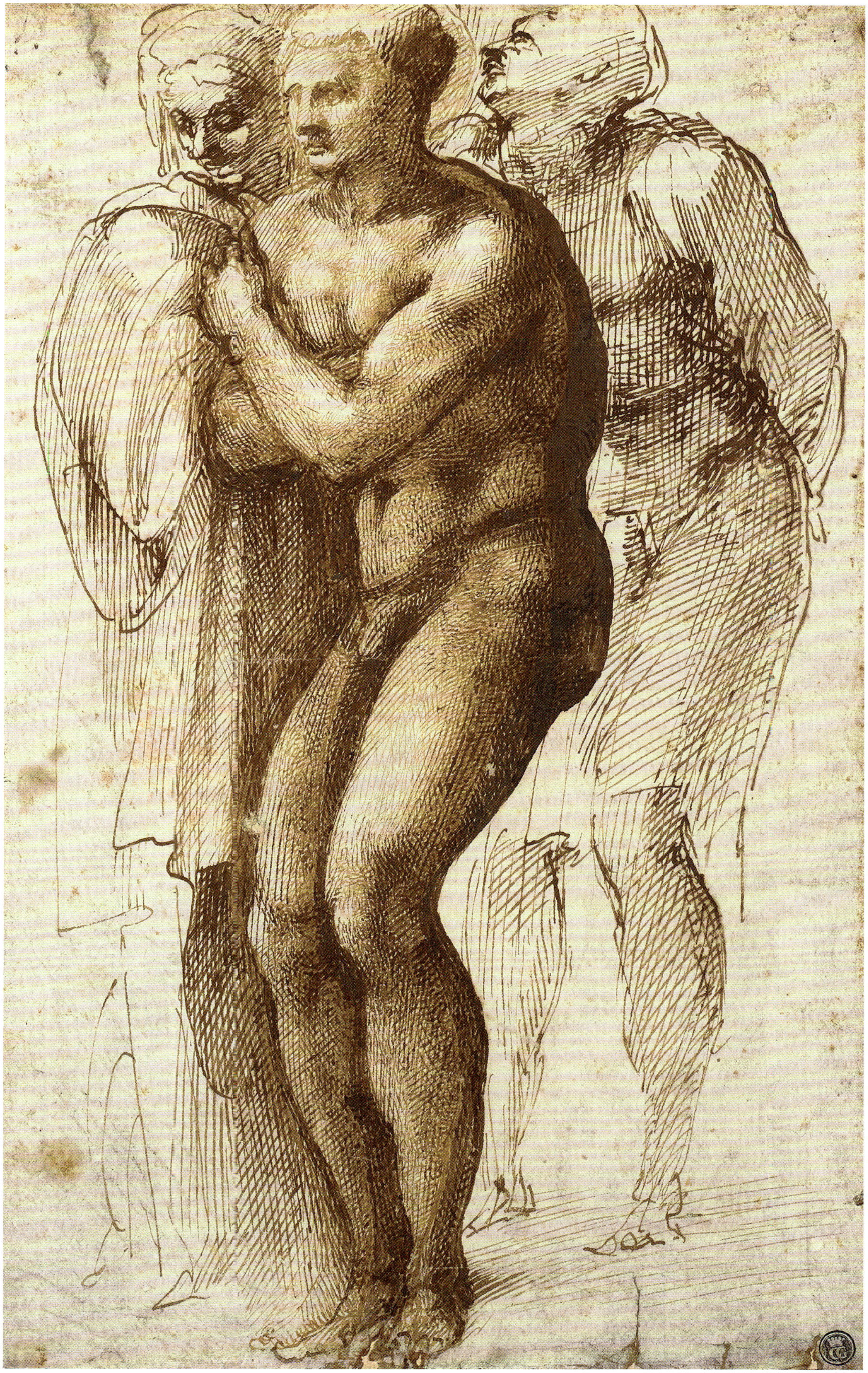

Michelangelo
Three Standing Figures,
ca. 1492–1496
Private Collection, USA

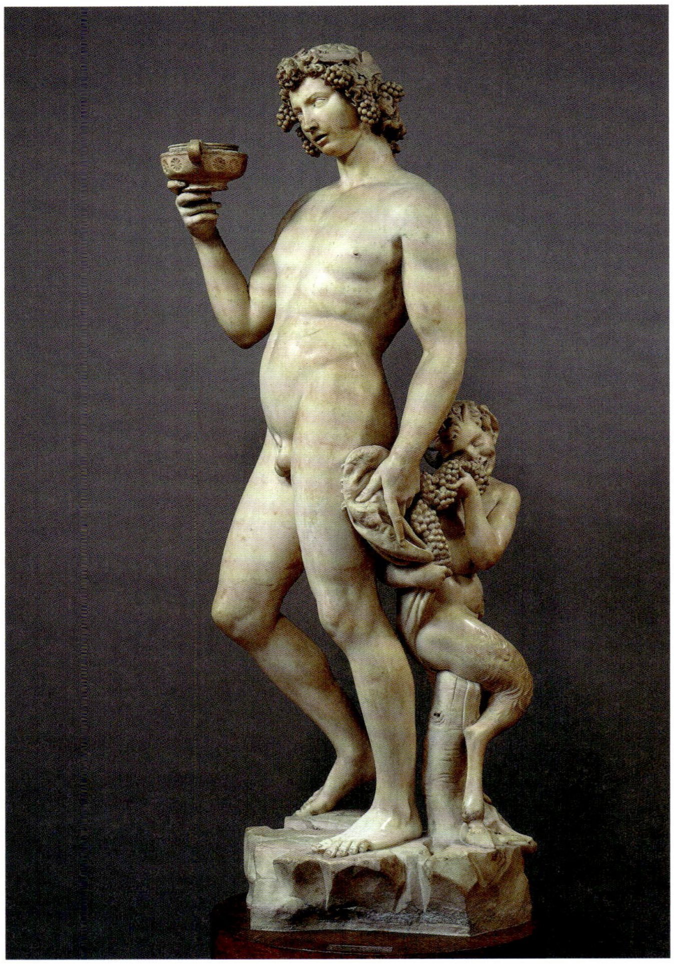

2 Michelangelo, *Bacchus*, 1496/97
Marble, h. 203 cm
Museo Nazionale del Bargello, Florence

One of his early sculptures, Michelangelo made his marble *Bacchus* (fig. 2) from 1496 to 1497. The work was commissioned by Cardinal Raffaele Riario, and from the time of its creation, this statue of the Roman god of wine was recognized as being on a par with the masterpieces of classical antiquity. Francesco I de' Medici acquired the figure in 1572 for display in the grand-ducal gallery in Florence alongside ancient sculptures already in his collection. In this early work, Michelangelo grapples with the ideal of the youthful male nude. Also, he takes a rather free approach to contrapposto: Bacchus, accompanied by a boyish faun, appears to step forward on unsteady legs. This is underscored by the curved line of the pose, suggestive of drunkenness. At the end of the seventeenth century, Massimiliano Soldani-Benzi made this same-size bronze copy for Hans-Adam I, Prince of Liechtenstein. Never before had Soldani created so ambitious a casting after a sculptural model.

LE

Massimiliano Soldani-Benzi
Bacchus, 1695–1703
LIECHTENSTEIN. The Princely Collections, Vaduz–Vienna,
Fürstliche Sammlungen Art Service GmbH

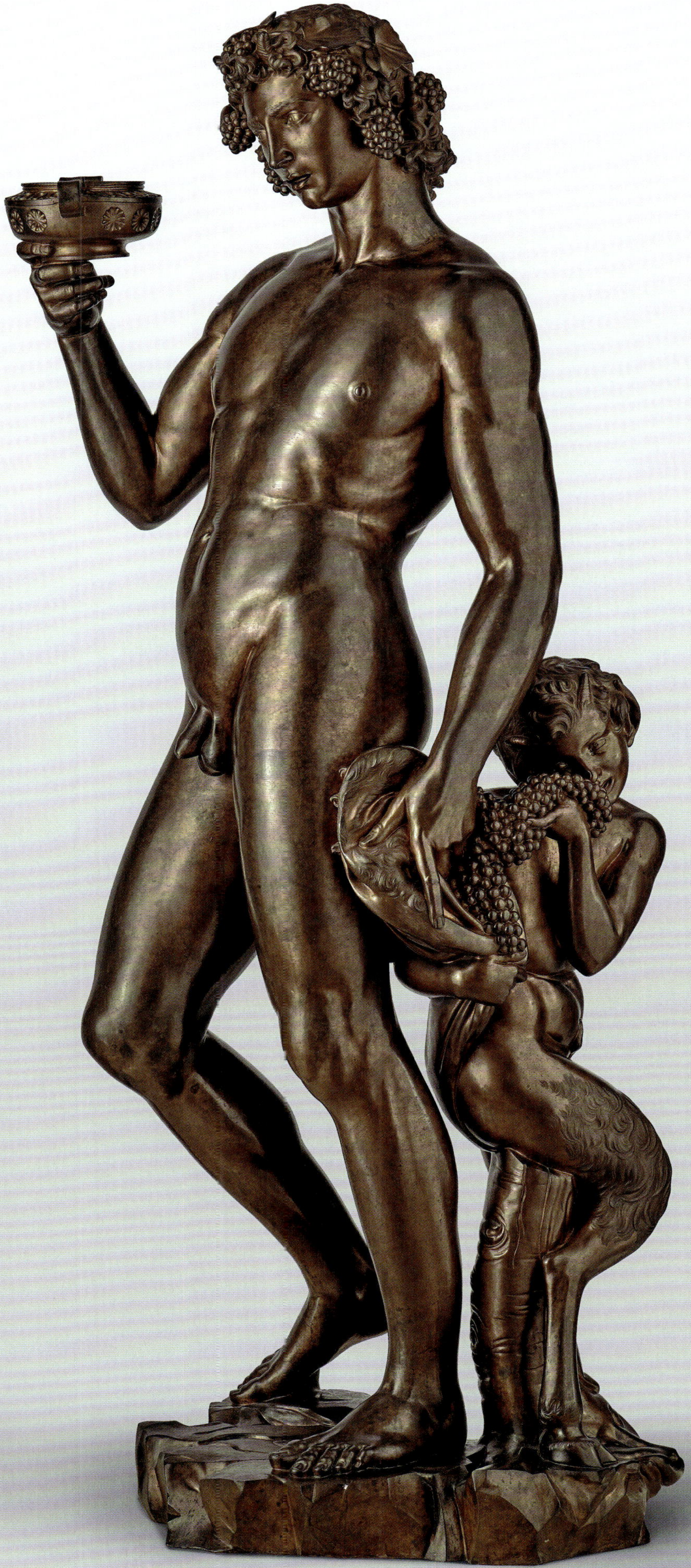

The Dancing Faun is among the most important statues from classical antiquity. The Roman marble copy after a lost Greek original shows a faun making music with cymbals and a scabellum, an ancient foot-operated clapper. It represents the ideal of a nude body in motion. The precise date of the statue's discovery is undocumented. The work was first mentioned, however, in the seventeenth century, and by the eighteenth century it had become one of the most influential antique sculptures. The significance of the Dancing Faun is underscored by its display in the Tribuna of the Medici gallery in the Uffizi of Florence. This elaborately decorated octagonal room is reserved for the most important and famous works of art in the grand-ducal collection, including the Medici Venus. In the nineteenth century, the claim was made that Michelangelo had carried out the restorations on the faun's head and arms. This assertion, later disproved, nevertheless provides an example of how the mythology surrounding Michelangelo's artistic genius developed after his death. This bronze copy made by Massimiliano Soldani-Benzi between 1695 and 1697 is the first in a series of casts after ancient models that Hans-Adam I, Prince of Liechtenstein, having returned from his Grand Tour, commissioned from the artist.

LE

Massimiliano Soldani-Benzi
Dancing Faun, 1695–1697
LIECHTENSTEIN. The Princely Collections, Vaduz–Vienna,
Fürstliche Sammlungen Art Service GmbH

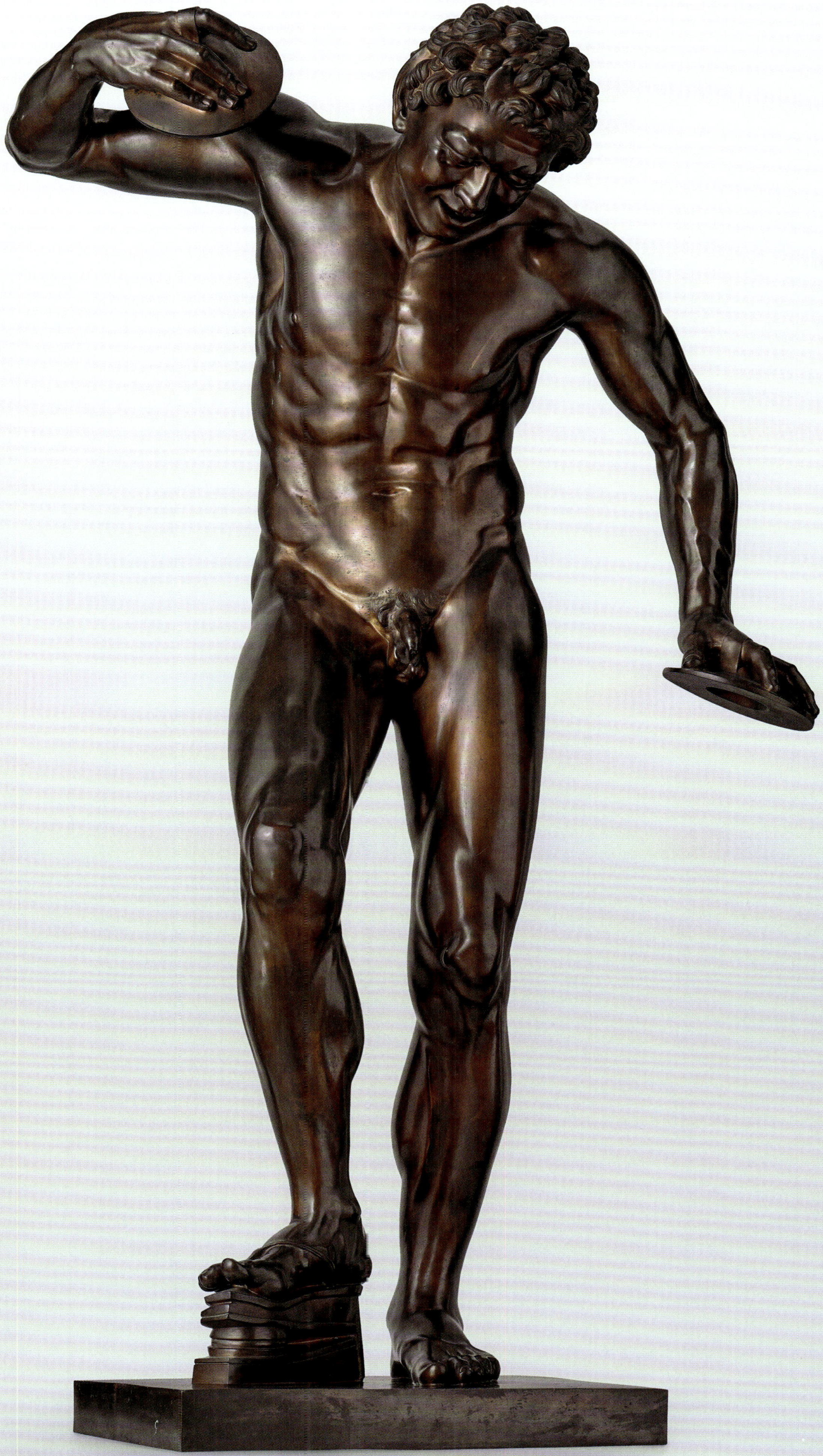

The Battle of Cascina, or Bodies in Tumult

Michelangelo's *Battle of Cascina* was to be executed as a monumental fresco on a wall of the Great Council Hall of the Palazzo della Signoria in Florence, in competition with Leonardo's *Battle of Anghiari*. The Signoria had approached Leonardo in the fall of 1503 with the request to paint the *Battle of Anghiari*, and the commission to Michelangelo likely occurred not much later. By the fall of 1504, when Michelangelo was assigned a room to produce the cartoon (a full-scale preliminary drawing), his project was certainly well underway. Unfortunately, these two battle scenes—the most famous of the Renaissance—were never completed: Leonardo's unfinished painting was lost to the remodeling of the hall, and Michelangelo's work never advanced beyond the preparatory stages. The *Battle of Cascina* cartoon is now lost, but a grisaille copy at Holkham Hall (fig. 3) illustrates its central scene. The background of the original showed a group of horsemen on the left and the actual battle on the right.

The famous battle depicted took place on July 28, 1364. Soldiers of the Florentine army were bathing in the Arno, seeking relief from the oppressive heat, when they were alerted to a surprise attack by Pisan troops, whom they fought back and defeated. Michelangelo divided the scene into three overlapping rows which reflect the sequence of events. The man rushing forward at the center is presumably Manno Donati, who raised the alarm. The soldiers in the immediate foreground scramble out of the river; those in the middle row dress themselves; and the ones in the upper zone prepare for battle. According to Vasari, some of the cartoon's nudes, which were over life-size, were outlined in charcoal and shaded with hatching, while others were modeled in graded tones and then heightened with white. In these figures, Michelangelo arrived at his new ideal of the heroic figure.

Artists flocked to the cartoon to sketch its motifs of bold action and the subtle foreshortening of the nude bodies. The figures displayed profound anatomical knowledge, having had been studied from live models. However, for Michelangelo, the depiction of musculature was not an end in itself; rather, it served to illustrate interior qualities of the human in action: irrepressible power, pulsating energy, determination, and strength of will—things no other artist had ever represented in this way. Leonardo writes in his treatise on painting that a good painter must portray two things: the human form and the intention of the mind. And while the first is easy, the second is difficult since it has to be expressed through the gestures and movements of the body.

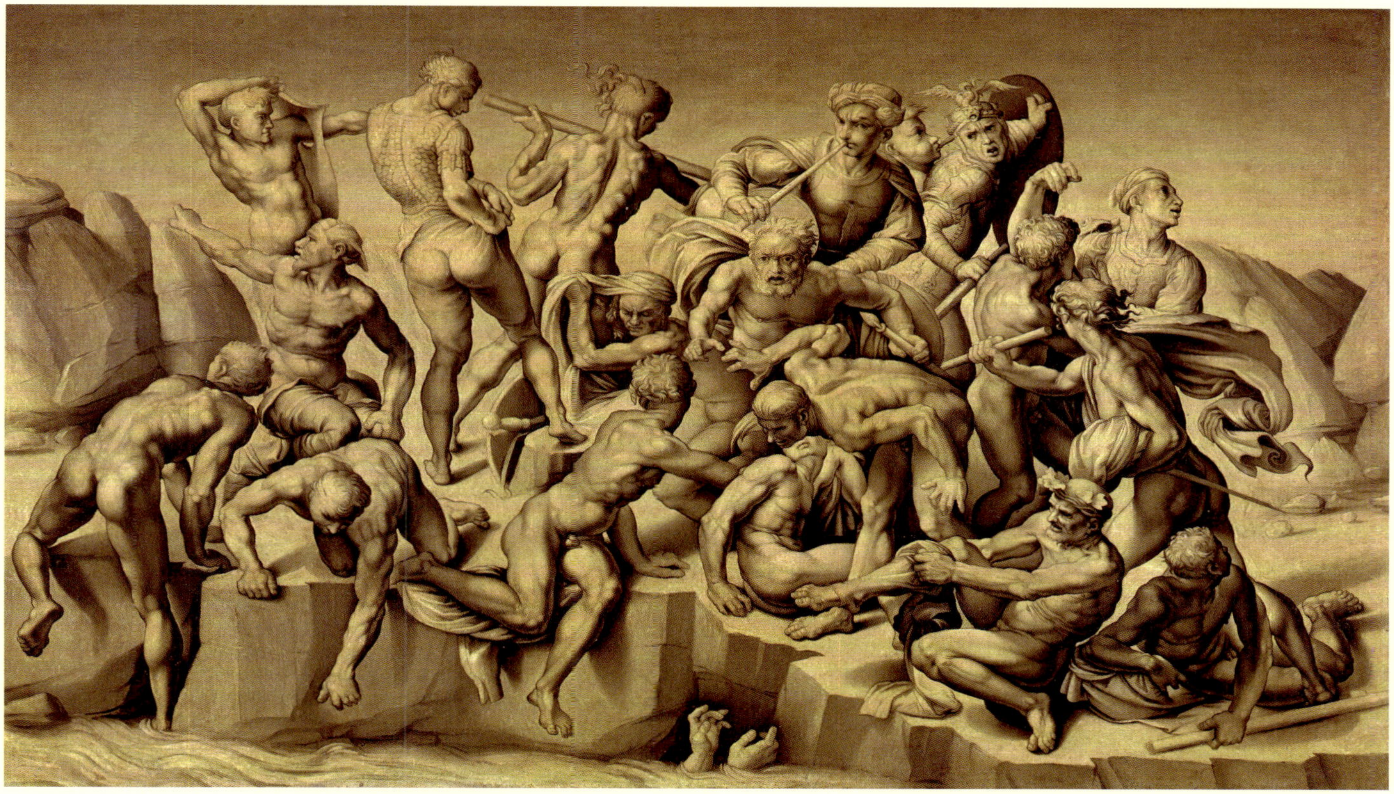

3 Bastiano (Aristotile) da Sangallo (after Michelangelo), *Battle of Cascina*, 1542
Oil on panel, 76.4 × 130.2 cm
Collection of the Earl of Leicester, Holkham Hall, Norfolk

The sculptor and goldsmith Benvenuto Cellini described the battle scenes by Leonardo and Michelangelo as paramount examples of the depiction of the human body—they were "the school of the world" (*la scuola del mondo*). Also, a change in Michelangelo's style can be observed in the *Battle of Cascina*. Whereas previously most of his figures seemed enclosed within their contours and were shown frontally, they now twist around their own axis and penetrate the space around them with bold, sweeping motions.

The Albertina's beautiful full-length male nude shown from behind has sometimes been associated with the marble *David* (fig. 4) commissioned from Michelangelo in August 1501; however, similar figures charging away from the viewer are found in early sketches for the *Battle of Cascina*. It was probably within that context that the drawing was made. Compared to the straight, stiffly applied strokes in the early copies after Giotto and Masaccio, the lines now flex and curve lightly as they model the musculature and flow harmoniously into the contours. They form an organic network that lends the movements a lively fluidity. In addition to the finely detailed technique of this work, Michelangelo used more summary means in other pen-and-ink drawings. Such is the case with the study of a Virgin and Child on the reverse of the present sheet, the pose of which would be used again for the *Medici Madonna* in the New Sacristy of San Lorenzo. In the drawing, the poses of Mary and the Christ Child are quickly defined with a few sketchy strokes, and the positions and

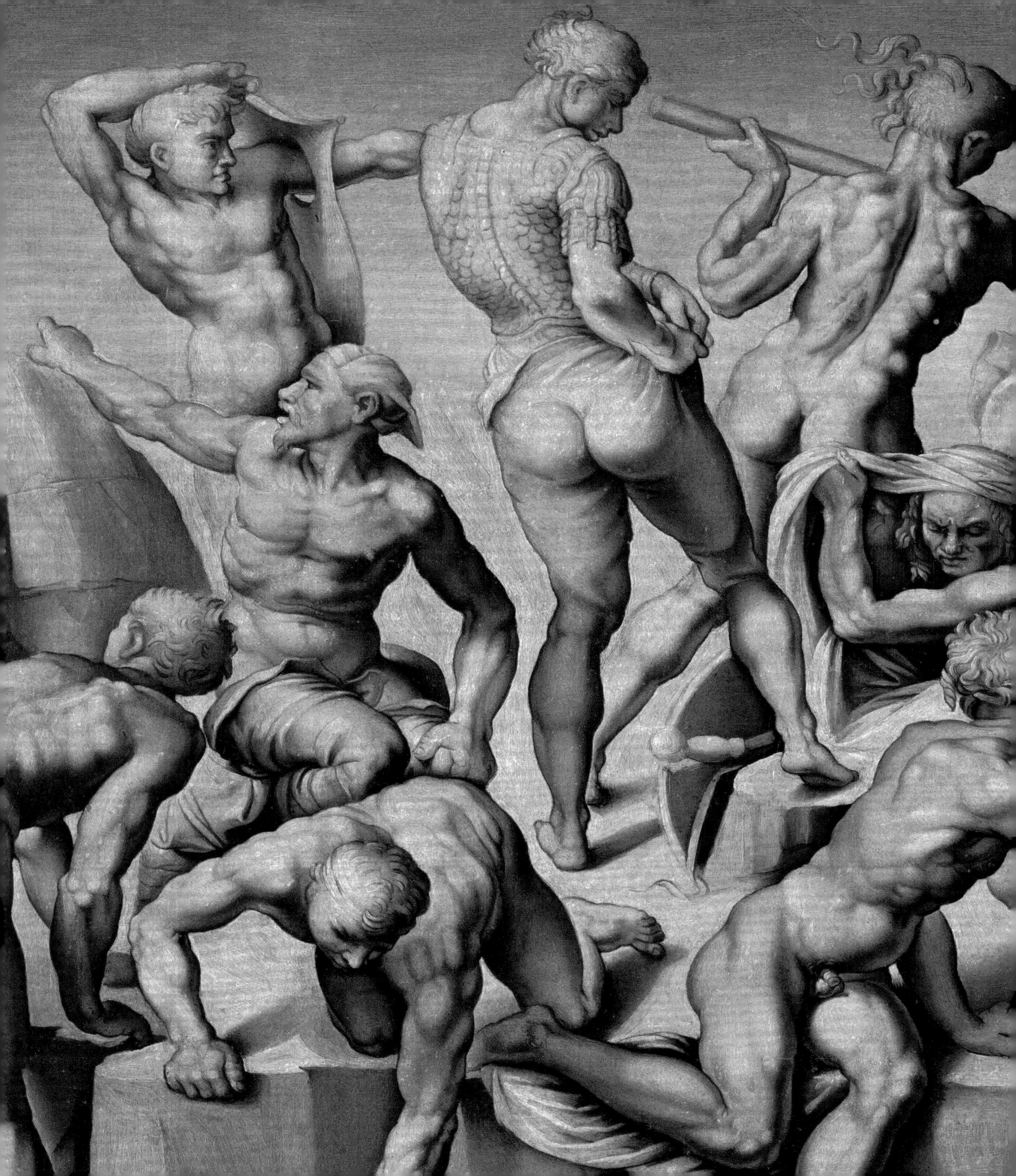

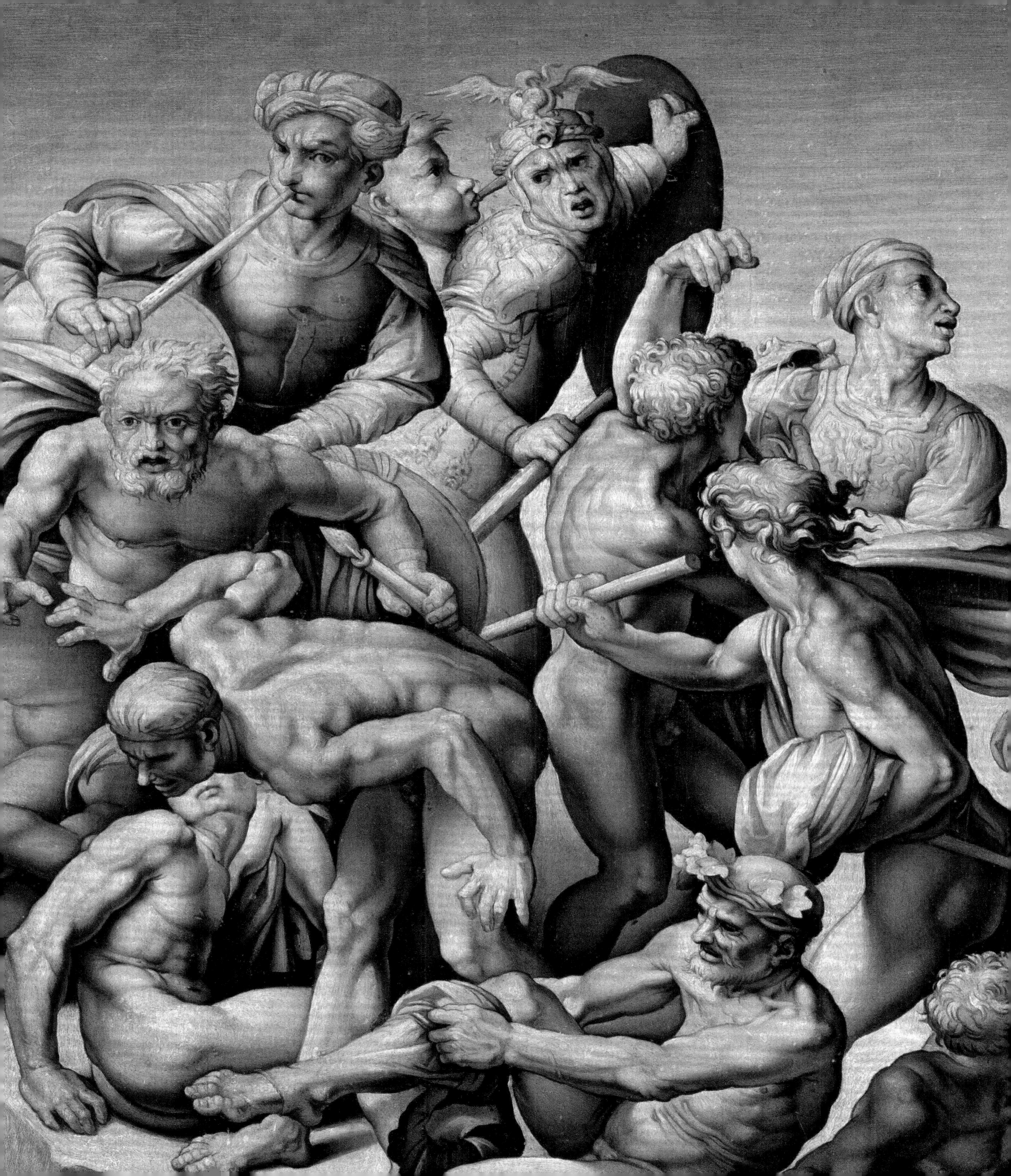

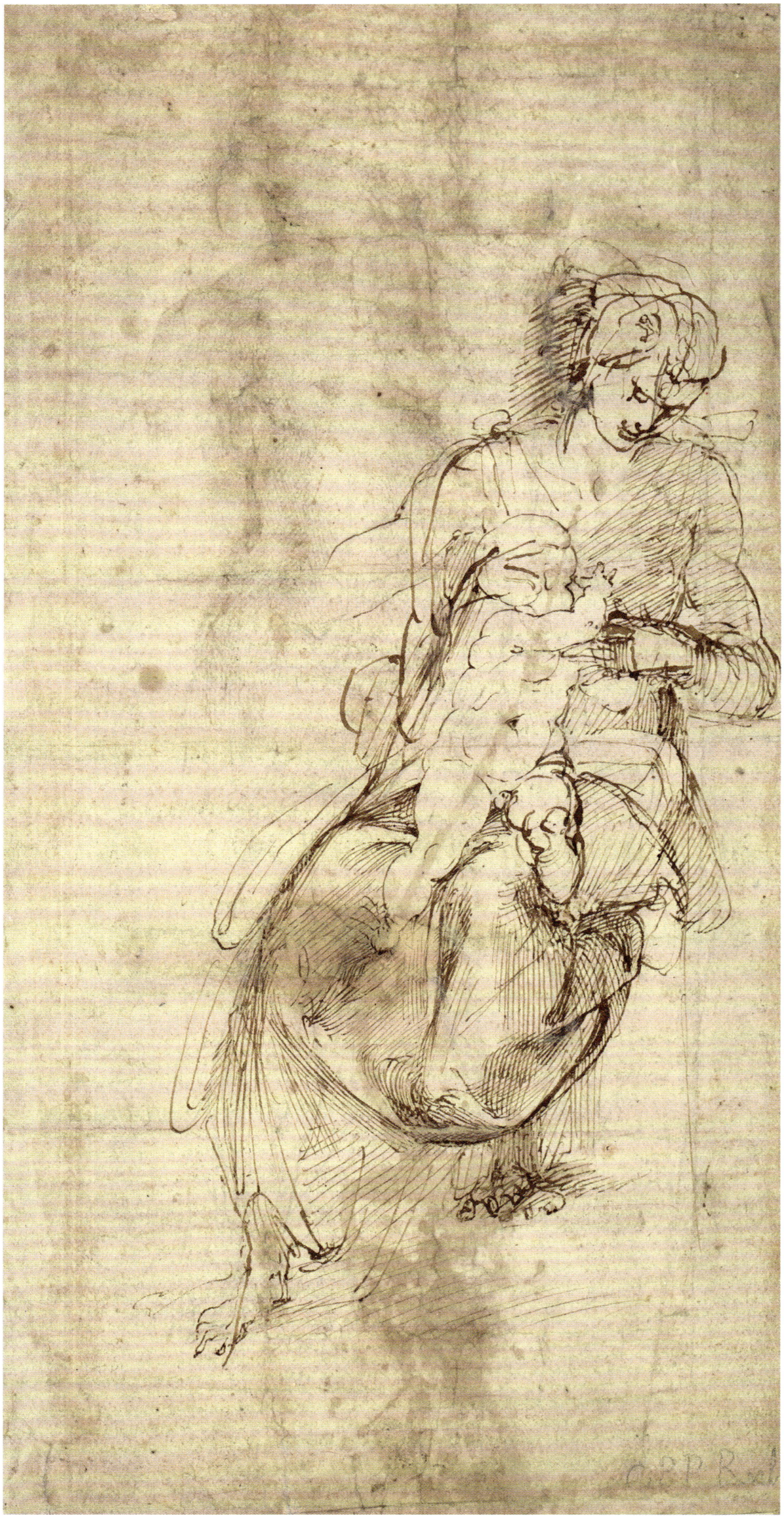

Michelangelo
The Virgin with the Child at Her Breast,
ca. 1503
The ALBERTINA Museum, Vienna

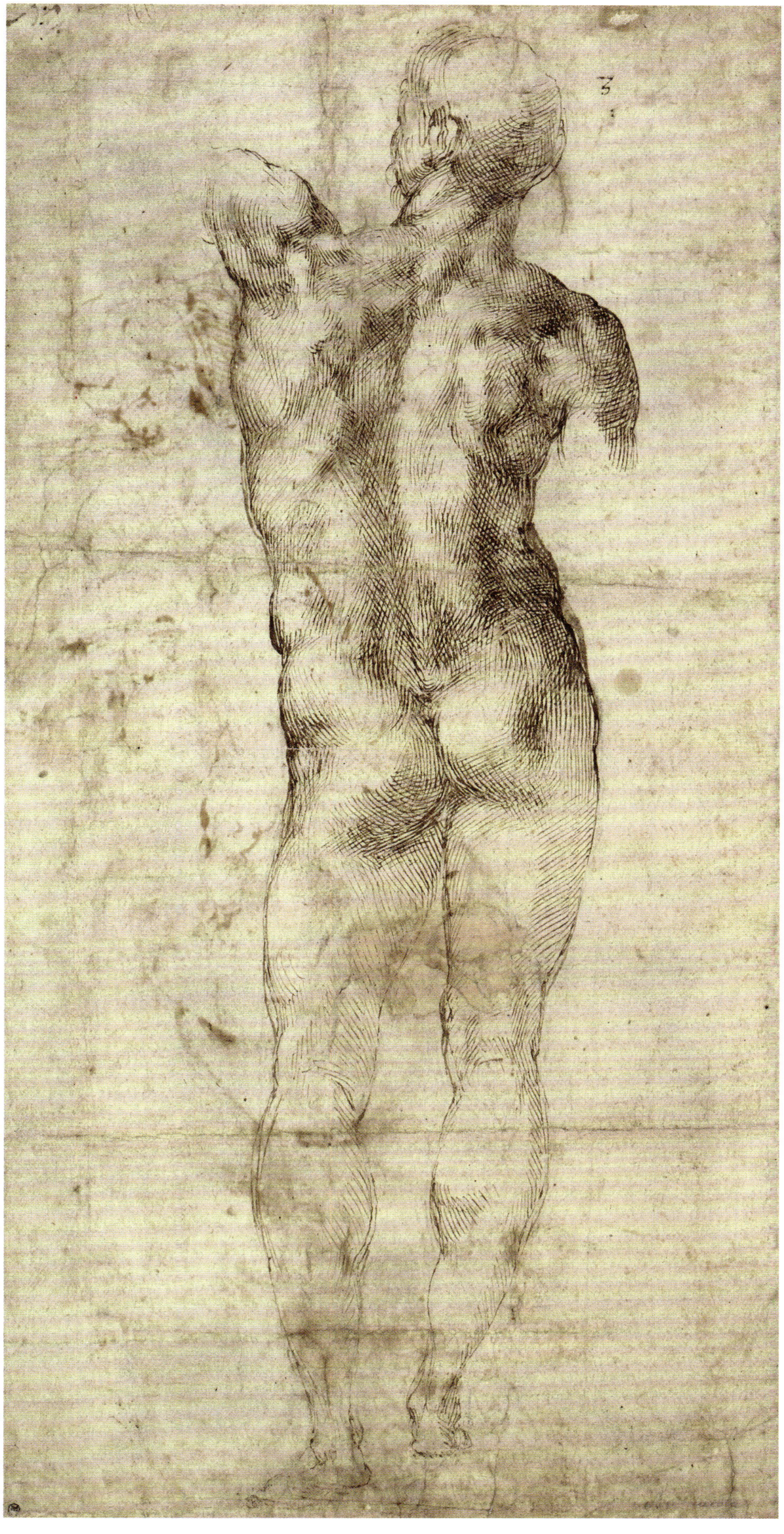

Michelangelo
Standing Male Nude Seen from the Rear,
ca. 1503
The ALBERTINA Museum, Vienna

foreshortening of the limbs are masterfully captured with a succession of short, curved lines.

On the front of another *Battle of Cascina* sheet in the Albertina, Michelangelo made studies for the soldier who rushes forward at the cartoon's center and, next to him, the one helping a comrade put on a cuirass. Working from live models, the artist began by outlining the body in black chalk, which he then carefully traced with a pen. The nude seen from the back on the other side of the sheet was preparatory to the soldier bearing a lance in the background of this scene of "bathers." In the drawing, Michelangelo slightly shifted the position of model's head (wearing a tight-fitting cap), and he gave only a general indication of the outstretched arm, since that limb would be overlapped by a neighboring figure in the cartoon. He used black chalk here, which from here on became his preferred material. This was related to the aforementioned change in style and the artist's endeavor to express a more spatial notion of the figure. The softness of the chalk enabled him to create fluid transitions and uniform fields of shadow, thereby achieving painterly effects. As in the cartoon, Michelangelo also applied white heightening to make the muscles stand out and accentuate their ability to move. The numerous tensed muscle groups create a lively relief that suggests tremendous interior exertion. The dynamic contour simultaneously contains the figure and directs energy outward.

The sheet with various arm studies documents Michelangelo's meticulous approach to producing anatomically precise representations of limbs. The three bent right arms in the lower portion are preparatory drawings for the soldier donning armor in the cartoon's upper left. As in the pen-and-ink study of two soldiers discussed above, the individual muscles are marked with reference lines and ciphers in order to clarify their positions from different angles and at different levels of tension. Perhaps Michelangelo planned to supply a legend with detailed descriptions for the ciphers and use that for a scientific exposition on the structures of the human body. In any case, according to his biographer Ascanio Condivi, Michelangelo intended to write a treatise dealing with human anatomy and all conceivable postures and movements.

AG

4 Michelangelo, *David*, 1501–1504
Marble, h. 517 cm
Galleria dell'Accademia, Florence

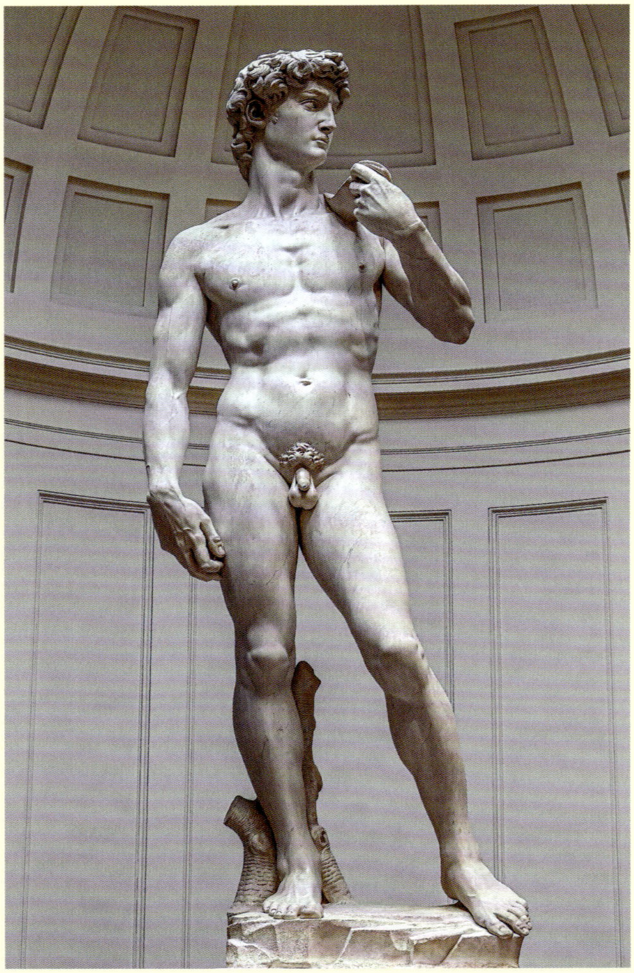

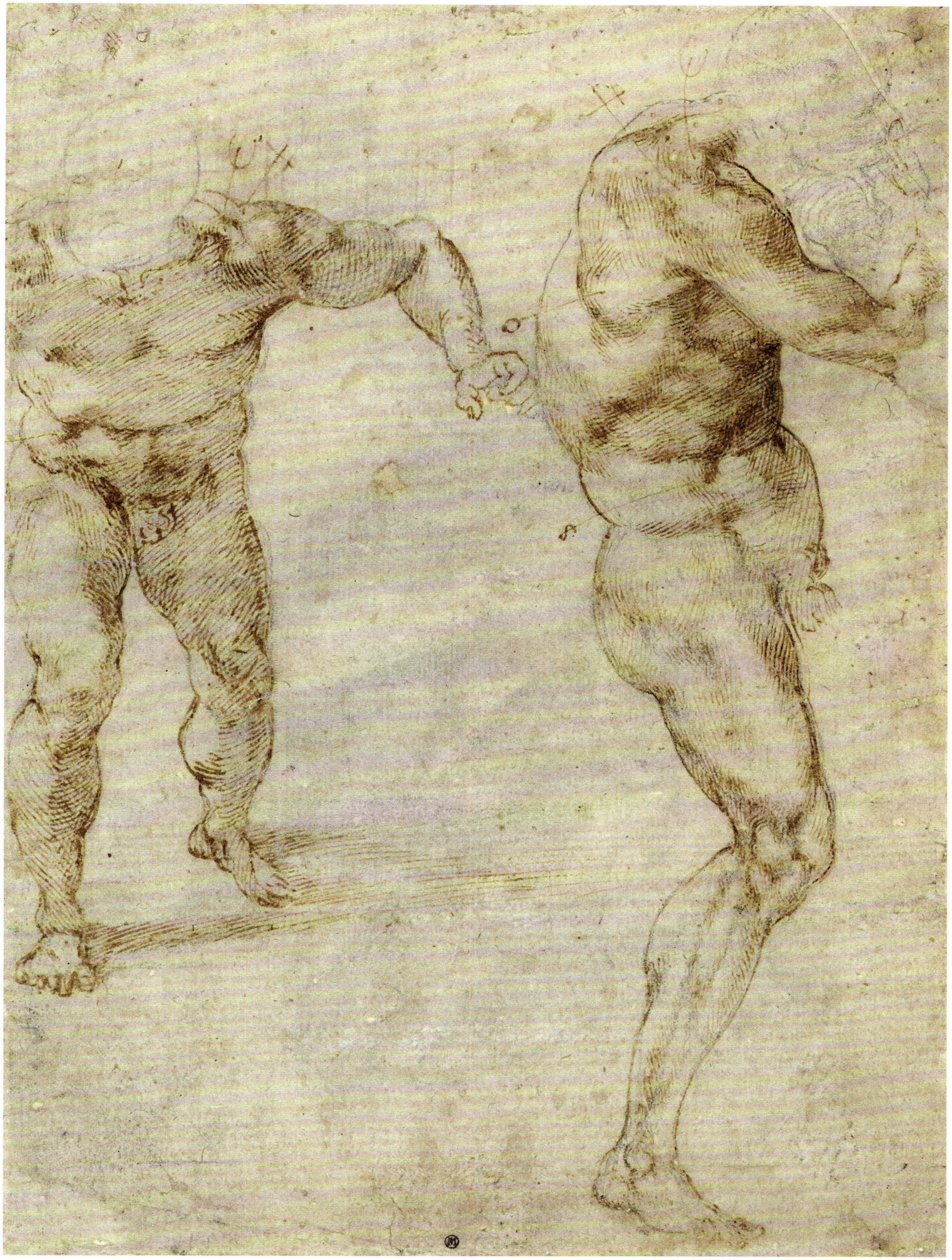

Michelangelo
Studies of Two Male Nudes, One Rushing Forward and One Facing Right, ca. 1504
The ALBERTINA Museum, Vienna

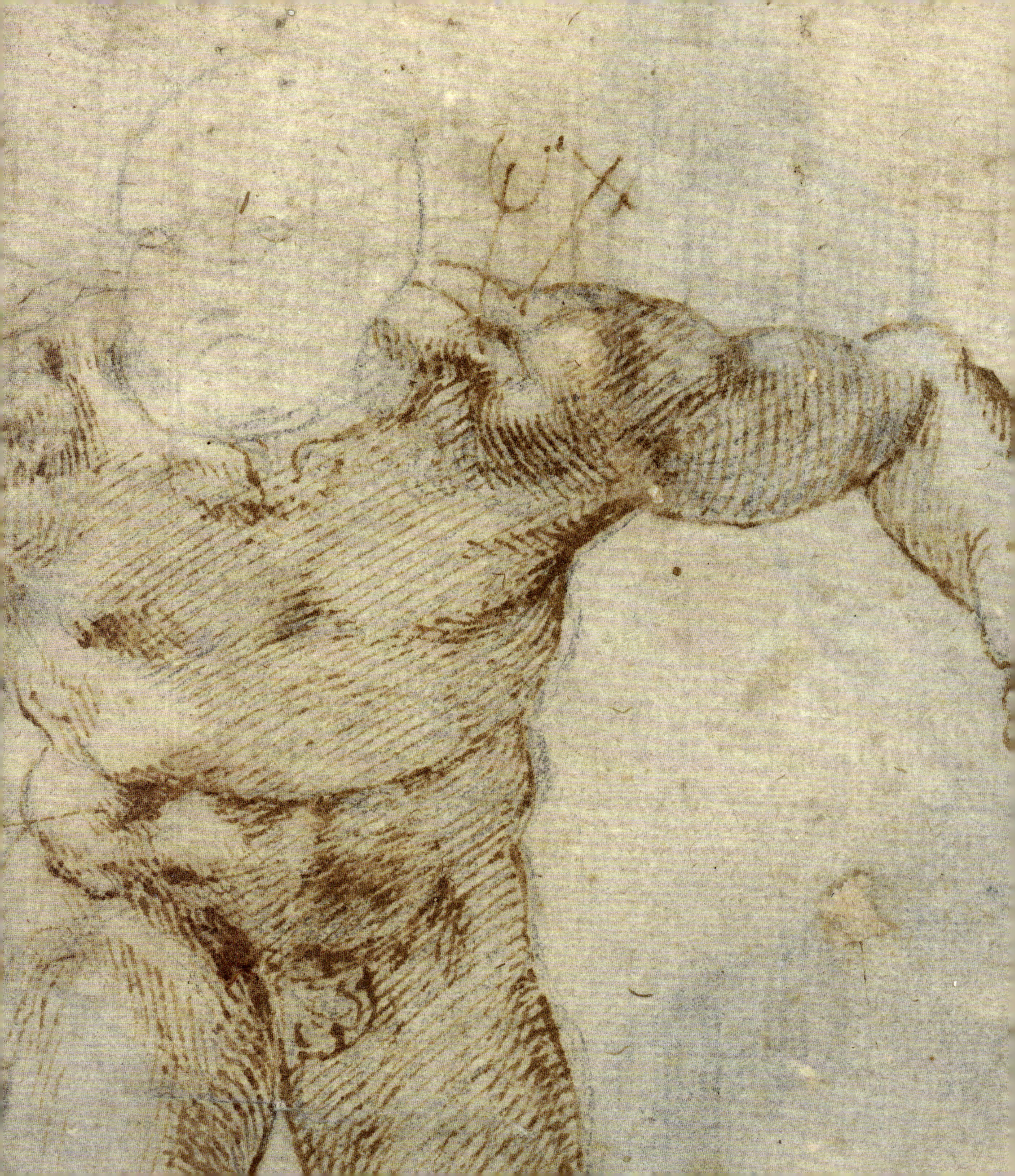

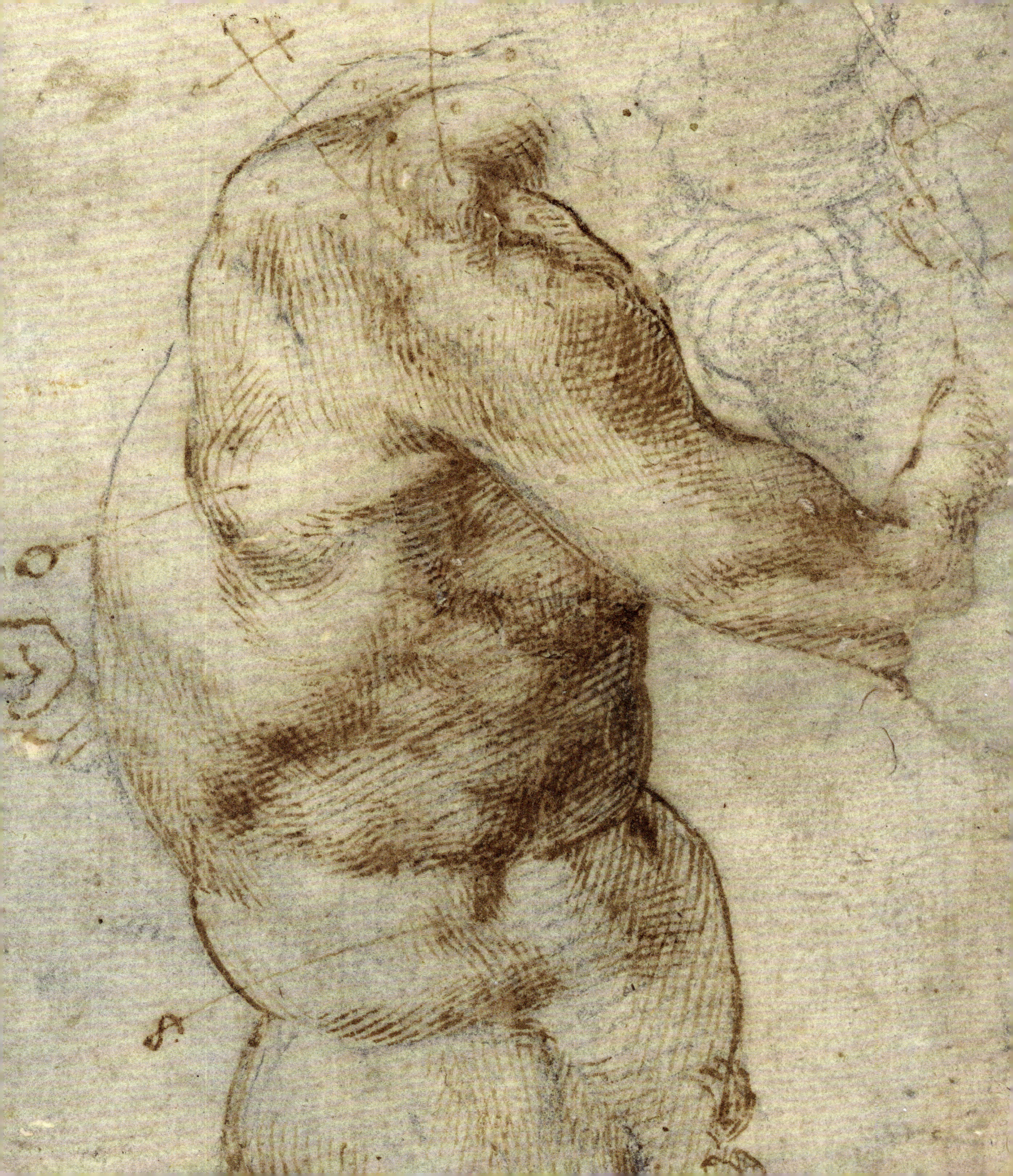

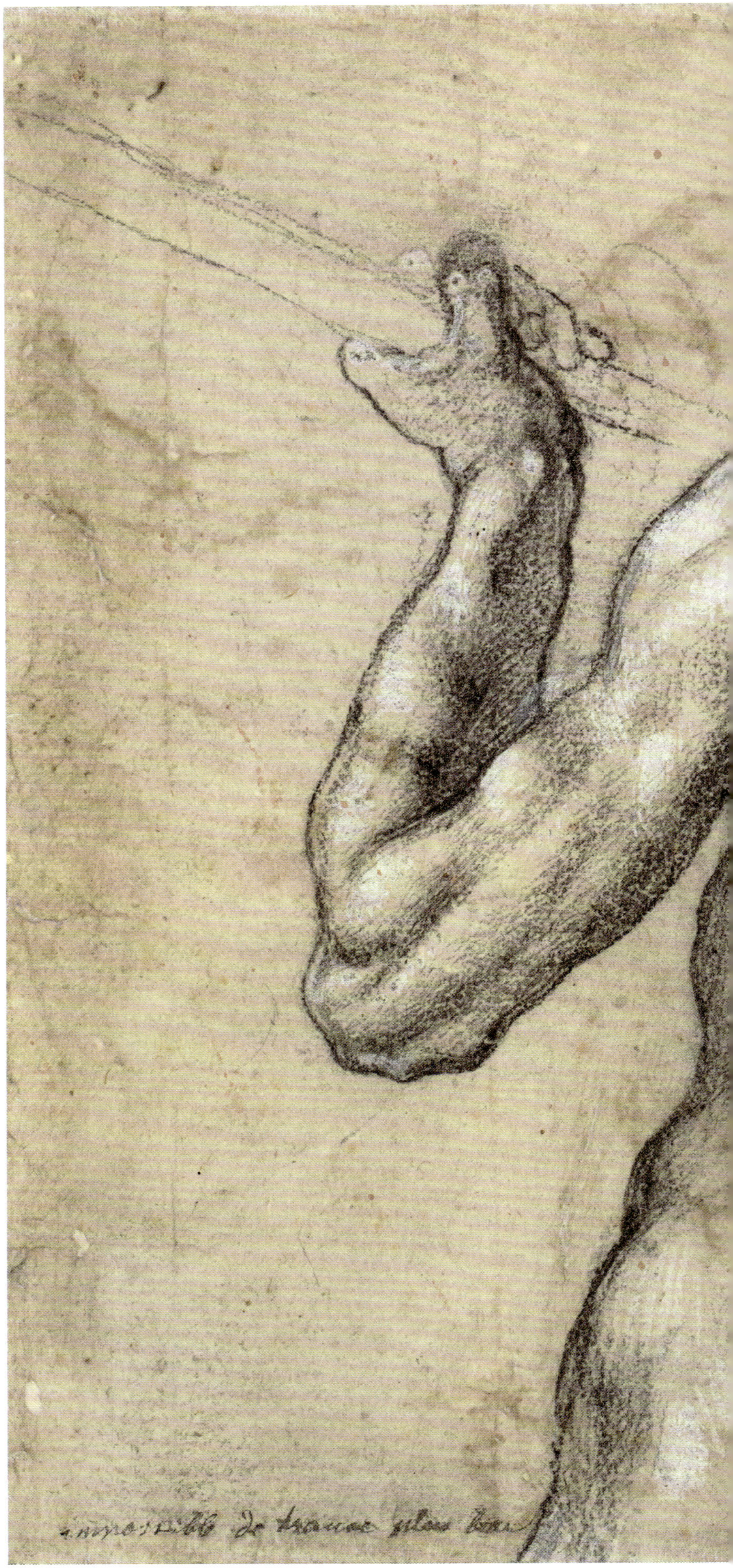

Michelangelo
Male Nude Seen from the Rear, ca. 1504
The ALBERTINA Museum, Vienna

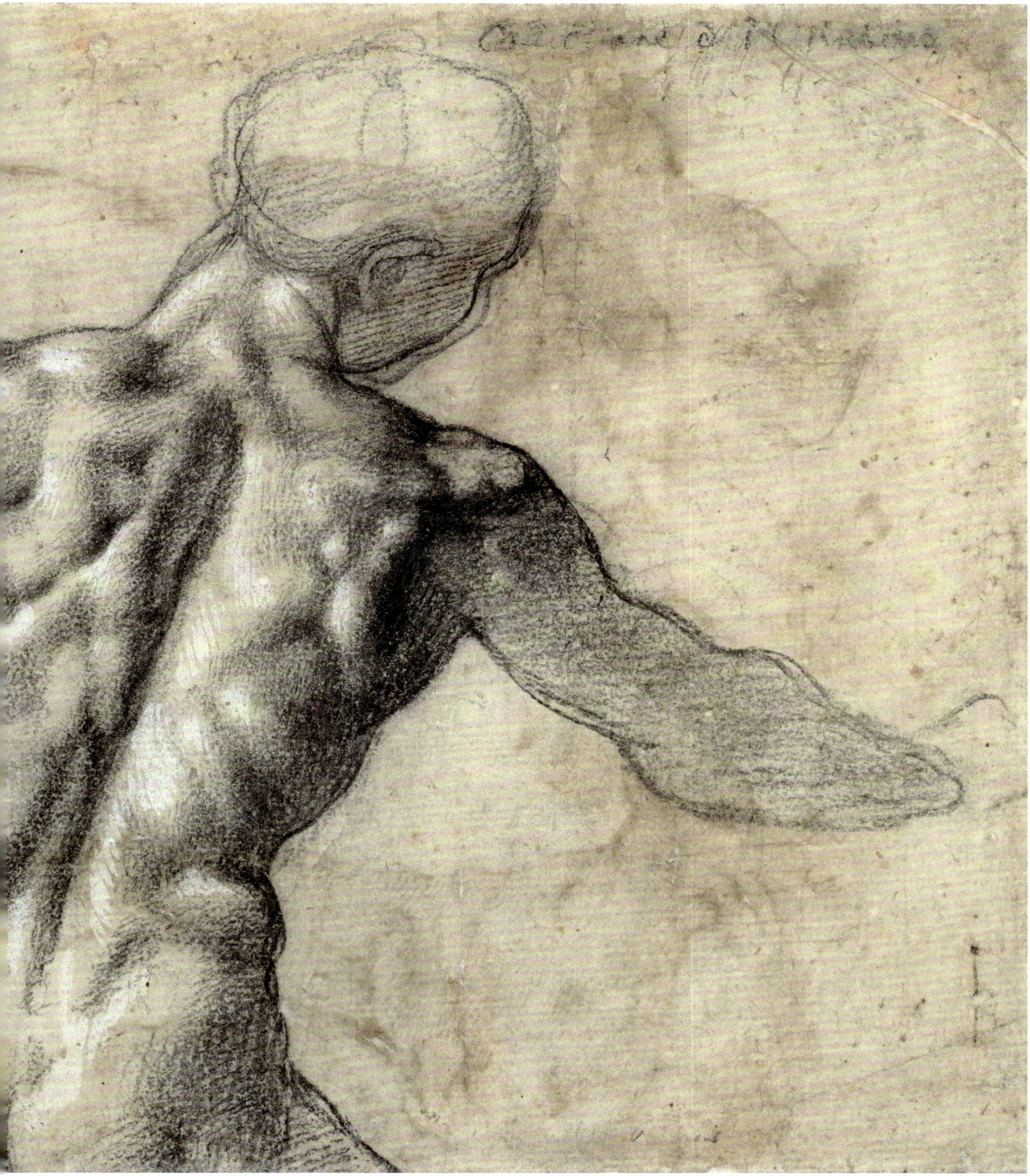

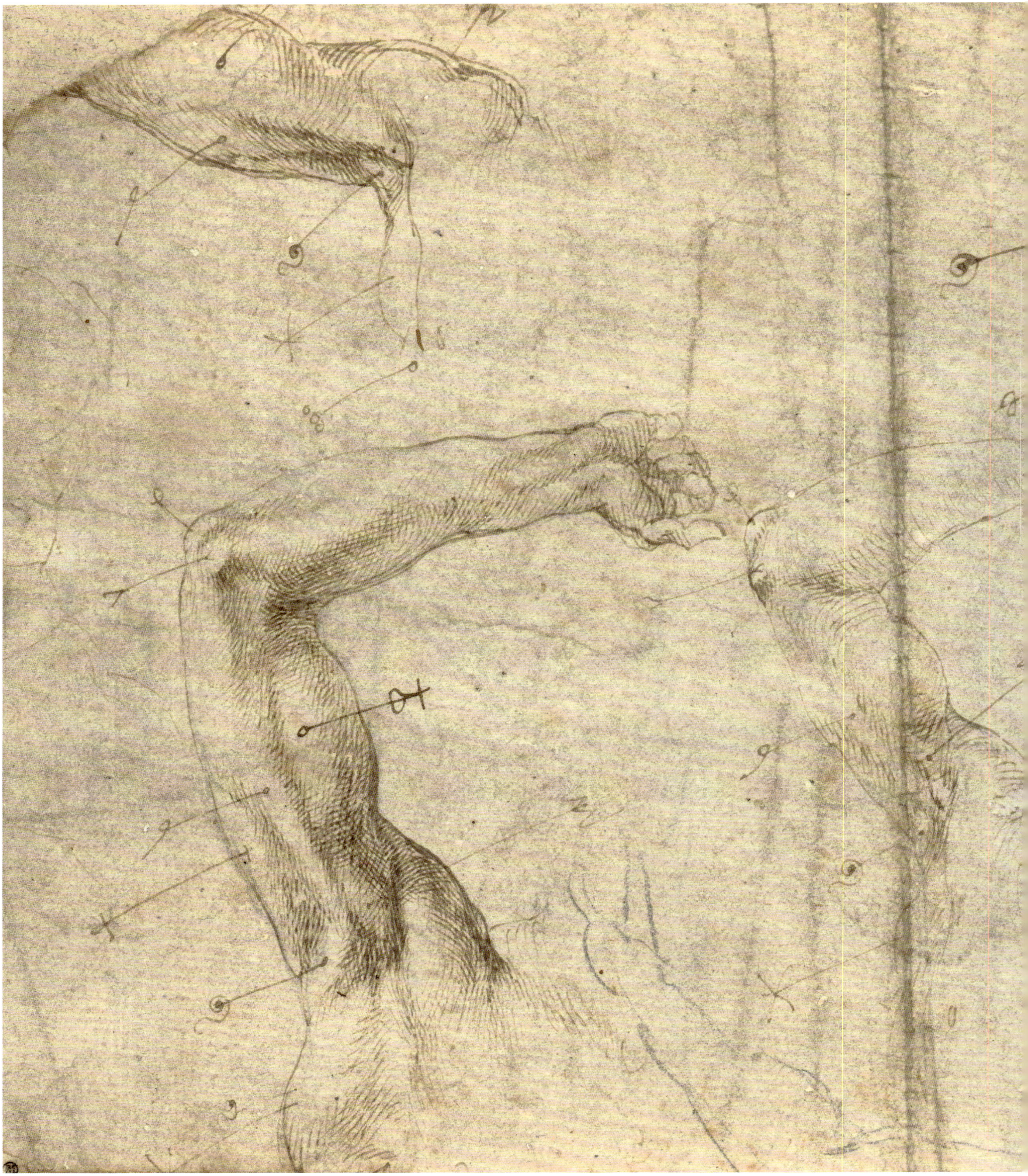

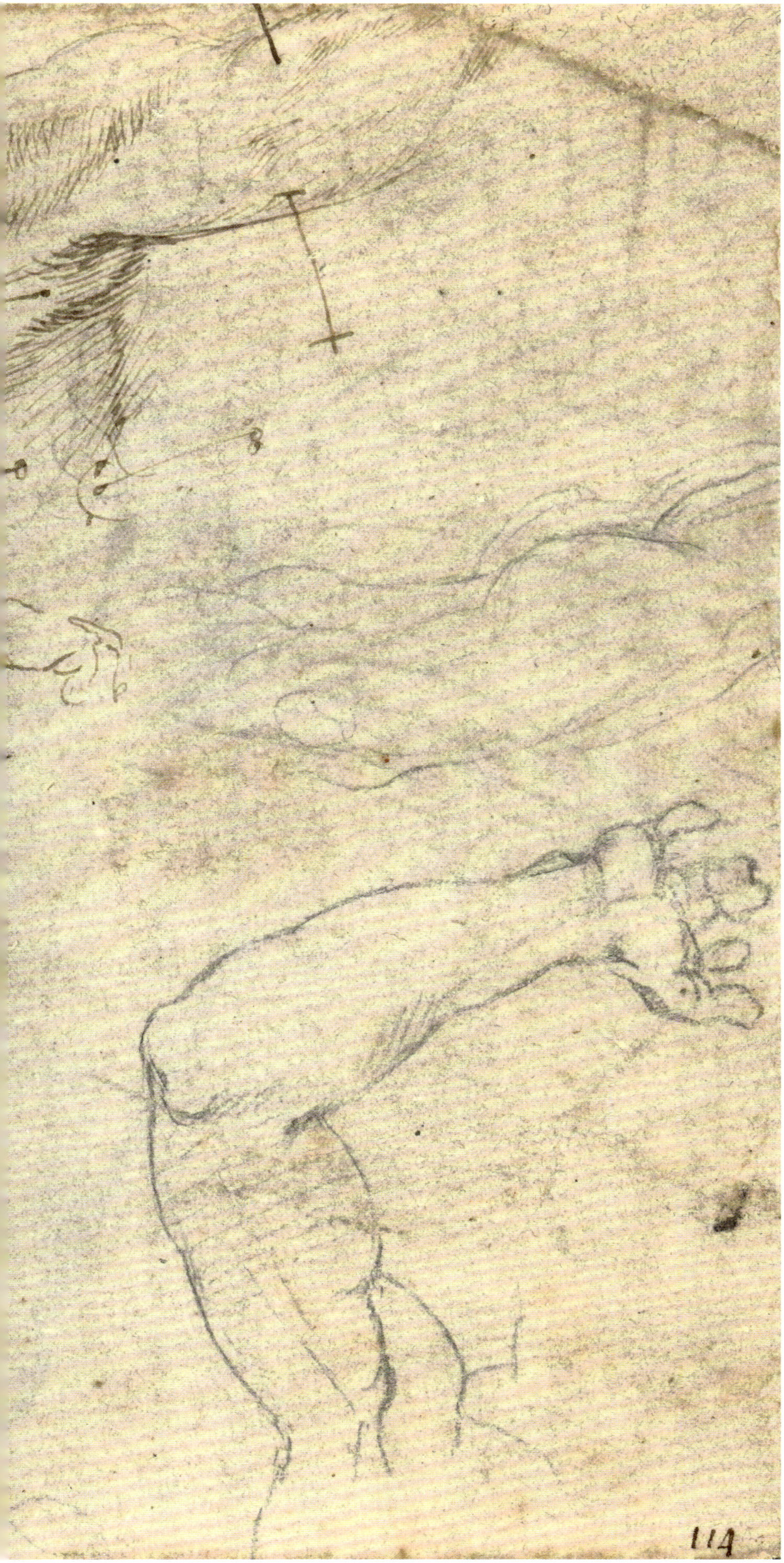

Michelangelo
Studies of a Raised Arm with Shoulder Joint, ca. 1504
The ALBERTINA Museum, Vienna

After Laocoön: 1506

The ancient Laocoön group was discovered in 1506 during excavations in a vineyard just outside the gates of Rome, causing a sensation. Michelangelo and his fellow artist Giuliano da Sangallo were among those who hurried to view the masterpiece. They agreed that the unearthed sculpture was the same Laocoön group that Pliny the Elder had mentioned in AD 79 in his *Naturalis historia*. The work represents the legend of the Trojan priest Laocoön, whom the gods punished with death for warning his fellow citizens about the Trojan Horse. The Roman marble copy after a lost Greek bronze shows Laocoön and his two sons struggling against deadly serpents set on them by the gods. Immediately after its discovery, the work was purchased by Pope Julius II and put on display among other sculptures in the Belvedere courtyard at the Vatican. Artists made pilgrimages to the Laocoön in order to draw from an antique original and study its human anatomy. The sculptural group was regarded as the quintessential portrayal of agony, as expressed in the figures' strained poses and intense facial expressions. The ancient ideal of human form embodied by this work had a decisive impact not only on Michelangelo but also on subsequent generations of artists, especially in the endeavor to represent the male nude at various ages.

LE

Giovanni Francesco Susini
***Laocoön*, second quarter of the 17th century**
LIECHTENSTEIN. The Princely Collections, Vaduz–Vienna, Fürstliche Sammlungen Art Service GmbH

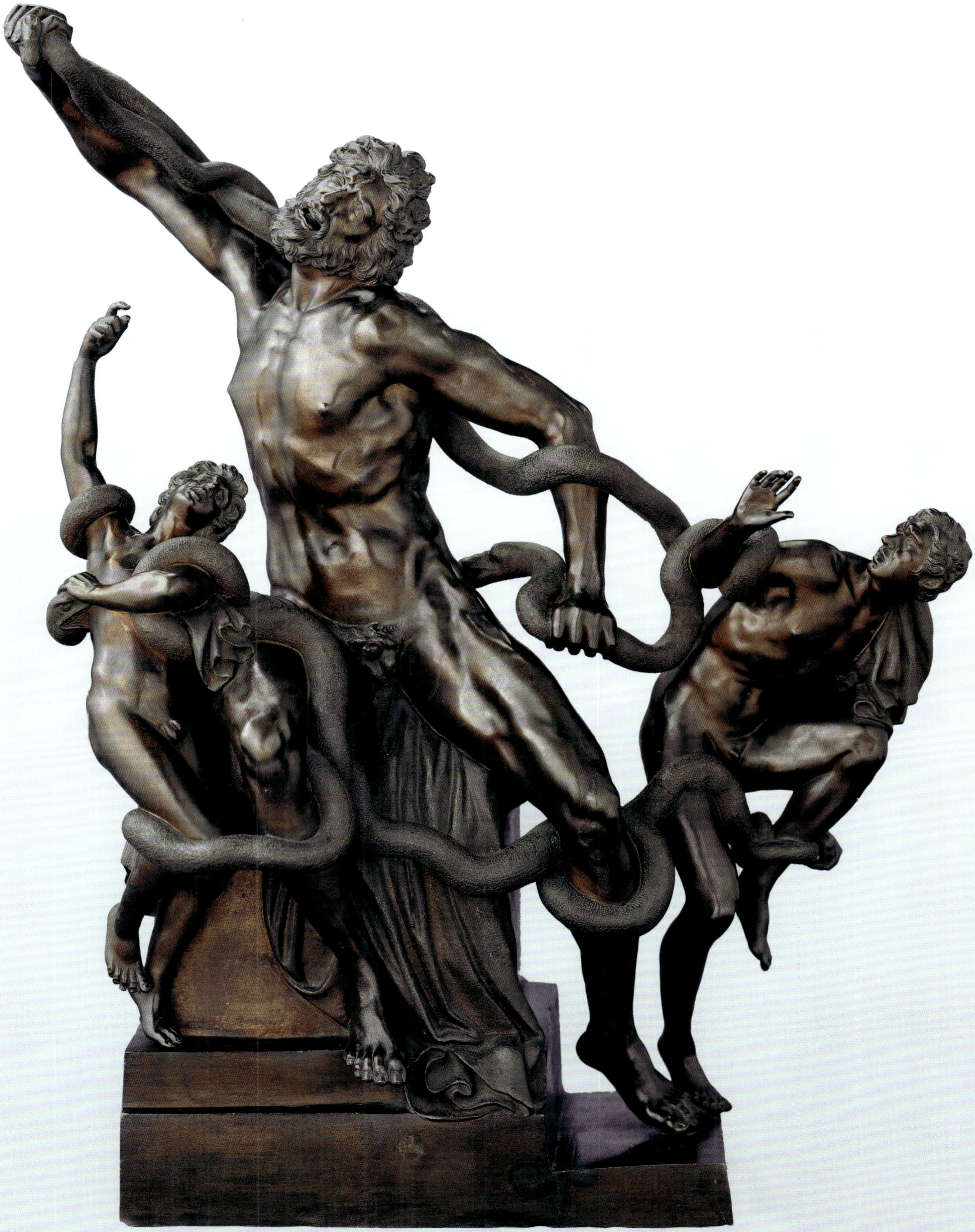

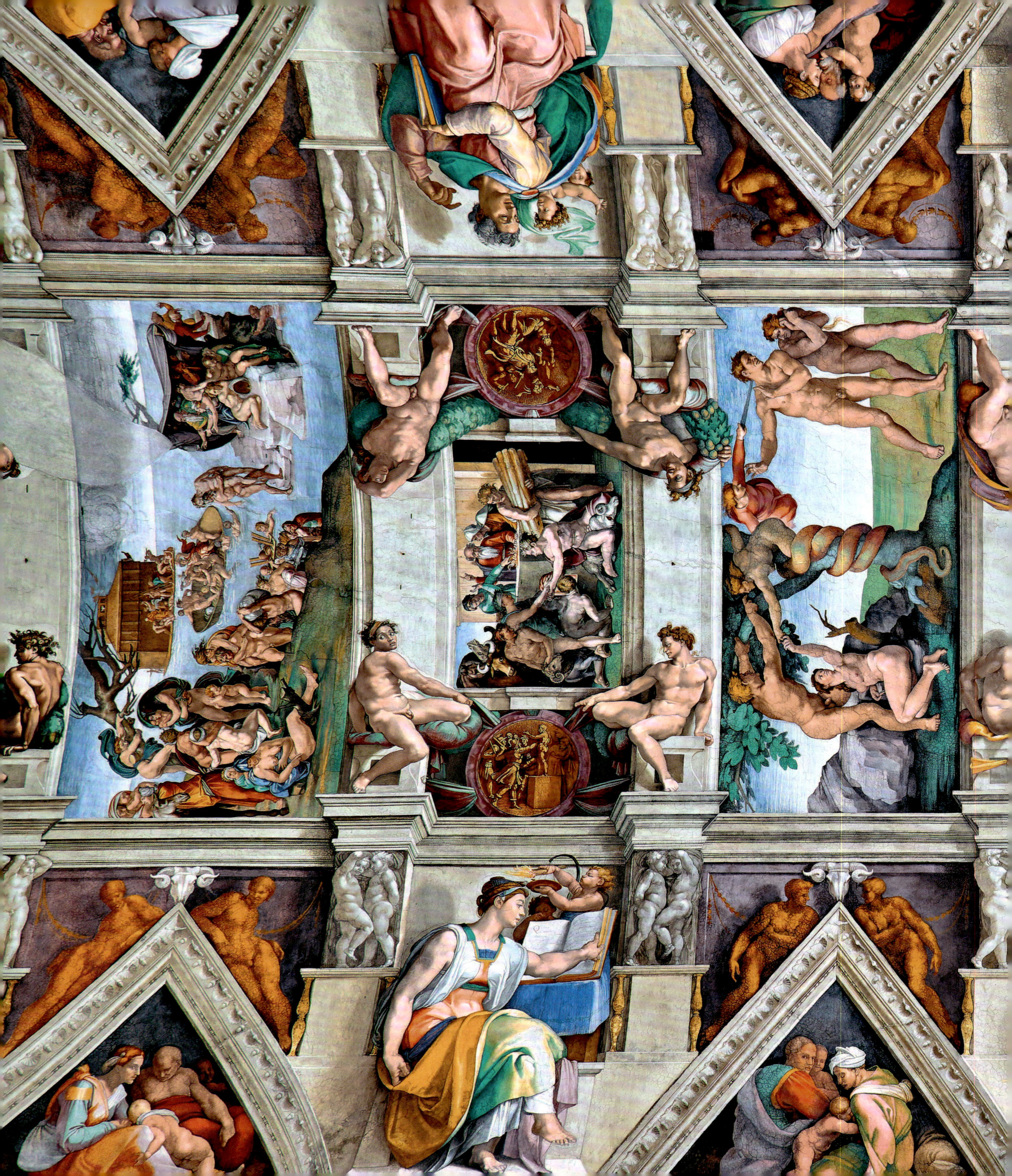

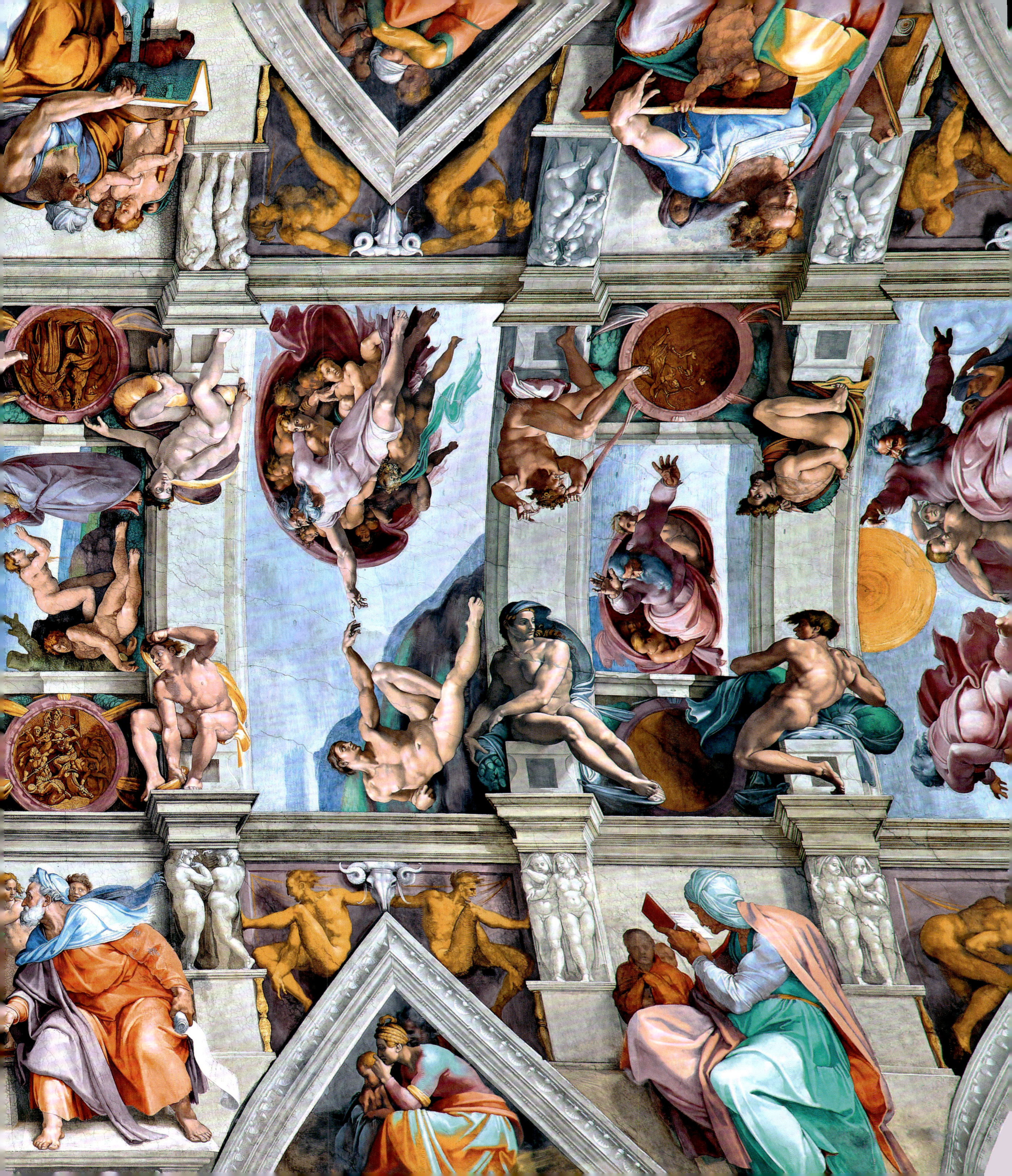

Naked in the Sistine Chapel

The ceiling decoration of the Sistine Chapel is not only Michelangelo's first surviving fresco and his most famous and influential painted work, it is also one of the greatest artistic creations of all time. Michelangelo gave the biblical figures heroic dimensions. In scenes from the Creation and the story of Noah, he illustrated the irreversibility of the divine plan of salvation and its implications for humanity, doing so in a pictorial way that still informs how we imagine those events today. He was initially reluctant to accept the commission. Pope Julius II had originally summoned Michelangelo to Rome in the spring of 1505 to erect a monumental free-standing tomb for him in Old St. Peter's Basilica. In the meantime, however, Julius had entrusted the architect Donato Bramante with rebuilding St. Peter's. From then on, all efforts were concentrated on that mammoth undertaking, and the tomb project was postponed, much to Michelangelo's regret. He began painting the Sistine ceiling in the late summer of 1508, completing the project only with great difficulty and largely alone. Numerous preparatory drawings offer insight into the process of planning the fresco decoration.

5 Michelangelo, *Ignudo*, 1508–1512
Fresco
Sistine Chapel, Vatican

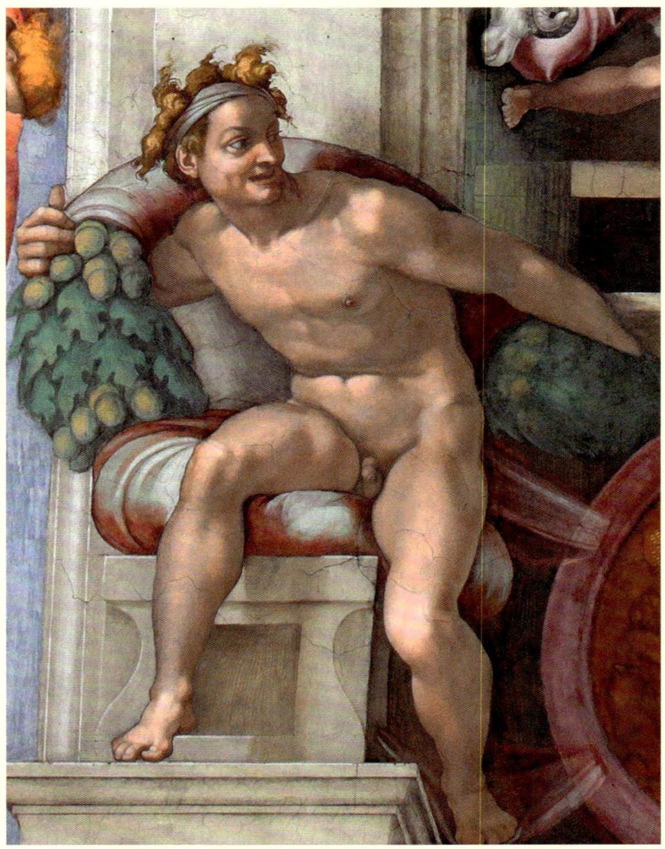

The drawing in the Louvre, in black chalk over lines incised with a stylus, served as a preparatory study for one of the *ignudi*, the seated youthful nudes arranged in pairs to either side of the central scenes. The *ignudo* in question (fig. 5), to the upper left of the prophet Isaiah on the ceiling, leans forward and directs a playful smile at his counterpart. The figure in the drawing largely corresponds to its execution in the fresco, although some details are absent in the study: the garland bearing acorns in reference to the Rovere family coat of arms of Julius II and the missing hands and feet, which however may have been lost to the sheet being trimmed. In the *ignudo*'s open pose, rendered with lively contours, the limbs extend in all directions and rotate dynamically within the surrounding space. The artist's effort to develop a sense of space around the figure also connects this study with the nudes of the *Battle of Cascina*. The soft, rubbed chalk lines allow light and air to circulate around the body, enveloping it in a *sfumato*-like veil that connects it to its surroundings in a painterly fashion.

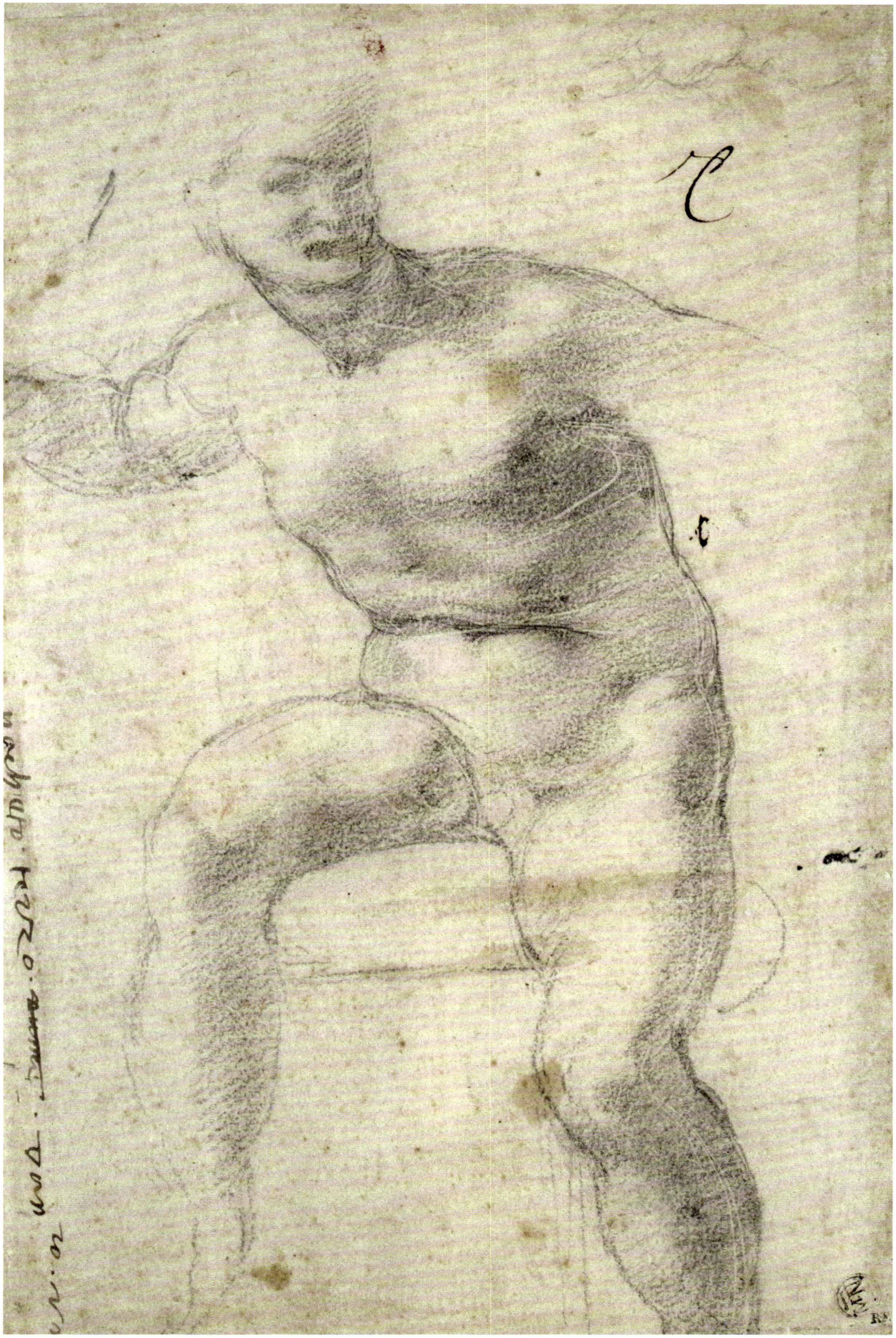

Michelangelo
Nude Youth, 1508/09
Paris, Musée du Louvre, Département des Arts graphiques

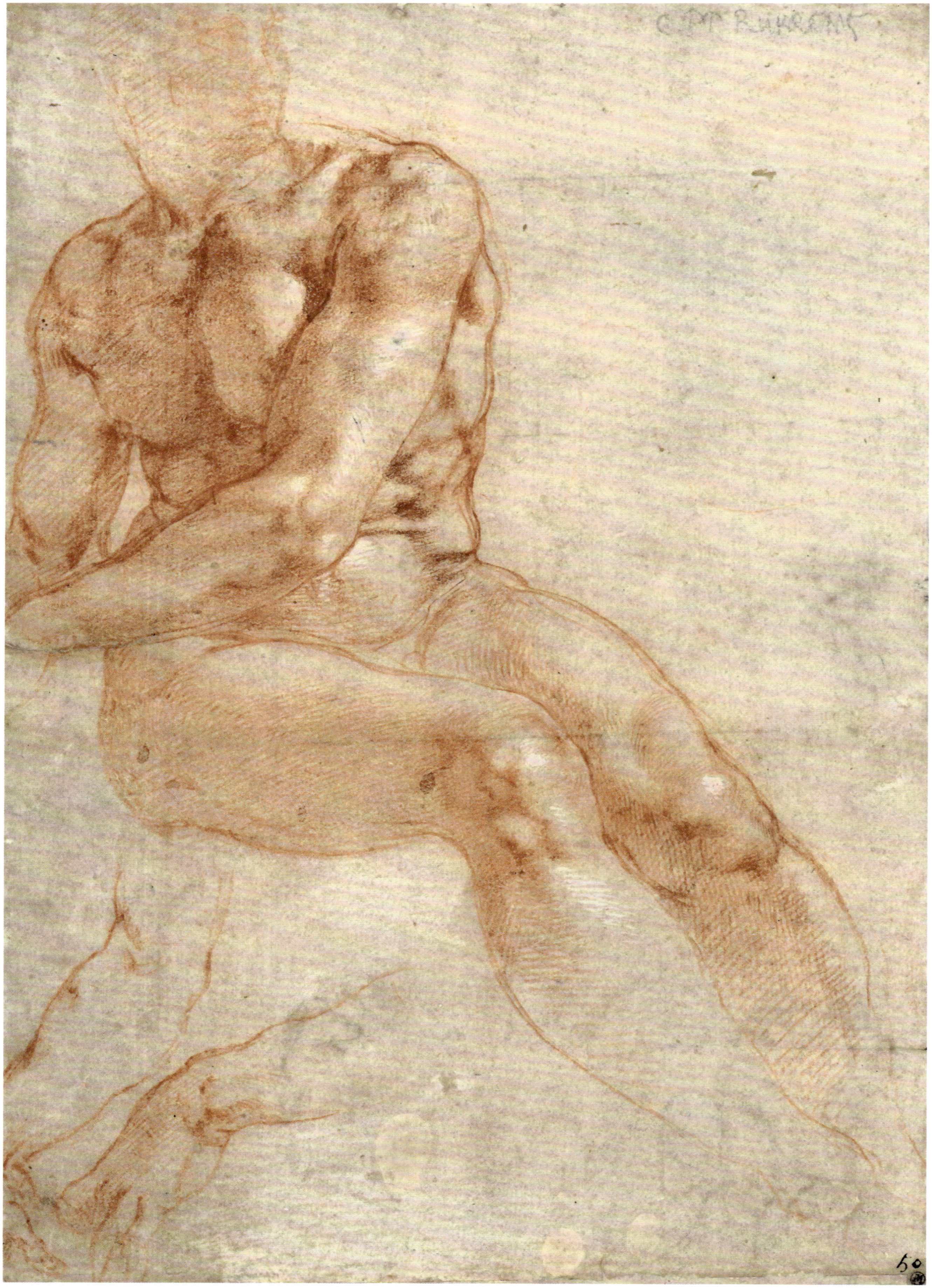

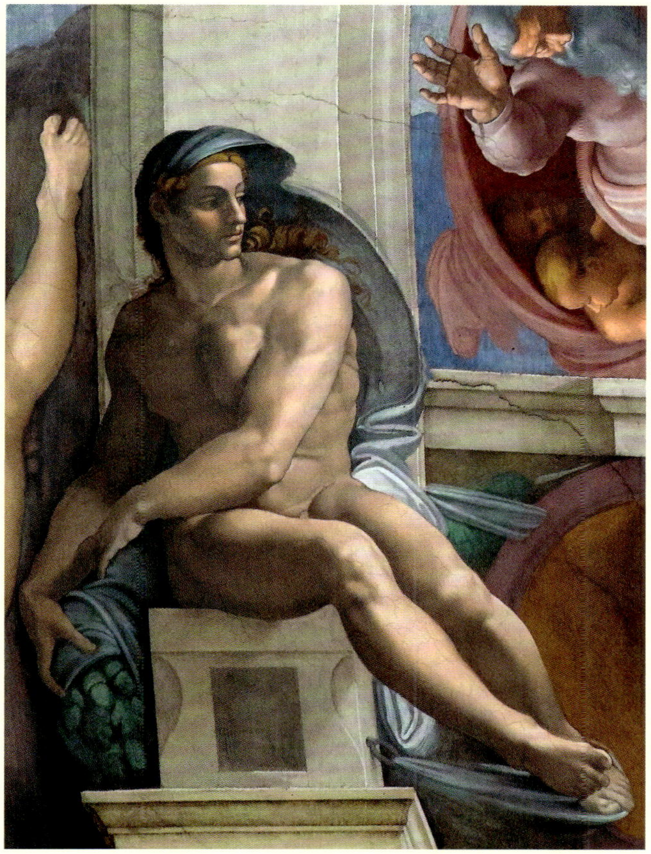

6 Michelangelo *Ignudo*, 1511/12
Fresco
Sistine Chapel, Vatican

In the summer of 1510, when Michelangelo was about halfway through the ceiling fresco, he stopped work, awaiting further instructions and funding from the pope, who was away from Rome at the time. After Pope Julius returned in June 1511, the first half of the ceiling was unveiled. That fall a second scaffolding was erected to continue the project, which came to completion in October 1512. The greater intensity and speed of the second phase of the work is evident in the execution. The figures became larger, the colors brighter and more luminous, and the modeling lighter and more transparent. At the same time, a change in style can be observed both in the fresco and its preliminary drawings. Instead of pen and ink and black chalk, Michelangelo turned to the red-chalk stick, a firmer medium which yields clear, fine lines. In the *Seated Nude Youth* of the Albertina, a study from life for the *ignudo* to the upper left of the Persian Sibyl (fig. 6), Michelangelo used fine hatching and slight variations in pressure to create rich tonal gradations. This emphasizes a sculptural tautness of the surface. The figure no longer extends outward like the *ignudo* in the Louvre; rather, its forces are concentrated within the muscular body, around which the surrounding space is now shaped. Instead of fusing the figure with the space, the outline sets it apart from the background. The short, curved strokes of the contours in the upper body consolidate the musculature, and the smoothly flowing contours of the outstretched legs create a convincing foreshortening. Because the upper and lower halves of the body turn in opposite directions, the resting pose exhibits an extraordinary dynamism.

The studies on the back of this sheet were made in preparation for Sebastiano del Piombo's *Pietà* in Viterbo (Museo Civico, Viterbo), for which Michelangelo is said also to have drawn the cartoon. Sebastiano had arrived in Rome from Venice in 1511, in the retinue of the rich Sienese banker Agostino Chigi. Michelangelo, in rivalry with Raphael, repeatedly provided Sebastiano with drawings as designs for his work as a way of countering Raphael's domination of the Roman art scene of the 1510s.

Among the most fascinating drawings for the Sistine Chapel ceiling is the sheet of studies for the Libyan Sibyl (fig. 8) in the Metropolitan Museum of Art in New

Michelangelo
Study of a Seated Nude Youth and Two Arm Studies, 1511/12
The ALBERTINA Museum, Vienna

York. As executed in fresco, the outstretched arms, sophisticated rotation of the body, and magnificent robe and coiffure make this sibyl the most graceful figure of the entire ceiling. She became an ideal model for Mannerist artists, who often elongated her pose and transformed it into something more decorative and planar. As he generally did for his female figures, Michelangelo used a male model for the sibyl. In the study at the center of the sheet, he precisely worked out the structure of the upper body, paying special attention to the ribs, the difficult foreshortening of the arms, and the tensions in the muscles. He aimed to gain a clear understanding of each detail. This would allow him, while painting the fresco, to concentrate on the overall impression and to unify anatomical details through color and modeling. The drawn pose largely corresponds to that of the fresco. There, however, the sibyl's gaze is directed further downward over her arm, and the angle at which her torso leans is increased. As is so often the case, Michelangelo used the paper very economically, filling in the remaining areas with further studies of the upper body, the head, the left hand, and the left foot.

7 Michelangelo, *Dying Slave*, 1513–1516
Marble, h. 215 cm
Paris, Musée du Louvre

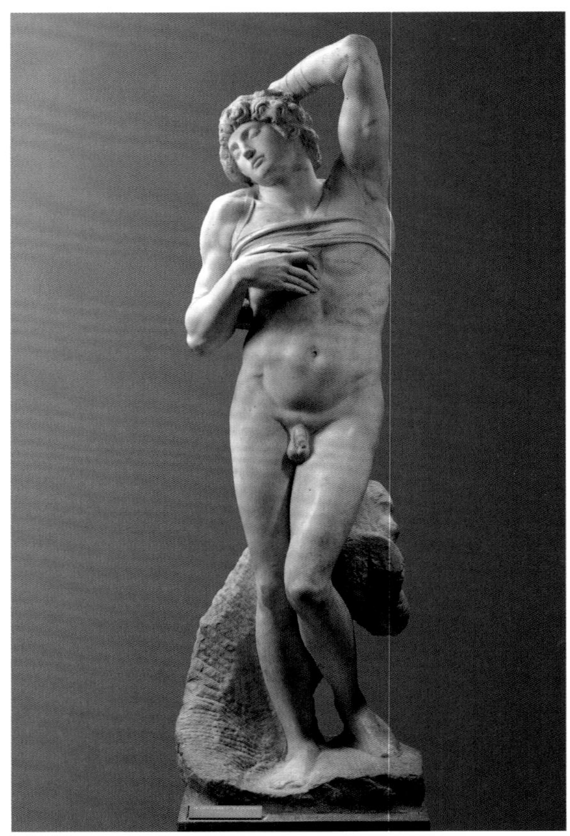

While he was painting the Sistine ceiling, Michelangelo's thoughts were still occupied with the tomb of Julius II. As initially planned, with its rich decorations, numerous reliefs, and about forty marble statues, the tomb's splendor and beauty would have surpassed those of any previous funerary monument. Another preparatory drawing for the Libyan Sibyl, this one in the Ashmolean Museum in Oxford, is accompanied by pen-and-ink sketches for statues of naked "slaves" or captives (*prigioni*) that were to decorate the base of the tomb alongside herm pilasters and Victories. According to Vasari, the captives represented the territories subjugated by Julius II, while Condivi interpreted them as personifications of the liberal arts, including painting, sculpture, and architecture. It was only after the death of Julius II, on February 21, 1513, that the tomb project received new impetus. The new contract drawn up with Michelangelo provided for a wall tomb instead of a free-standing monument. He worked on the sculptures of *Moses* and, in 1513, the two *prigioni* now in the Louvre—the *Dying Slave* (fig. 7) and the *Rebellious Slave*—as part of the revised plan. This project and various subsequent undertakings were, however,

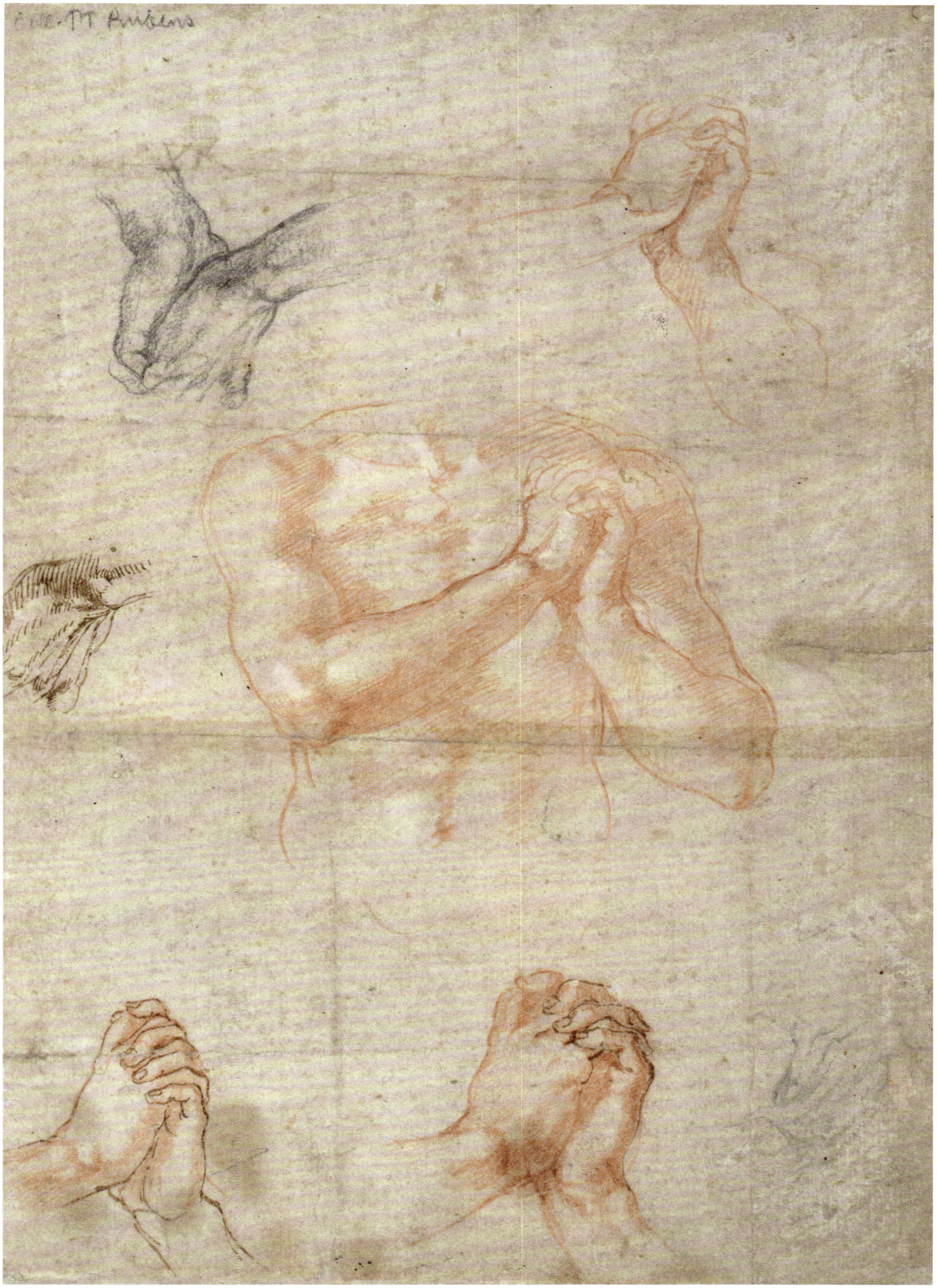

Michelangelo
Male Upper Body with Folded Hands and Studies of Hands, 1511/12
The ALBERTINA Museum, Vienna

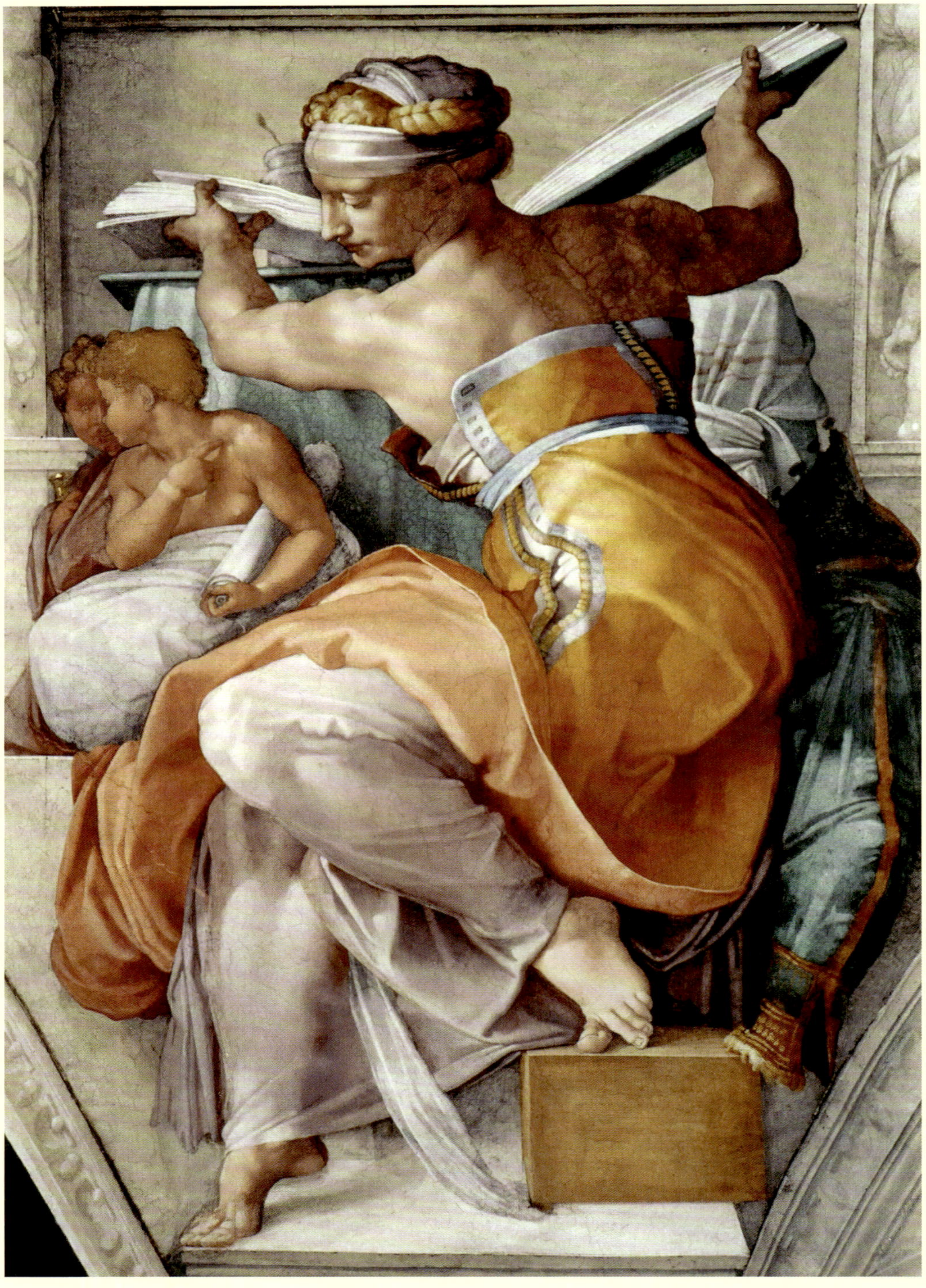

8 Michelangelo, *Libyan Sibyl*, ca. 1510–1512
Fresco
Sistine Chapel, Vatican

not completed. The aspirations for this tomb became the great tragedy of Michelangelo's life. The monument was ultimately erected in a much-reduced form in the Roman basilica of San Pietro in Vincoli between 1532 and 1545.

AG

Michelangelo
***Studies for the Libyan Sibyl*, ca. 1510/11**
The Metropolitan Museum of Art, New York, Purchase, Joseph Pulitzer Bequest, 1924

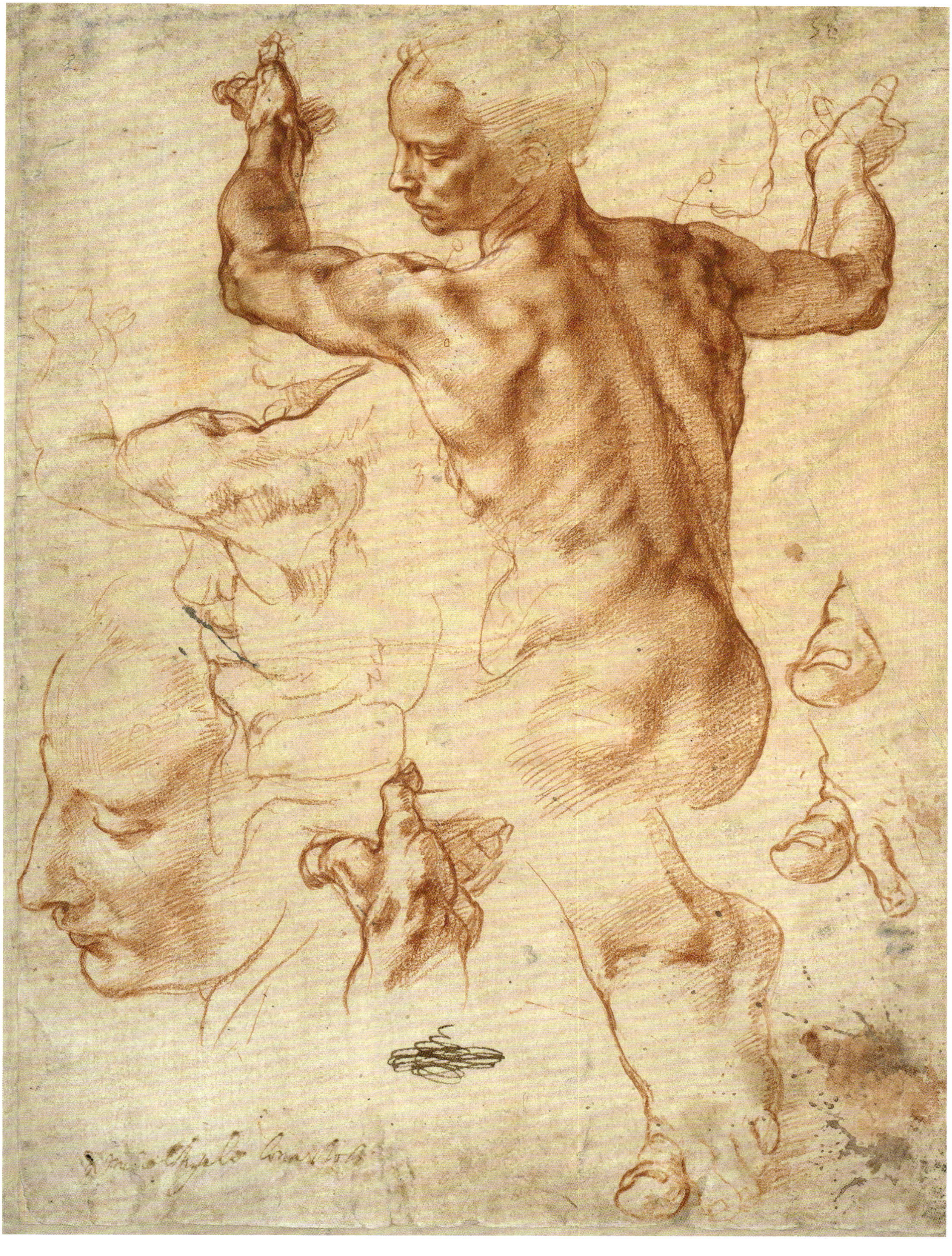

Raphael: Under the Spell of Michelangelo

The brilliant Michelangelo was highly sensitive in character, while also melancholic and reserved. Possessed of an almost superhuman creative power, he drew more inspiration from the inner world of his mind than he did from exterior artistic influences, which he concealed in his work. Raphael, on the other hand, was fully receptive to the art that surrounded him. He learned from it and borrowed from it in his paintings. These external stimuli, however, always underwent adaptation to Raphael's own ideas, which gave rise to completely new and individual creations. One reason for his move to Florence in late 1504 may have been a desire to study Leonardo's and Michelangelo's battle scenes firsthand. The soldiers in the *Battle of Cascina*, worked up in great anatomical detail, attuned him to the importance of studying musculature in order to depict sequences of movement and inner exertion correctly. Raphael made drawings after Michelangelo's marble sculptures of *David* and *Saint Matthew* (Galleria dell'Accademia, Florence), as well as after the *Taddei Tondo* (Royal Academy of Arts, London). Furthermore, Raphael's paintings of the Madonna take inspiration from the Virgin and Child now in the Church of Our Lady in Bruges, and his *The Deposition* (Galleria Borghese, Rome) was influenced by Michelangelo's unfinished painting of the same subject (National Gallery, London). Through Michelangelo's example, Raphael's figures became more organic in regard to their physical form and more powerful and solid in their bearing. After arriving in Rome in the second half of 1508, Raphael's art underwent a breathtaking development. His engagement with ancient sculpture and his more intensive study of live models resulted in a monumental conception of the figure, equal to that of Michelangelo's heroic nudes.

The two red-chalk drawings in the Albertina served as preparatory studies for *The Fire in the Borgo* fresco (fig. 9) in the Stanza dell'Incendio at the Vatican, which was painted from 1514 to 1517 under Pope Leo X, successor to Julius II. For the decoration of this *stanza*, events were chosen that took place during the lifetime of important papal predecessors who bore the same pontifical name—i.e., the popes Leo III and Leo IV. The fresco in question depicts the fire that broke out in the Roman district of Borgo in 847, at the beginning of Leo IV's pontificate, and which was extinguished upon a benediction from the pope. The present study for the youth escaping over a wall from a burning building is modeled with fine, dense lines that detail every rise and fall of the musculature. It clearly displays the influence of Michelangelo's red-chalk studies for the Sistine Chapel ceiling. The distinct tension

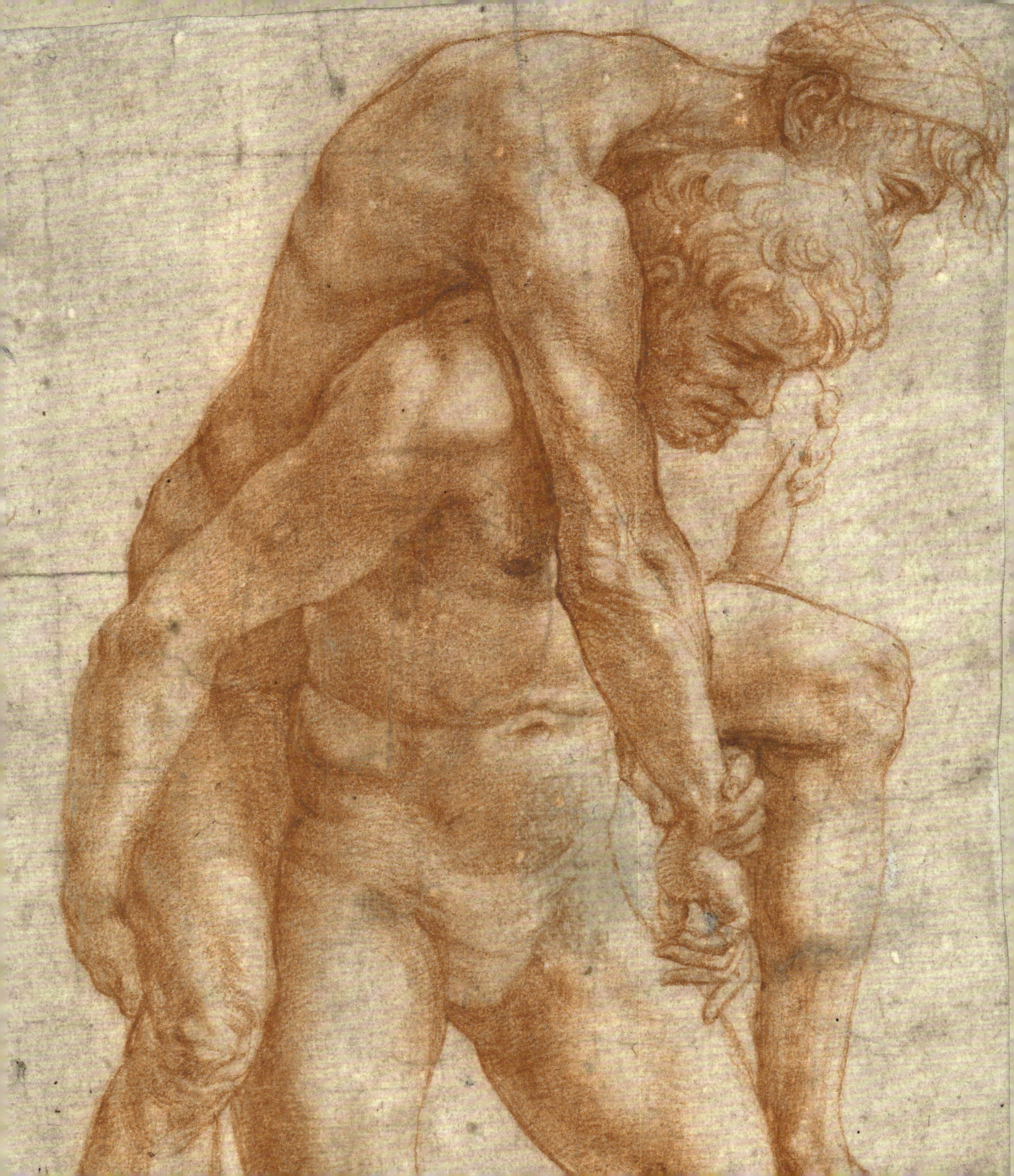

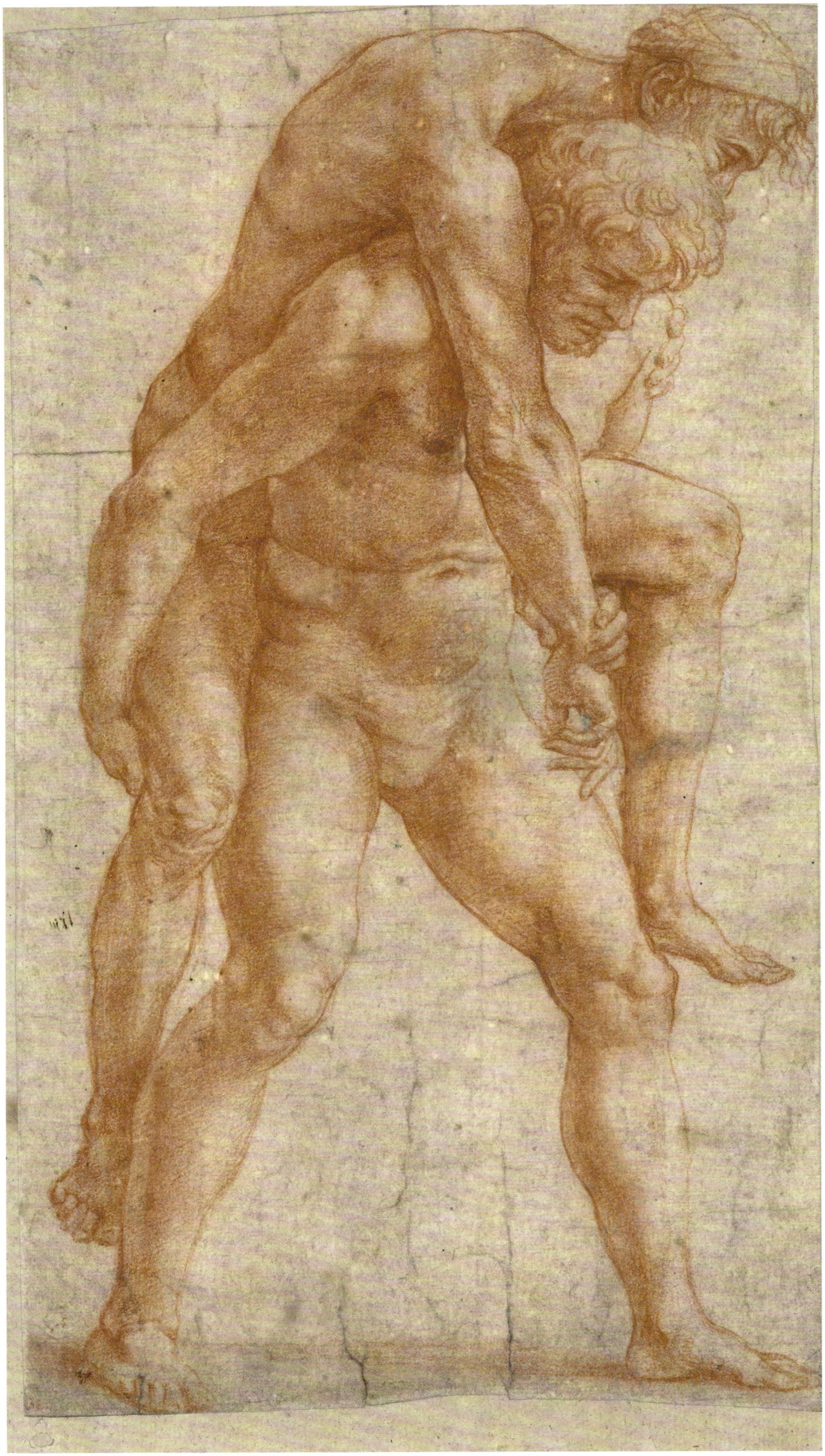

Raphael
A Young Man Carrying an Old Man, 1514
The ALBERTINA Museum, Vienna

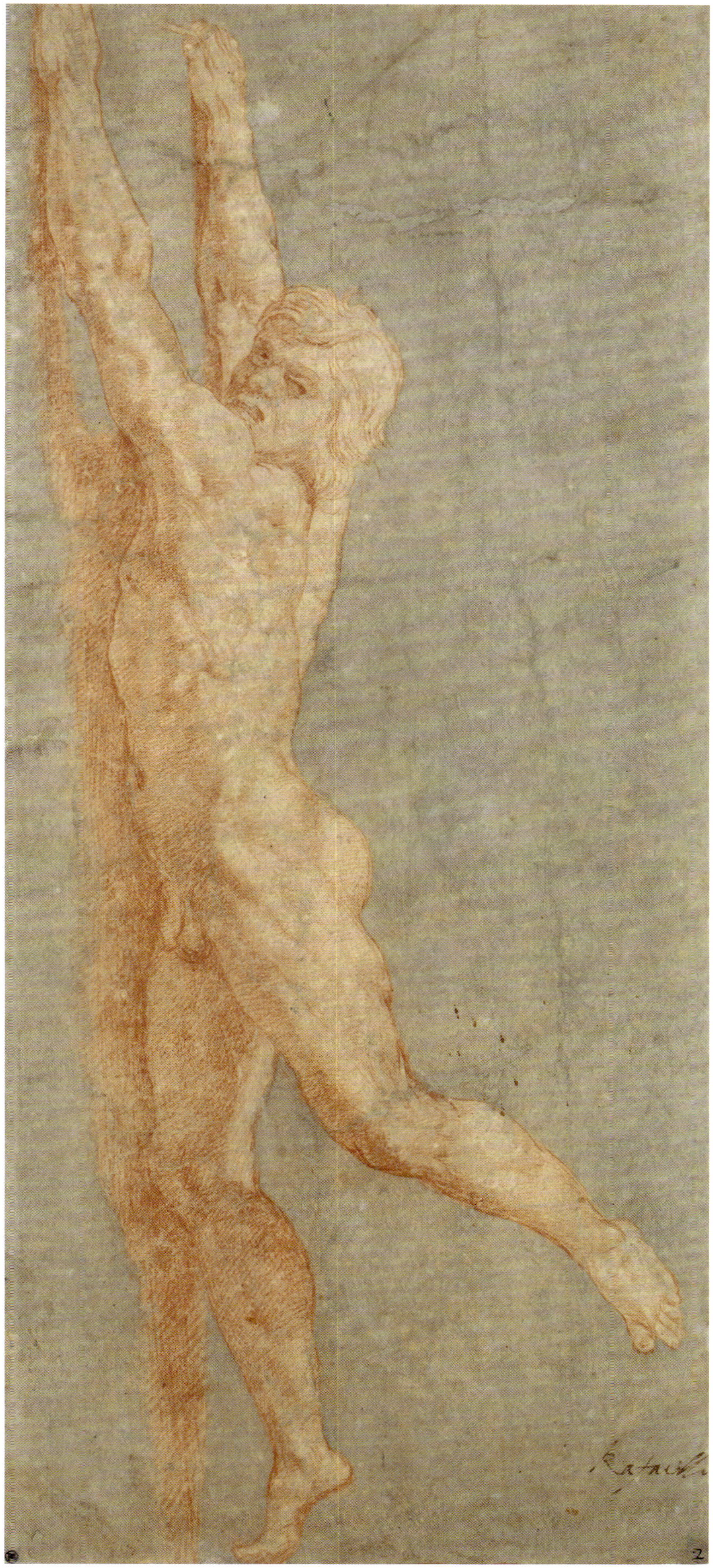

Raphael
Nude Youth Hanging from a Wall,
1514
The ALBERTINA Museum, Vienna

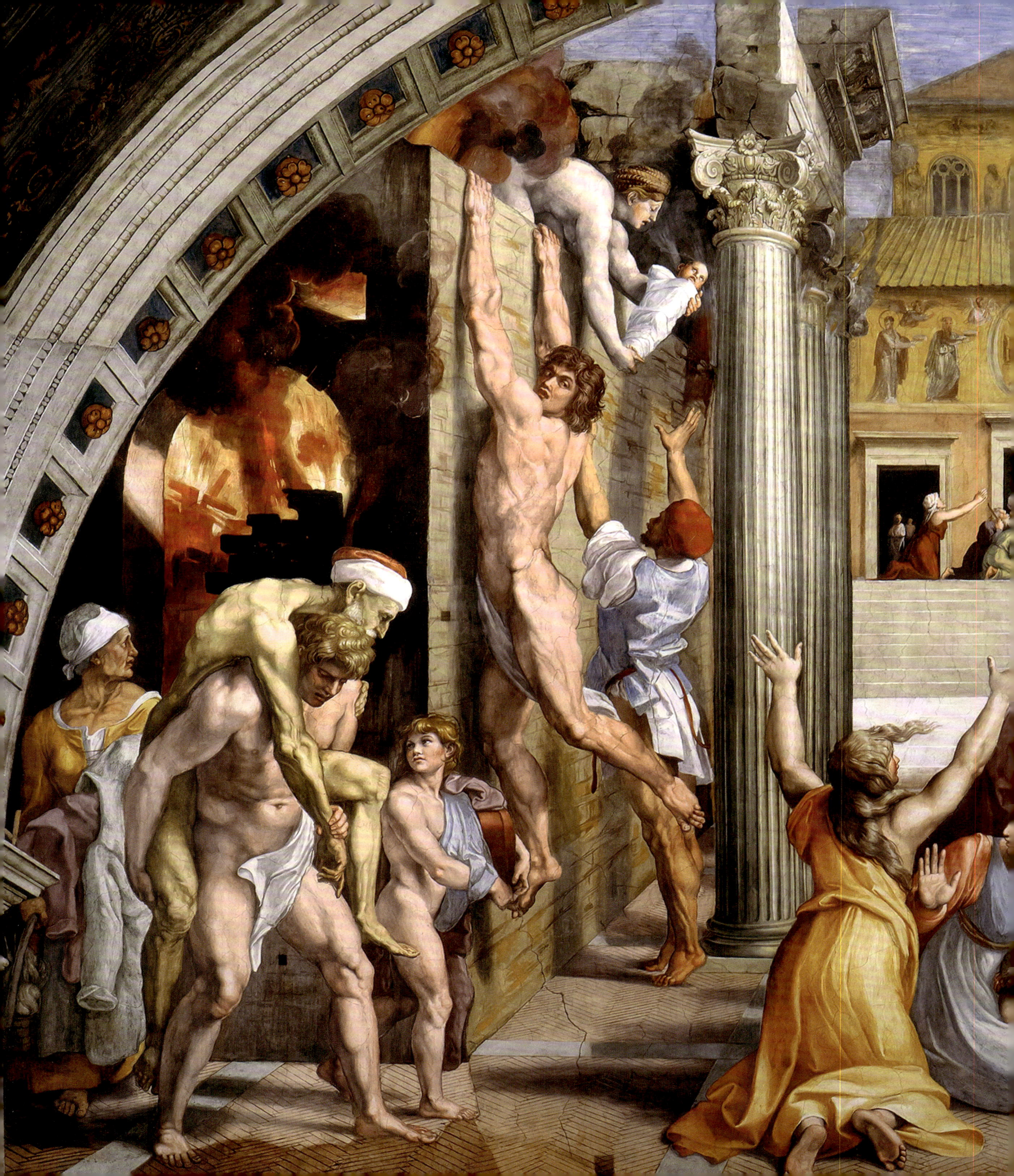

throughout and the striking contours of the scissor-like pose are, above all, reminiscent of the preparatory drawings for the crucified Haman in Michelangelo's ceiling fresco. Raphael underscored the vivid expressiveness through the fearful contortions of the face, the strained shoulder, and the protruding pelvic bone. In Michelangelo's studies, areas of light and shade are juxtaposed to emphasize relief-like qualities, and the modeling is concerned entirely with the body. By contrast, in the present drawing, the figure's limbs are encircled by light and air, which connects them with their surroundings. Whereas Raphael's figures seek contact with the outside world and move freely within space, Michelangelo's remain separated from their surroundings by closed contours.

The other red-chalk study by Raphael was a preparatory drawing for the figural group at the fresco's left edge. Early on, this group was already likened to the scene described by Virgil in which Aeneas carries his father, Anchises, away on his shoulders from burning Troy. The careful, densely spaced lines and the subtle tonal gradations achieved by slight variations in pressure are equally reminiscent of Michelangelo's studies for the *ignudi*. Raphael succeeded masterfully in distinguishing age—the younger man's smooth, taut skin contrasts with the old man's sags and wrinkles—and in fusing the two intertwined bodies into one marvelous unit. In contrast to the drawing style of the sculptor Michelangelo, who emphasized surface relief and set figures apart from the ground, it is striking to note how the figures in Raphael's study appear to be enveloped by space through which they seem to move freely. While the characters that Michelangelo created are forced to rely on themselves and bear the burden of fate, which they must do in isolation, Raphael's are characterized by a greater emotional and interpersonal connectedness. In the figure of Aeneas, one senses the protagonist's self-sacrificing love for his ill father, who, unable to walk, has fully put his trust in his son. Michelangelo's figures are governed by the enormous willpower of their creator, whereas Raphael's lead full lives marked by mutual exchange and by attentiveness to their fellow humans and the outside world.

AG

9 Raphael, *The Fire in the Borgo*, 1514 (detail)
Fresco
Stanza dell'Incendio, Vatican

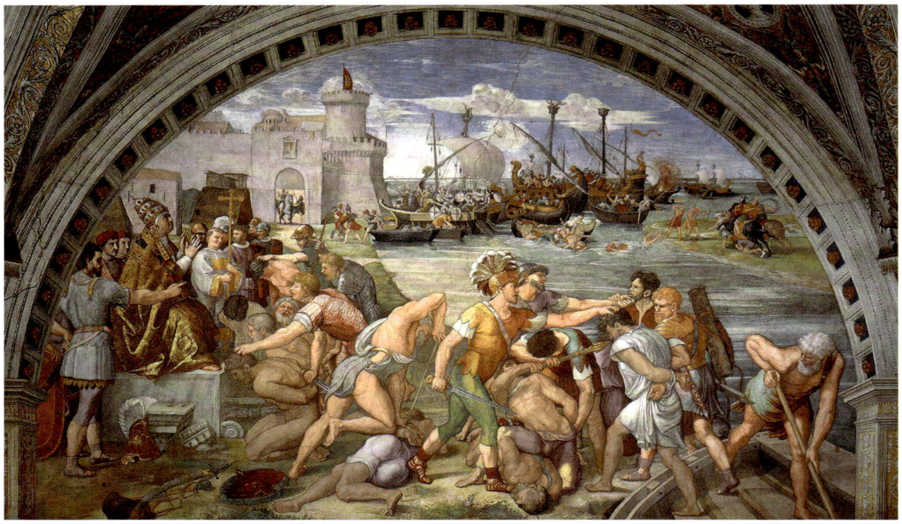

10 Raphael and Workshop, *Battle of Ostia*, 1516/17
Fresco, Stanza dell'Incendio, Vatican

In this famous drawing, the figure on the right with one arm extended is a preparatory study for the captain at the left edge of the *Battle of Ostia* fresco (fig. 10), located on the east wall of the Stanza dell'Incendio, adjacent to *The Fire in the Borgo*. Raphael did not include either the nude at the left or the fragmentary background figure in his finished work. Using the same live model for all three figures, Raphael studied and drew the poses one by one. Light, gently curved strokes envelop the individual forms, precisely rendering the musculature. Areas in which force is concentrated are worked up to an especially high finish: the left figure's lean on the staff and the right figure's placement of his hand on his hip. Although the modeling in red chalk is less dense than in the study for Aeneas and Anchises, in that aspect, too, Raphael may have been prompted by Michelangelo's drawings, for example, his studies for the captives (*prigioni*) meant for the tomb of Pope Julius II. Yet Raphael aligned himself with the ideal of ancient sculpture more than Michelangelo did, and he infused new life into antique approaches to form. His intensive study of antiquity enabled him to create figures with greater solidity and a more statuesque quality, which in turn allowed them to exude an air of freedom and self-determination. The majestic poise of the commanding officer, while based on the pose of Raphael's live model, also clearly draws inspiration from ancient sculptures such as the Apollo Belvedere. In that way, Raphael's art combines models from life and classical antiquity into a new image of a Christian ideal in a living human form. This nude study has unique historical importance, as it documents not only an exchange of works between Albrecht Dürer and Raphael but also the two artists' mutual admiration.

The drawing was once owned by Dürer. His inscription on it notes that Raphael of Urbino, highly esteemed by the Pope, sent it to him in Nuremberg in 1515 in order "to show him his hand" (*Im sein hand zw weisen*). According to Vasari, Dürer had sent Raphael a watercolor self-portrait on thin canvas, in which all highlights were left unpainted and the support exposed, instead of being added in white paint, so that the work could be viewed from the front and back. Raphael's assistant Tommaso Vincidor, who oversaw the production in Brussels of tapestries that Raphael had designed for the Hall of Constantine at the Vatican, met Dürer in Antwerp in October 1520 after the death of his master. He gifted the German artist an ancient ring and drew a portrait of him. Dürer in turn gave Vincidor a set of his prints in exchange for which he hoped to receive a series of prints by Raphael. It is likely that Raphael intentionally selected this sheet, and presumably others, as gifts for Dürer, knowing that, for one thing, the study of nature was dear to the Nuremberger. Moreover, Raphael was probably aware that Dürer, inspired by theoreticians and artists of the Italian Renaissance, whose nudes ("nacketn Bildern") he praised, sought to determine the ideal proportions of the human figure.

AG

Raphael
Studies of Nudes, 1515
The ALBERTINA Museum, Vienna

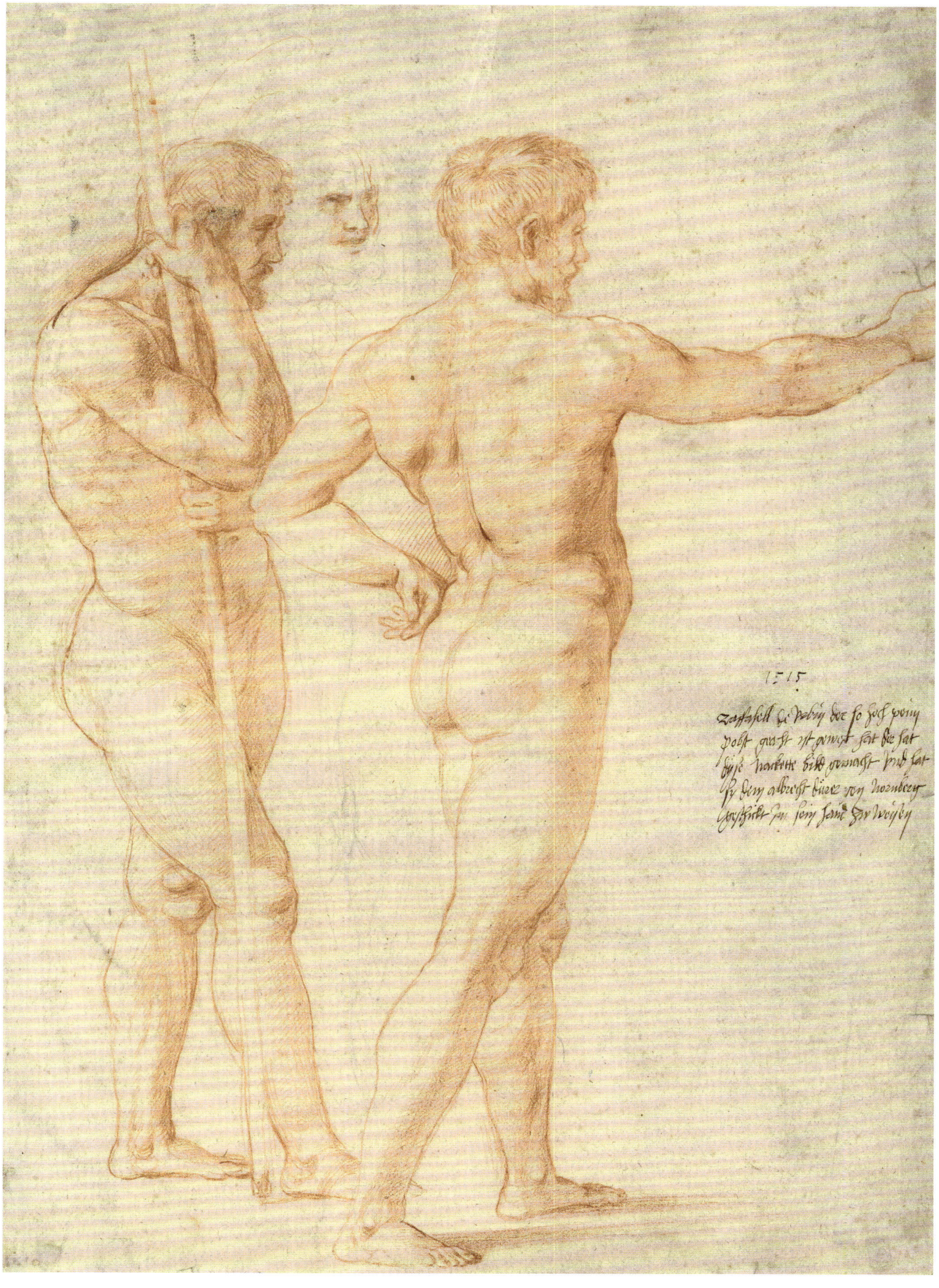
1515

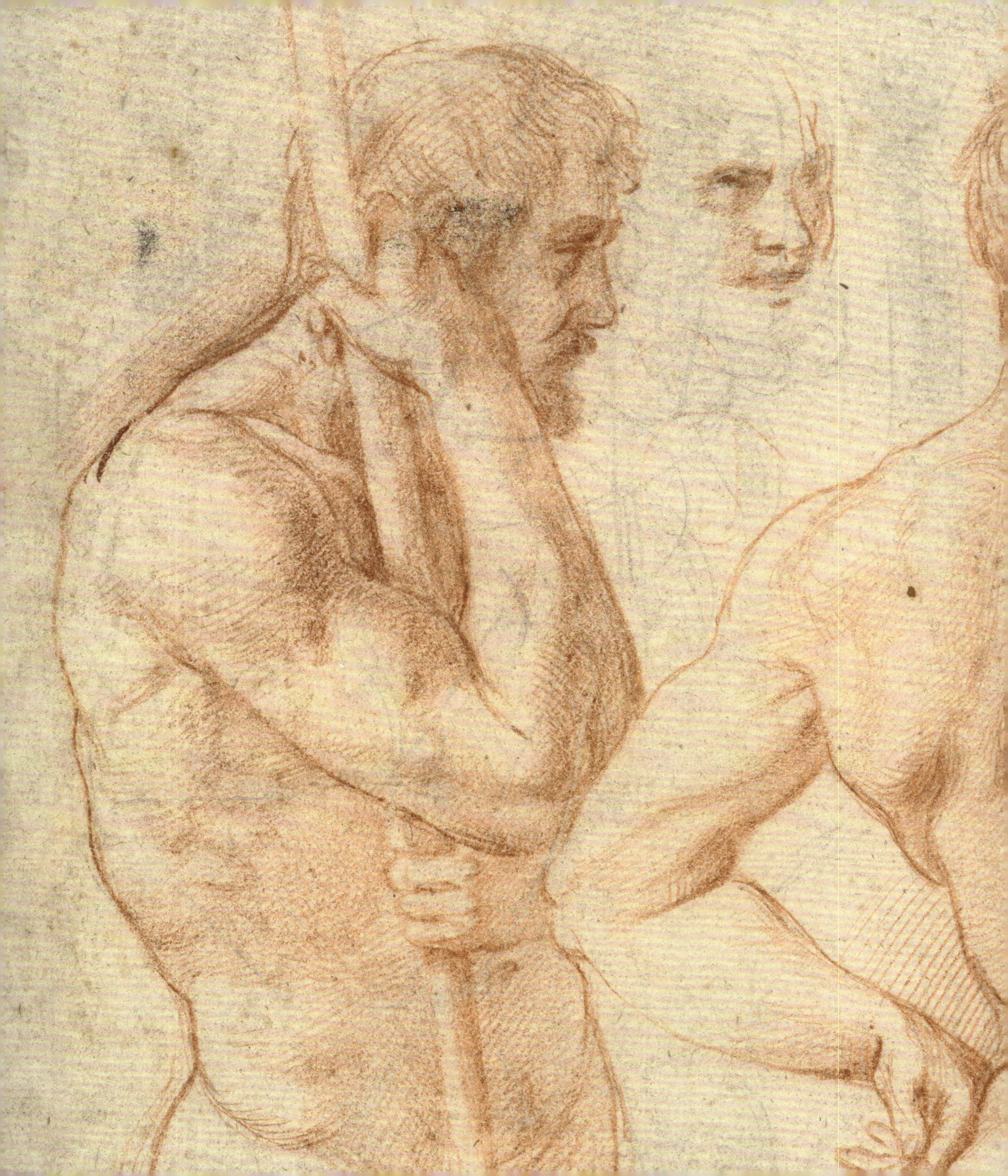

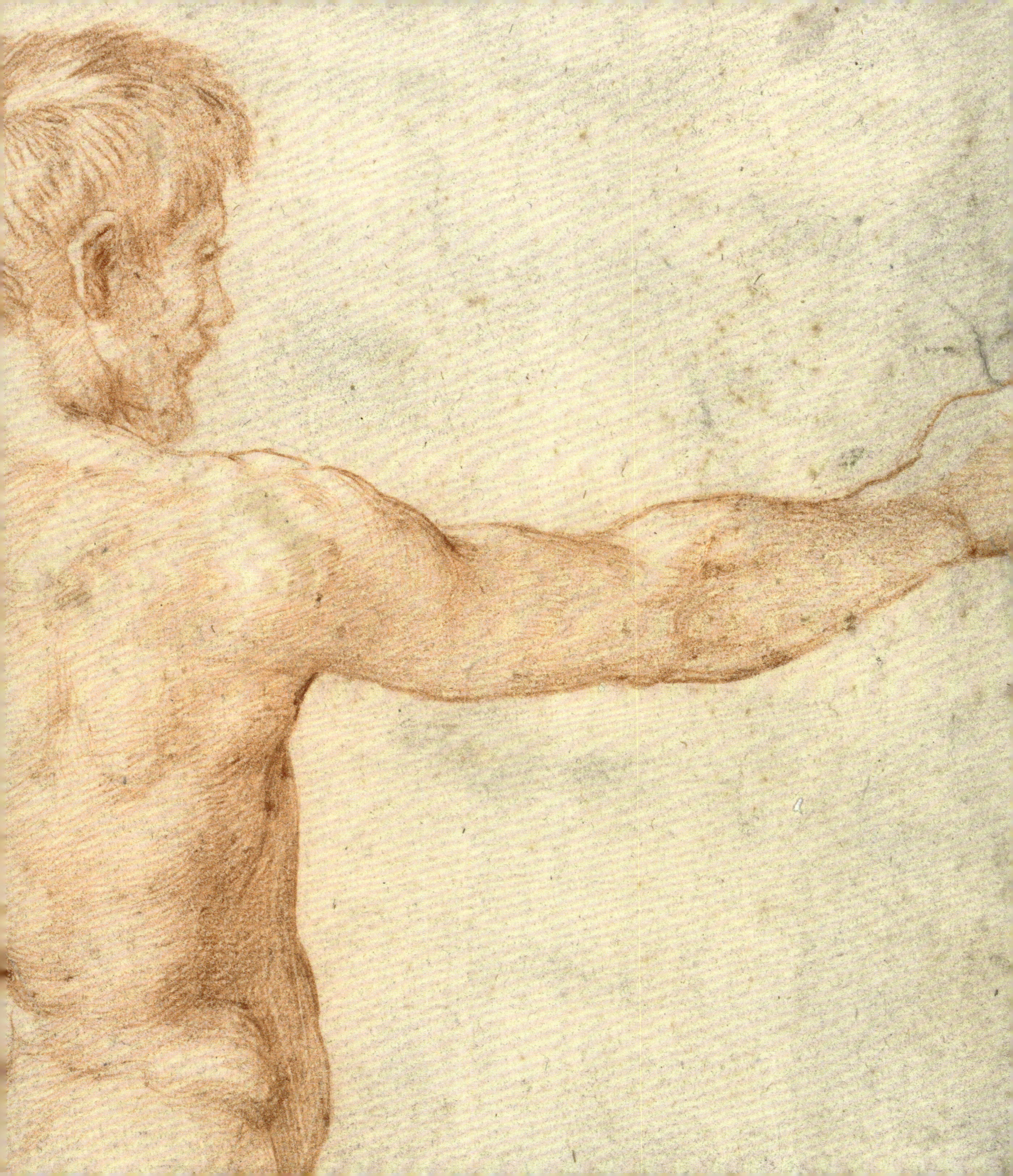

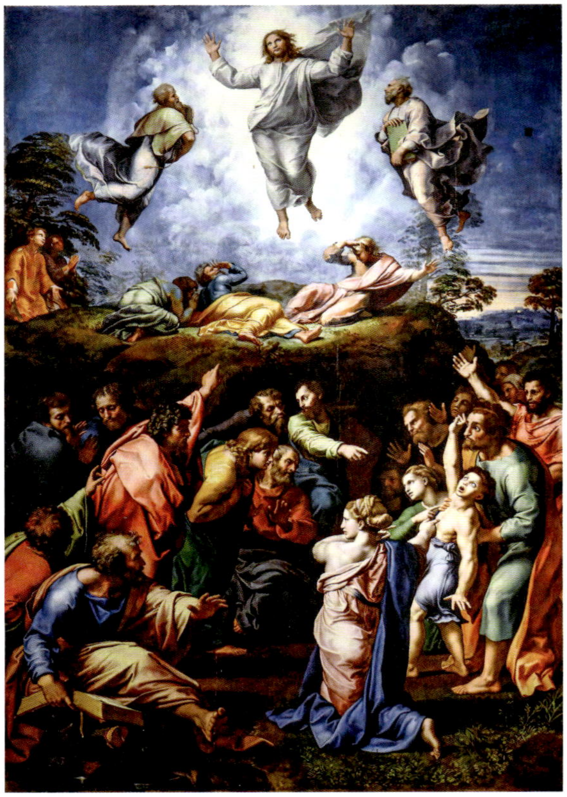

11 Raphael, *Transfiguration*, 1516–1520
Oil on panel, 405 × 278 cm
Musei Vaticani, Vatican

Raphael drew these nudes in red chalk in preparation for the *Transfiguration* (fig. 11), his last large-scale panel painting. Cardinal Giulio de' Medici commissioned the work in 1516 for the cathedral in his diocese at Narbonne, and shortly thereafter he turned to Sebastiano del Piombo for a second painting, *The Raising of Lazarus* (National Gallery, London), for the same episcopal church. Sebastiano is known to have received preparatory drawings for this work from Michelangelo, who at that time was working in Florence. The two artists joined forces in opposition to the mighty position held by Raphael, who dominated the art world in Rome at the time. Sebastiano executed the muscular, anatomically detailed nudes of Michelangelo's drawings in a highly painterly manner. In so doing, with his paintings, he achieved a harmonious fusion of the Florentine's heroic figural ideal and the atmospheric coloring of his own Venetian training. Ultimately, however, Raphael's *Transfiguration* triumphed in this competition, and the picture was near completion when the artist died on April 6, 1520, at the age of thirty-seven. The present drawing is a study by Raphael for three apostles located in the center middle ground, who react to the possessed boy at the right of the picture with amazement, curiosity, and skepticism—that is, with spontaneous human interest. Raphael had the same live model take a series of different poses, while leaving a space in reserve for the fourth apostle who in the completed painting is leaning forward, overlapping the seated one. Although the apostles wear long robes in the painting, Raphael's studies are after nudes. While this was consistent with his design methods at the time, for this work he attached special importance to careful study of the nude, since he knew that his rival, Sebastiano, was benefiting from the aid of Michelangelo's drawings. He therefore did his utmost to ensure that his apostles could withstand comparison with the grand figural ideal of the Florentine artist. In this sheet, he handled the red chalk with great economy, restricting the modeling to just one or two layers of hatching and setting broad areas of light against fields of shadow. In those aspects, among others, there are connections with several studies by Michelangelo among those drawings for the *ignudi* of the Sistine Chapel ceiling that are cursorily executed. In his apostle group, Raphael was mainly concerned with defining the individual poses in spatial relationship to one another and with clarifying the difficult uses of foreshortening, such as in the legs positioned at various angles. Raphael devoted special attention to harmonizing the apostles' emotional reactions with their bodily movements. Thus, he made the incredulous seated figure shift slightly to the side, and he expressed the doubtfulness of the figure at the rear through a hunched pose and tensed shoulder muscles. Later in the design process, Raphael worked up his figures in greater detail and then created marvelous drawings of the heads of the individual apostles.

AG

Raphael
Apostle Group, 1518–1520
The ALBERTINA Museum, Vienna

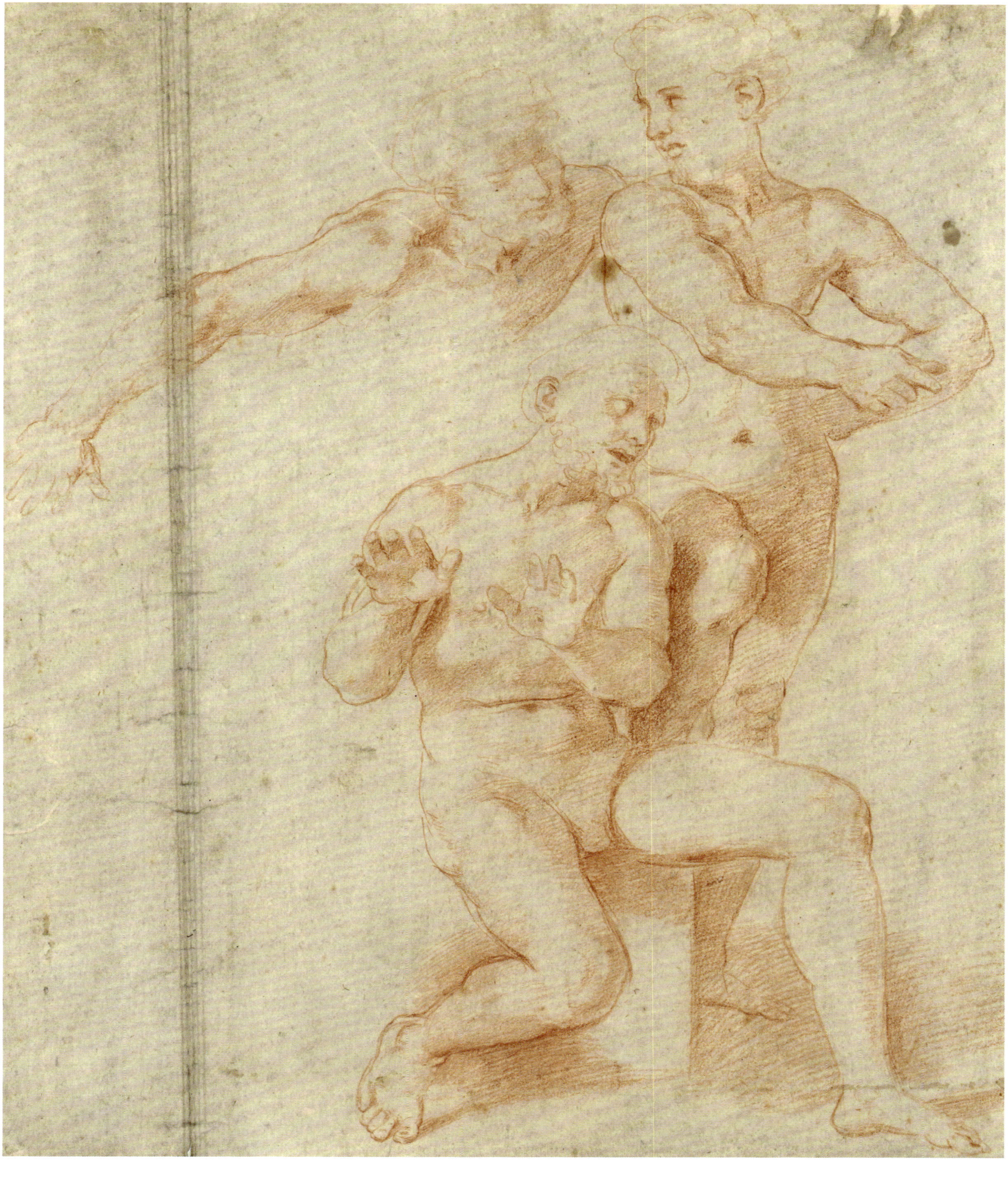

The Death of Christ, or The Beauty of the Immortal

Michelangelo explored the subjects of the Pietà and the Lamentation of Christ throughout his career, in painting, drawing, and most notably sculpture. His early masterpiece is the marvelous *Pietà* in Saint Peter's Basilica (fig. 12), which he created at the young age of twenty-three or twenty-four as a commission from the French cardinal Jean Bilhères de Lagraulas. The marble sculptural group was influenced by Northern Pietà sculptures of the fourteenth and fifteenth centuries. Carried out to utmost perfection, it was soon copied by other artists in various media. The younger generation of painters active in Rome after the death of Raphael were among those who drew inspiration from it, for example, Parmigianino (fig. 13), who hailed from northern Italy, and the extravagant Rosso Fiorentino, both of whom worked in the Eternal City from 1524 to 1527.

Rosso's admiration for Michelangelo is evident in the pen-and-ink drawing of a recumbent nude in the Albertina. He made this study after a live model in preparation

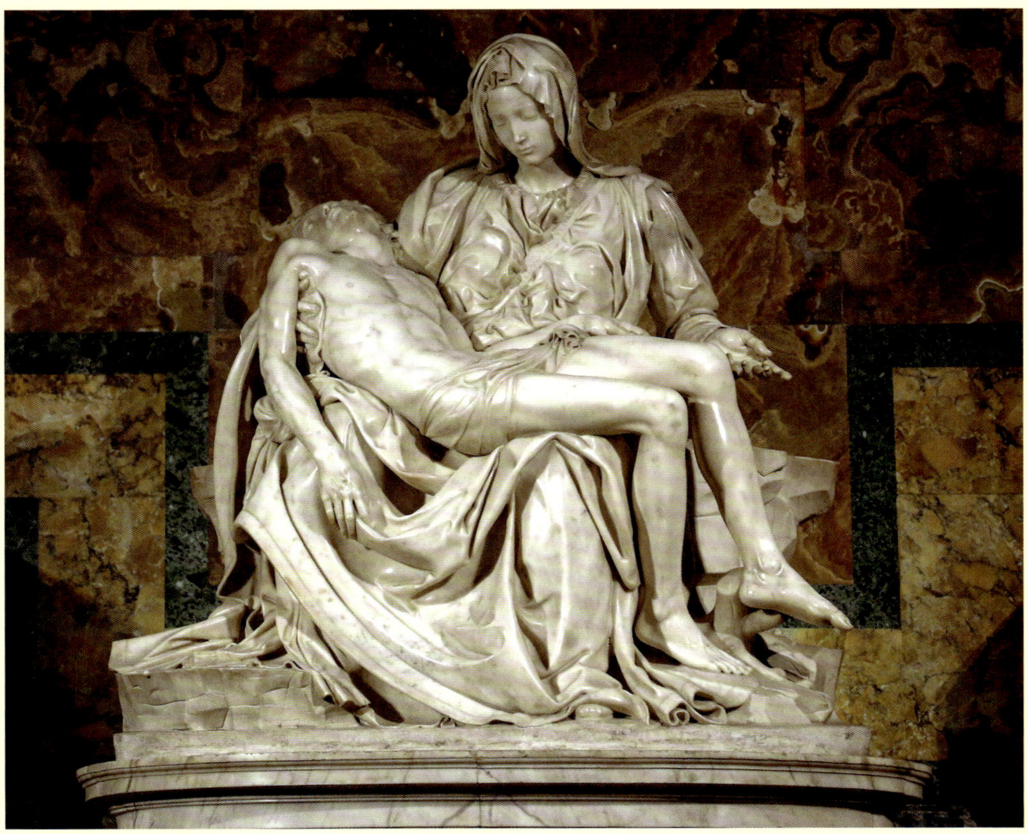

12 Michelangelo, *Pietà*, 1498/99
Marble, 174 × 195 × 69 cm
St. Peter's Basilica, Vatican

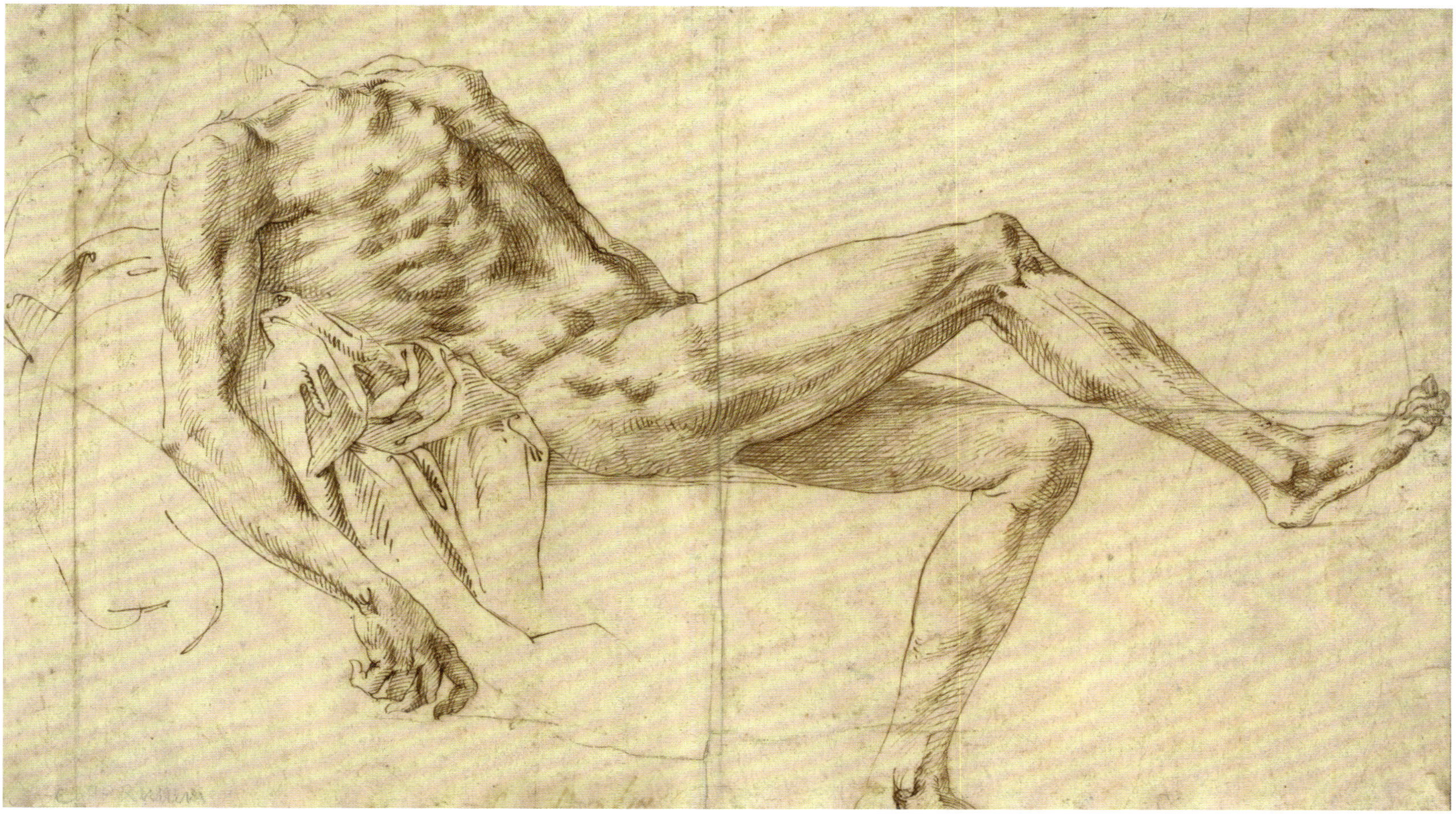

Rosso Fiorentino
Reclining Male Nude, 1527/28
The ALBERTINA Museum, Vienna

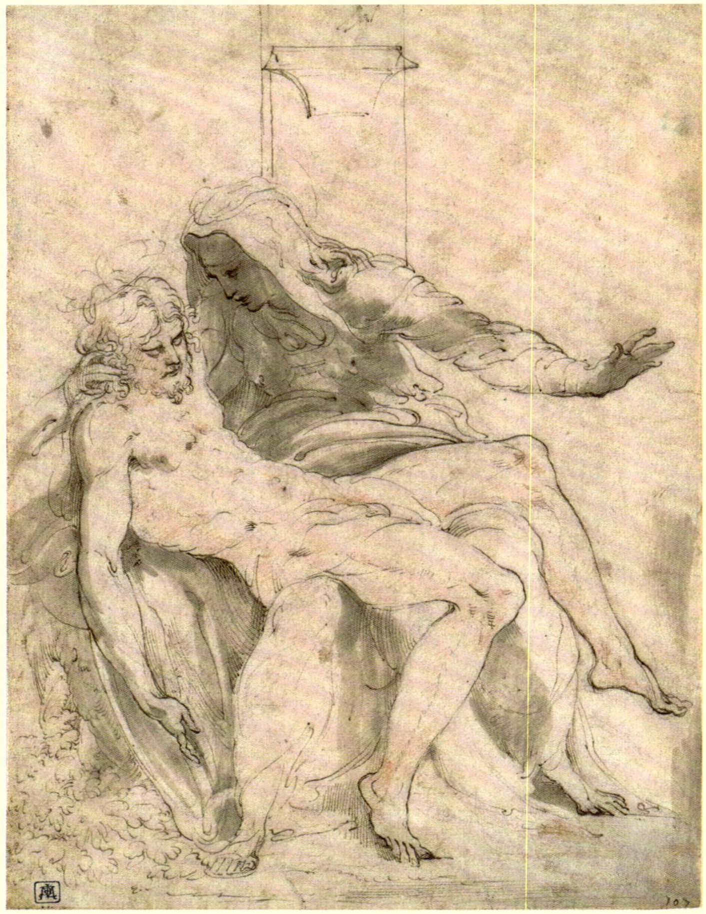

13 Parmigianino, *Pietà*, 1524/25
Pen and brown ink, gray wash, red chalk, over black chalk, 29 × 21.4 cm
The Morgan Library & Museum, New York
Purchased by Pierpont Morgan in 1909

for the dead Christ in his panel painting, *The Descent from the Cross* (1527/28), at the church of San Lorenzo in Borgo Sansepolcro. In Michelangelo's *Pietà*, the Christian Messiah, who lies in his mother's lap in repose, evinces a feeling of protection and security in her care. A sense of inner life is conveyed by one leg swung slightly forward and the drooping right arm with its delicately formed hand, the fingers brushing against a drapery fold as if by chance, as well as by the pulsing muscles of the torso. A graceful curve runs through the whole body. In contrast, the pose of Rosso's Savior consists of diagonals that work in opposition; angular contours enhance the tension. The artist satisfied his inclination toward the bizarre and unsettling by depicting the martyred body with chest swelled, ribs stabbing against the skin, and fingers bent claw-like, all of which drastically evoke the agonies preceding death. Rosso was among the artists who had schooled themselves on the cartoon for the *Battle of Cascina*, and the nude study in the Albertina furthermore betrays knowledge of the pen-and-ink drawings of Michelangelo, to whom the study was once even attributed. Whereas Michelangelo's lines interweave organically, flow into the contours, and create a sculpturally taut surface, those of Rosso combine into clusters of cross-hatching that abut areas of light without transitional modeling. This produces a faceted compartmentalization of forms that is typical of Rosso's style.

In Michelangelo's multi-figure *Lamentation* scene in red chalk, the Savior, shown frontally, is drawn in greater detail than the sketchier figures supporting him. With great refinement, the supple curve of Christ's torso and the buckling of his legs create an impression of downward movement, which is underscored by the succession of standing, kneeling, and crouching poses among the accessory figures. In this *Lamentation*, which is reminiscent of a Descent from the Cross, Michelangelo no longer emphasized the drama of the narrative through pronounced musculature but rather through expressive and memorable poses, maximizing the passion and intensity of the figures' actions. Michelangelo probably made this drawing, and the one discussed subsequently, in the early 1530s.

Michelangelo
The Lamentation of Christ, ca. 1530–1535
The ALBERTINA Museum, Vienna

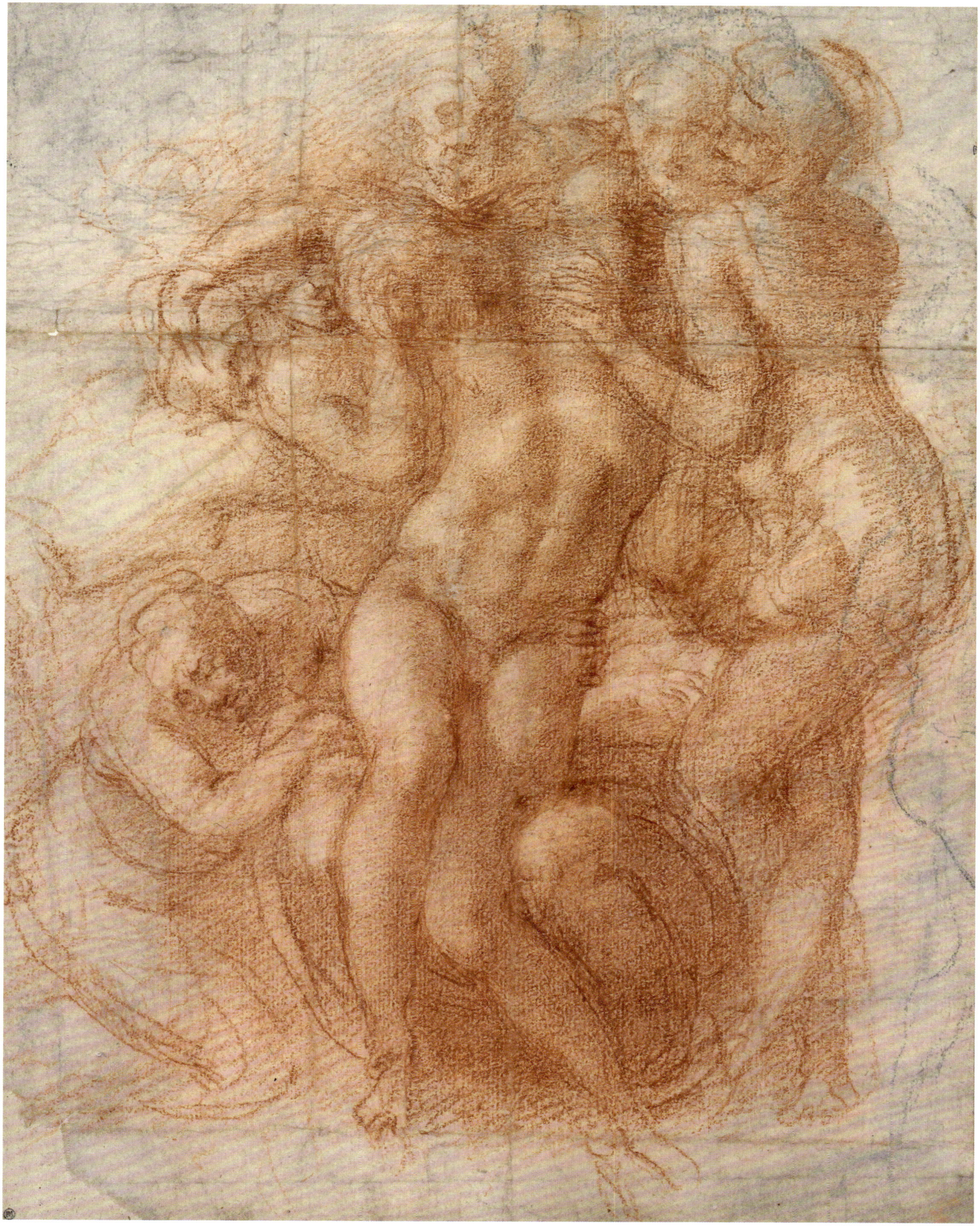

In this drawing, the dead Christ is seated on a sarcophagus and supported from behind by a kneeling figure, probably the Virgin Mary. In the frontal display of Christ's body, Michelangelo employed an iconographical type that was common in the late Middle Ages and early Renaissance, and which he later revisited in the marble sculpture known as the *Rondanini Pietà* (fig. 14). He established the form of the Savior with a stylus and then worked up the modeling with black chalk, followed by red chalk in countless short strokes which are hardly perceptible individually. After that, he sparingly sketched in the Virgin. Her earthbound nature and painful grief find expression in angular, coarse forms. In contrast, the deeply soulful figure of Christ is free of all tension, shows no wounds, and radiates a supernatural power and beauty. The body of this man without sin is immaculate and impervious to decay, even though life has departed it. Michelangelo was often occupied with thoughts of death and resurrection. Such drawings are thus to be understood as personal confessions of faith in which the artist gave visual form to his own perception of salvation through divine grace and his hope that the Messiah might offer succor in the face of death.

AG

14 Michelangelo, *Rondanini Pietà*, 1552–1564
Marble, h. 195 cm
Castello Sforzesco, Milan

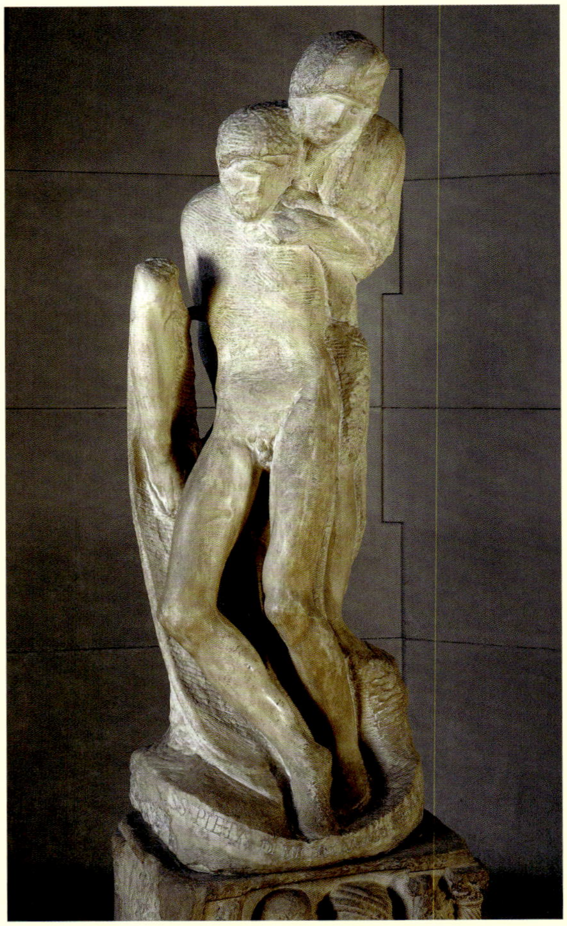

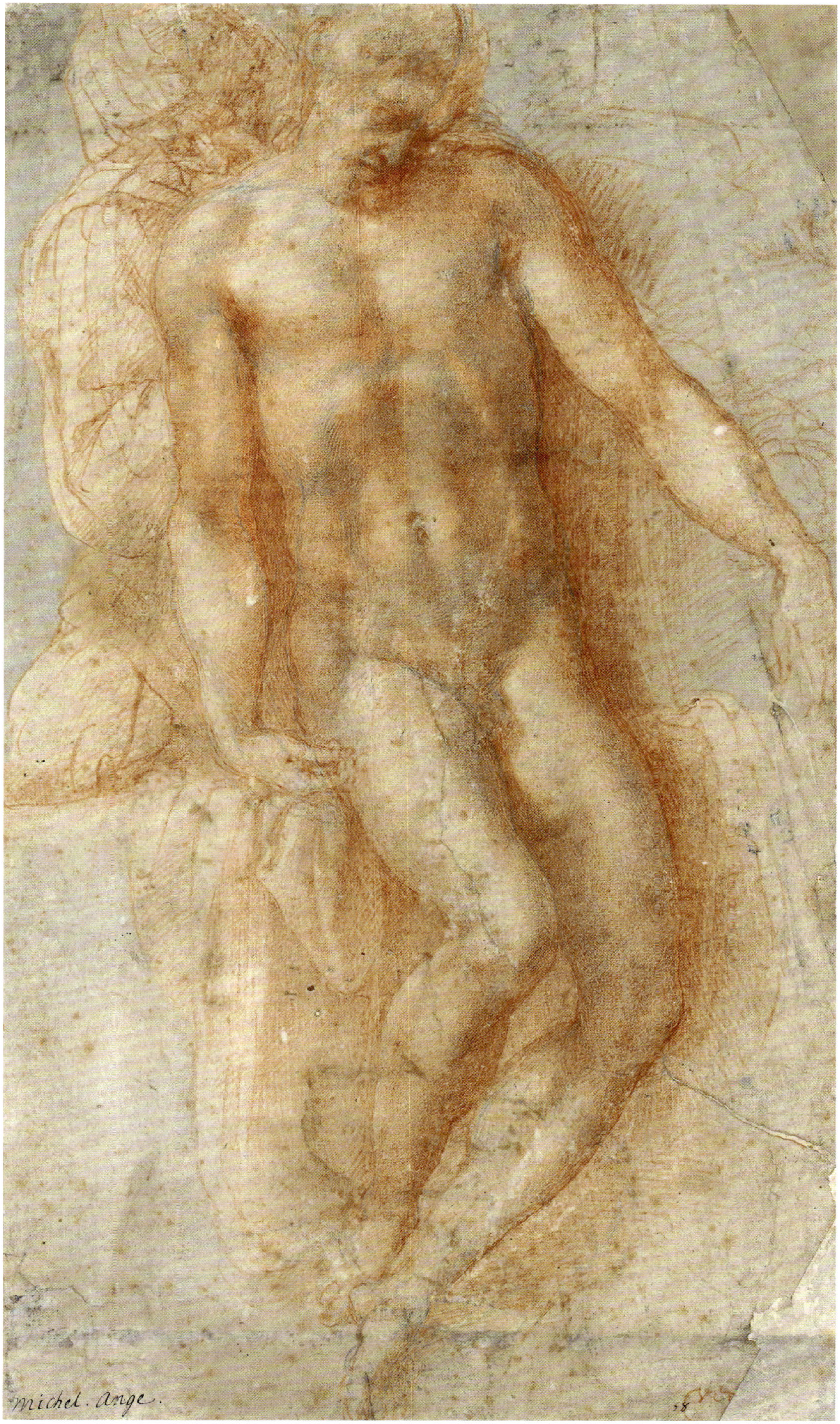

Michelangelo
Pietà, ca. 1530–1536
The ALBERTINA Museum, Vienna

Of Struggle and Passions

Michelangelo rendered the two wrestling nudes in broad, quick strokes of red chalk. He added diagonal hatching to set them off from the page. The sketchiness of the multiple deviating lines reveals that Michelangelo was experimenting with the arrangement of the figures and only determined their final positions in the process of drawing. He refrained from articulating the anatomy in detail, and he devoted attention to depicting the movements of muscles only in areas of light. The subject matter has been interpreted in two ways. One proposal sees the drawing as representing the Old Testament story of the patriarch Jacob wrestling with a man, often identified as an angel (Gen. 32:23–33). The contest was equal until the angel hit Jacob's hip, throwing it out of joint. One of the nudes in the drawing does in fact grasp at his opponent's pelvis with his right hand. When his adversary demanded to be released, Jacob is said to have responded, "I will not let thee go, except thou bless me." Michelangelo is known to have treated this subject in small sketches in chalk on the reverse of a drawing at the École des Beaux-Arts in Paris. In those, however, the angel is clearly identifiable by his wings. Alternatively, it is more probable that the Louvre drawing represents the battle of Hercules and Antaeus. The combatant on the left, who appears to have the upper hand, would thus be Hercules, the ultimate victor. With both feet planted firmly on the ground, he attempts to lift his rival by grasping him under the thigh. The distraught opponent clenches Hercules's neck and uses a leg to try to bring him down. According to the legend, Hercules realized during the struggle that the giant Antaeus drew his strength from his mother, Gaia (the Earth). He thus lifted Antaeus off the ground and held him in a crushing grip until he died. The red-chalk study is similar in style to sketches that Michelangelo made around 1524/25 for a planned marble sculpture of Hercules and Antaeus meant to be placed before the Palazzo della Signoria in Florence as a pendant to his *David*. Following heated arguments with the Signoria and various modifications of the subject matter, the project was ultimately entrusted to Michelangelo's archrival, Baccio Bandinelli, who sculpted a marble group of Hercules and Cacus. Although the present sketch could hardly have been meant to serve as the model for a colossal sculptural group of Hercules and Antaeus, Michelangelo may have created it while he was occupied with designing that marble sculpture. In addition, scholars have noted that Michelangelo's inscriptions on the back of the sheet suggest an approximate date of 1524/25.

AG

Michelangelo
Two Nude Men Wrestling,
ca. 1524/25
Paris, Musée du Louvre, Département des Arts graphiques

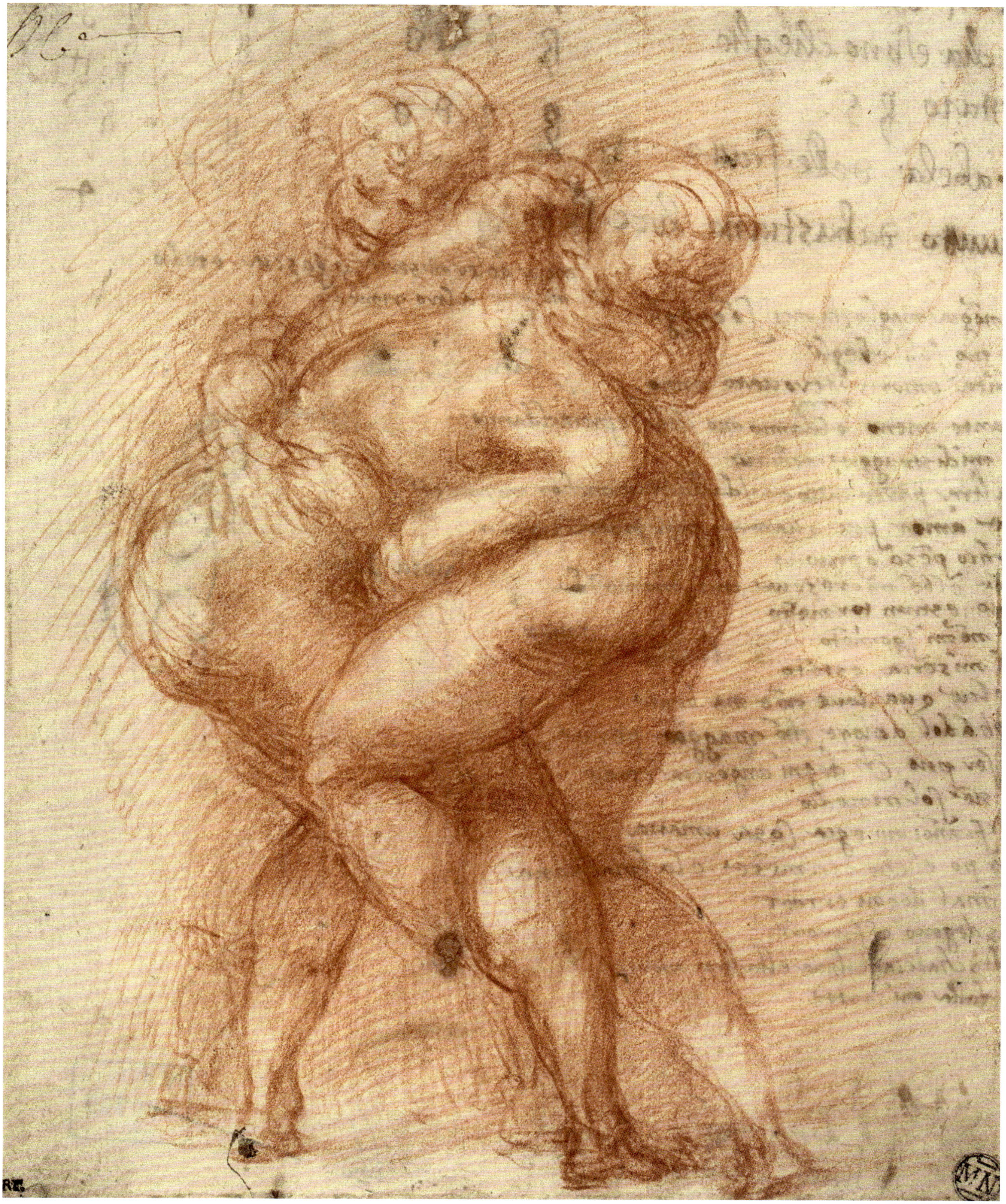

The Albertina sheet is based on a drawing by Michelangelo, the original of which in red chalk is kept at Windsor Castle (Royal Collection, inv. no. 912778). The subject of this famous composition has not yet been precisely identified. A group of nudes, which includes women and children, appears to burst forth, unbound, surging toward the right. Some float, some take broad strides forward, while others kneel or crouch. The figures are posed as archers, but only a few arrows have struck their mark—a target attached to the torso of a youthful herm. Inspired by a stucco relief in the Domus Aurea, the composition betrays knowledge of Neoplatonic sources possibly imparted to Michelangelo by a learned scholar. The allegory's general meaning is that "blind and passionate desire will not reach the true target" (Johannes Wilde). Among the more elaborate interpretations, one proposes that the subject matter derives from passages in Cristoforo Landino's *Disputationes Camaldulenses* (1472–1474) and Mario Equicola's *Libro di natura d'amore* (1525). In both, people who are driven by their desires are likened to archers. Equicola contrasts worldly passions, which aim to satisfy sensual desires, with heavenly love, which only finds true happiness in God as the highest goal. The two putti at the left, blowing on a burning bundle of sticks, stoke the flames of human passion. Above them, a satyr holds his bow backwards and, thus, will never hit the mark. The sleeping Cupid at the opposite end personifies heavenly love, the only pathway to contemplation of divine things. According to Erwin Panofsky, the artist omitted the bows to express the idea that the archers are themselves instruments of a power that lies beyond their will and consciousness.

Michelangelo executed his drawing, which is datable to about 1530, in fine strokes which vary subtly in their impression and in delicate gradations of hatching. The work belongs to a group of highly finished sheets that have been termed "presentation drawings." In contrast to earlier studies, such as those for the *Battle of Cascina* or the Sistine Chapel ceiling, in which each of the figures' muscles stand out more individually, this work gives the impression of an extraordinary tension arising from within the body, through which surges an almost irrepressible force. The sequence of movements thus appears more fluid and coherent. Michelangelo's composition was copied in numerous drawings, an engraving, and a fresco. The Albertina sheet is one of the highest-quality versions, even though it is probably not based directly on Michelangelo's red-chalk drawing but instead on a lost copy.

AG

Copy after Michelangelo
Archers Shooting at a Herm, 1530–1560
The ALBERTINA Museum, Vienna

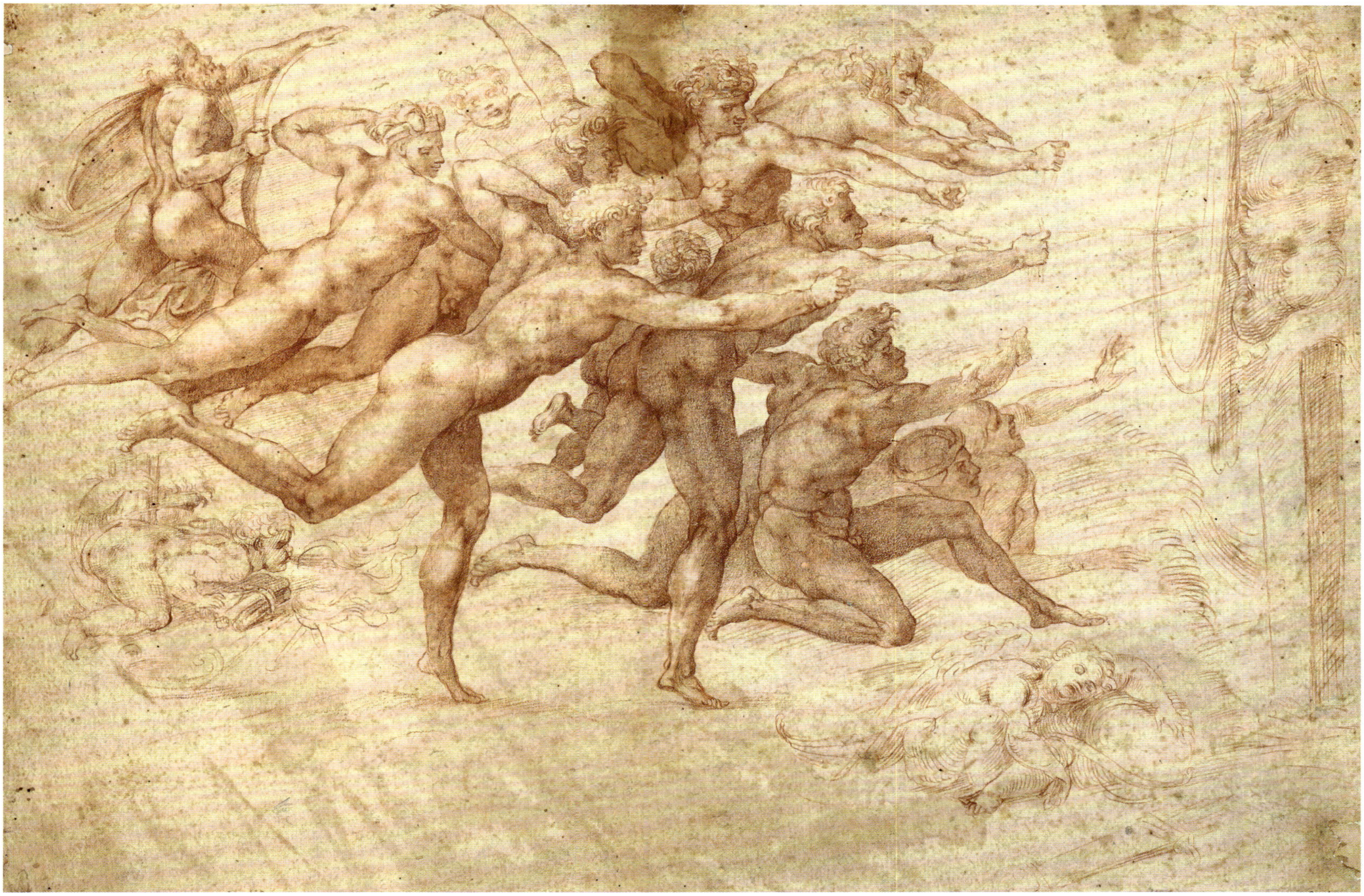

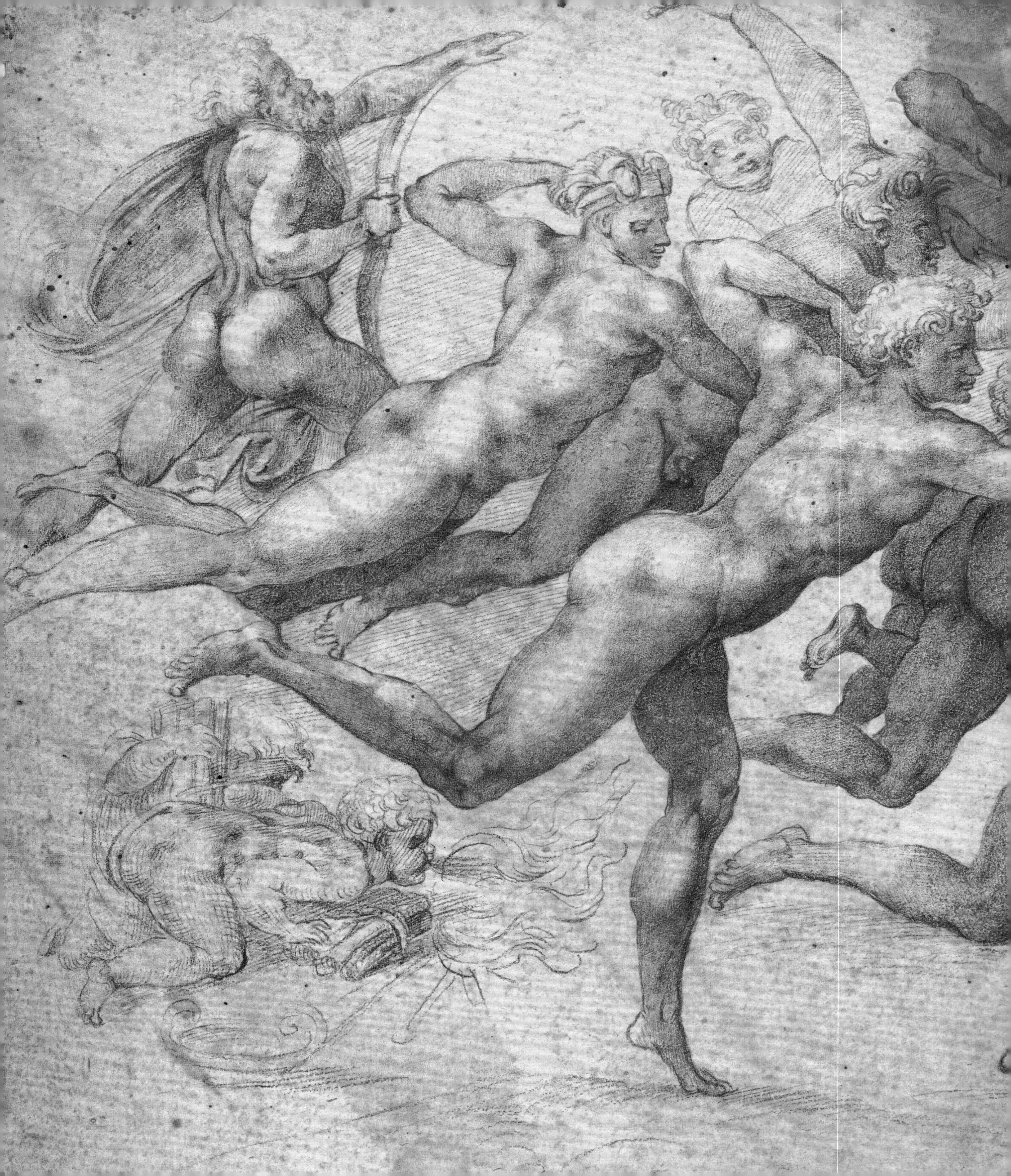

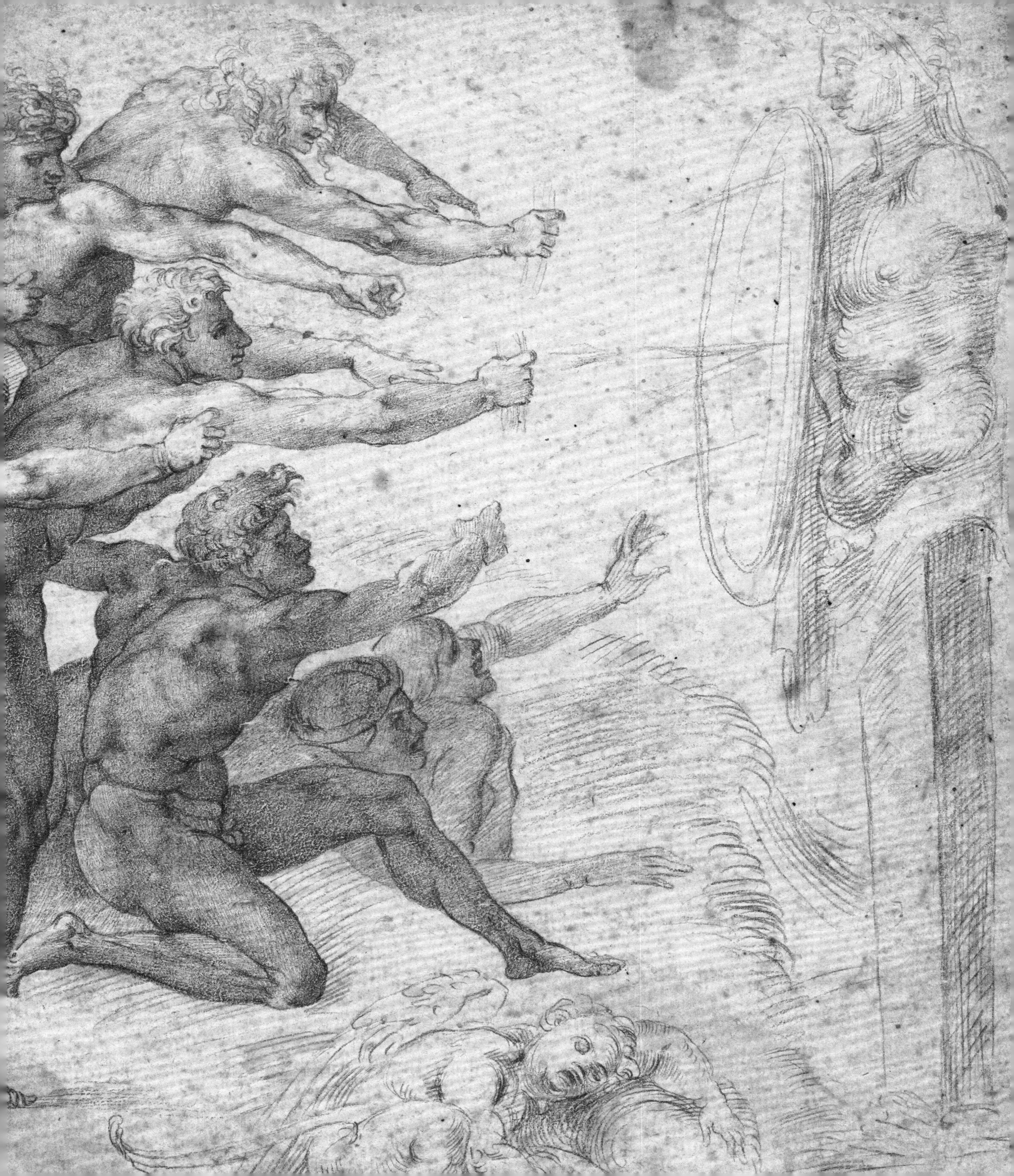

This sheet formerly attributed to Michelangelo contains studies in red chalk over preliminary sketches in black chalk. The motifs are not necessarily related to one another. The lower extremities of a nude seen from behind at the center of the sheet has been associated with Michelangelo's studies for the *Battle of Cascina*, even though a concrete connection is lacking. The careful modeling of the markedly contoured leg with its dense cross-hatching more closely resembles Michelangelo's pen-and-ink technique than it does his use of red chalk. Also, the somewhat elongated proportions suggest that the sheet was created later than the studies used for the battle scene cartoon. The youth at the lower right, who holds a pair of glasses to his eyes, is sketchier in execution. The peculiar crest on his head is sometimes found in representations of devils or demons. In the area of the neck and collarbone, the detailed indication of muscles and sinews betrays knowledge of Michelangelo's anatomical studies. The fluid handling of line calls to mind his drawings of the late 1520s and the 1530s. However, this sheet cannot have originated from Michelangelo's hand as the strokes of hatching are too uniform, schematic, and coarse. At the left edge, there is a grinning personification of Death as an écorché, a figure with its skin removed. The skeletal form appears to wear a cloak, and it holds up a crown and presumably a bag of money hanging from a chain. The other end of the chain is attached to a large collar that encircles the figure's neck. These are insignia of human dominion and wealth subject to the power of Death and thus quite literally chained to it. The draftsman was likely an artist active in the second quarter of the sixteenth century and perhaps also later, presumably in Florence, whose identity remains elusive.

AG

Circle of Michelangelo
Study Sheet with a Leg, Skull, and Young Man in Bust-Length, ca. 1525–1540
The ALBERTINA Museum, Vienna

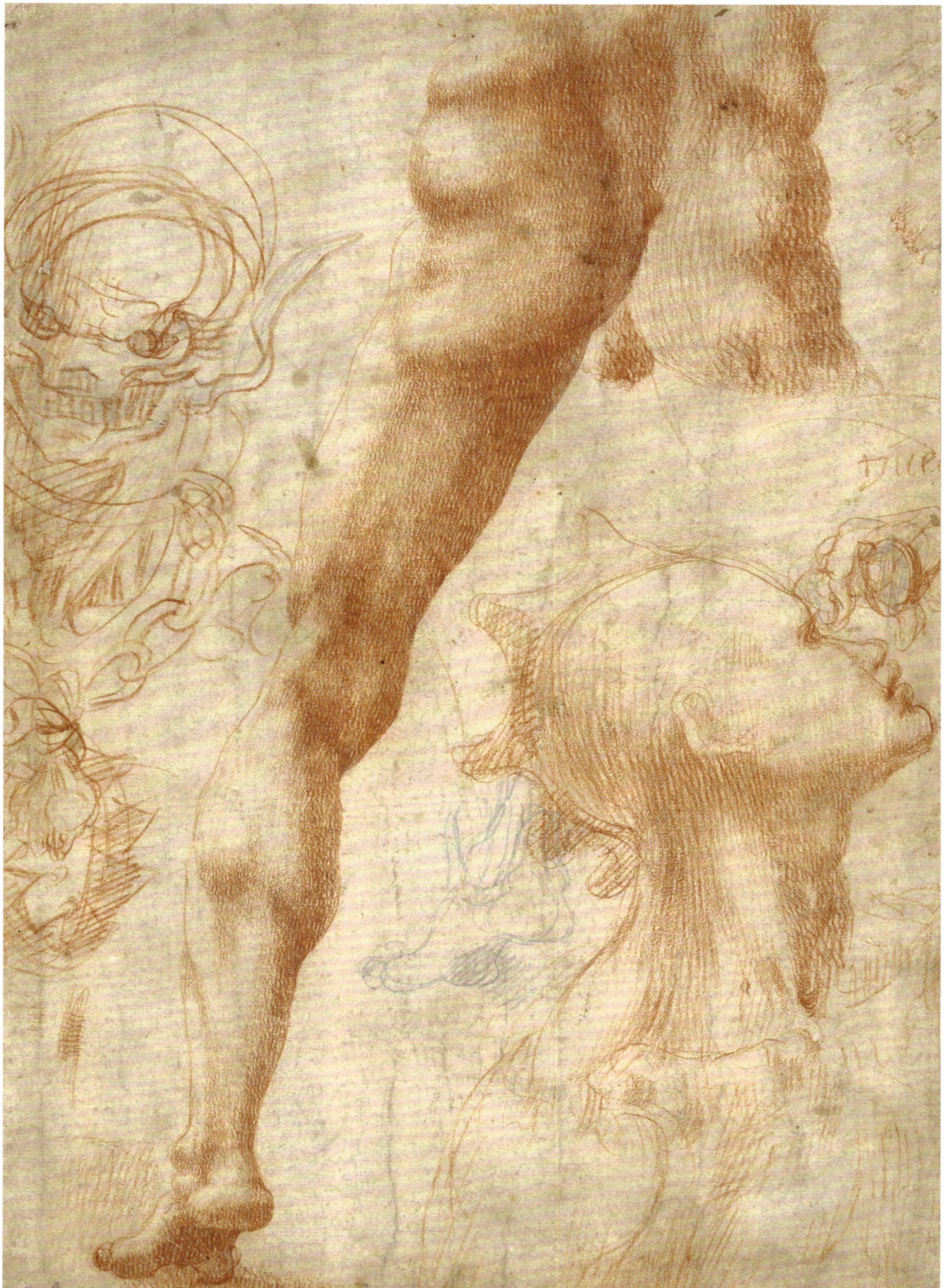

Michelangelo's Ideal: The Woman in the Man

The drawing in the Louvre of a standing female nude seen from the back, which dates from 1524/25, shows Michelangelo's engagement with the female body. In this sheet, Michelangelo may have drawn not only from life but also from an ancient statue of Venus. He is said to have owned a cast of an ancient female torso, itself possibly a fragmentary statue based on the Capitoline Venus type (fig. 15), the rear view of which shows similarities to the figure in the drawing. Michelangelo added the missing arms of the torso, merging the study of antiquity with drawing from life. The organic modeling of the musculature with its closely spaced diagonal hatching and its interplay with areas of blank paper gives the skin a sensual aura. Fluid outlines create the impression that one is observing a moving, living figure rather than a sculpture. At the same time, Michelangelo's athletic, muscular ideal of the body is also apparent. That ideal applies not only to the artist's male nudes; it also became an essential feature of his female nudes. For one thing, this is because Michelangelo's knowledge of human anatomy was based mainly on the male model. For another, the bold physiognomies he used for female figures made them heroic in character.

15 Rear view of the Capitoline Venus, AD 96–192
Roman copy after a Hellenistic recreation of an original by the Greek sculptor Praxiteles, 4th century BC
Marble, h. 193 cm
Musei Capitolini, Rome

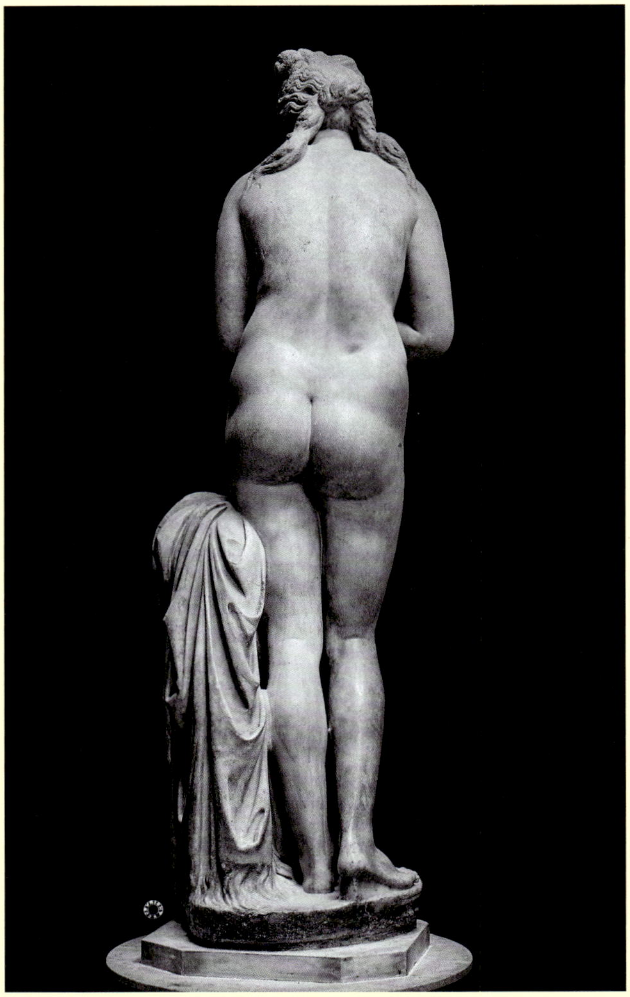

Michelangelo again took the male body as a starting point for the Albertina sheet with several studies of a female nude seen from behind, which dates from the first half of the 1530s. The black-chalk drawings document the implementation of an idea in different degrees of finish—from schematic outlines to a more thoroughly defined motif. The subject is a woman seated with a crouched posture, leaning on a support covered in fabric. Michelangelo was particularly interested in the back muscles, which he modeled in fine shades of chalk. In this work, the strength and muscularity of the woman's physique is again conspicuous. Both sheets are reminiscent of well-known examples of Michelangelo's representation of the female body, such as the sibyls on the ceiling of the Sistine Chapel in Rome, the Medici tomb sculpture of *Night* (fig. 16) in the New Sacristy

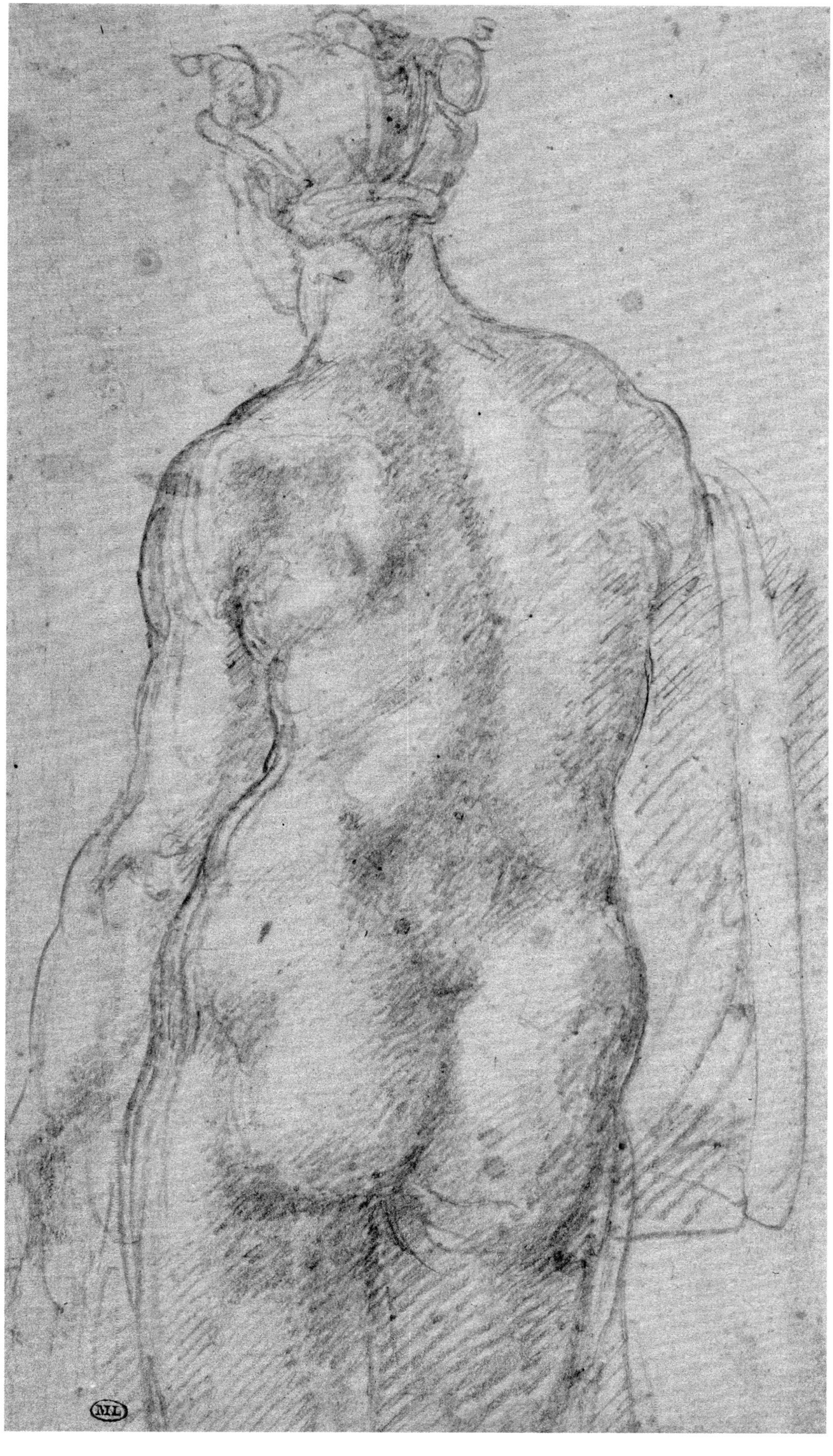

Michelangelo
Female Nude Seen from the Rear,
1524/25
Paris, Musée du Louvre
Département des Arts graphiques

of San Lorenzo in Florence, and the lost *Leda and the Swan* painting, known only through copies and engravings. Those figures represent a heroic female type that is on a par with the artist's powerful male nudes.

LE

16 Michelangelo, *Night*, 1526–1531
Sculpture for the Tomb of Giuliano di Lorenzo de' Medici
Marble
San Lorenzo, Florence, New Sacristy

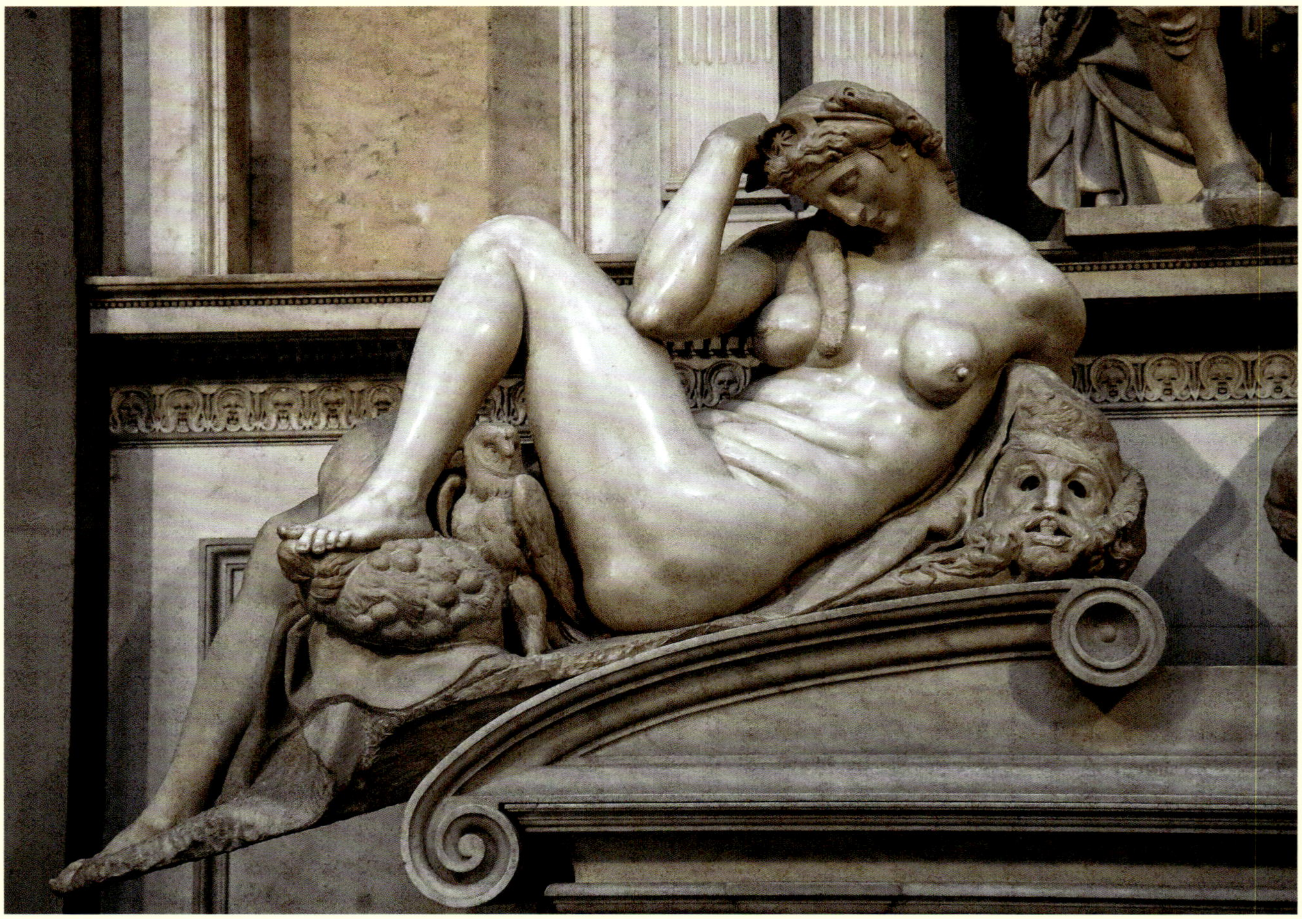

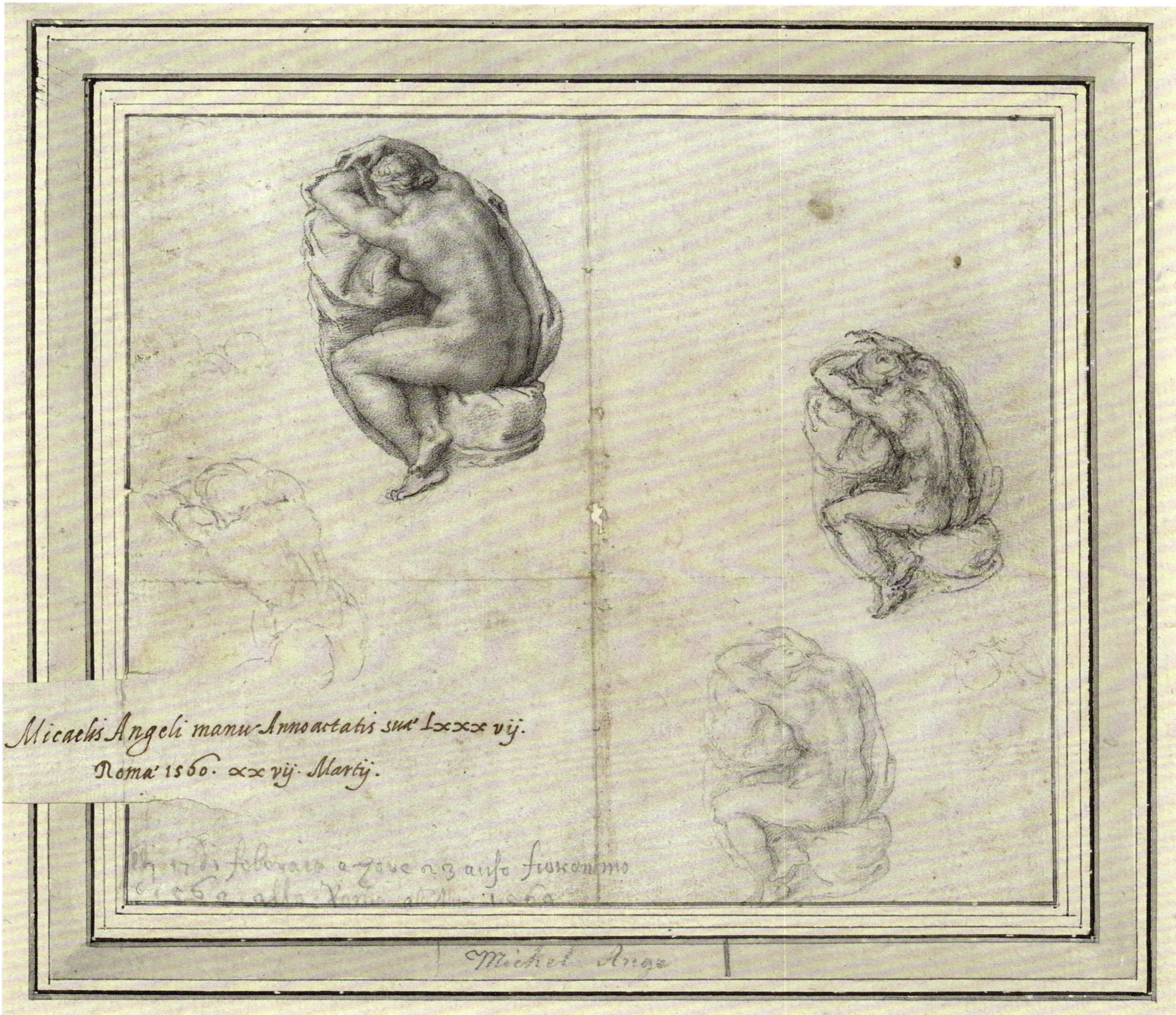

Michelangelo
Study for Seated Female Nudes
Seen from the Rear, ca. 1530–1536
The ALBERTINA Museum, Vienna

The Suffering God

In this Albertina drawing, Christ is depicted as already deceased, even though his delicate body is imbued with inner life. His head bearing the crown of thorns has sunken to his left, while his tightly clasped legs are turned in the other direction. The highly detailed handling of line, the use of the thinnest of strokes, and the finely nuanced modeling recall Michelangelo's representations of Christ from the 1530s and so-called "presentation drawings" that the artist made for his friend Tommaso de' Cavalieri. The graceful curve that runs through the Savior's body is reminiscent of the drawing of Christ on the Cross from about 1538–1541 (British Museum, London), which Michelangelo gave to Vittoria Colonna, the famous poet he admired. In that work, however, Christ is shown as still alive. In the Louvre (inv. no. 843) there is a copy after a lost drawing of the Crucifixion, possibly also made for Colonna, and in that work the pose is even closer to that of the Christ figure in the Albertina drawing. According to the old inscriptions on the sheet, it was owned by the artist Biagio Betti, who was born about 1545 in Cutigliano, near Pistoia, and who joined the Theatine Order as a lay brother at the convent of San Silvestro al Quirinale in Rome in 1573. According to Giovanni Baglione, Betti was a gifted musician, an experienced physician, and an artistically well-rounded person, who created miniatures on parchment and models in wax and clay. Yet the Vienna drawing does not relate to any works attributed to him. Betti was a pupil of Daniele da Volterra, part of whose collection of drawings he inherited. Daniele's drawings are finished to a similarly high degree, but his strokes remain individually distinguishable. His modeling is less cohesive, which results in a hardening of forms. Also, the movements of his figures lack fluidity since the limbs sometimes appear almost tacked on. The present drawing is therefore also not by Daniele, and its author must remain anonymous for the time being.

Particularly in his late period, Michelangelo treated the subject of the crucified Christ in numerous drawings. At the age of eighty-two, he made the chalk drawing now in the Louvre, which can be dated precisely to 1557 thanks to a study on the reverse for the vault of the chapel for the French king at St. Peter's. Christ is shown in the throes of death, yet his agony is expressed neither through a strong torsion of the body nor forced movements of the limbs. Instead, Michelangelo lent the figure a fully unified form. Christ's suffering and pain find expression in a massive shudder at the body's core, which reverberates outward in the repeatedly retraced contour lines. His agony is clearly legible in the face, with its deeply recessed, half-closed eyes, raised eyebrows, furrowed brow, and drawn-down corners of the mouth. Rising

Circle of Michelangelo
The Crucified Christ,
second third of 16th century
The ALBERTINA Museum, Vienna

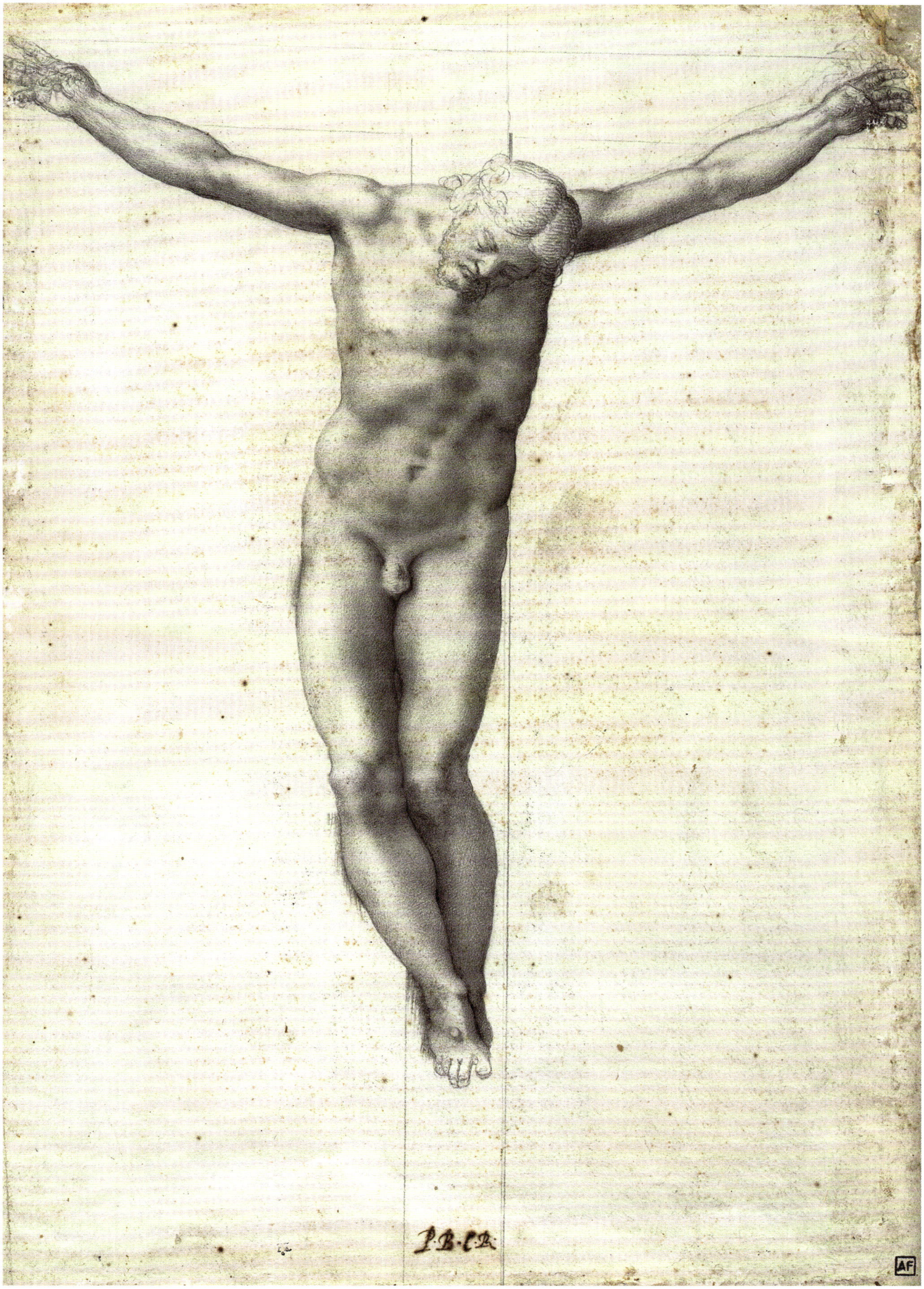
AF

up once more before death, Christ strains outward and takes one last, deep breath, as if about to say, "It is finished," before bowing his head and giving up the ghost (John 19:30).

Such drawings give a sense of Michelangelo's intense compassion for the suffering of Christ. In these moving depictions, the deeply pious artist articulated not only his fear of death but also his vision of salvation through divine grace. Michelangelo also expressed these thoughts repeatedly in his poetry, for example, in the verses of one of his late sonnets: "Painting and sculpture soothe the soul no more, / its focus fixed on the love divine, outstretching / on the cross, to enfold us closer, open arms" (qtd. *The Complete Poems of Michelangelo*, trans. John Frederick Nims 1998).

AG

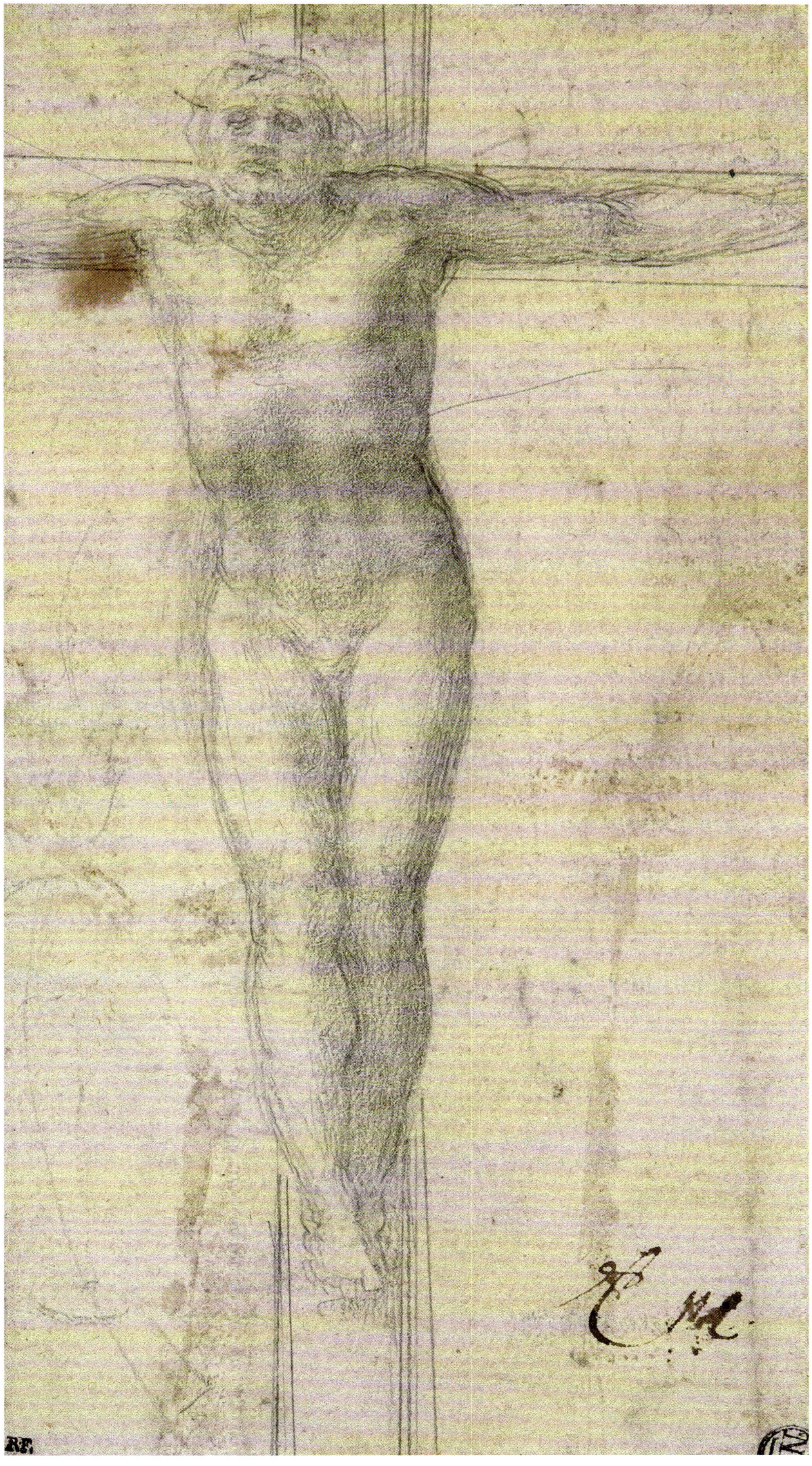

Michelangelo
The Crucified Christ, 1557
Paris, Musée du Louvre
Département des Arts graphiques

Mad about Michelangelo

The brilliant block cutter Ugo da Carpi introduced the chiaroscuro woodcut to Italy. This novel printmaking technique had been recently developed by Hans Burgkmair and Jost de Negker in Augsburg and by Lucas Cranach in Wittenberg. It produces a color print made from two or more blocks. For the so-called tone block, the composition's highlights are cut out so that the white of the paper remains visible in those areas of the print. The line block, often inked in black, is printed second; it contains all the lines of the composition, as in a normal woodcut. Ugo worked first in Venice, reproducing drawings by Titian, and from 1516 to 1518, he was in Rome, where he established contacts with Baldassare Peruzzi, Raphael, and the printmakers in Raphael's workshop. He translated various preparatory drawings that Raphael made for paintings and tapestries into marvelous chiaroscuro prints. While his early sheets were printed with just two blocks, the later ones involve three or more tone blocks, a process by which the line block, previously most important, gradually became unnecessary. Ugo's achievement was in liberating the chiaroscuro woodcut from its linear constraints; the composition could be modeled solely with color and light, producing a remarkably painterly effect.

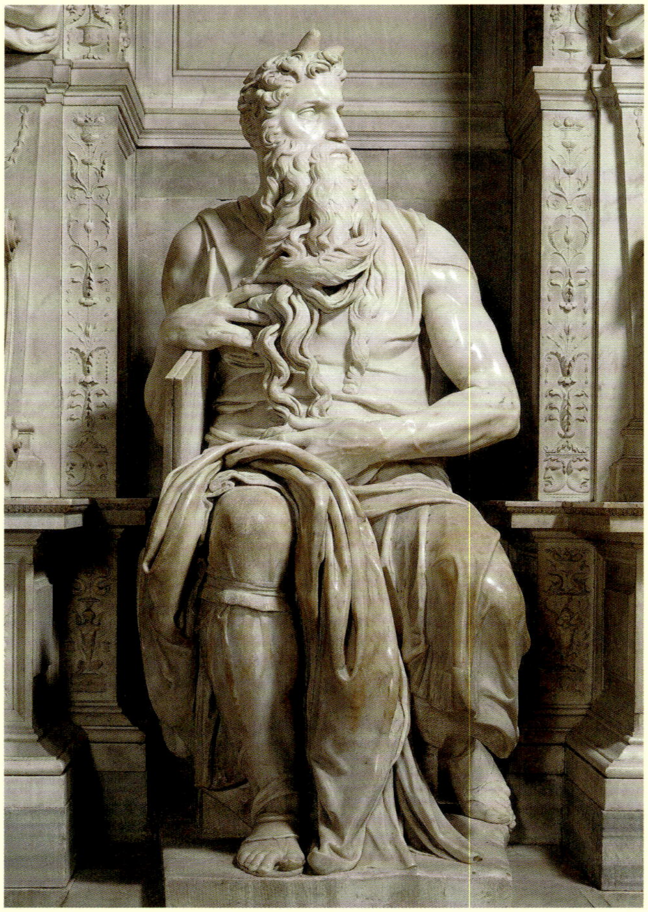

17 Michelangelo, *Moses*, 1513–1515
Marble, h. 235 cm
San Pietro in Vincoli, Rome

After the death of Raphael, Ugo began a collaboration with Parmigianino, who spent the years 1524 to 1527 in Rome. Like Perino del Vaga, Baccio Bandinelli, and Rosso Fiorentino, Parmigianino studied the frescoes of the Sistine Chapel ceiling and made decisive contributions to the planar, decorative style of the 1520s seen in Rome. His drawing style was particularly suited to Ugo's chiaroscuro prints because of its diffuse painterly qualities and emotional elegance of line. Their joint masterpiece is the *Diogenes* of about 1526/27. This work unites the monumentality of Michelangelo's figures with Parmigianino's pursuit of a refined buoyancy of line and graceful design. While the dynamism of the pose derives from the *ignudi*, the inner tension and great force of will perceptible throughout the figure of Diogenes may have been inspired by Michelangelo's *Moses* (fig. 17). The bent posture of the left arm and the vigorous gesture of that hand may have also derived from the *Moses*. Although the sculpture was not publicly

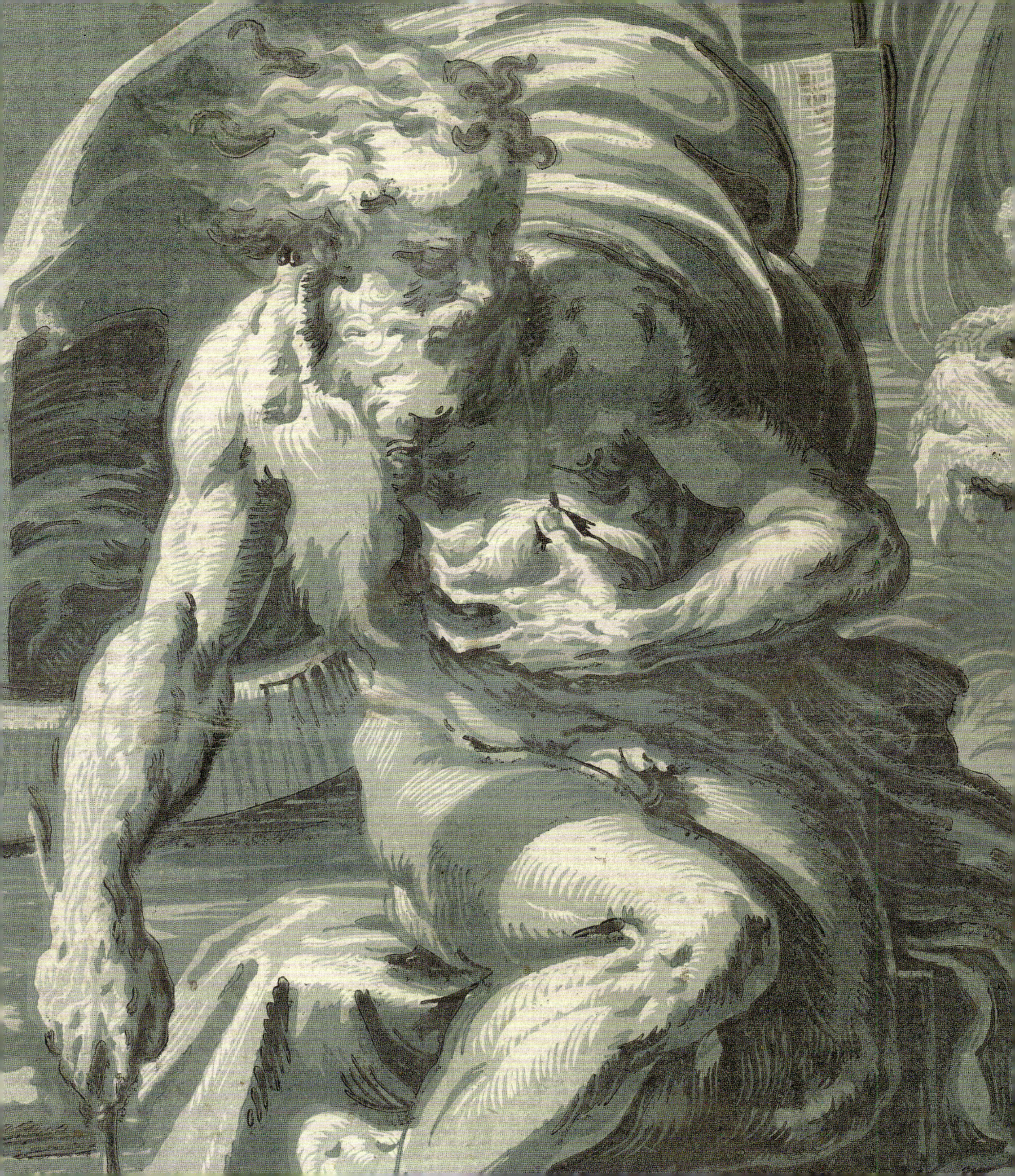

accessible at that time, Parmigianino was presumably aware of its appearance, particularly because certain aspects of his later grisaille fresco of Moses in Santa Maria della Steccata in Parma even more closely resemble the model provided by Michelangelo. Diogenes's violent mental agitation is expressed through the vehemently twisting motion of the figure. This force pulsates outward, into the blown-back shock of hair and the billowing cloak, ultimately channeled into the circular form of the barrel in the background. Even the chicken, with which the Cynic mocked Plato's definition of humans as featherless bipeds, is alarmed and on the run. The painterly richness of this chiaroscuro woodcut is wonderful. Irregular tonal areas and sparing black lines, used only as accents, combine to create a coherent image and fully model the forms, as if they had been applied with a brush. The white of the visible paper support convincingly describes such details as the highlights on the body, the bulging veins on the arms, the wrinkled skin of the chicken, and the wood grain of the barrel. Parmigianino also had the *Diogenes* engraved, after a variant design, by Giovanni Jacopo Caraglio. In doing so, Parmigianino ensured that his invention would be disseminated in both a detailed monochrome engraving and a broadly executed color chiaroscuro woodcut.

AG

Ugo da Carpi
Diogenes, ca. 1526/27
The ALBERTINA Museum, Vienna

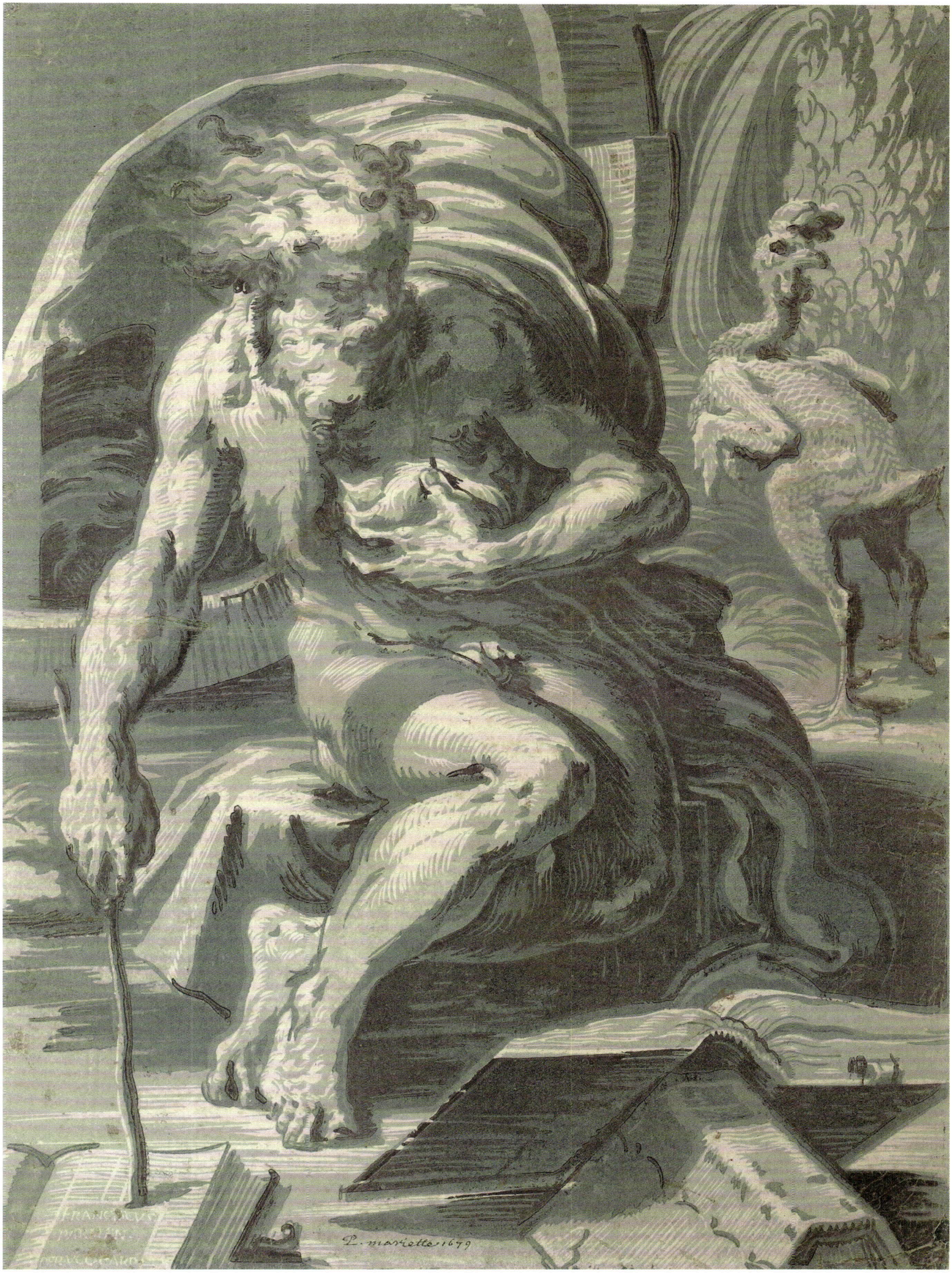

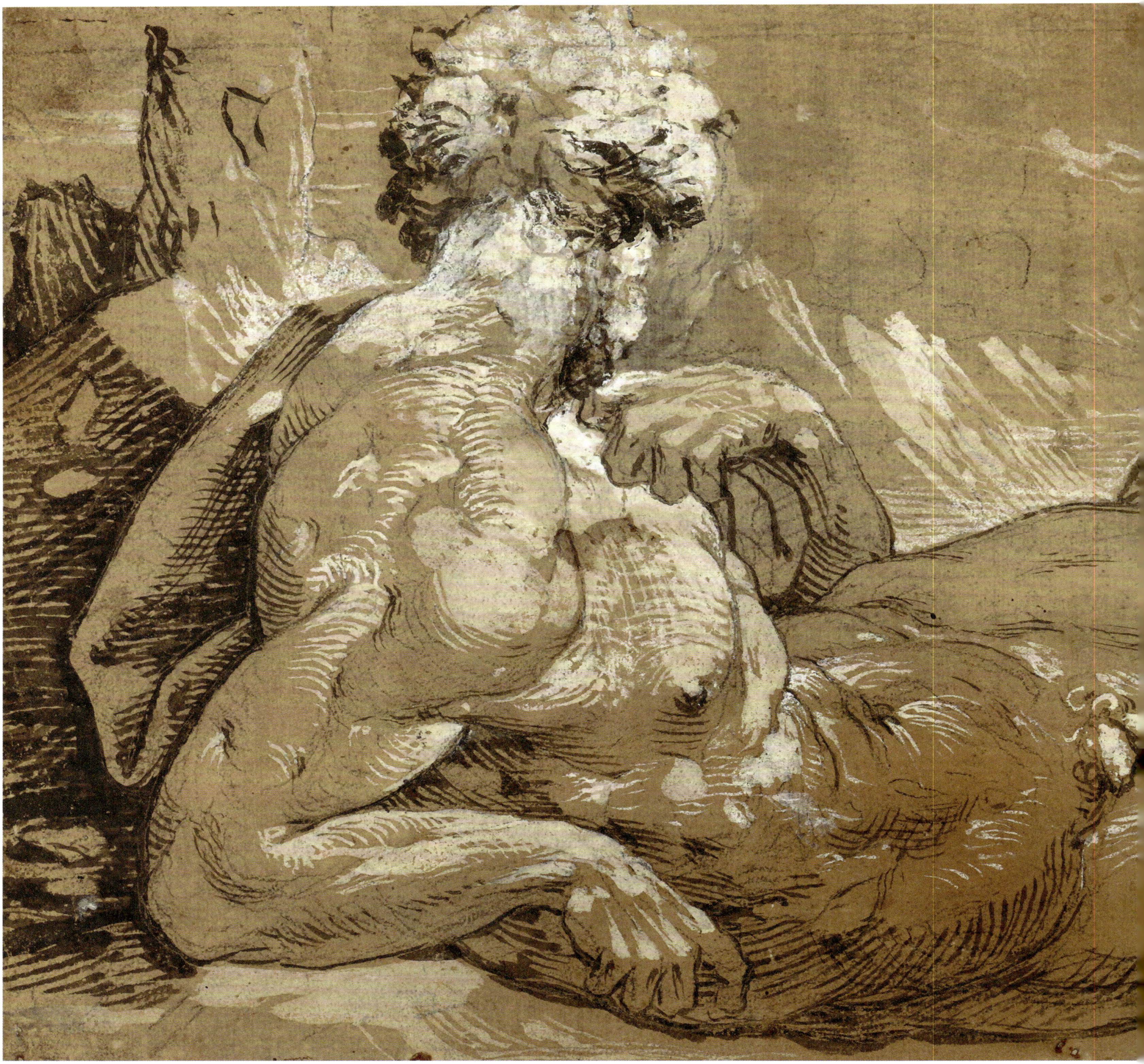

Domenico Beccafumi
Reclining Male Nude in a Landscape,
ca. 1540–1544
The ALBERTINA Museum, Vienna

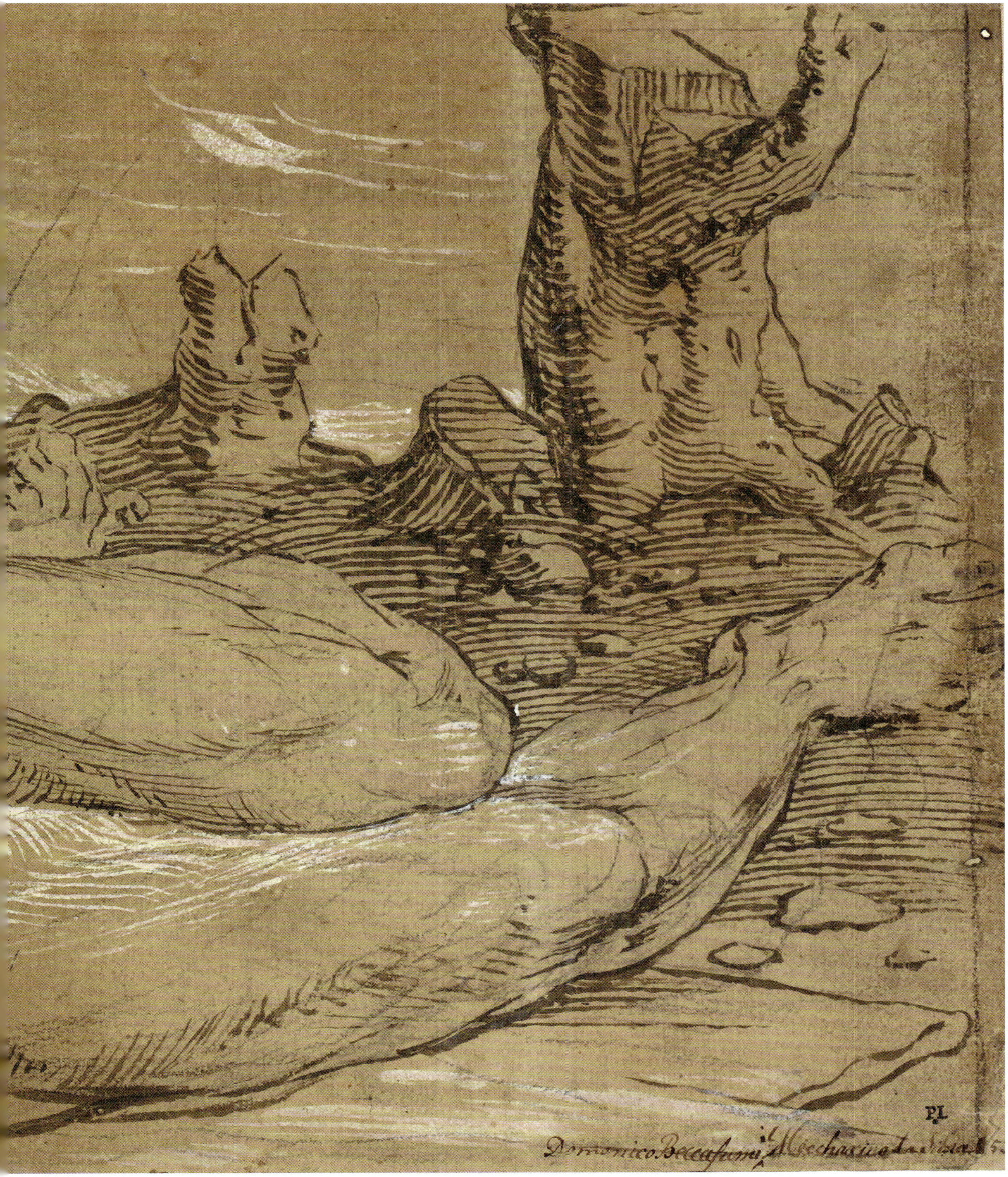
PL
Domenico Beccafumi

Domenico Beccafumi's highly individual style is characterized by an exaggerated expressiveness in which the eccentric and the fantastical are emphasized. This penchant for the fabulous, unreal, and expressive is underscored in his pictures by a flickering chiaroscuro and by bright, phosphorescent colors. Beccafumi is thought to have stayed in Rome for the first time in the early 1510s. There, he studied the works of Michelangelo and Raphael before returning to his native Siena in the fall of 1512.

In its bulky proportions, this male nude, lying on the ground in the pose of an antique river god, betrays the influence of Michelangelo's mature figural ideal as represented, for example, by the allegorical sculpture of *Dusk* in the New Sacristy of San Lorenzo in Florence. Yet Beccafumi introduces Mannerist adaptations to this model: in the swelling musculature and in the posture that twists strongly while also giving the impression of being fully at rest. In this pen-and-ink drawing, which diverges somewhat from its underlying black-chalk sketch, the upper body stands out because of the contrast created by lavish applications of white heightening. The handling of line has no direct relationship to sheets by Michelangelo. Similar poses are found among Beccafumi's figures in the inlaid marble pavement of Siena Cathedral, for example, in his depictions of *Moses on Mount Sinai* and *The Sacrifice of Isaac*. A probable connection with chiaroscuro woodcuts that the artist may have made in the 1540s has also been noted. The painterly character of the Albertina sheet, which incorporates the paper's brown tone as a color value, is indeed reminiscent of such woodcuts. The clouds and mountains resemble the recessed areas of a tone block, where the white of the paper would shine through. The drawing is especially close to an etching by Beccafumi with an accompanying tone block, in which three male nudes are wedged into a similarly low horizontal format. In the print, the figures also recline in a deep landscape with rocky mountains in the distance. A pen-and-ink sketch in the Uffizi probably represents an initial idea for the drawing, and in the Louvre, there is an autograph replica, once owned by Vasari, which Beccafumi possibly made for the purpose of presentation.

The youthful nude in the other Albertina drawing by Beccafumi derives from one of Michelangelo's *ignudi* on the Sistine Chapel ceiling: the figure above and to the left of the Persian Sibyl. Also, the head is closely related to that of Adam in the depiction of his creation on that ceiling. Yet, whereas Michelangelo's *ignudo* extends into the space surrounding it, Beccafumi's figure spreads across a shallow plane. At the same time, the refined thinning and elongation of the figure does have a certain affinity to the bronze-colored nudes in the spandrels of the Sistine ceiling. In this nude, Beccafumi gave general indications of the musculature without much anatomical articulation. The body's strong curvature therefore seems less a Mannerist exaggeration of Michelangelo's heroic figure ideal than an echo of the Gothic S-curve. The stone tablet held by the young figure presumably identifies him as a prophet. The presence of putti would be consistent with that, as the prophets and sibyls on the Sistine Chapel ceiling receive their divine inspiration from similar figures. The sheet likely dates from the first half of the 1540s, especially given the connections with the prophets and sibyls in the floor mosaic of Siena Cathedral, carried out in 1544. Beccafumi made several versions of the figure in this drawing, and the composition proved popular, as various copies attest.

AG

Domenico Beccafumi
Seated Nude Youth with a Stone Tablet and Two Putti, ca. 1544/45
The ALBERTINA Museum, Vienna

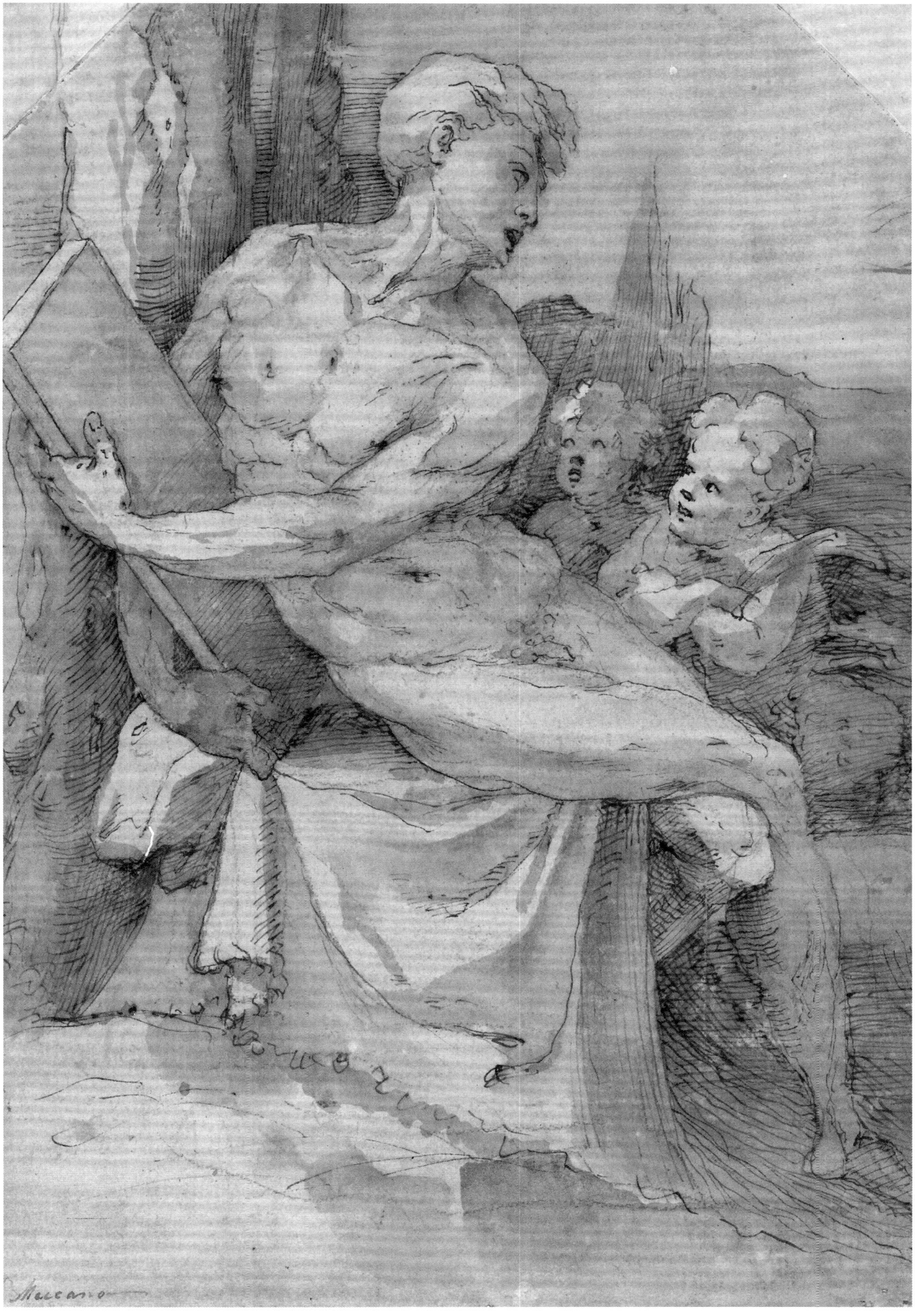

The sculptor and painter Baccio Bandinelli was initially a great admirer of Michelangelo. He was among the artists who made drawings after the *Battle of Cascina* cartoon. Although Vasari held him responsible for the cartoon's dismemberment, he also praised Bandinelli for his precision of line and modeling in the depiction of nudes, which Vasari thought surpassed that of all other artists. The highly ambitious Bandinelli sought to outdo even Michelangelo, and ultimately became the master's archrival. The red-chalk drawing in the Albertina belongs to a series of academic nudes that were inspired by Michelangelo. Possibly dating from the first half of the 1520s, they are not connected with any of Bandinelli's painted or sculpted works. This male nude takes inspiration from the *ignudo* to the upper right of the Erythraean Sibyl in the Sistine Chapel. Its powerful, bulging musculature is particularly striking. Bandinelli, a keen student of anatomy, attended dissections and made drawings of the corpses. Michelangelo used subtle gradations of tone in his red-chalk drawings for the *ignudi* in order to represent gatherings of force, emphasize the areas of the joints, lend the muscle movements an organic fluidity, and animate the figures from within. In contrast, Bandinelli employed rigid parallel strokes in a somewhat more uniform manner throughout the figure. His juxtaposition of areas of hatching with areas of light creates an impression of sculptural tautness, and the raking fall of light across the body emphasizes the relief-like character of the pose. Bandinelli was concerned exclusively with exterior form and was incapable of imbuing the figure with human emotions or real passions. Whereas the power of Michelangelo's figures resides not only in the physical but also in the psychological and moral, Bandinelli's concept of muscularity in this drawing was purely athletic. Bandinelli made the magnificent pen-and-ink drawing of *The Creation of Adam* in connection with a project for the Florence Cathedral. Filippo Brunelleschi had erected a large octagonal wooden choir enclosure in the crossing, which he had intended to replace with a marble structure. Bandinelli was able to convince Duke Cosimo I de' Medici to carry out the planned project in close conformity with the old model. Yet Bandinelli's choir was also to be more splendid in design, thanks both to richer articulation of the architecture and to decoration with numerous sculptures and reliefs. For the eight exterior surfaces of the marble screen, Bandinelli planned twenty-one bronze reliefs with Old Testament scenes. These were never carried out, but the designs are partially preserved in drawings of about 1545–1548. The arch in the east side of the screen was meant to accommodate the marble group *Adam and Eve with the Tree of Knowledge* (Museo Nazionale del Bargello, Florence), and the area beneath that sculptures was meant to display a marble or bronze relief of the creation of this original human couple. The drawing in the Albertina shows the design for the scene of Adam's creation, and its style is typical of Bandinelli's works in pen and ink. The handling of line shows the influence of Michelangelo, who himself prized Bandinelli's draftsmanship. In Michelangelo's pen-and-ink studies, however, the flow of line is more complex, following the forms of the body and lending them roundness. His lines smoothen transitions and form overlapping clusters of hatching. Bandinelli, in contrast, used straight, firm, widely spaced lines which, instead of combining in a fluid manner, cover the body like loosely knit patches of fabric. Because the clusters of hatching abruptly adjoin areas of light, the forms appear hard and sculptural. In the present drawing, Bandinelli intentionally contrasted his bold hatching with the bare paper to heighten the relief effect. The depiction shows God the Father, enthroned on clouds, alighting on Earth and bringing Adam to life by touching a rod to his knee. Here, the Creator is the *deus artifex* who frees the first human, like a statue, from a block of stone—an expression of Bandinelli's understanding of himself as a sculptor with godlike creative power.

AG

Baccio Bandinelli
Seated Male Nude with Right Leg Raised to the Left, 1520–1525
The ALBERTINA Museum, Vienna

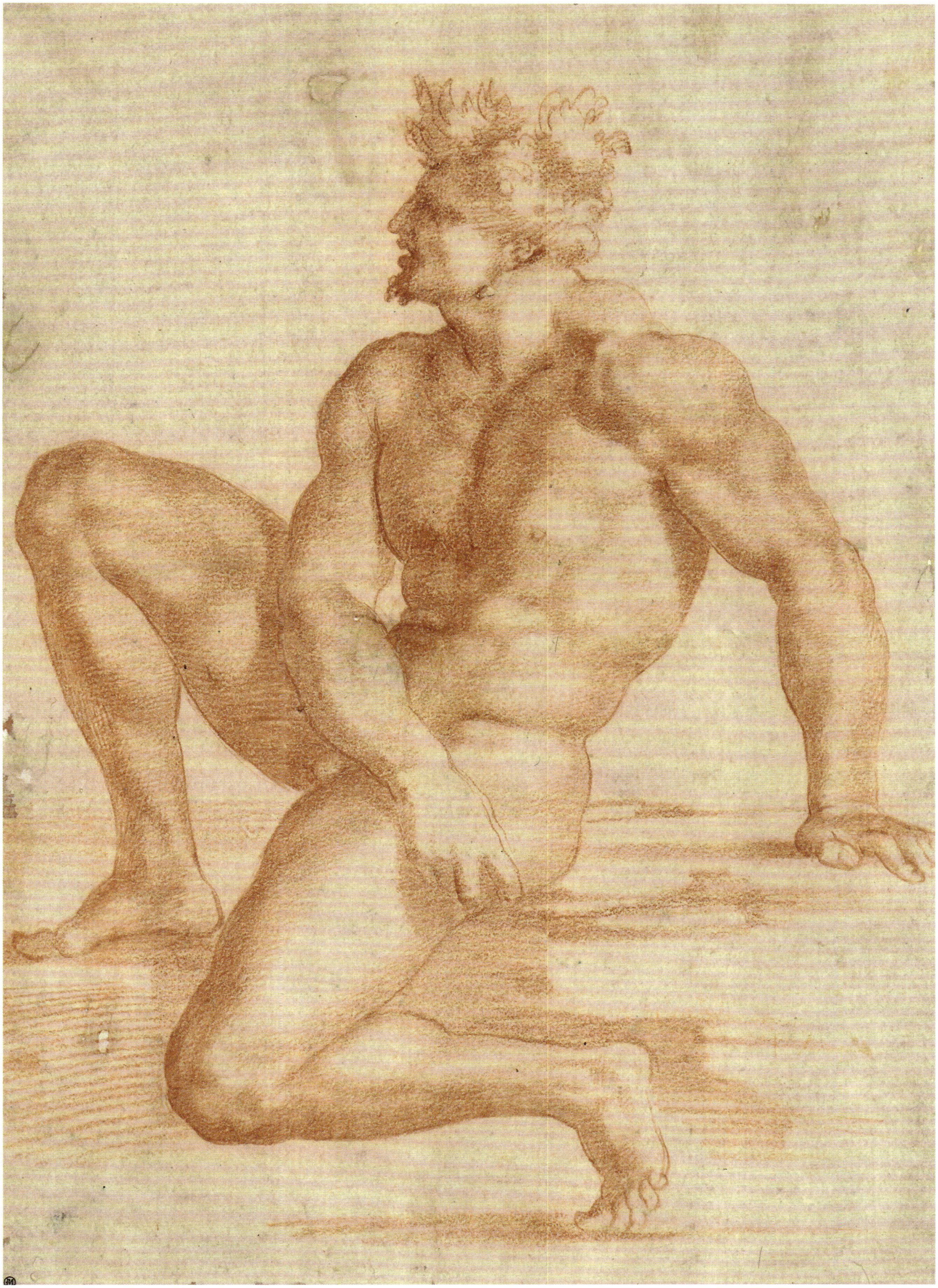

Baccio Bandinelli
The Creation of Adam, 1545–1548
The ALBERTINA Museum, Vienna

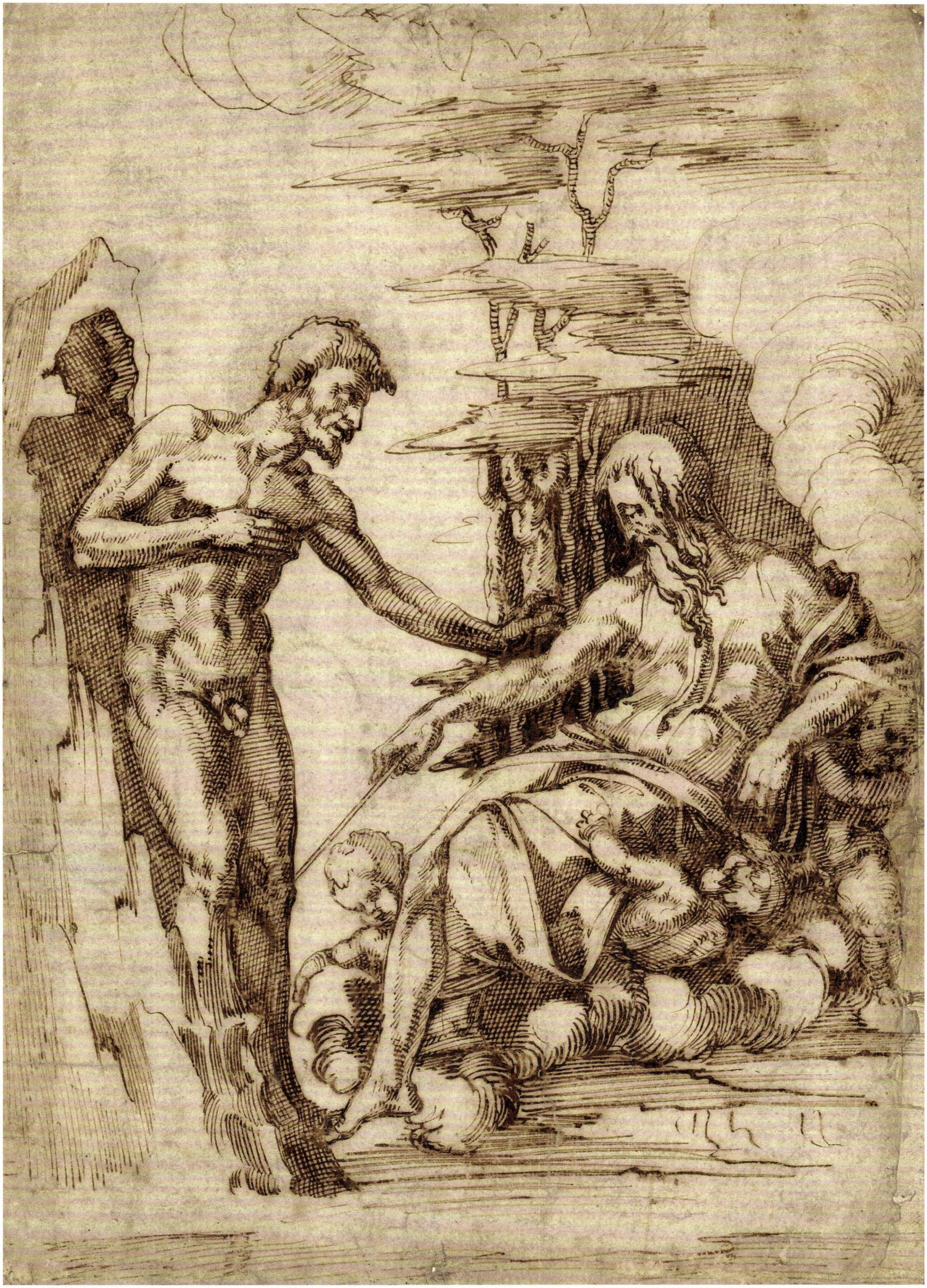

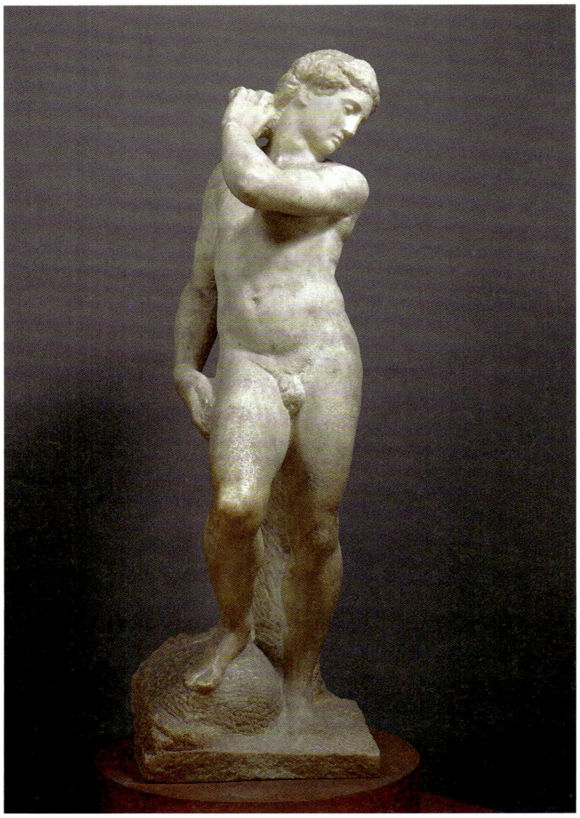

18 Michelangelo, *Apollo/David*, 1530
Marble, h. 146 cm
Museo Nazionale del Bargello, Florence

Salviati's admiration for Michelangelo is most evident in his copies after the master. These include studies after the allegorical sculptures, the Times of Day, in the New Sacristy of San Lorenzo in Florence. In addition, Vasari mentions a colored copy after one of Michelangelo's drawings of the Fall of Phaeton as well as studies after *The Last Judgment*. The drawing in the Albertina is based on the graceful marble statue of *Apollo* (fig. 18) that, according to Vasari, Michelangelo made to gain the friendship of Baccio Valori, the papal governor of Florence installed by Clement VII in August 1530. In the inventory of the art collections of Cosimo I de' Medici (1553), it should be noted, the unfinished statue is listed as a David. These conflicting identifications have sparked intense debate. Furthermore, it has also been proposed that Michelangelo began carving the work even earlier, about 1525/26, with the original intention of placing it in the New Sacristy of San Lorenzo. Current scholarship mostly agrees that Vasari's description is correct and that the statue shows Apollo reaching for an arrow in his quiver.

Salviati also interpreted the subject as Apollo. Modifications that he introduced include replacing the spherical object beneath the foot of Michelangelo's sculpture with the serpentine dragon Python, changing the stone in the god's right hand into a corner of drapery, and elongating the standing figure. Otherwise, his drawing adheres closely to the model. By including a dark area between the legs, he even gives an intimation of the tree stump that supports the statue from behind. Salviati employed delicate, carefully controlled lines; they run diagonally, overlap one another, and through small variations in pressure, create fine tonal gradations. In places that required emphasis, Salviati reinforced the contours. The handling of line resembles that of Michelangelo's highly finished studies in black chalk from the second half of the 1520s and the 1530s, such as the drawings created for Gherardo Perini, the designs for a Risen Christ, and the sheets made as gifts for Tommaso de' Cavalieri. The Mannerist Salviati was captivated less by the sculpture's spatially convincing torsion and dynamic movement than he was by the graceful elasticity of the pose, which gives the impression of effortlessness. Salviati's angle of view was not fully frontal but rather from slightly to the left, and he reduced the foreshortening in the limbs and in the overall spatial relations, causing the figure to spread more fully across the picture plane. This planar, decorative aspect is accentuated by the piece of drapery wafted sideways as well as by the refined silhouette of the dragon.

AG

Francesco Salviati (Francesco de' Rossi)
Apollo Standing on the Dragon Python,
ca. 1543–1548
The ALBERTINA Museum, Vienna

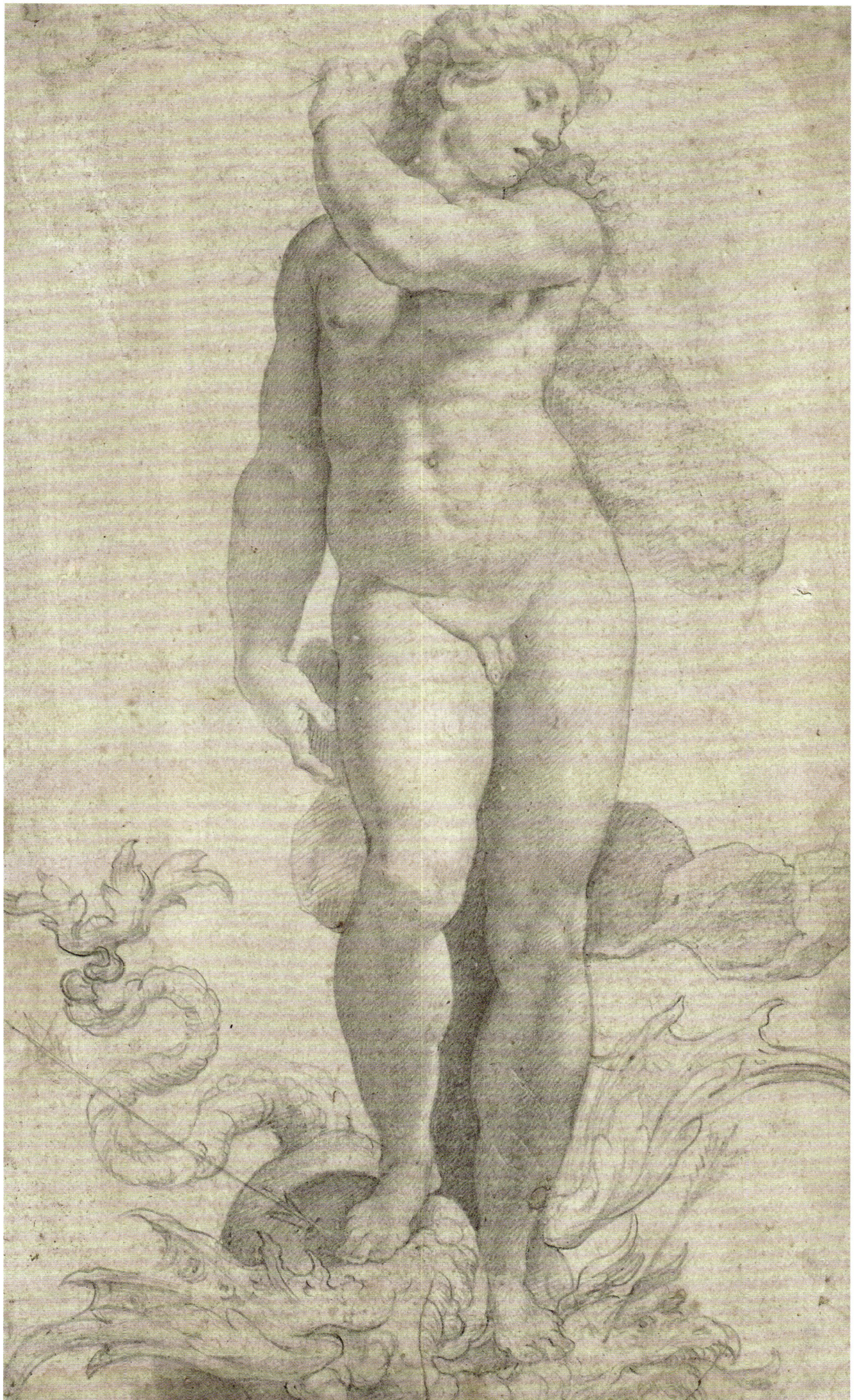

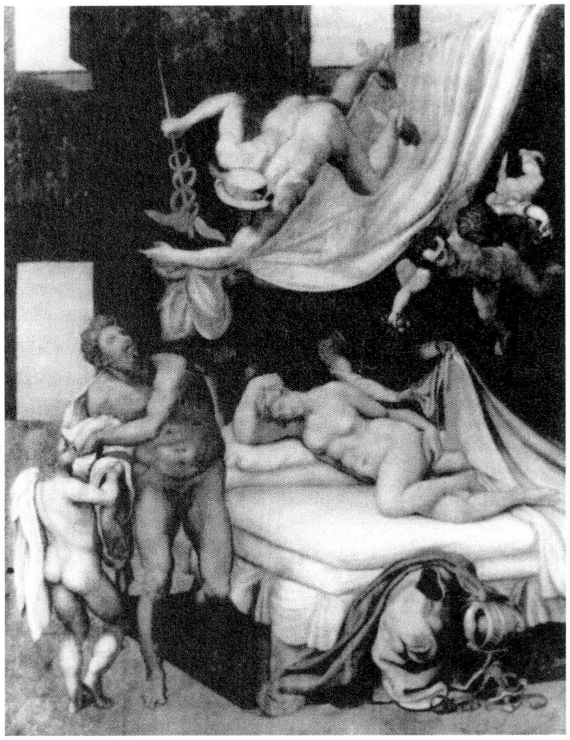

19 Daniele da Volterra (or copy after the same), *Mercury Commanding Aeneas to Leave Dido*, ca. 1555/56, oil on panel, 65 × 47 cm
Whereabouts unknown (formerly in a Swedish private collection)

At the advanced age of seventy-five, Michelangelo stopped painting and devoted all his energies to ambitious architectural commissions. As he had already done for Sebastiano del Piombo, he continued to supply drawings to artist friends of his, such as Ascanio Condivi, Marcello Venusti, and Daniele da Volterra, who then immortalized Michelangelo's inventions in paintings. The drawing of a nude man and boy in the Albertina is a study for Daniele da Volterra's painting *Mercury Commanding Aeneas to Leave Dido*, made for Monsignor Giovanni della Casa, papal nuncio to Venice and author of the famous *Galateo* (published 1558). Della Casa probably commissioned the work from Daniele sometime between his return to Rome on June 22, 1555, after a four-year stay in Venice, and his death on November 14, 1556. The painting, now lost, was possibly the one that was once in a Swedish private collection and is known through a photograph (fig. 19), even though that work was painted on wood, contrary to Vasari's mention of a canvas support. Daniele executed no fewer than five paintings for Giovanni della Casa, and preparatory drawings by Michelangelo are known for three of them. Wherever possible, Michelangelo supported his colleague and devoted friend and secured important commissions for him. Several of Michelangelo's studies for *Mercury Commanding Aeneas to Leave Dido* have survived; these were elaborated on and possibly further developed by Daniele. The image on the Vienna sheet, which shows a boy helping Aeneas to undress, corresponds almost exactly to the same two figures as executed in the painting. Through the disrobing and Aeneas's turn toward Mercury, who flies in from above to urge the Trojan hero to depart, Michelangelo wonderfully expresses the inner conflict between the hero's love for Dido and his painful decision to leave her. The heavy, block-like forms of the bodies are characteristic of Michelangelo's late style. In his late works, the energy of the figures is increasingly bundled within, and the modeling creates a unified appearance, placing less emphasis than before on details such as the bulges of individual muscles. In the present drawing, the manner of execution in countless short, closely spaced strokes of chalk, hardly discernible individually, is consistent with the style of late, highly finished drawings by Michelangelo, such as the small cartoons (*cartonetti*) for paintings by Marcello Venusti. It is thus conceivable that Daniele did not elaborate a mere sketch by Michelangelo but rather relied on a comparably detailed drawing. Compared to typical figures by Michelangelo, Daniele's figures lack something of the internal energy and fluid movements; they appear to be as if assembled more from pieces. The musculature does not convey an inner tension; instead, it forms rhythmic, almost decorative surface patterns. Also, the hair and beard are depicted with strong curved strokes which produce a chiseled look. Nevertheless, in sheets such as this one, Daniele demonstrated a nearly unsurpassed ability to assimilate and build upon Michelangelo's late drawing style.

AG

Daniele da Volterra
Aeneas with a Boy, ca. 1555/56
The ALBERTINA Museum, Vienna

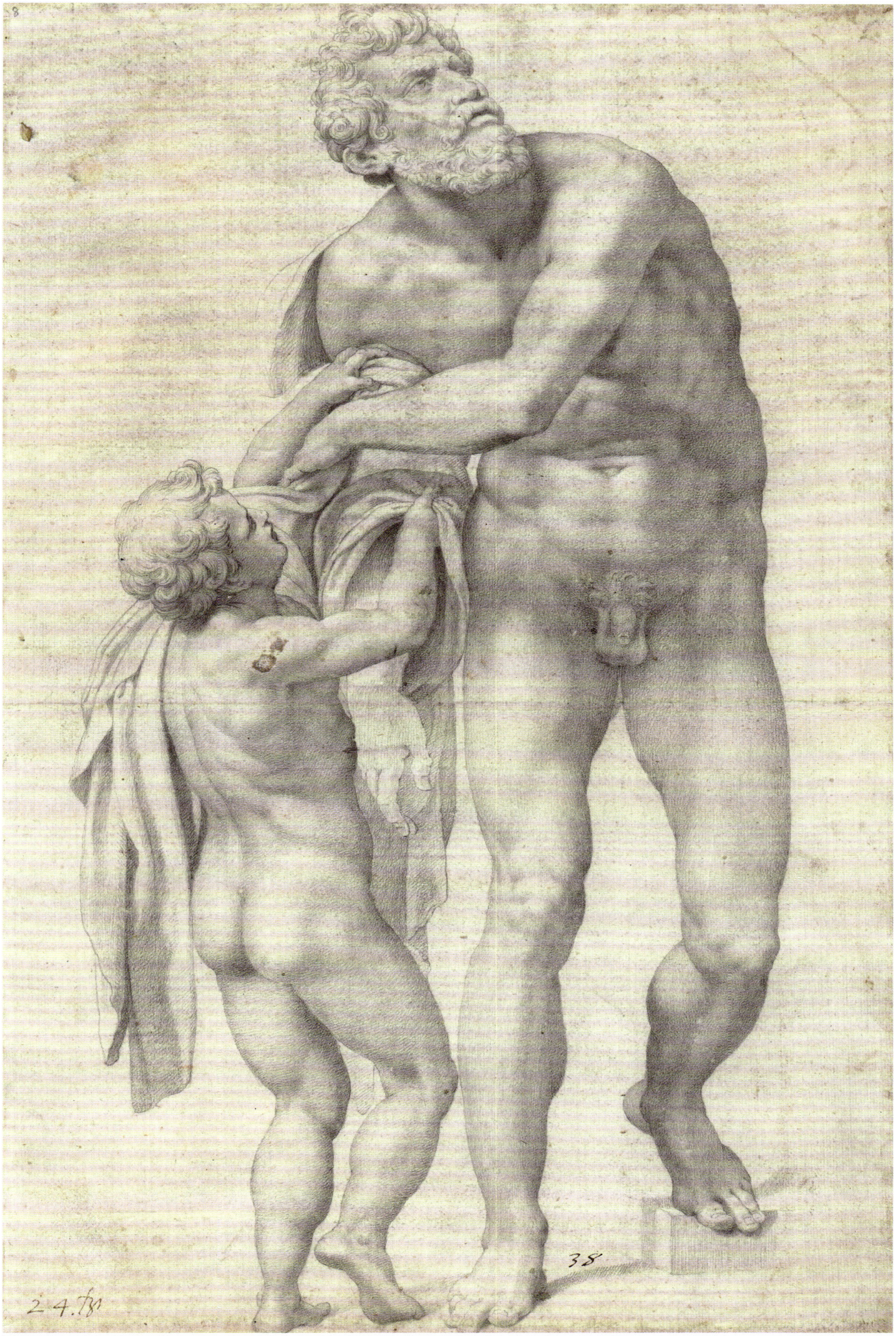

Bolognese Artist (after Bartolomeo Passarotti)
Seated Male Nude in Profile to the Right, ca. 1600
The ALBERTINA Museum, Vienna

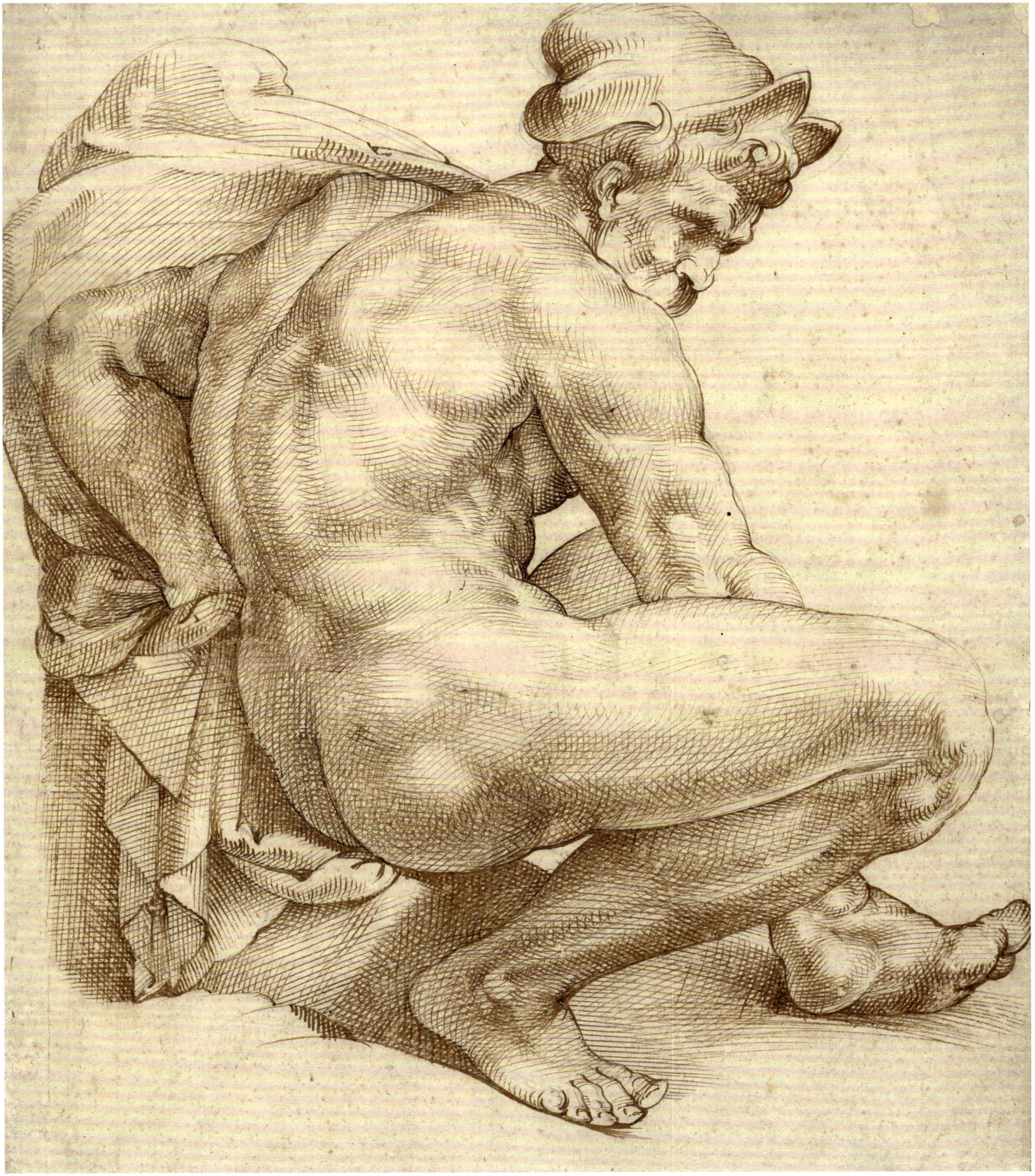

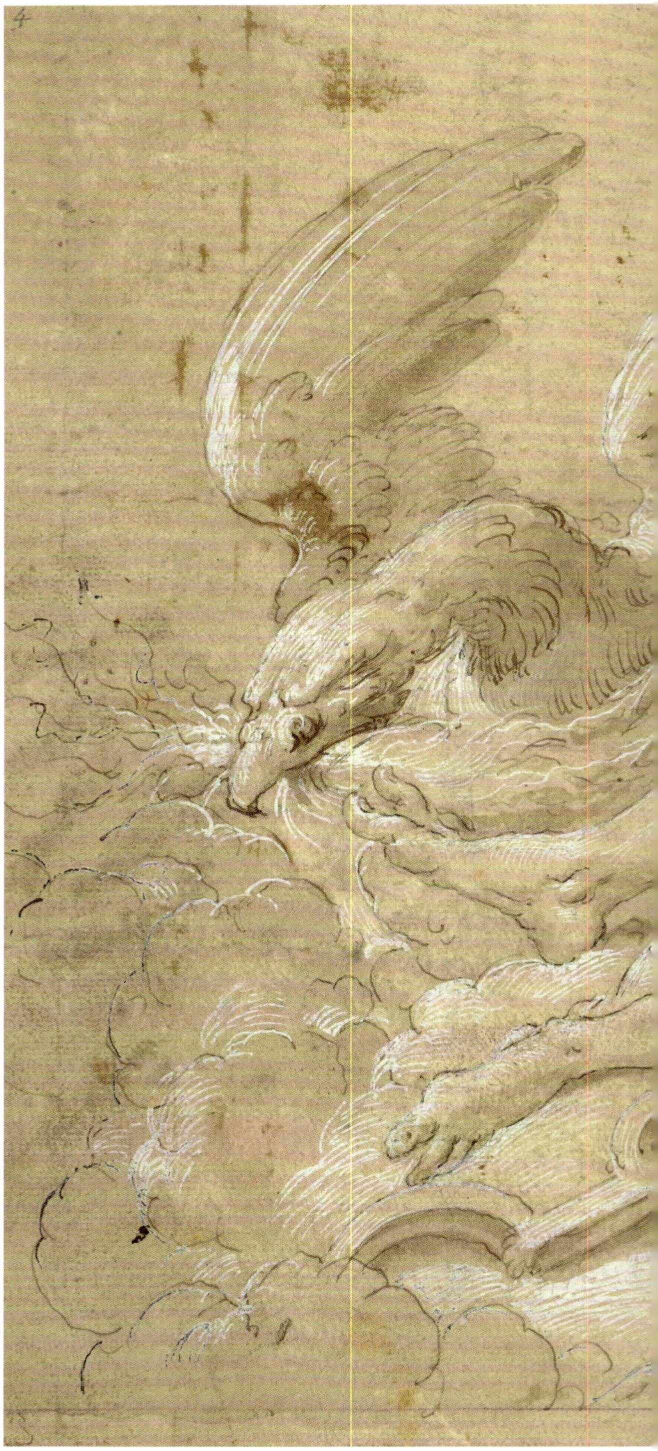

Niccolò dell'Abate
Jupiter and Cupid, ca. 1560–1570
The ALBERTINA Museum, Vienna

Niccolò dell'Abate, a representative of the Bolognese school, was active mostly in the regions of Emilia and Romagna. In 1552, King Henry II of France called the artist to the royal court at Fontainebleau to assist in the workshop of Francesco Primaticcio. Abate became Primaticcio's foremost collaborator and one of the most important artists of the school of Fontainebleau, playing a decisive role in shaping the Mannerist style cultivated there. His pen-and-ink drawing *Jupiter and Cupid*, for example, which dates from between 1560 and 1570, shows characteristics typical of Mannerism: a highly ornate vocabulary of form, anatomical elongation, and complex movements. The sheet is distinguished by its fine ductus of line and its precise and detailed accents of white heightening. As was commonly

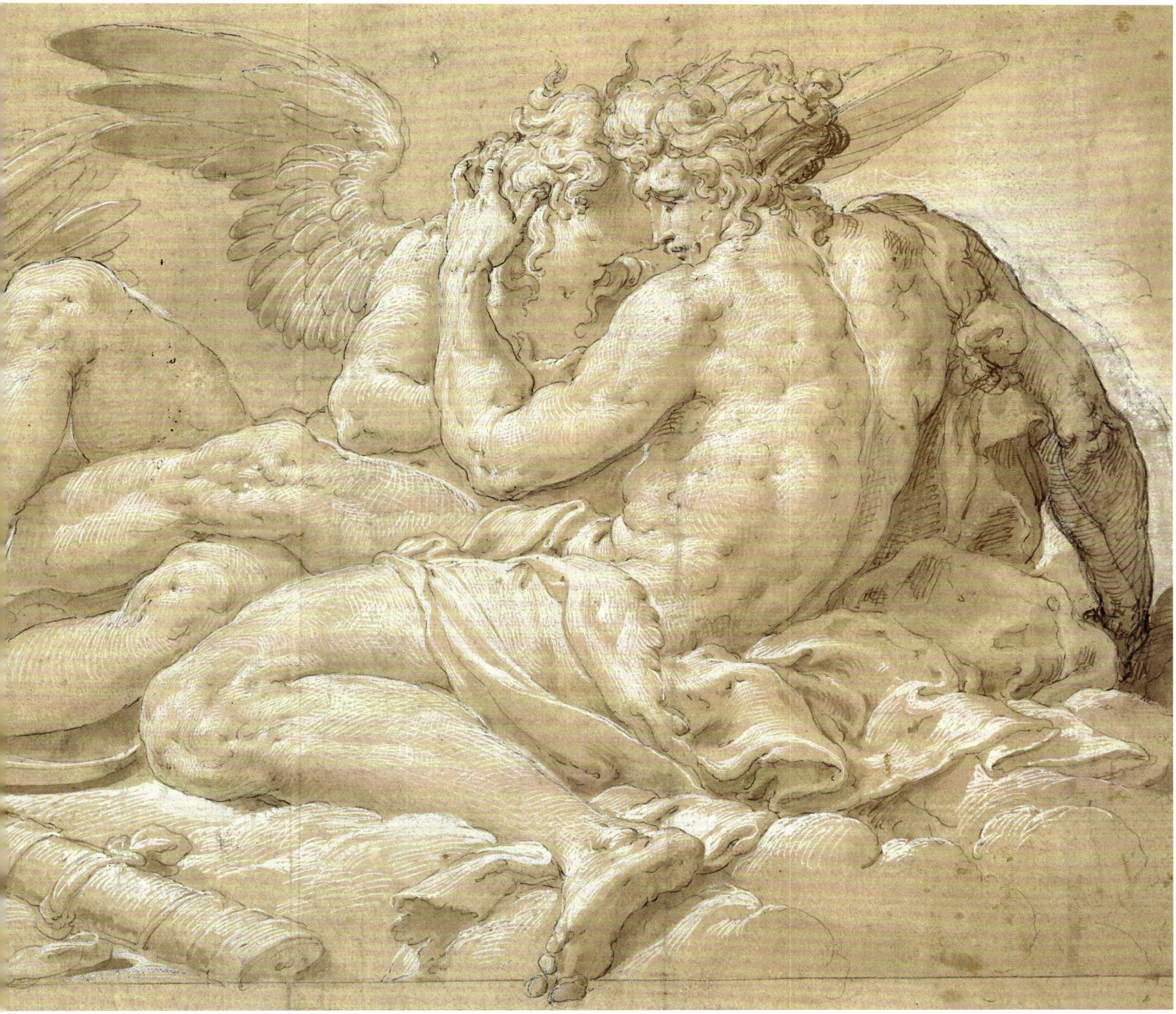

done, the artist used a mythological subject to erotic effect. The eagle at the left identifies the male figure seen from behind as Jupiter. The attributes in the foreground, a bow and quiver, indicate that the youth in a tender embrace with the divine patriarch is Cupid, the god of love. His adolescent body contrasts with Jupiter's broad frame and powerful physique, which is accentuated by its pronounced, even exaggerated, musculature. This figure of Jupiter is reminiscent of Michelangelo's ideal of the male nude, though Abate was less concerned with anatomical accuracy.

LE

Un sacco di noce, or Nature Distorted

Mannerist representations of the human form are characterized by unnaturally elongated and distorted proportions as well as complex twists of the body—often drastic, sometimes grotesque. Artists who practiced the style were concerned less with fidelity to nature than with heightened expressivity. The latter was not least achieved through a deliberately unusual vocabulary of form and a renunciation of harmony in favor of compositional tension.

Mannerism emerged in the early sixteenth century; outside Italy, it persisted beyond 1600. Alongside other progenitors of this style, Michelangelo is an important point of reference. His late oeuvre, including such works as the *Last Judgment* fresco on the western wall of the Sistine Chapel, is particularly relevant since it displays incipient tendencies of the new *maniera*. The complicated, dynamic, and sometimes overwrought twisting motions of figures in the late works of Michelangelo also appear in the art of the Mannerists.

One such Mannerist artist who studied the works of Michelangelo was the Venetian Jacopo Tintoretto. He occupied himself intensively with Michelangelo's oeuvre, making drawings after such works as the tomb sculptures of the New Sacristy of San Lorenzo in Florence, which, however, he only knew through bronze copies rather than firsthand. Like Michelangelo, he was interested in portraying the human body in poses that were both complex and to some extent unnatural. Tintoretto's drawings of nudes are distinguished by his use of wavy lines to render single groups of muscles, creating the impression of an uneven surface. This manner of depiction is often referred to with the Italian expression *sacco di noce* (bag of nuts). Tintoretto's exploration of human anatomy after live models resulted in a free interpretation of the figure, which departed from realistic representation in favor of a Mannerist ideal.

LE

Jacopo Tintoretto
Study of a Male Nude, ca. 1590
The ALBERTINA Museum, Vienna

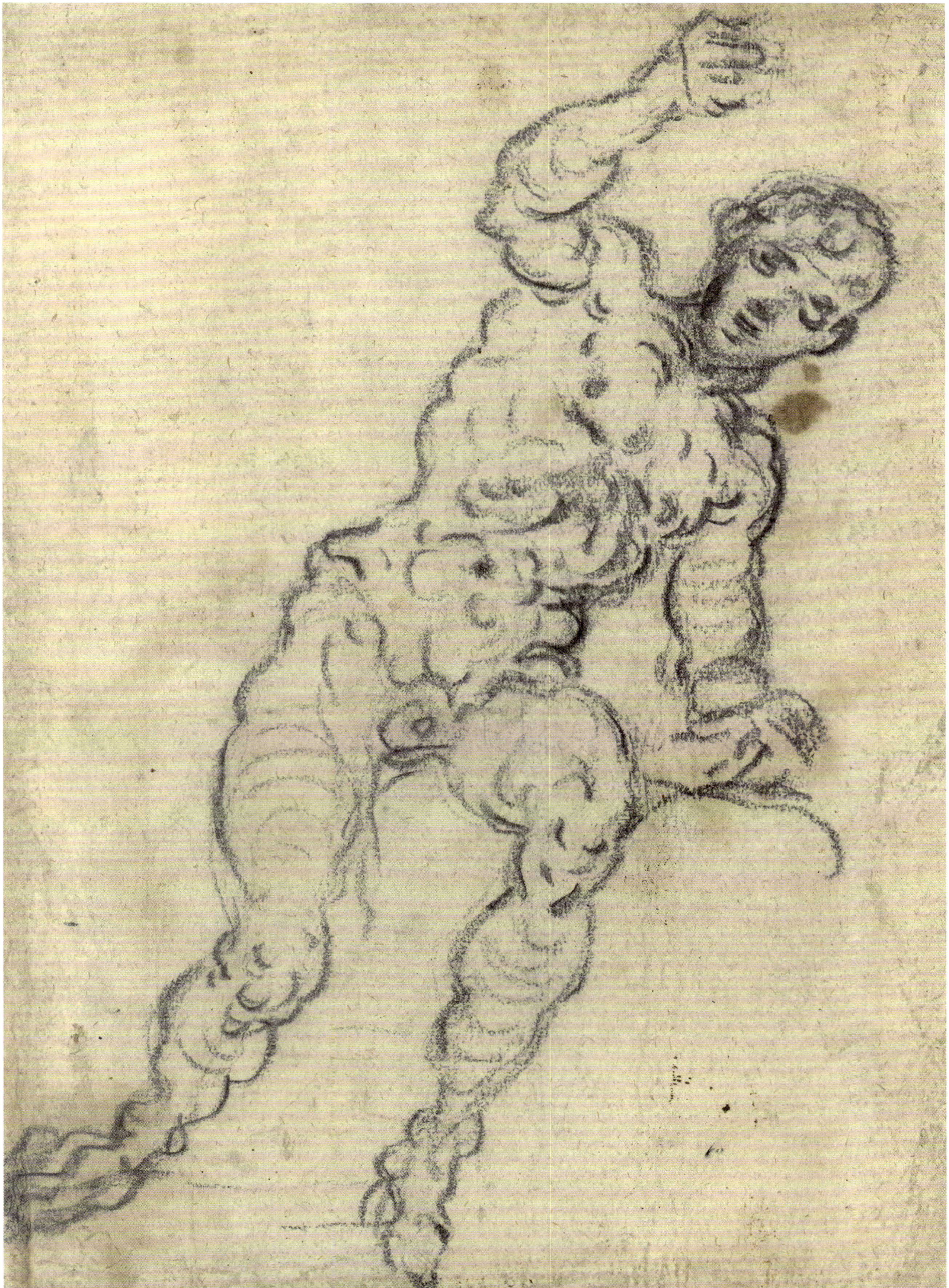
G. Tintoretto

According to legend, Saint Sebastian served as a captain at the court of the Roman emperor Diocletian. When the sovereign learned, however, of Sebastian's Christian devotion, he ordered the soldier bound to a tree and shot with arrows. This muscular nude, bent gracefully to one side and encircled by a swirling length of drapery, almost hides the fact that the scene represents a martyrdom. Only on closer inspection does it even become apparent that the body is pierced by arrows. In place of the severe realism of earlier depictions, from the Renaissance onward, the faithful were presented with the beautiful body of the saint, unharmed by torture or death. Executed in chiaroscuro technique on a colored ground, the drawing acquires much of its visual impact through the contrast between the elegance of the martyr's sinking motion and the physical strength of his body. The contrived pose, the elongated proportions of the limbs, and the torso's exaggerated musculature are typical of Mannerism—certainly this artist's stylistic idiom, despite the fact that his identification remains an open question. Attempts at attribution have ranged from Pieter Jansz. Pourbus to the circle of Frans Floris to Michiel Coxie (according to Otto Benesch); although Coxie's classical style, strongly influenced by Raphael's works, clearly differs from that of this *Saint Sebastian*, even though the figure's athletic physique betrays knowledge of Italian treatments of the motif.

The Italian ideal of the human figure was adopted by additional Netherlandish Mannerists. Cornelis Cornelisz. van Haarlem, one of the most important Haarlem Mannerists, has been dubbed the "Dutch Michelangelo." Proceeding from the achievements of the Italians, he and others, such as Abraham Bloemaert in Utrecht, created muscular nudes in complex, twisted poses, while also using dramatic perspectival views and foreshortening. Cornelis depicts the mythological giant Tityus—eternally beset by liver-devouring vultures in punishment for the attempted rape of the goddess Leto—splayed across a rock in an elaborate and spectacular backward fall. In such works, even gruesome subjects were made aesthetically palatable.

EM

Netherlandish Artist
Saint Sebastian, last third of the 16th century
The ALBERTINA Museum, Vienna

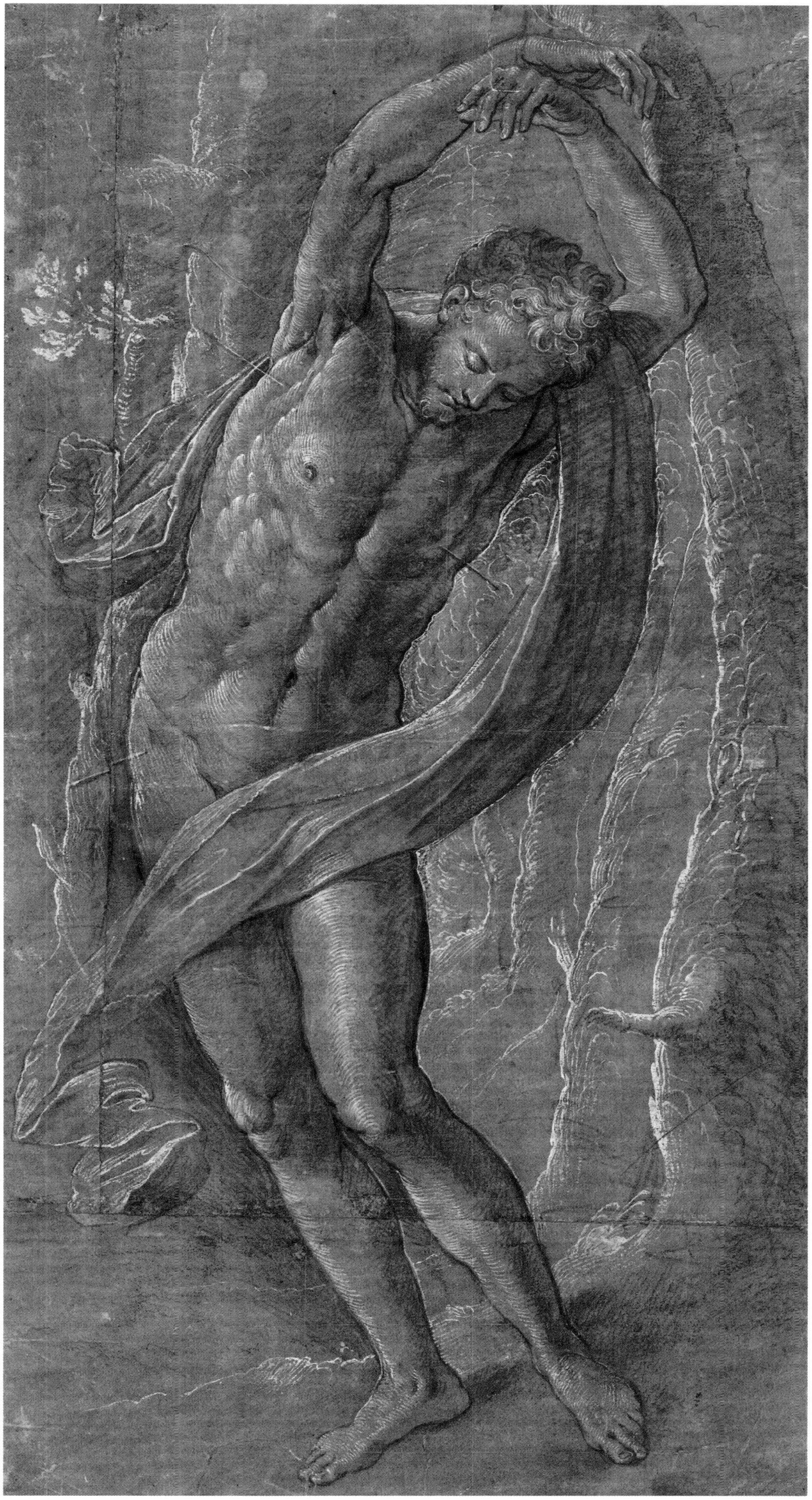

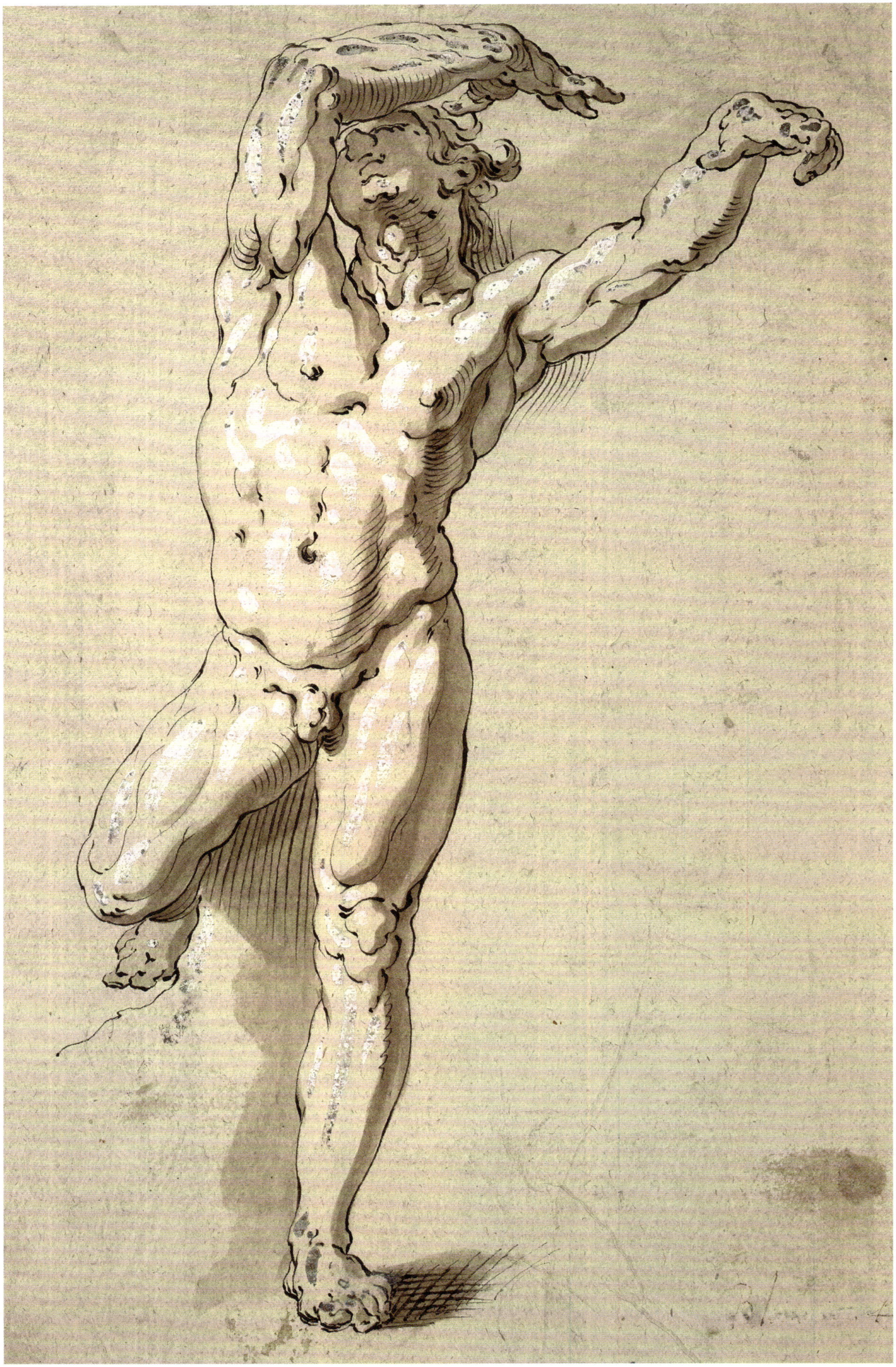

Abraham Bloemaert
Study of a Nude, 1592/93
The ALBERTINA Museum, Vienna

Cornelis Cornelisz. van Haarlem
Tityus, 1588
The ALBERTINA Museum, Vienna

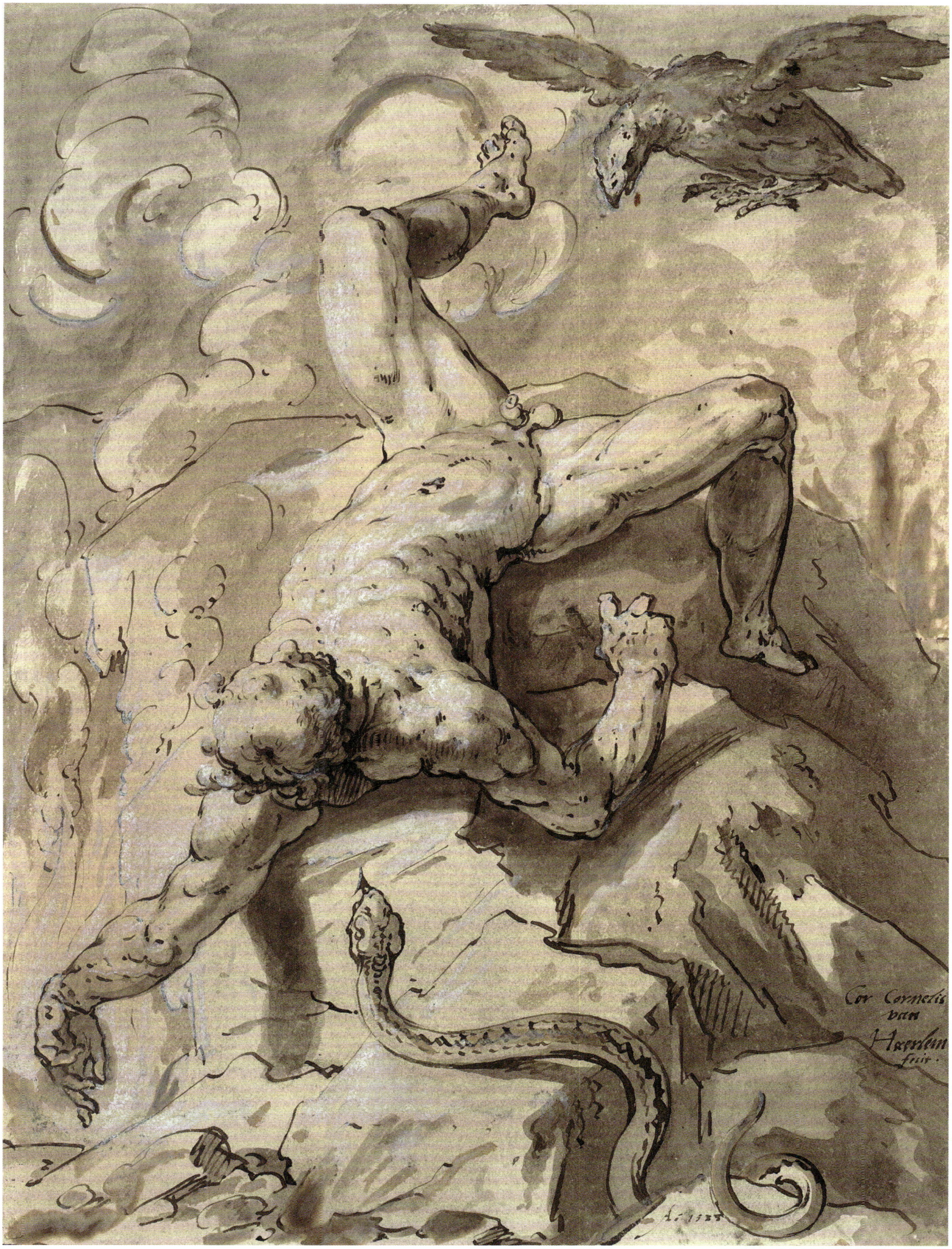
Cor Cornelis
van
Haerlem
fecit.

Adriaen de Vries's bronze *Christ at the Column,* created between 1613 and 1615, is an outstanding example of Mannerist sculpture. The Son of God is posed in a dynamic S-curve, in contrast to the severe straightness of the column displaced behind him from the center of the base. This compositional counterweight provides stability and seeks to balance the lively movement. Furthermore, the work exhibits a tension between delicacy and massiveness: the highly detailed execution of certain parts, such as the hair, creates fine textural effects, while the hefty corporeality imparts presence and weight to the figure. The powerfully muscular, idealized, and apparently unblemished body is at odds with the subject matter of the martyred Messiah. In that regard, De Vries's Christ recalls the Michelangesque nude, characterized by an idealized portrayal of the beautiful but suffering body. The tensions within the De Vries bronze hark back to Michelangelo's representations of the dying or deceased Messiah in his drawings of the Crucifixion and the Pietà.

LE

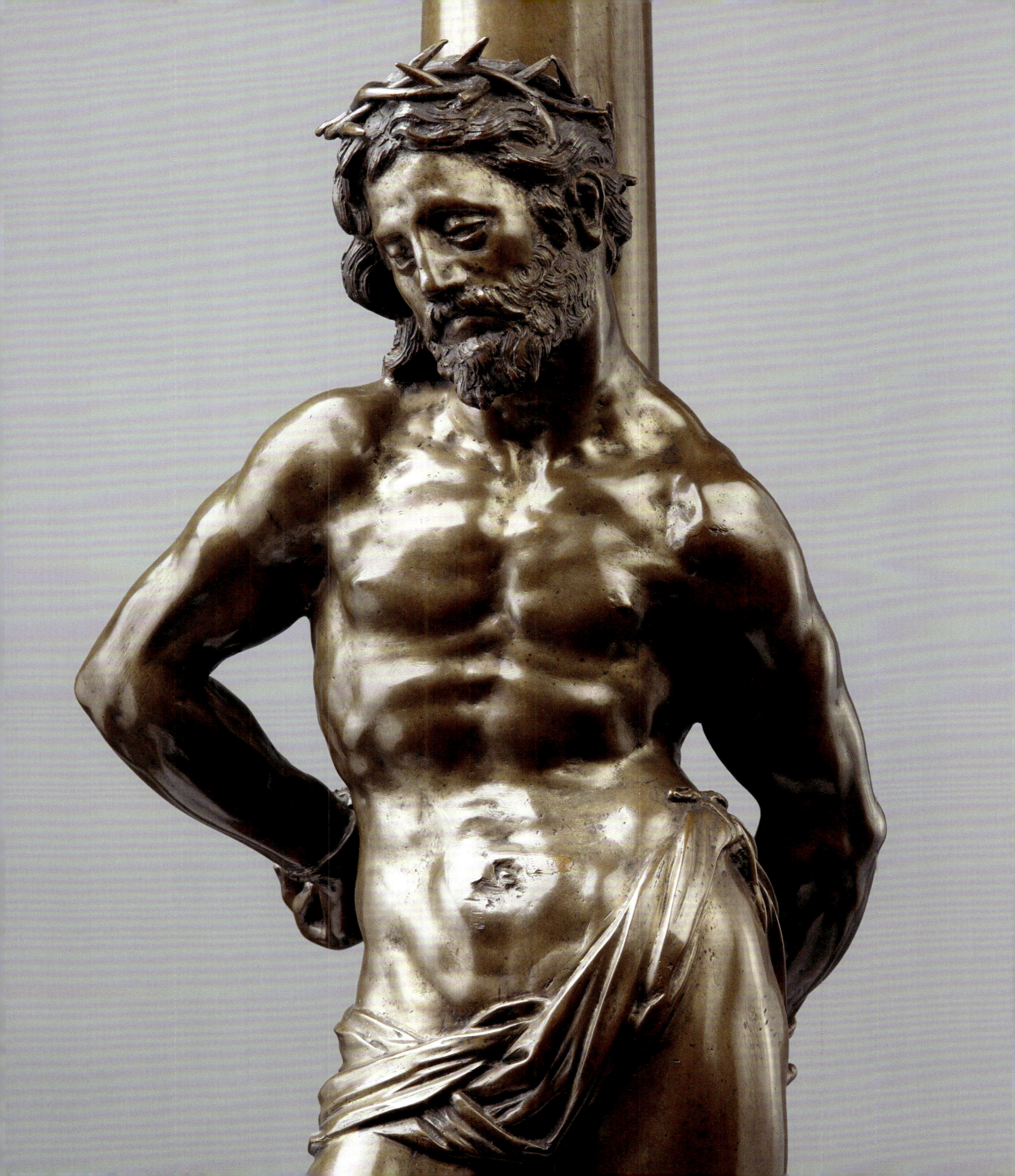

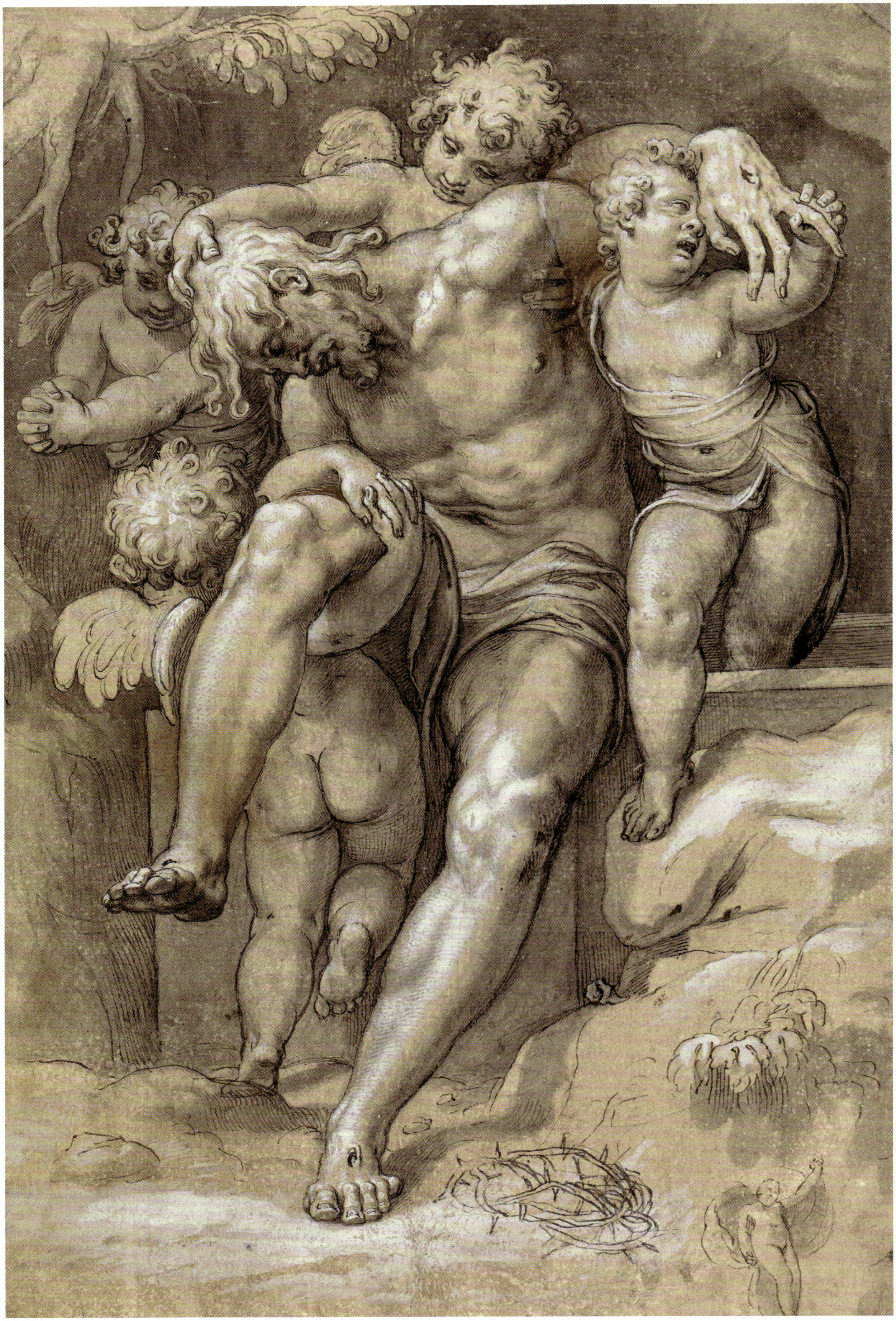

Paolo Farinati
Four Angels Lamenting the Dead Christ, second half of the 16th century
The ALBERTINA Museum, Vienna

Adriaen de Vries
Christ at the Column, ca. 1613–1615
Kunsthistorisches Museum, Vienna, Kunstkammer

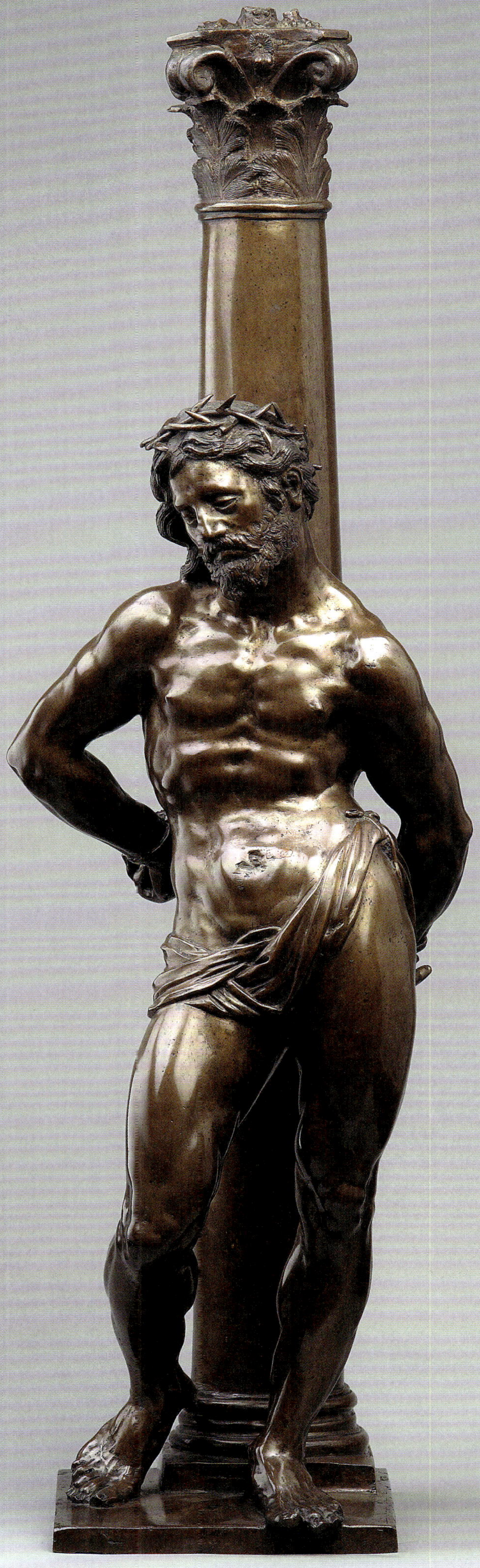

La serpentinata: Beautiful from All Sides

Giambologna's *The Rape of the Sabine Women* is a prime example of sculpture meant to be viewed from all angles. The three figures are carved out of a single block of marble—a particularly difficult technical challenge met here with virtuosic skill. In 1583, the work was put on display in the Loggia dei Lanzi of Florence to great public acclaim. This sculpture group depicting a scene of abduction also exemplifies the so-called *figura serpentinata*, a figural composition, characteristic of the late Renaissance and Mannerism, which spirals snakelike around its own central axis. Because of the exceptional qualities of its composition and execution, Giambologna's *The Rape of the Sabine Women* was repeated in numerous copies and casts, for example, this bronze in the Princely Collections of Liechtenstein dating from about 1600 and attributed to Antonio Susini, a pupil of Giambologna.

LE

Attributed to Antonio Susini
***Rape of a Sabine Woman*, ca. 1600**
LIECHTENSTEIN. The Princely Collections, Vaduz–Vienna, Fürstliche Sammlungen Art Service GmbH

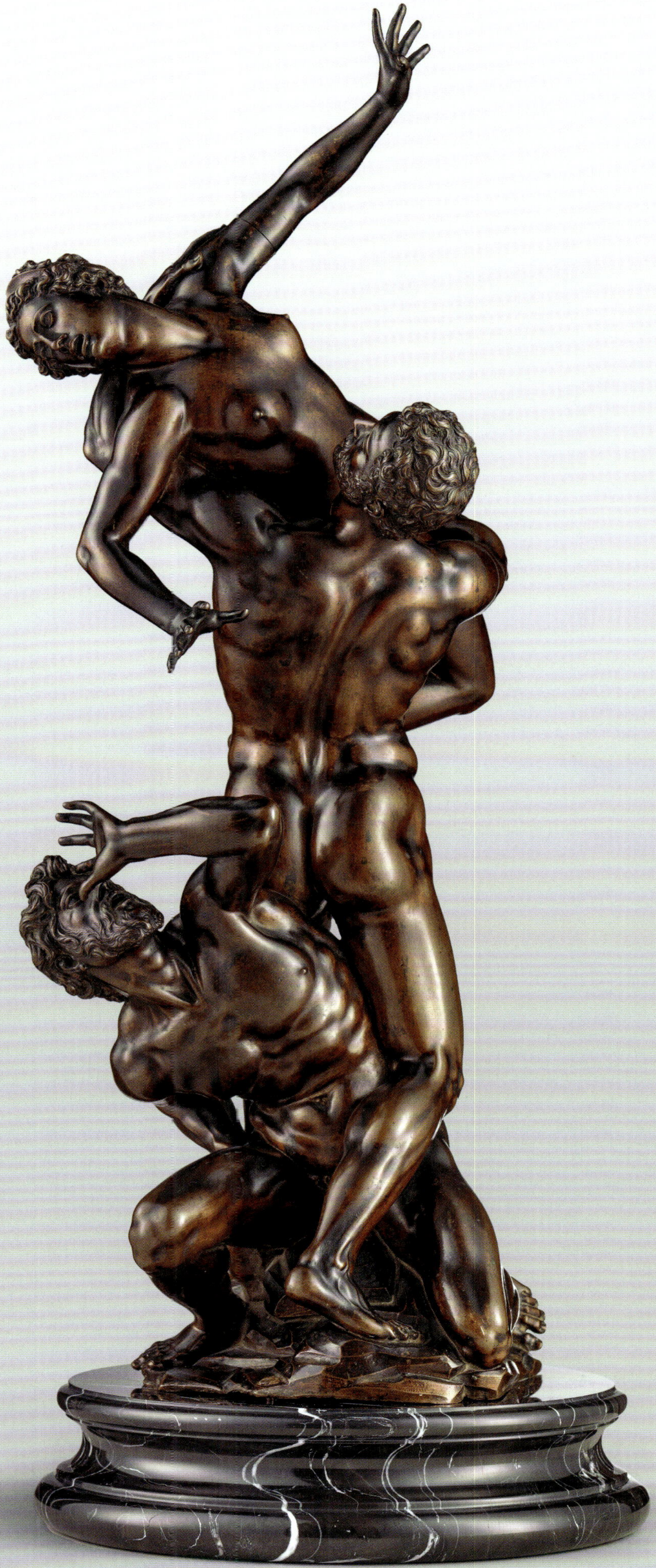

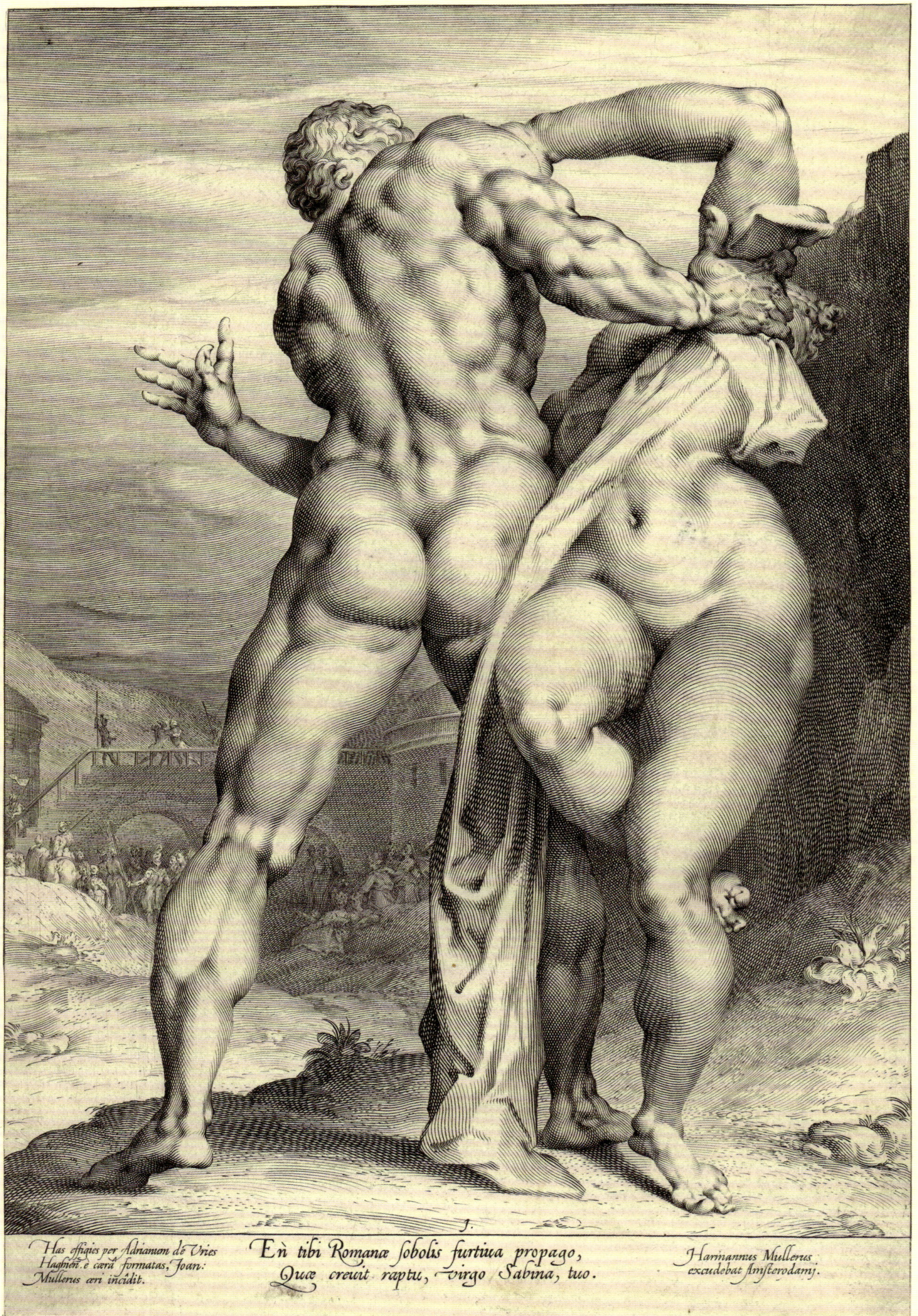

Jan Harmensz. Muller
Rape of a Sabine Woman,
ca. 1598
The ALBERTINA Museum,
Vienna

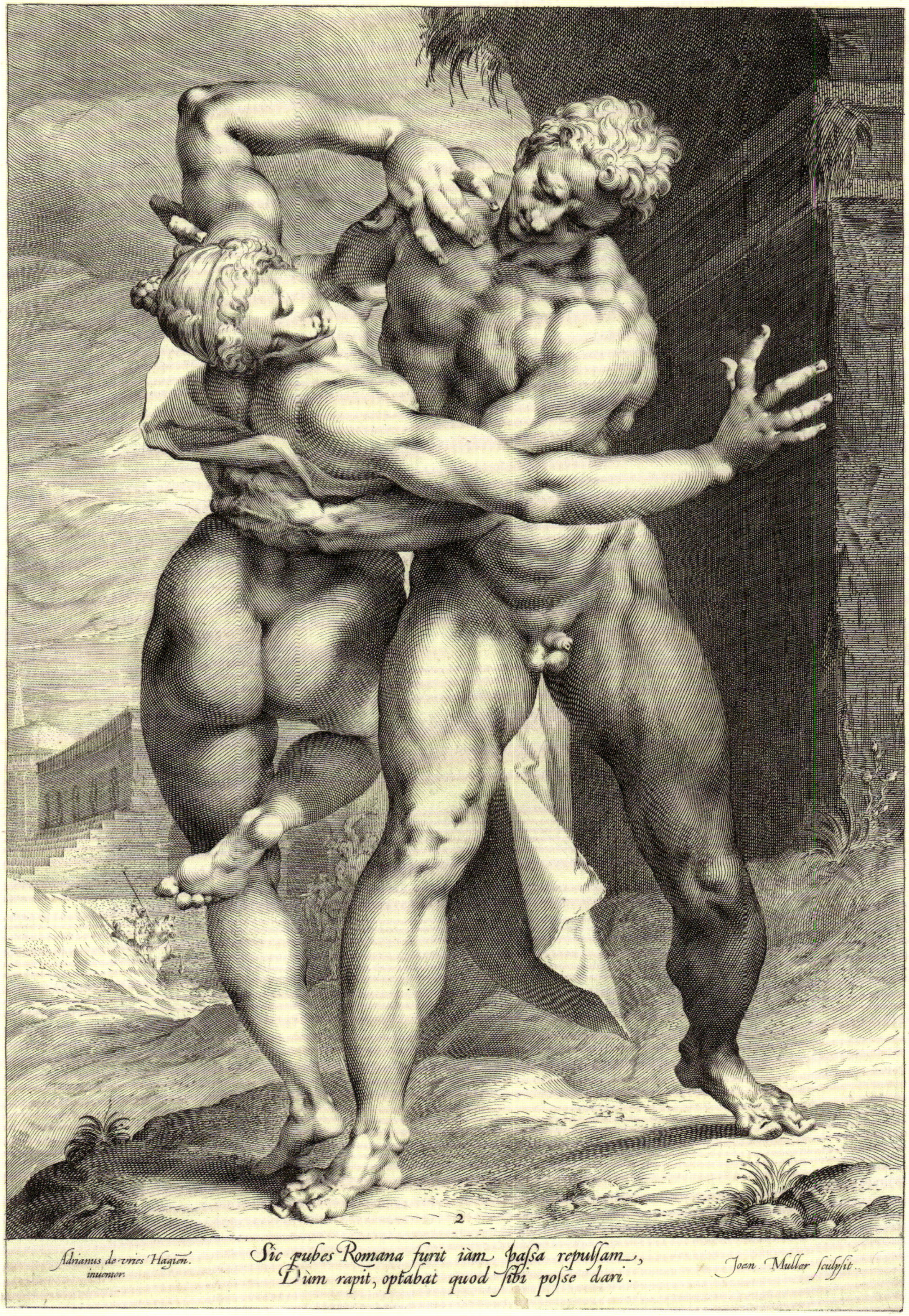

Jan Harmensz. Muller
Rape of a Sabine Woman,
ca. 1598
The ALBERTINA Museum, Vienna

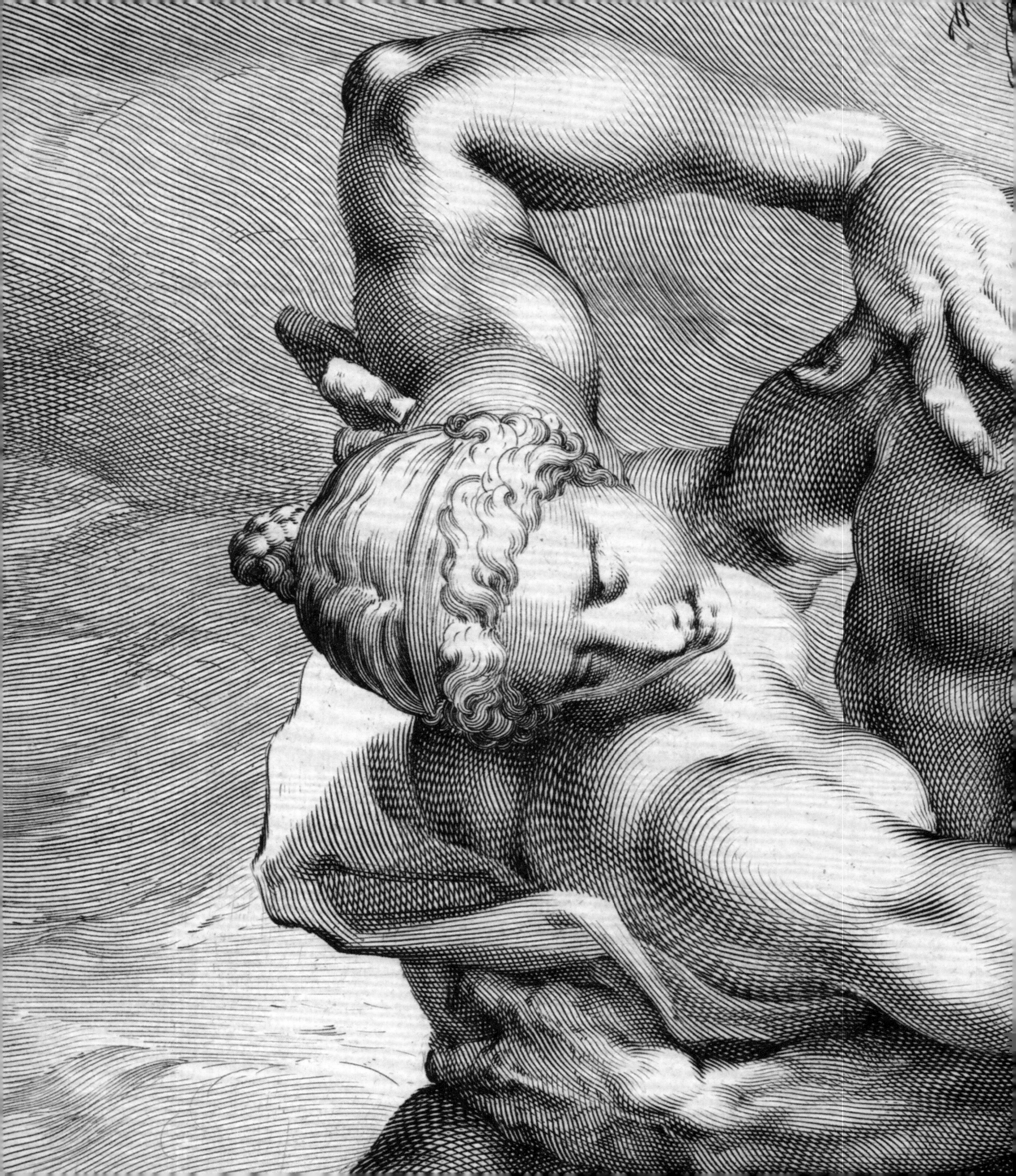

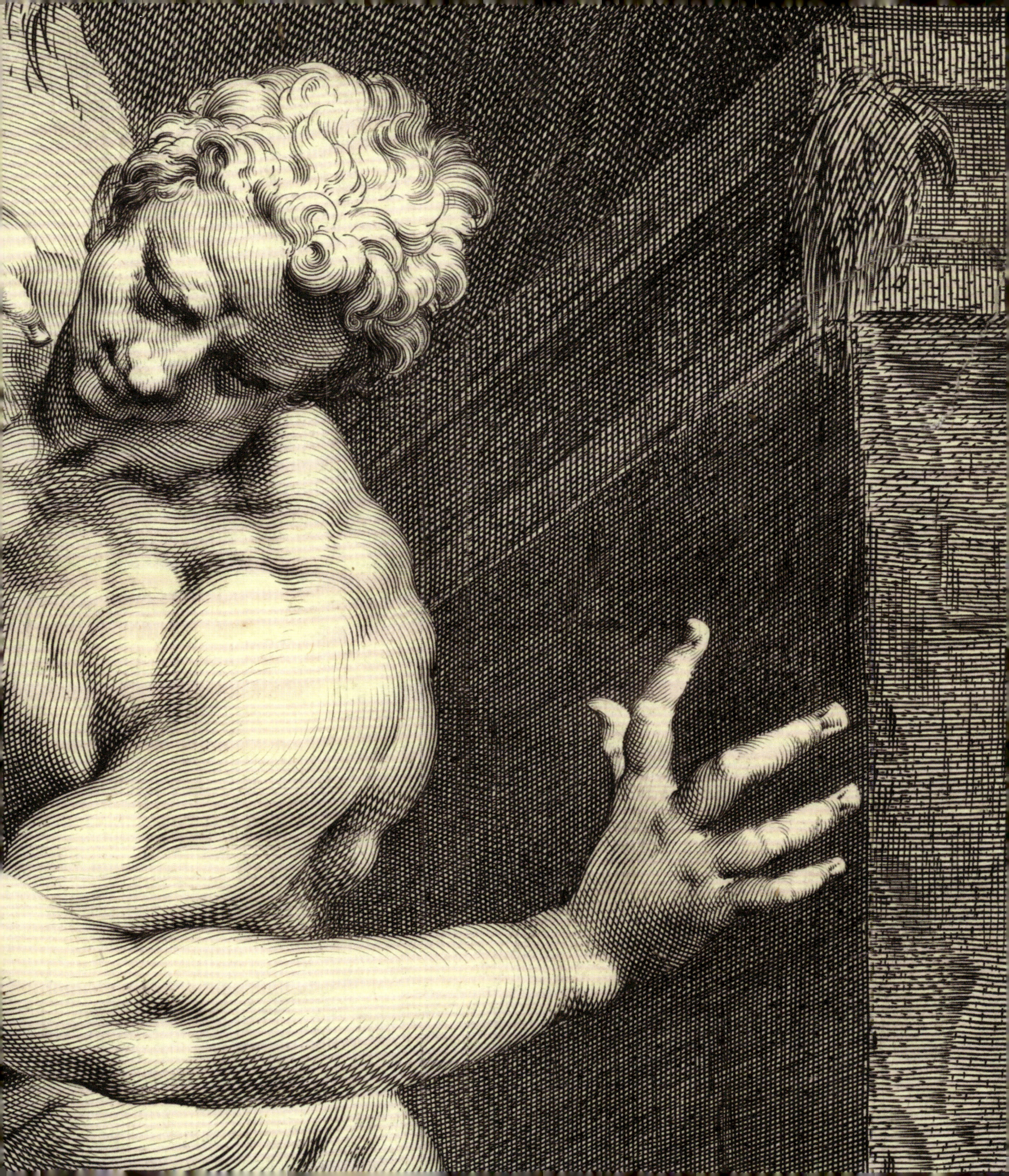

The Body, Measured and Planned

In the works of Albrecht Dürer, systematization based on the study of human proportions and the pure study of nature do not stand in contradiction. Instead, he used the two elements to construct a field of tension within which he could experiment. Throughout his career, he developed a broad spectrum of the unclothed human form—from naturalistic naked figures all the way to elaborated images of the nude.

For Dürer, the study of nature was the foundation of all art. Gradually, human figures constructed according to measure and plan supplanted those based on empirical observation. Around 1500, he became preoccupied with the development and visualization of human proportions and attempted to develop a set of principles devoted to the perfected depiction of the human figure.

The *Reclining Female Nude,* which is dated 1501, is regarded as Dürer's first constructed figure and represents his earliest attempt at the metrication of human form. Visible beneath the delicately executed chiaroscuro drawing on green prepared paper are traces of silverpoint lines guided by compass and ruler. Running through the navel is a line that intersects two other construction lines to form a point situated above the navel. Here, in his choice of motif, Dürer had recourse to depictions of recumbent figures he had executed several years earlier. But in one essential respect, these are distinguishable from this sheet: in the latter from 1501, he avoids any type of rotation, overlapping, or foreshortening in order to arrive at clearly measurable body parts and distances.

The engraving of *Adam and Eve,* produced just three years after the *Reclining Female Nude,* is the key document for Dürer's extraordinary achievement in adopting the depiction of the nude human figure—both masculine and feminine—as a primary purpose of art, ennobling it in the process. The engraving was preceded by construction drawings which depict the first parents separately. The two preliminary drawings of Adam and Eve were executed on both sides of the paper: clearly recognizable on one side is the construction of the figures according to the dimensions derived from preceding proportional studies; on the versos, Dürer has elaborated the figures within the external and internal contour lines from the rectos. He has darkened the backgrounds in order to emphasize the sculptural qualities of the individual figures of the first parents more effectively through the hard contrast. The archetype for the figure of Adam is the Apollo Belvedere, which had been disseminated through prints

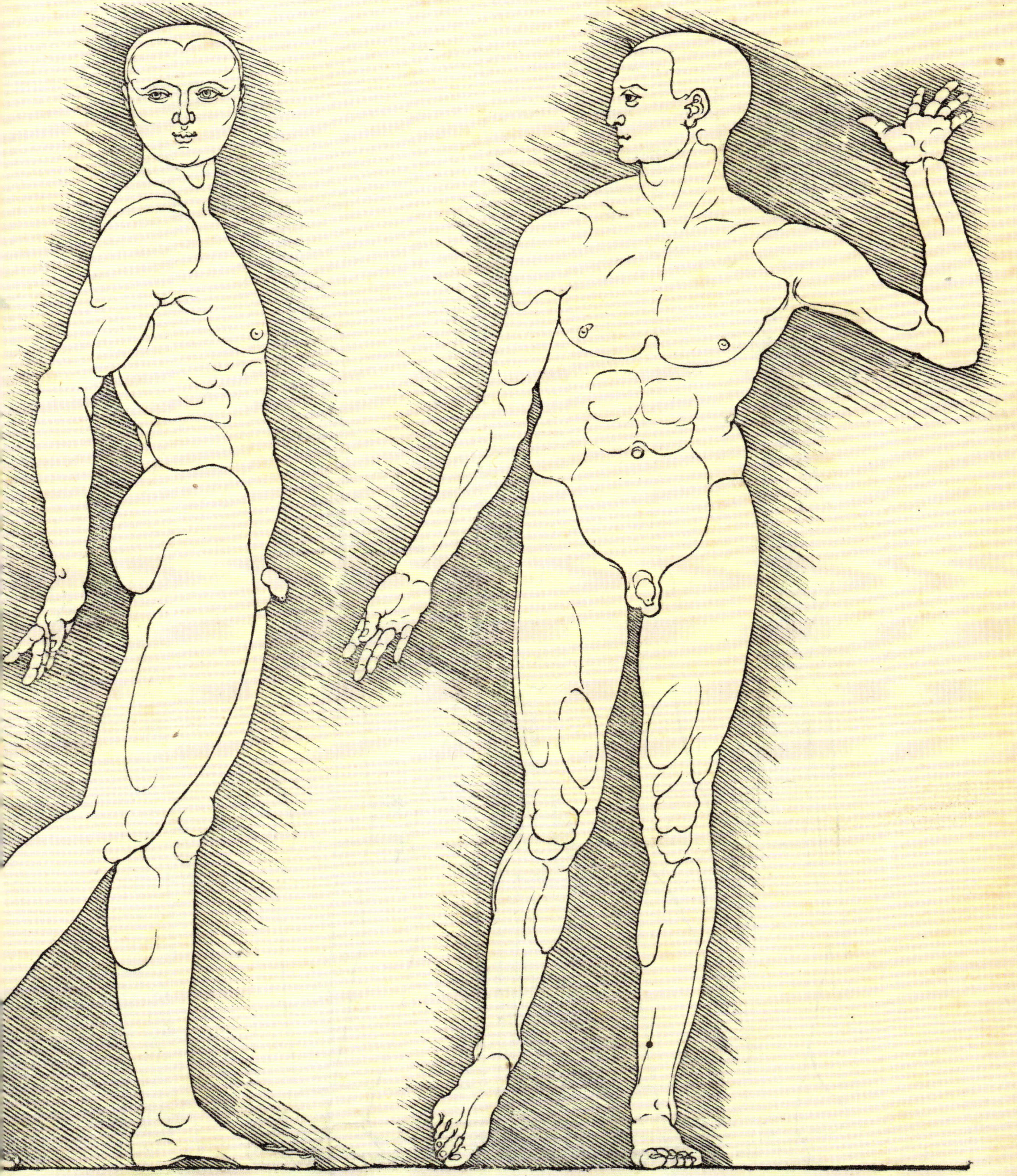

Albrecht Dürer
Reclining Female Nude, 1501
The ALBERTINA Museum, Vienna

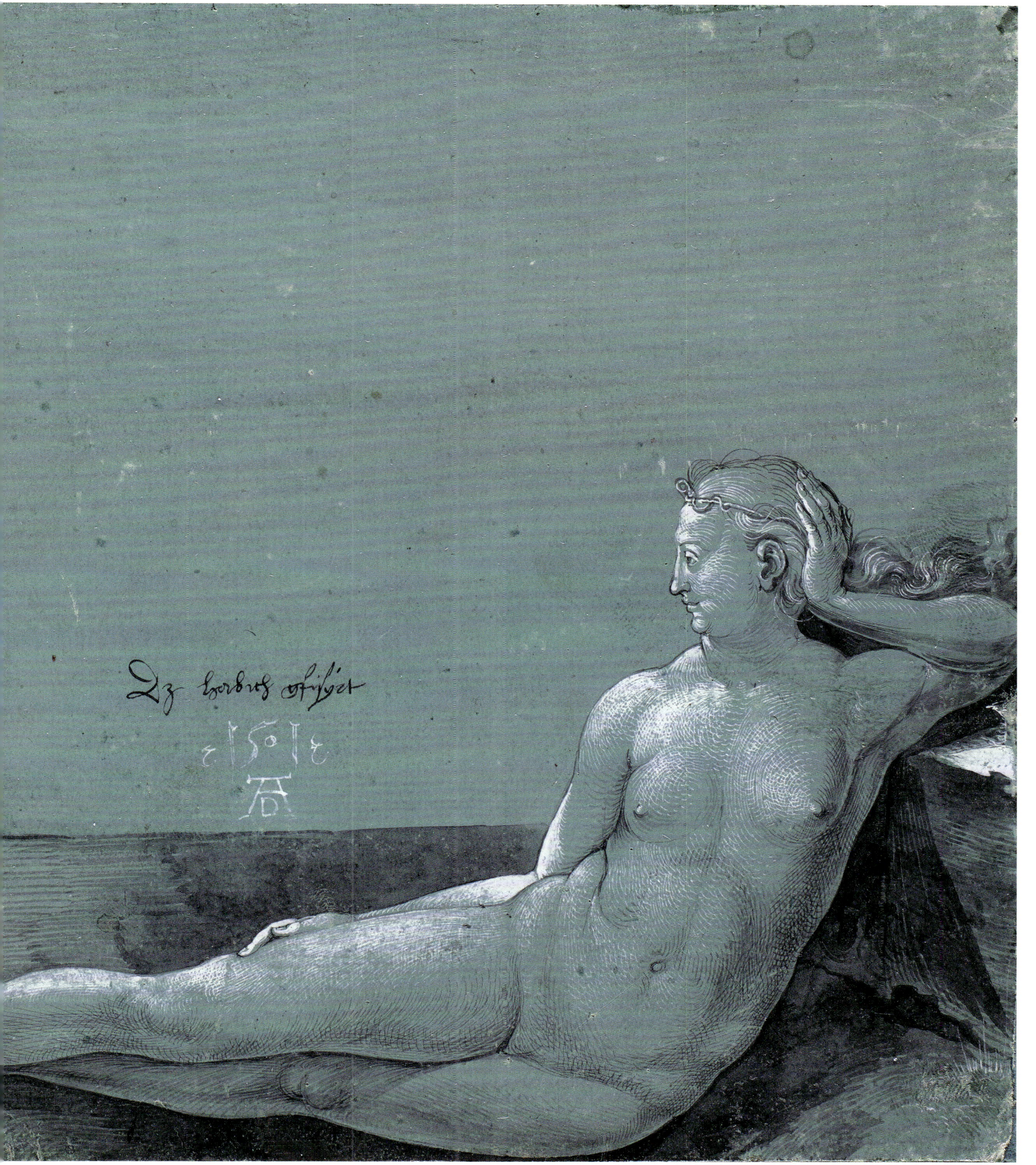

by Italian engravers beginning in the final decade of the fifteenth century. The antique figural ideal for Eve was derived from depictions of Venus, although no precise prototype has been identified.

In the early sixteenth century, in particular after his two journeys to Italy, Dürer sought to orient himself in relation to Italian artists; he also made use of archaeological finds in Augsburg to arrive at a rough conception of the figural ideal of antiquity. Soon, however, he developed his own solutions for the self-appointed task of representing the ideal nude figure—and that following a different path from Michelangelo, who, according to his biographer Ascanio Condivi, was critical of Dürer's studies of proportion.

Around 1513, Dürer's search for what he referred to as humans drawn "according to measurement" or "a canon of proportions" (*aus der Maß*) culminated in his preparations for the long-planned publication of his theory of proportion. Over a period of years, he assembled the materials for his *Vier Bücher von menschlicher Proportion* (Four Books on Human Proportions) but did not live to see its actual publication: the first printing appeared only shortly after his death in 1528.

Dürer's initial nude studies were also iconographically grounded in relation to Adam and Eve as the first couple; in 1513, he constructed anonymous, schematized bodies, both male and female, seen for the most part from three primary views. His meticulously analytical approach is exemplified by the *Study of Male Proportions in Profile and Front View,* dating from around 1513. Displayed on one side are the construction drawings, shown here, and on the other, a fair drawing. The broadly proportioned man is rendered from two views (in profile on the left, frontally on the right), in a way that would become the standard in the print version of his theory of proportion. In order to construct and calculate such depictions of the human figure, Dürer required empirical data, which he derived from measurements taken of numerous live models. Based on these, he arrived at mean values for those limbs and body parts he deemed important, elaborating a human figure based on ideal proportions. Drawings like this one are graphic reflections of the data he compiled and processed on such a grand scale—a singular undertaking even among the efforts of natural scientists of his age.

In his theory of human proportions, Dürer formulates the central perception of his thinking on art theory as follows: "art is embedded in nature. Whosoever can extract it, has it" ("die Kunst [steckt] in der Natur. Wer sie heraus kann reißen, der hat sie"). And it is this perception that defines his approach to the depiction of the human nude and its elevation to the vital purpose of art, for his strivings toward the human "according to measurement."

CJM

Albrecht Dürer
Study of Male Proportions in Profile and Front View, ca. 1513
The ALBERTINA Museum, Vienna

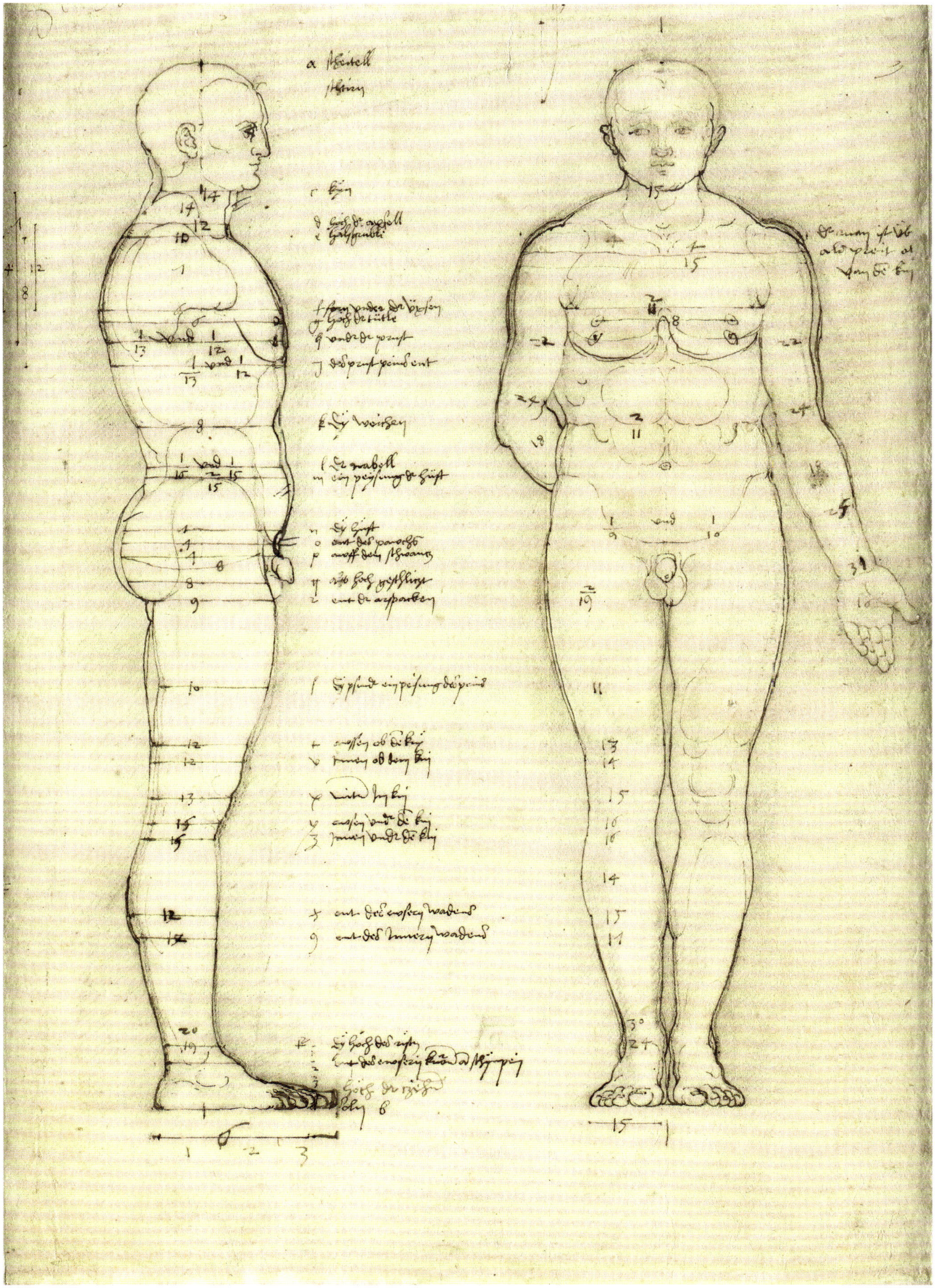

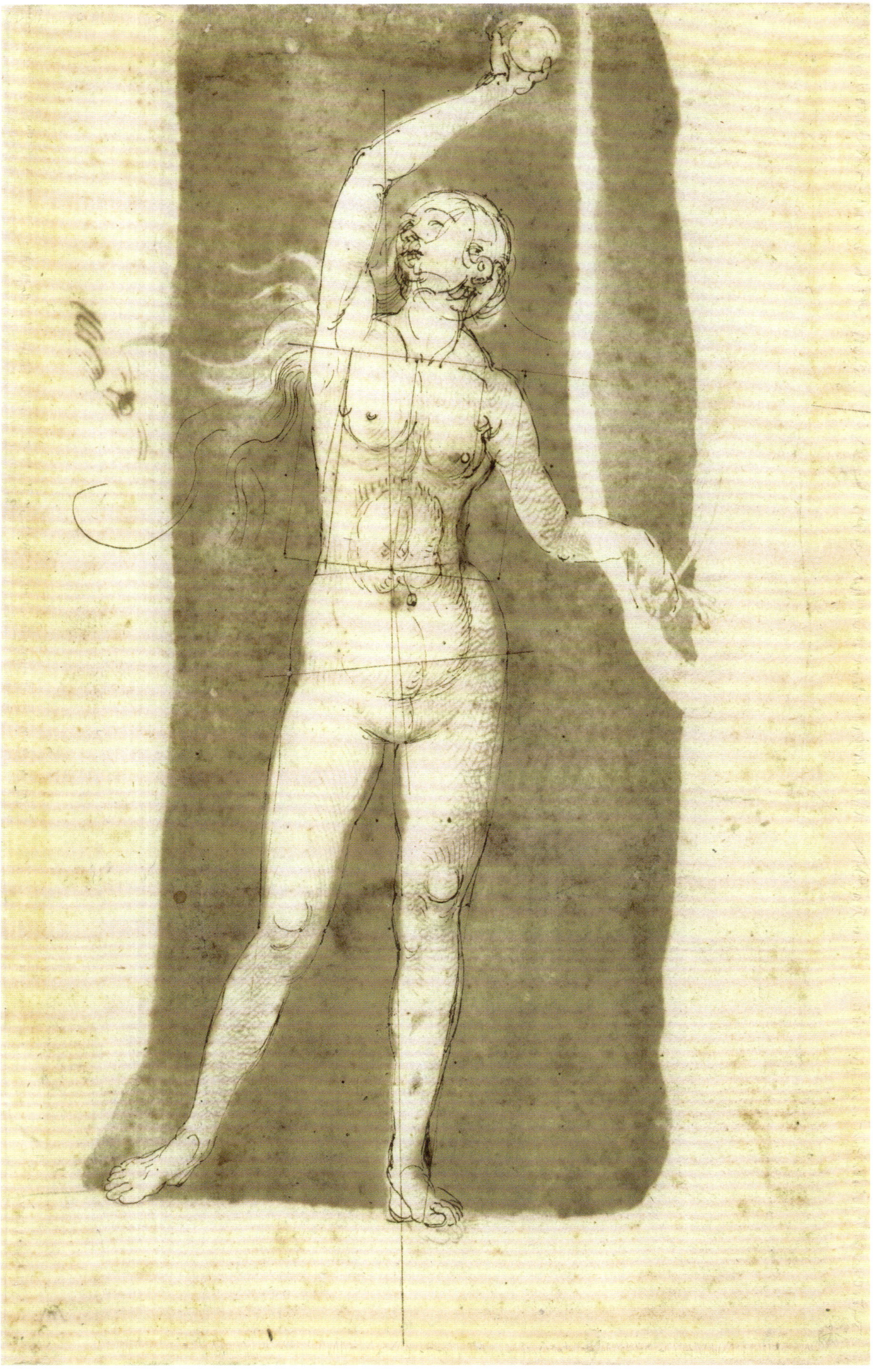

Albrecht Dürer
Eve (construction drawing),
1504
The ALBERTINA Museum, Vienna

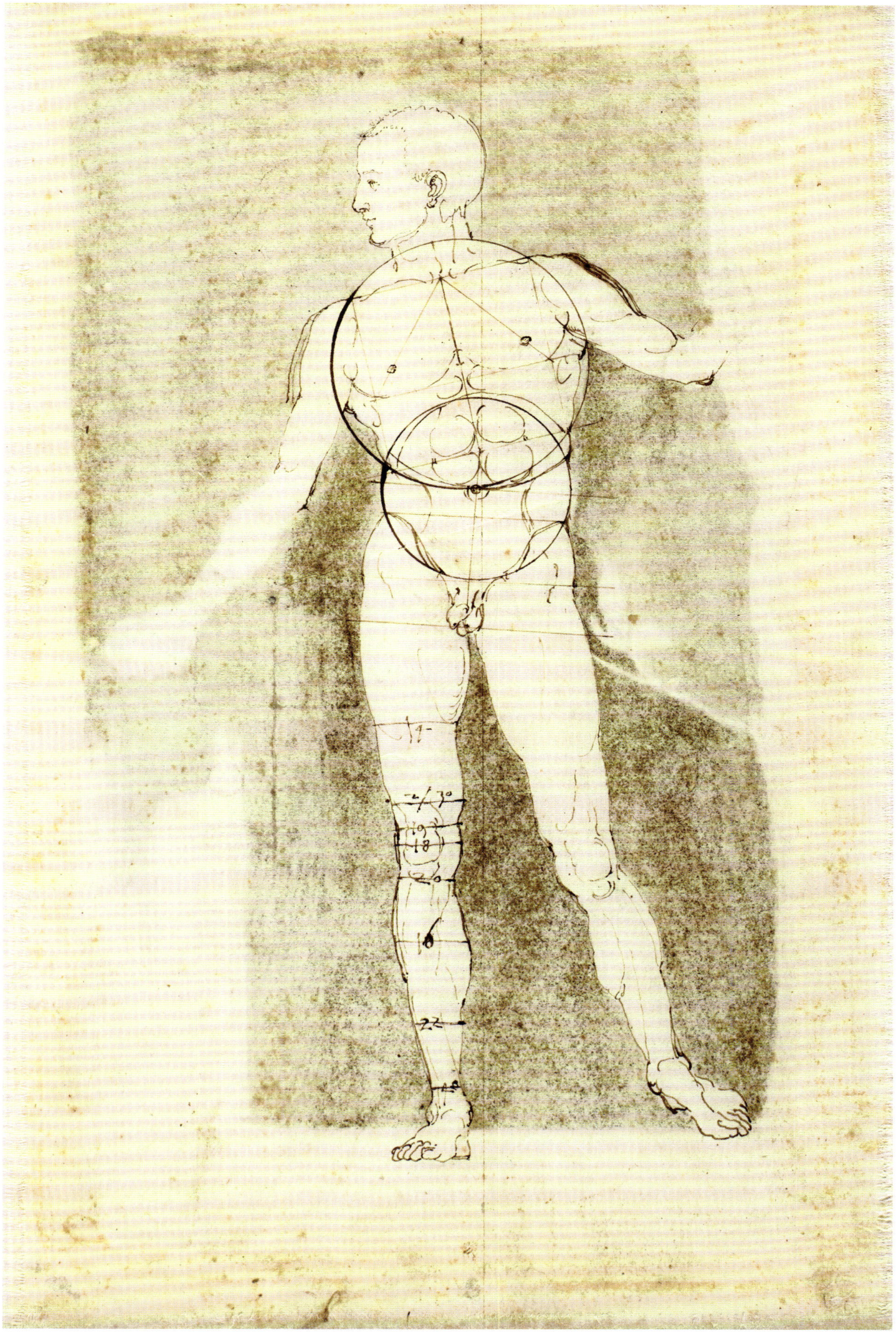

Albrecht Dürer
Adam (construction drawing), 1504
The ALBERTINA Museum, Vienna

In 1504, with his *Adam and Eve,* Albrecht Dürer created an icon of the idealized modern image of the human form—and, in a sense, the incunabula of male and female nudes. This artistic depiction of the first parents—which was preceded by a number of construction drawings depicting Adam and Eve separately, and far removed from any narrative scenario—represents the first autonomous representation of the nude north of the Alps.

For the first time, Adam and Eve are shown not chiefly in relation to a specific biblical scene, which does however become perceptible to viewers upon closer inspection, but instead strongly exemplify the artistic ambition of conceiving the ideal human figure. While the bodies of the protagonists are turned frontally to face the viewer, their heads are turned toward one another and thus seen in profile. Their nudity signals that the two still embody a state of divine innocence. Illustrated is the brief moment just before the Fall from Grace—Adam's seduction. He still grips the tree of life firmly with one hand, but his solemn gaze is already directed fixedly at Eve. She, however, avoids his eyes, observing instead the serpent pensively; the forbidden fruit still hidden from Adam in her left hand. This allows Dürer to generate a sense of tension in the moment—a state of suspense between the paradisial, ideal God-given form of existence and the Fall into sinful, ephemeral human fate.

Dürer succeeds here in condensing the Fall of Man into a singular instant, only hinting at its momentous significance through the gazes and gestures of its protagonists. In this way, he propels the salvific context so far into the background in favor of an artistic emphasis on the idealized human figure that the result must be regarded, de facto, as an autonomous depiction of the nude.

CJM

Albrecht Dürer
Adam and Eve, 1504
The ALBERTINA Museum, Vienna

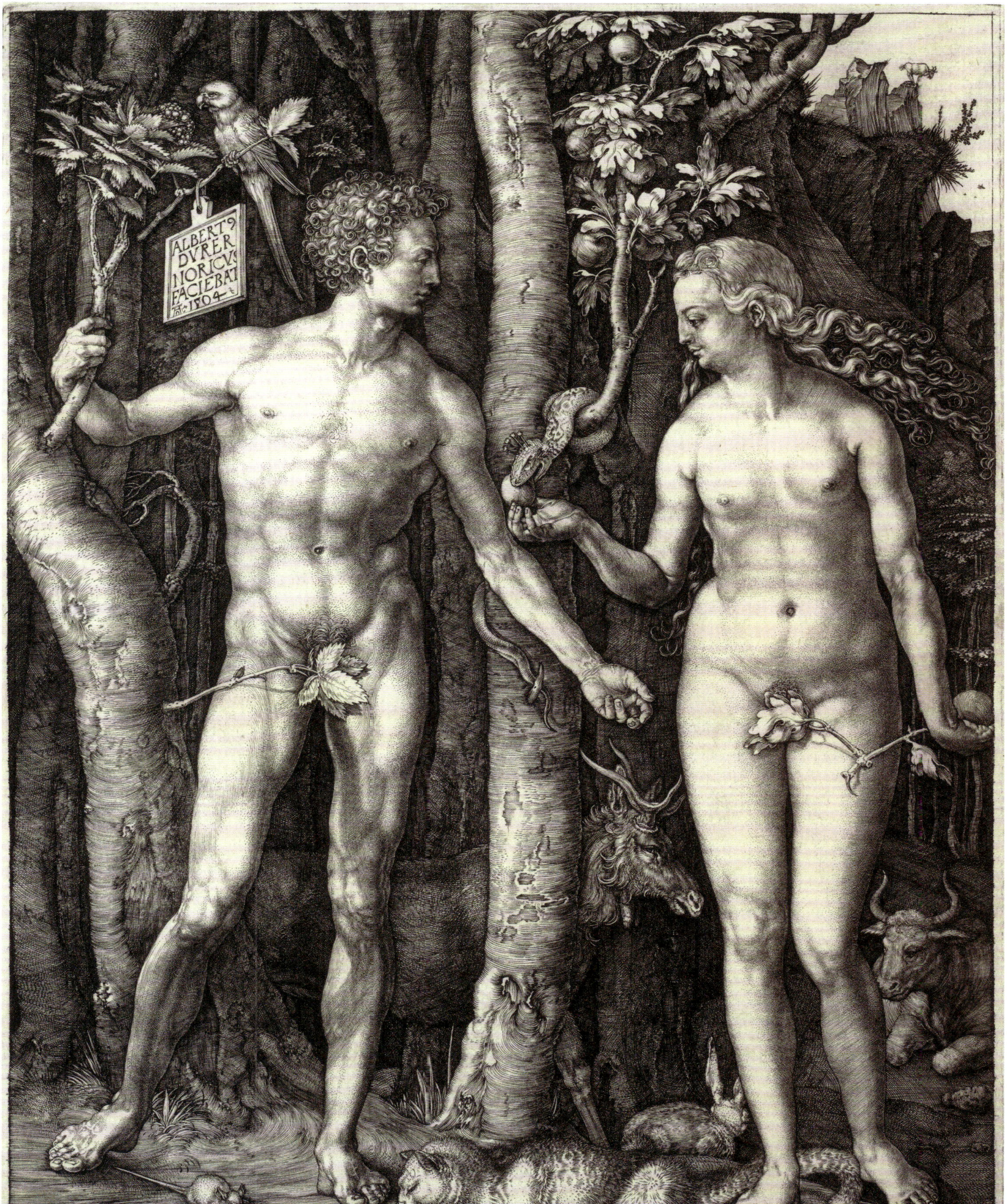
ALBERTꝰ
DVRER
NORICVS
FACIEBAT
AD 1504

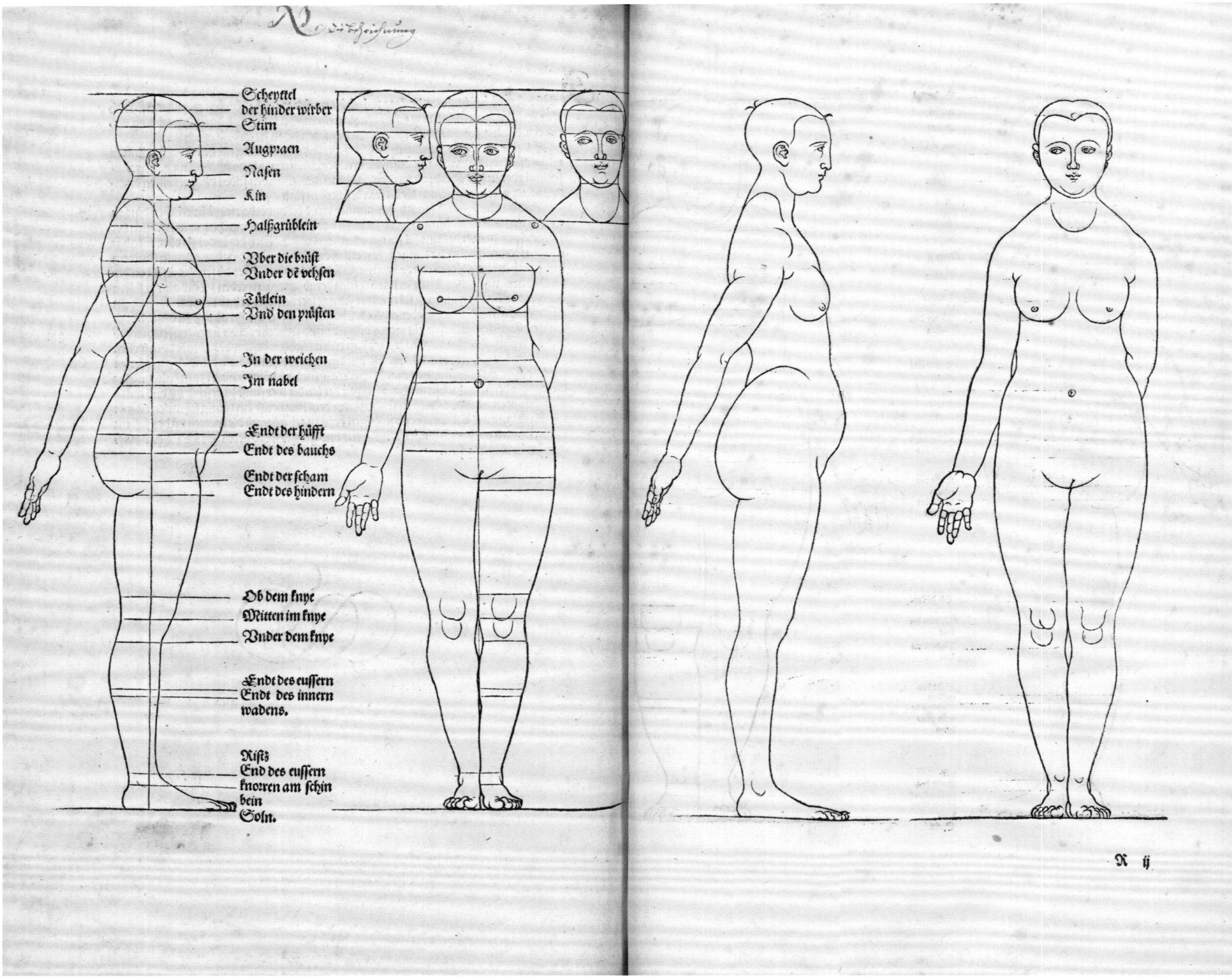

Albrecht Dürer
Human Proportion Studies from
Vier Bücher von menschlicher Proportion
(Four Books on Human Proportions), 1528
The ALBERTINA Museum, Vienna

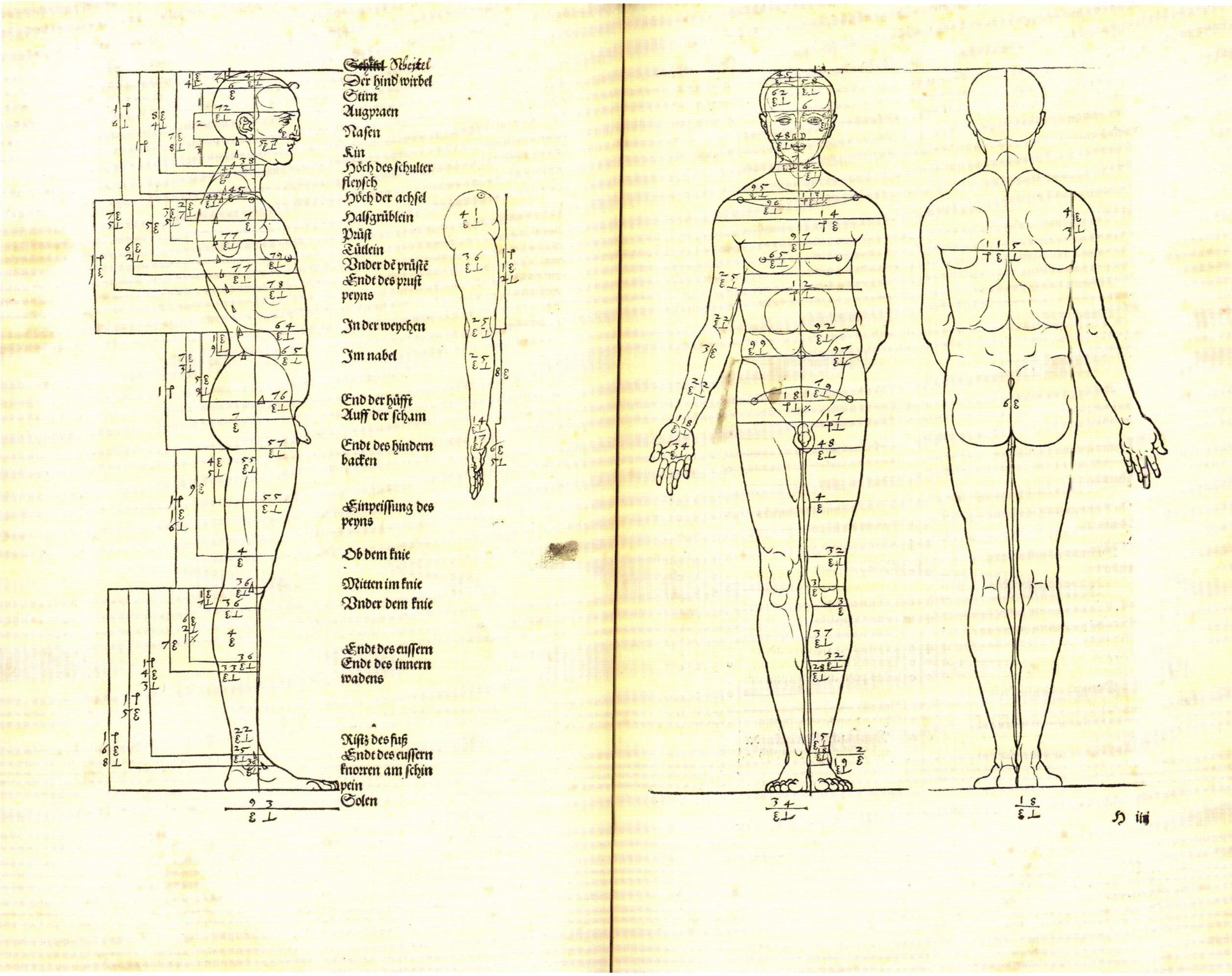
Scheitel
Der hind' wirbel
Stirn
Augpraen
Nasen
Kin
Höch des schulter
fleysch
Höch der achsel
Halsgrüblein
Prüst
Tütlein
Vnder dẽ prüstẽ
Endt des prust
peyns
In der weychen
Im nabel
End der hüfft
Auff der scham
Endt des hindern
backen
Einpeissung des
peyns
Ob dem knie
Mitten im knie
Vnder dem knie
Endt des eussern
Endt des innern
wadens
Ristz des fuß
Endt des eussern
knorren am schin
pein
Solen
H iiij

The Strongest Man, a Demigod

Giovanni Francesco Susini
Farnese Hercules, second quarter of the 17th century
LIECHTENSTEIN. The Princely Collections, Vaduz–Vienna, Fürstliche Sammlungen Art Service GmbH

As the personification of physical strength and virtuous heroism, Hercules (Heracles) was one of the most popular figures of Greco-Roman mythology. He used strength, courage, and cunning to complete twelve seemingly impossible feats, and after his death, he ascended to Olympus as a god. The most famous of all ancient representations of this hero is the Farnese Hercules (fig. 20), named after the family in whose palace it was once displayed—the Palazzo Farnese in Rome. Standing with one foot forward, Hercules leans with his muscular left arm on his club, which is draped with the pelt of the Nemean lion he slew. In his right hand, rested behind his back, he holds three golden apples stolen from the garden of the Hesperides. This fascinatingly naturalistic portrayal shows not an active warrior but instead a muscular hero tired from his labors, resting in deep thought. The over life-size statue, 3.17 meters tall, was created by the sculptor Glycon after a now lost original by the famous Hellenistic artist Lysippos (fourth century BC) for the Baths of Caracalla, which were opened in AD 216. The statue was rediscovered on that same site in 1546, although without its legs and head. The head was found in Trastevere, and the missing legs were initially refashioned by Guglielmo della Porta, a pupil of Michelangelo. Pope Paul III (Alessandro Farnese) had secured his family exclusive rights to all excavated finds. And so, in 1556, the Hercules was put on display in the Farnese family's magnificent palace, where it became one of the most renowned antiquities. After the male line of the Farnese died out in the eighteenth century, the exquisite collection came into the possession of the Spanish Bourbons. In 1787 the Hercules—fitted with the original legs, which had been rediscovered—was brought to Naples, where it is now kept in the National Archaeological Museum.

20 Glycon, Farnese Hercules, AD 216
Roman copy after a Greek original by Lysippos, ca. 320 BC
Marble, h. 317 cm
Museo Archeologico Nazionale, Naples

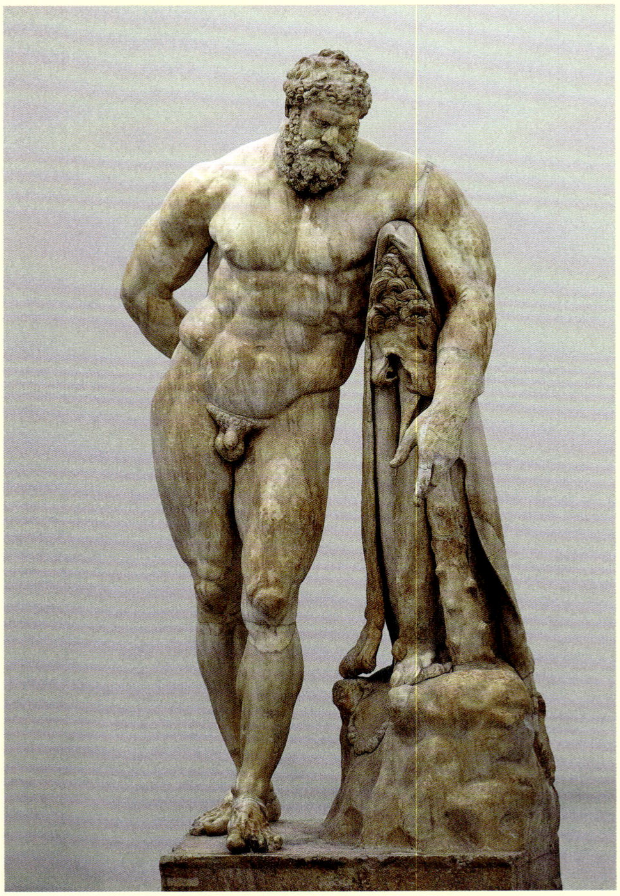

Numerous large- and small-scale copies and variations of the Farnese Hercules were made since ancient times. Following the statue's rediscovery, the Palazzo Farnese became a place of pilgrimage for artists, and the Hercules was expressly recommended as an object of study in artists' treatises and travel guides. The Dutch artist Hendrick Goltzius was among those

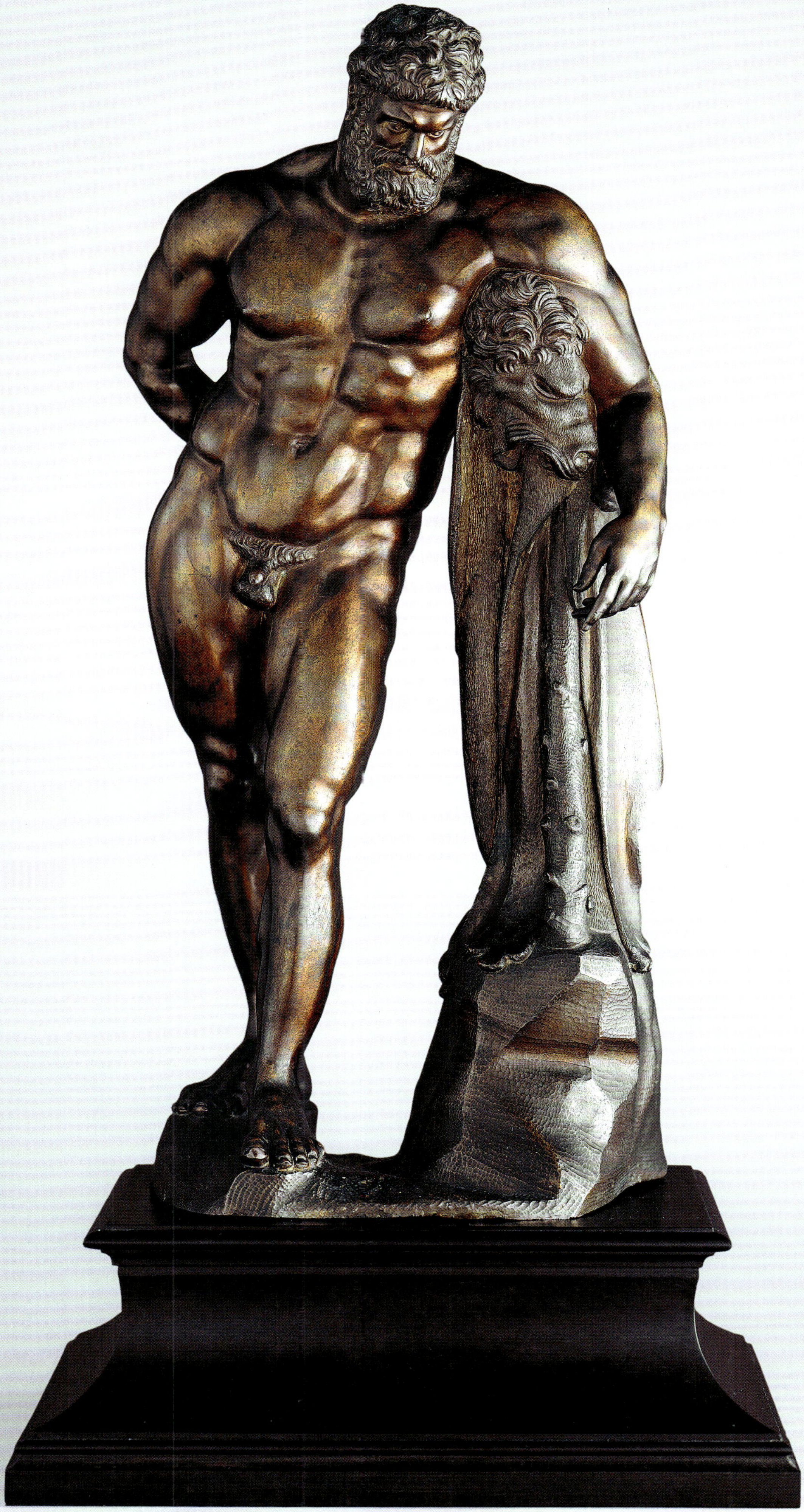

who admired the work firsthand. His engraving inventively stages the famous sculpture with a rear view—a highly original choice, which makes the hero appear more alive than statue-like. Hercules seems to gaze down at the two upward-glancing observers beside his pedestal, who look tiny by comparison. Goltzius's *The Great Hercules*, on the other hand, does not follow the Farnese type. In the background, it shows scenes of Hercules battling the river god Achelous in the form of a bull and wrestling with Antaeus the giant. The sheet owes its title not only to its unusually large format but also to the subject's grotesquely exaggerated muscles, which earned this work the epithet "Knollenman" (bulbous man) as early as the seventeenth century. The nickname alludes symbolically to the national strength of the Dutch Republic, founded in 1581, a united Netherlands in its struggle for independence from the Spanish Habsburgs. In 1606, Peter Paul Rubens made several drawings of the Hercules in the Farnese collection, and these were later copied by associates and pupils in his Antwerp workshop. The Florentine sculptor Antonio Susini, an assistant to Giambologna, was allowed to produce five reduced-scale bronze casts after the Farnese Hercules during a stay in Rome. Antonio Susini's casts, in turn, probably served as models for the bronze figure by his nephew Giovanni Francesco. Anton Raphael Mengs stayed in Rome from 1741 to 1744 to study ancient sculpture and the old masters, especially Raphael and Michelangelo. His red-chalk drawing of the Farnese Hercules is of utmost refinement. In these cases, the point was not to study human anatomy after the live model in the mold of Michelangelo but instead to reproduce and circulate the famous ancient exemplar. As the epitome and prototype of the powerful male body, the Farnese Hercules formed a distinct canon for representations of Hercules that remained influential for centuries.

EM

Hendrick Goltzius
Farnese Hercules, ca. 1592
The ALBERTINA Museum, Vienna

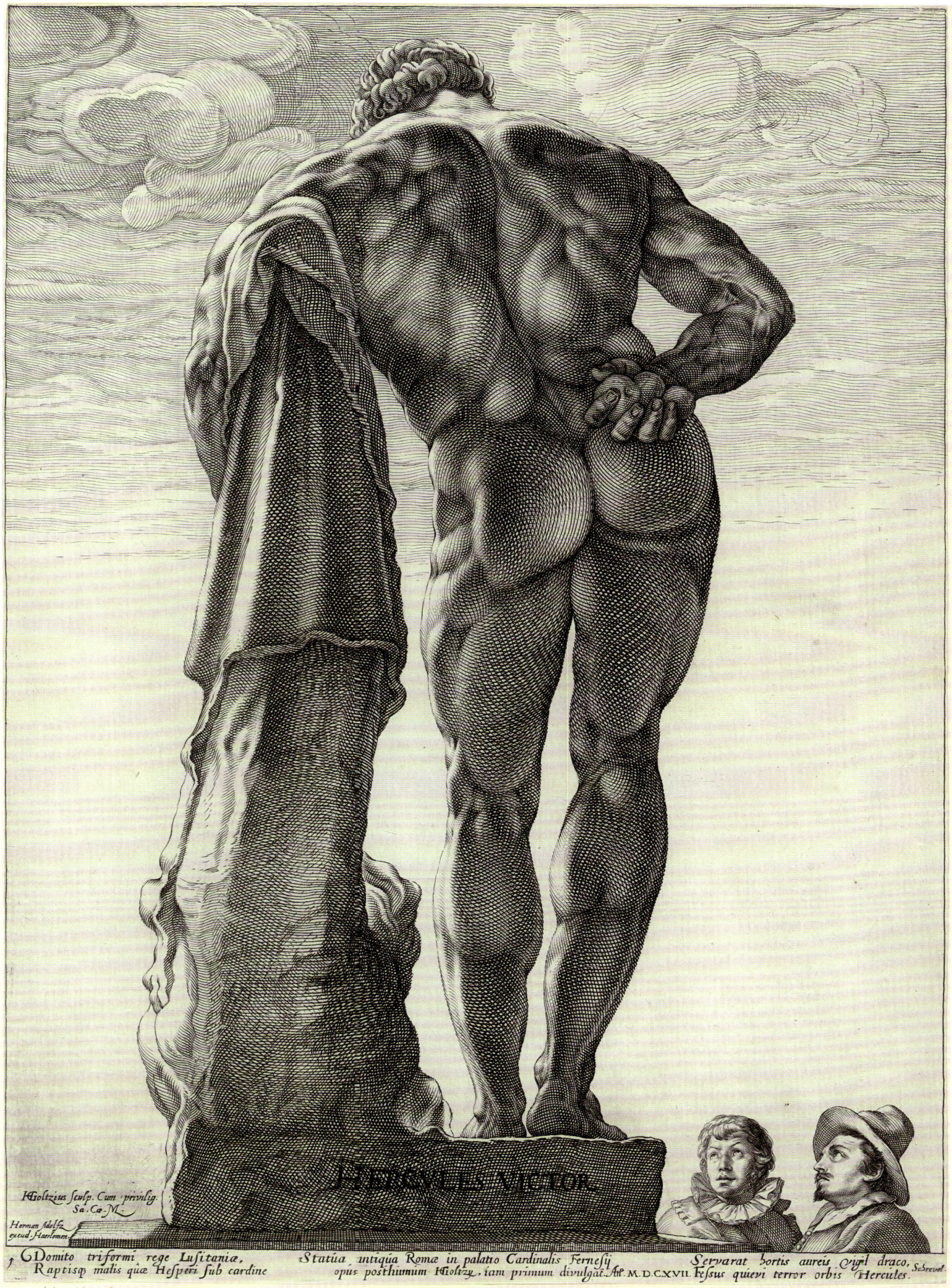
HERCVLES VICTOR
HGoltzius sculp. Cum privilig. Sa. Cæ. M.
Herman Adolfz excud. Haerlemen.
Domito triformi rege Lusitaniæ, Raptisq malis quæ Hesperi sub cardine
Statua antiqua Romæ in palatio Cardinalis Fernesij opus posthumum HGoltzy, iam primum divulgat. Aº. M.D.CXVII.
Servarat hortis aureis vigil draco, Fessus quievi terror orbis Hercules.
Schrevel.

Hendrick Goltzius
The Great Hercules, 1589
The ALBERTINA Museum, Vienna

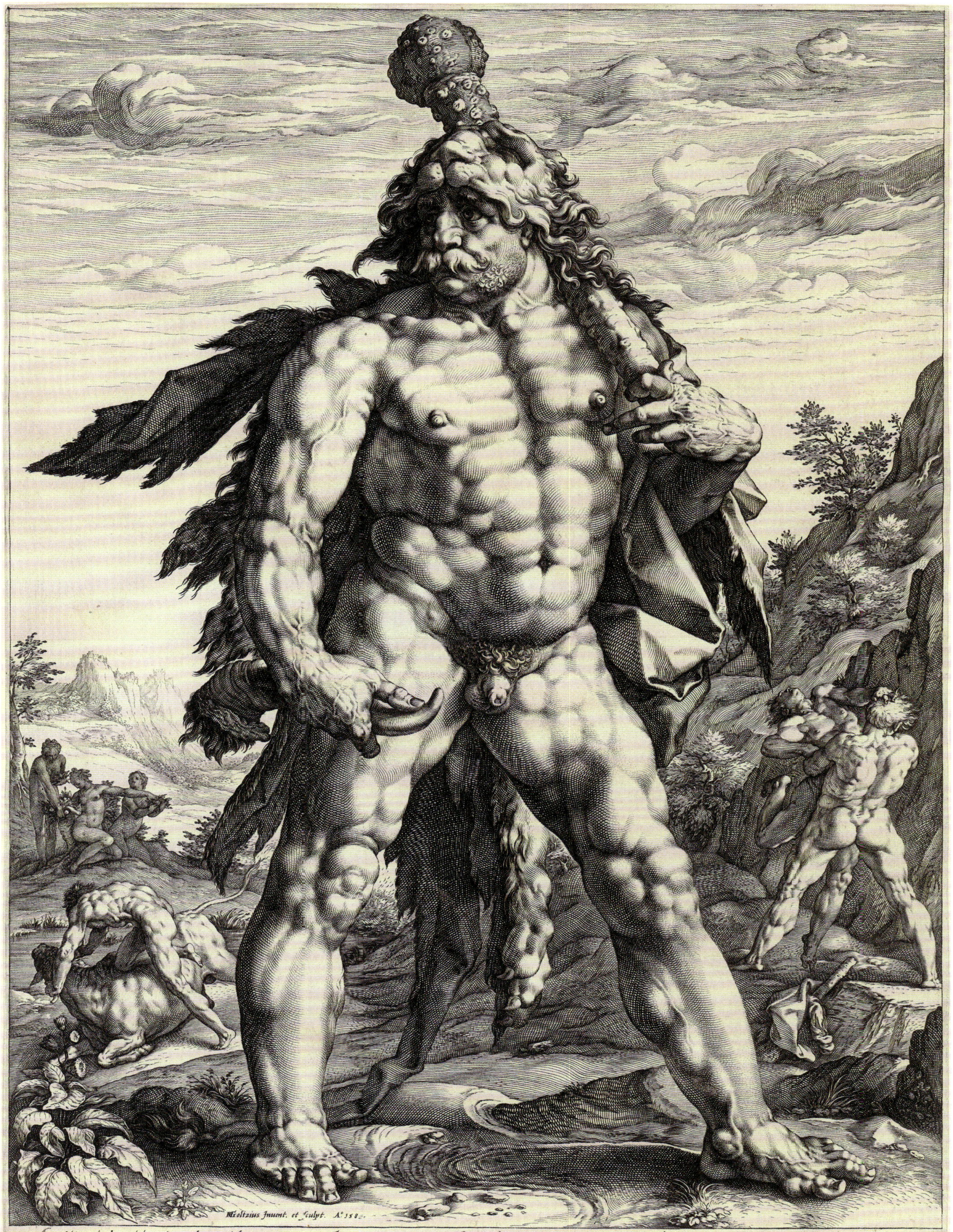
HGoltzius Inuent. et sculpt. A° 158
Amphitryoniade virtus terraqꝫ mariqꝫ
Quem latet? et tanti sæua nouerca mali?
Ille tot expositus monstris, Hydreqꝫ, tricorpor
Geryon atqꝫ tibi, flammiuomoqꝫ Caco.
Ille hic Anteum, et superat te Acheloe bicornis;
Naiades at truncum fruge ferace beant.

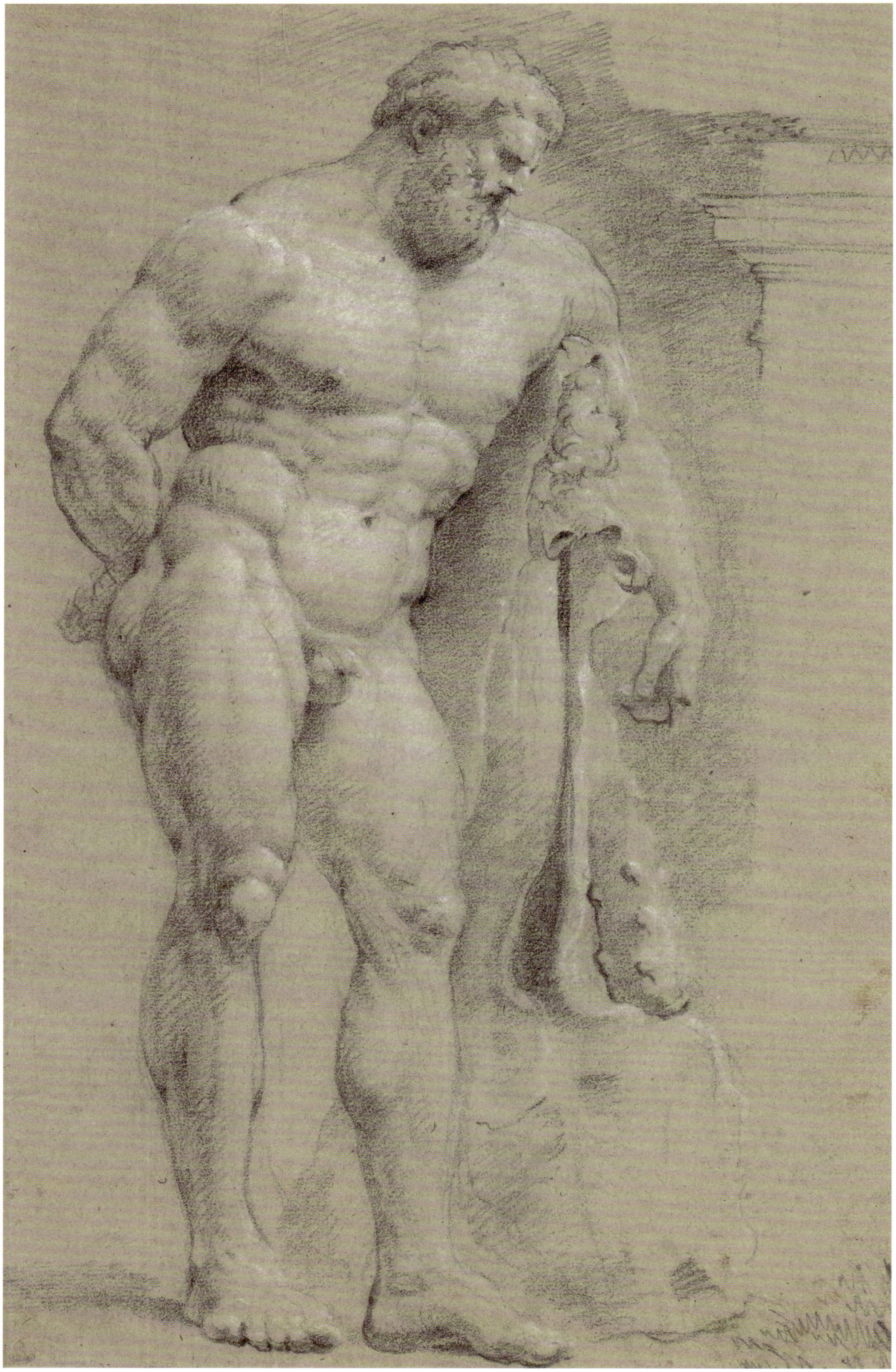

Copy after Peter Paul Rubens
Farnese Hercules, second third of the 17th century
The ALBERTINA Museum, Vienna

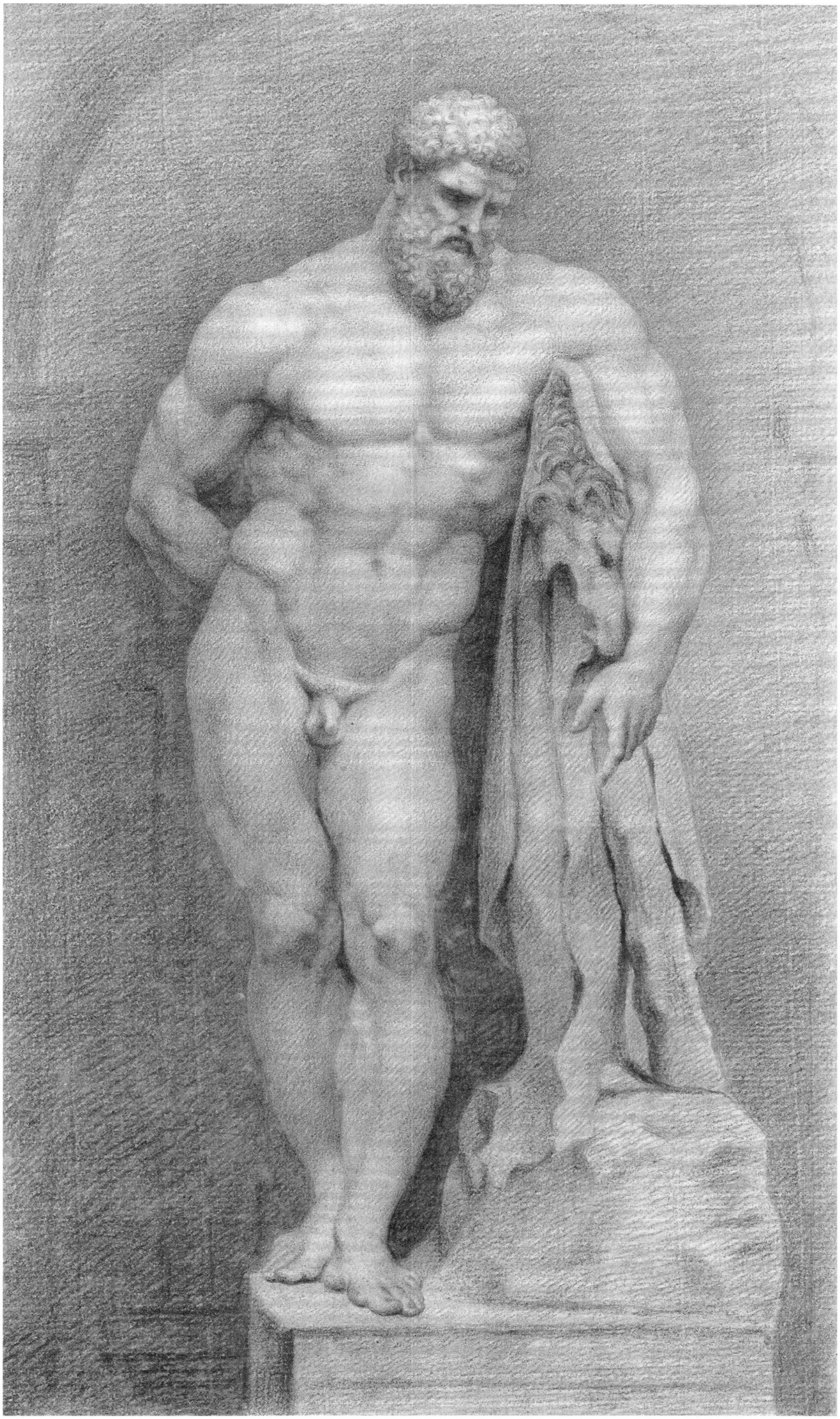

Anton Raphael Mengs
Farnese Hercules, early 1740s
The ALBERTINA Museum, Vienna

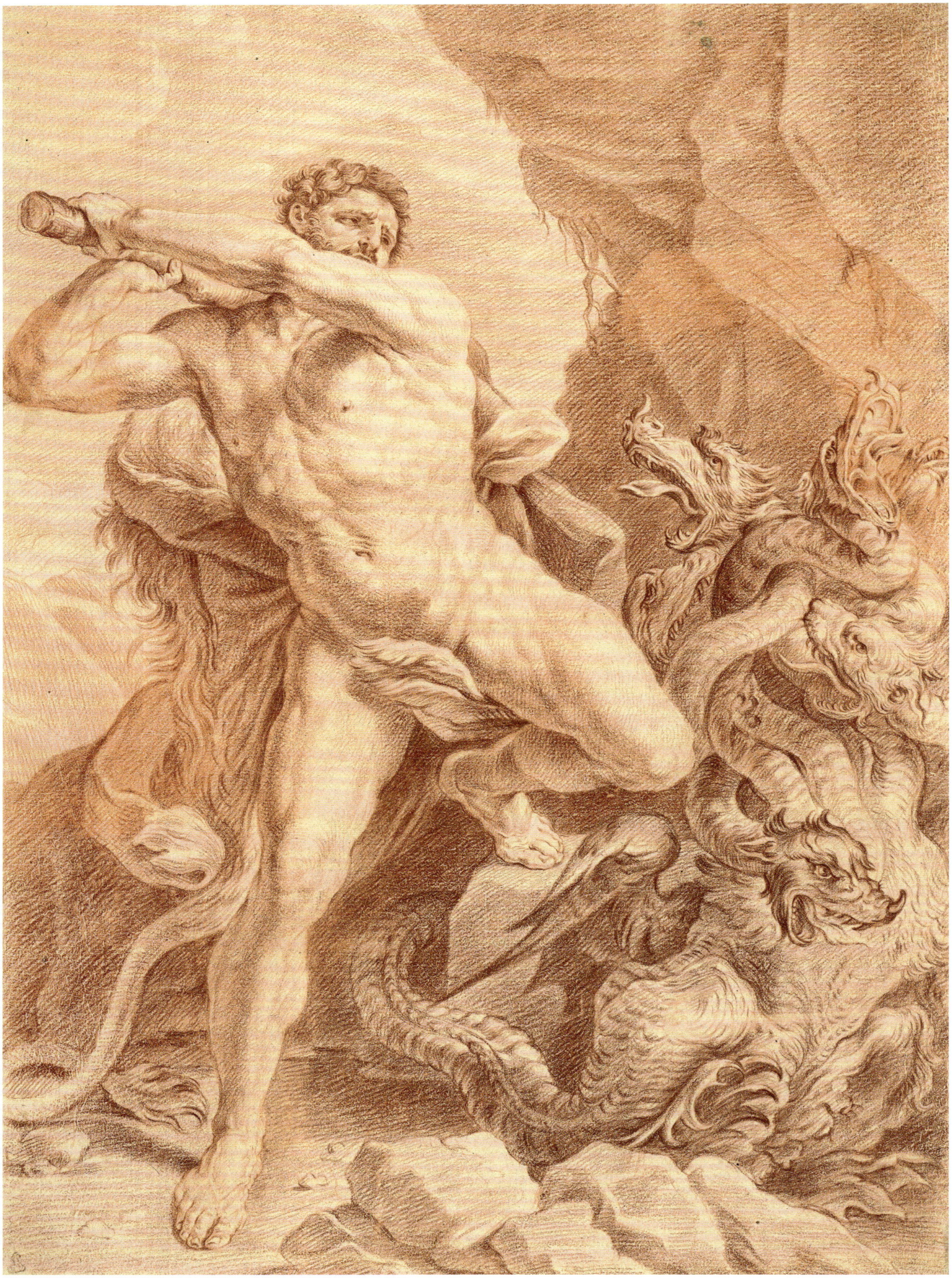

French Artist
(after Guido Reni)
Hercules and the Hydra, second third of the 17th century
The ALBERTINA Museum, Vienna

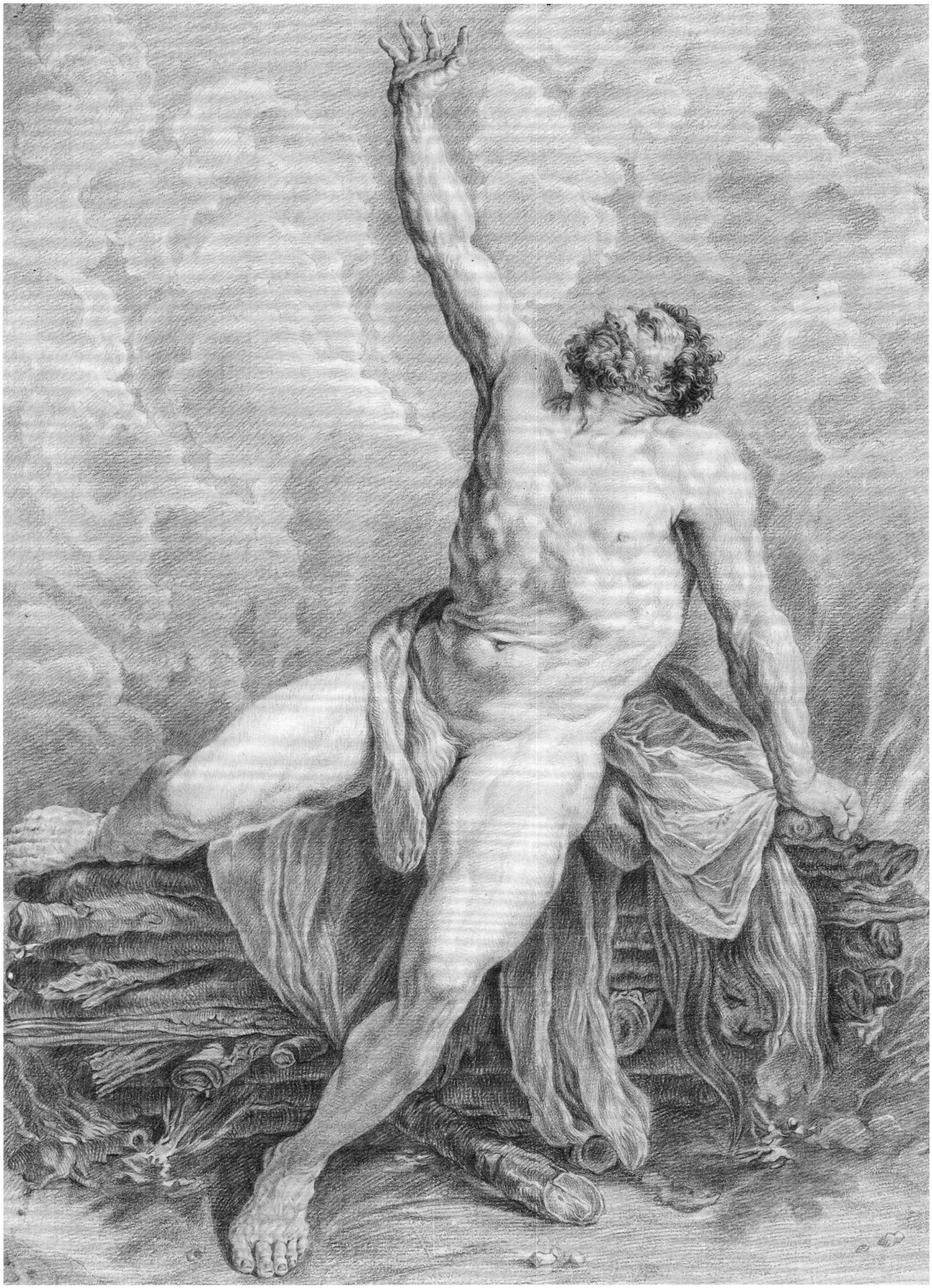

French Artist
(after Guido Reni)
Hercules on the Pyre,
second third of the
17th century
The ALBERTINA
Museum, Vienna

Rembrandt: The Anti-Michelangelo, or The Naked Truth

Like Michelangelo, Rembrandt also drew after the live model. But his nudes depart from classical notions of beauty and thus differ fundamentally from the athletic figures of the Italian artist; they are rendered with great realism, free of any idealization. For example, in Rembrandt's *The Fall of Man* (Gen. 3:1–6), Adam and Eve are presented completely naked in glaring backlight. Contrary to pictorial tradition, they are not shown as a beautiful young couple. Eve casts an annoyed glace at Adam, who reaches with his left hand for the forbidden fruit in her grasp while raising his right hand in a gesture of admonishment, in awareness of their guilt. The combined naturalism and ugliness of Adam and Eve serve as a stylistic means of pointedly representing both the moral conflict between seduction and guilt and the loss of paradisal harmony.

Two etchings from about 1631 showing solitary female figures belong to the earliest nudes by Rembrandt. Because of the quiver of arrows beside her and the wooded setting, one is thought to represent Diana, goddess of the hunt and chastity. She turns her body away, for the sight of the nude goddess was forbidden to mortals. The naked woman on the other sheet faces us openly. Due to the format being almost identical to that of the *Diana*, this figure is described as a nymph (perhaps Callisto) from the goddess's retinue. Both women look straight out of the picture, which gives them great immediacy. The isolated position of the "nymph" before the minimally etched light background lends her portrayal a sketch-like character. The models Rembrandt chose were no slender beauties; this, too, was a break with tradition, especially in the depiction of goddesses. His women lack ideal proportions and are realistically rendered down to the smallest detail. In the bright light, the "nymph" clearly shows her bulging belly (perhaps no longer firm due to multiple past pregnancies), wrinkles and fleshy folds, and the imprints of garters on her legs. The combination of unidealized, unsparing naturalism and the sensual appeal of the skin, subtly modeled with the finest hatching, is a continuing source of fascination. Yet, Rembrandt met with little understanding from an art criticism shaped by classical norms: early authors were surprised that a man of such genius and intellect drew so persistently after life instead of selecting from what is most beautiful—namely, Italian or ancient prototypes. "Flaccid breasts, distorted hands, yes the pinches of the laces, of the corset on the belly, of the garters on the leg, it all had to be followed, or nature was not satisfied, at least his [nature], which tolerated neither rules, nor

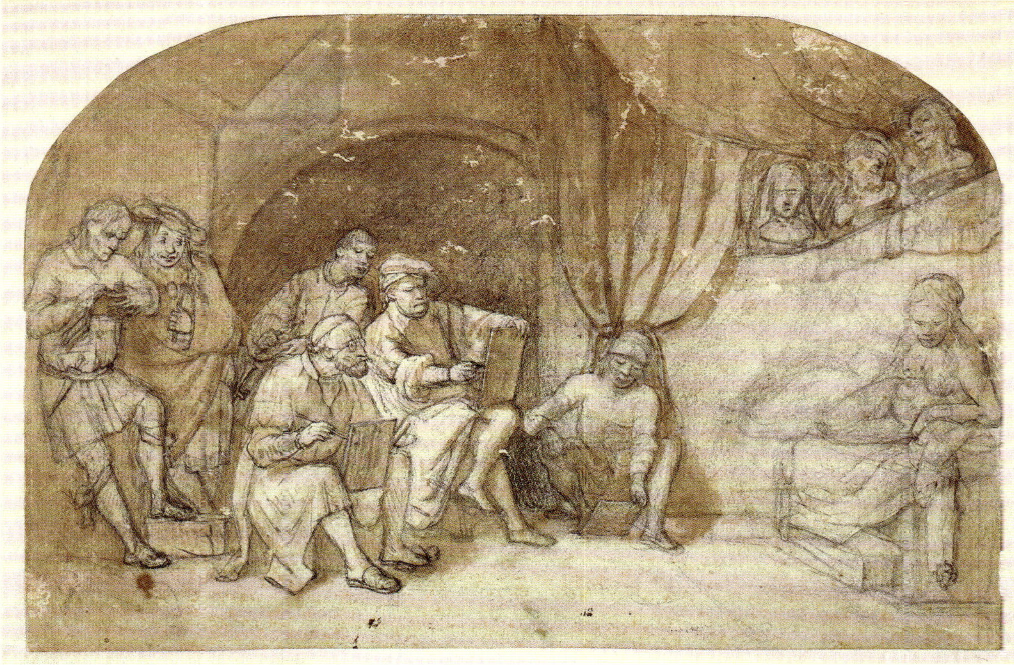

21 Constantijn van Renesse, *Rembrandt and His Pupils Drawing from a Nude Model,* ca. 1649
Brush and brown ink, black chalk, heightened with white, brown wash
18 × 26.6 cm
Hessisches Landesmuseum Darmstadt

any reason of proportion in a body's members" (Andries Pels 1681, qtd. Arnold Houbraken 1718–1721; trans. Hendrik J. Horn and Rieke van Leeuwen 2021).

A contrast to the two female nudes found in nature is offered by three etchings of male nudes, worked up as direct studies after live models in the studio. These are not muscular athletes but lanky youths, perhaps the artist's workshop assistants. Rembrandt employed various associates and pupils, and drawing together from models was part of artistic training (fig. 21). On the first sheet, the model, clad only in a loincloth, sits on a chair; in the second, the model is on the floor; in the third, two nudes, one sitting, the other standing, were later supplemented with a delicately sketched background scene in which a woman coaxes a baby forward in a walker (*rolwagentje* in Dutch). This latter scene is a didactic allusion to the importance of studying nature: just as the child only learns to walk through continued practice and only matures through learning, so too does the aspiring artist only achieve mastery through diligent drawing and practice. Rembrandt intended these etchings for a wide audience. They were perhaps also meant as illustrations for a small artists' manual, but no copy of any such publication has survived. A drawing showing the standing model from the *Het Rolwagentje* print in reverse has been attributed to Rembrandt or one of his pupils (possibly Carel Fabritius). Other student drawings show the same model from slightly different angles, which suggests that teacher and students worked side by side. This offers evidence of the importance that Rembrandt placed on group drawing sessions after the live model.

EM

Rembrandt Harmensz. van Rijn
Adam and Eve (The Fall of Man), 1638
The ALBERTINA Museum, Vienna

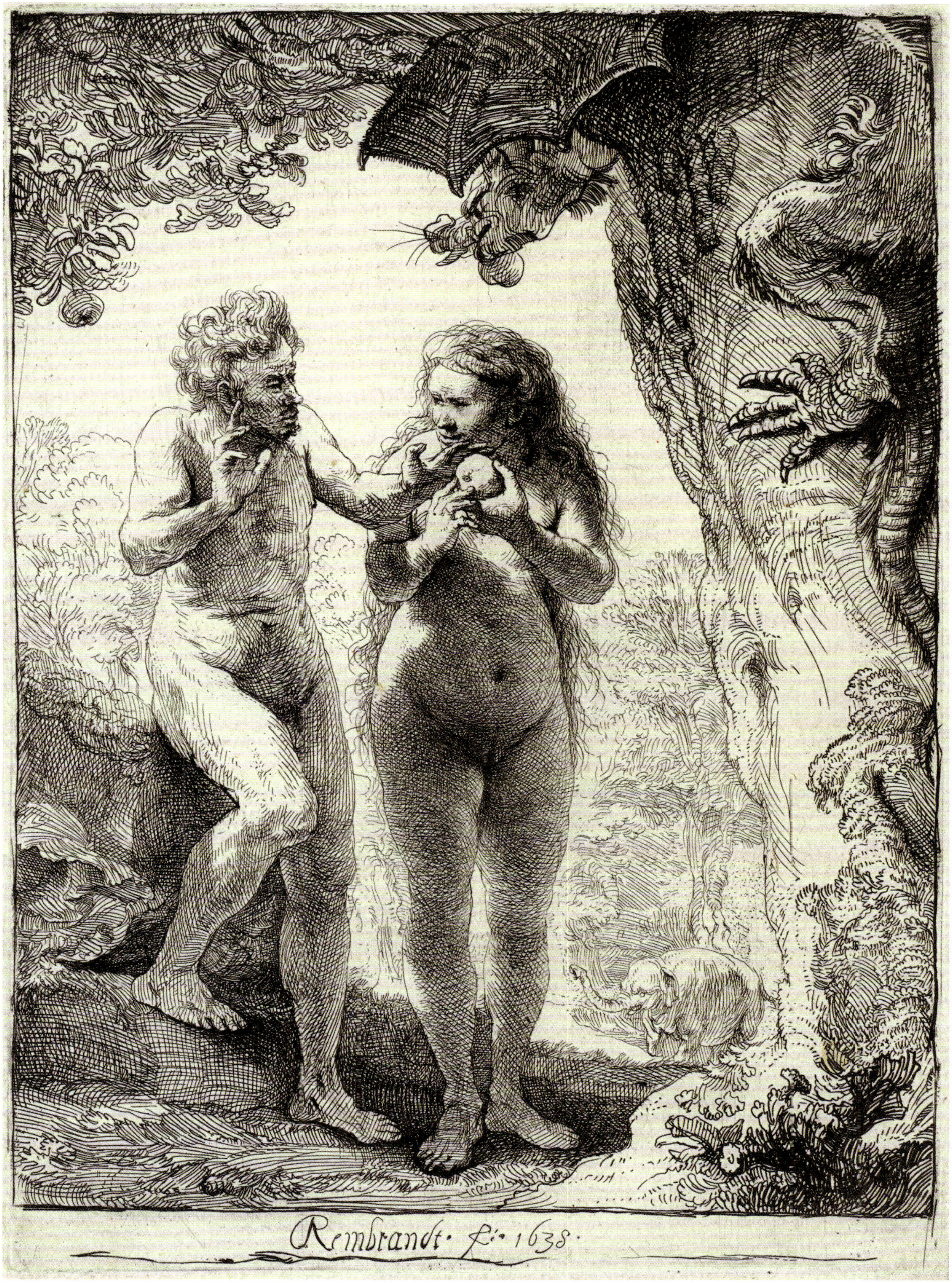
Rembrandt· f.· 1638·

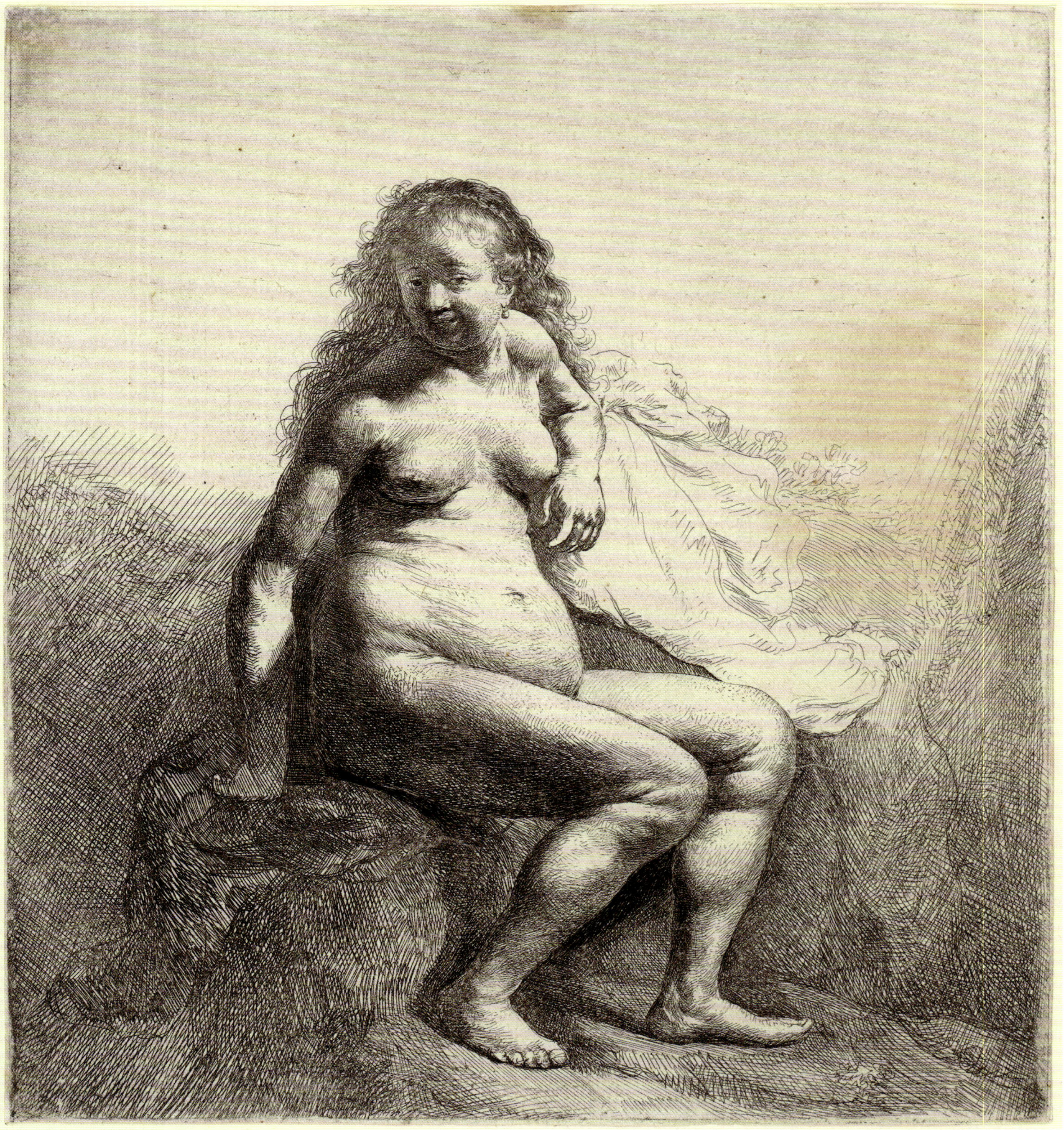

Rembrandt Harmensz. van Rijn
Seated Female Nude (Naked Woman Seated on a Mound), ca. 1631
The ALBERTINA Museum, Vienna

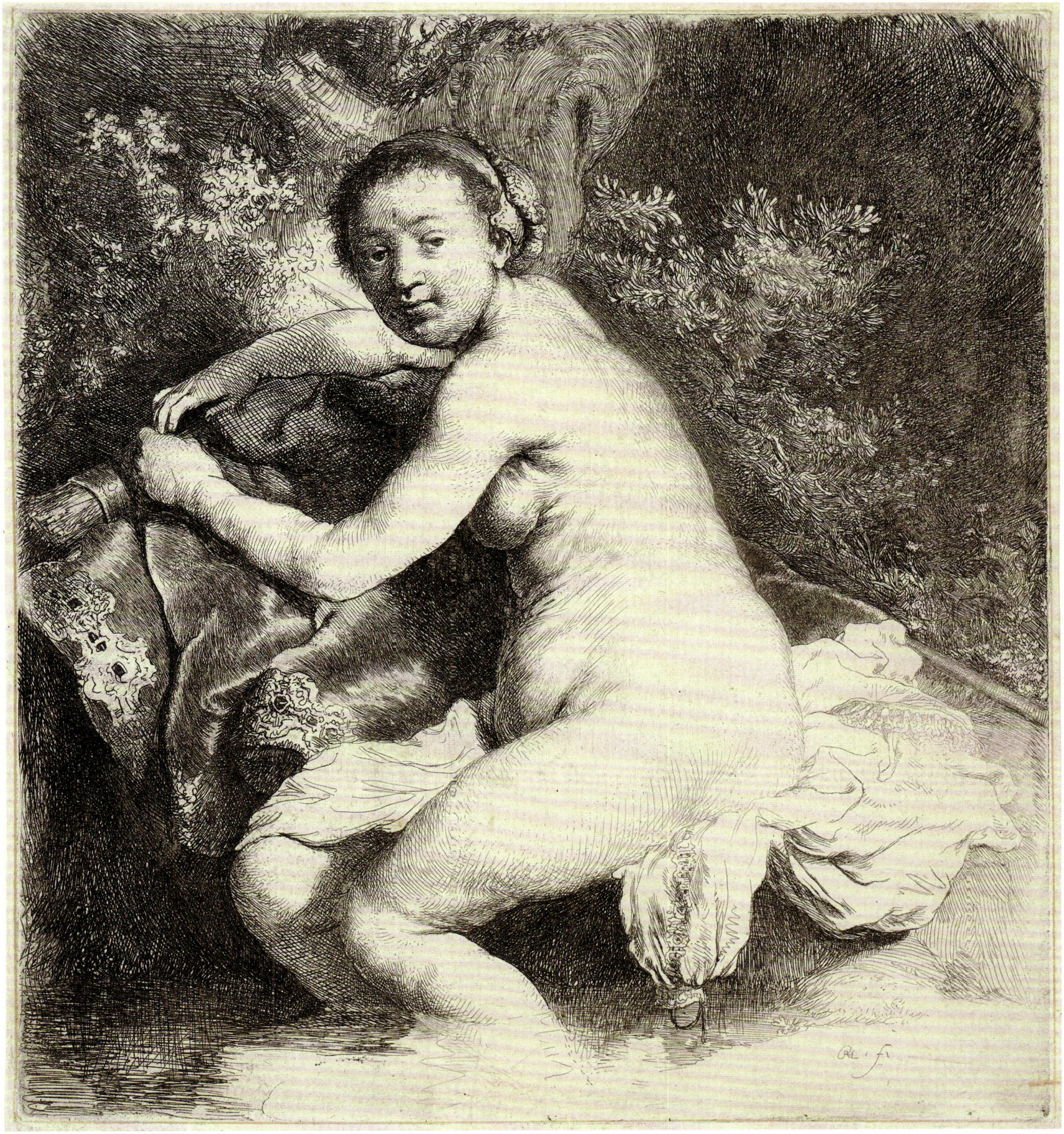

Rembrandt Harmensz. van Rijn
Diana at the Bath, ca. 1631
The ALBERTINA Museum, Vienna

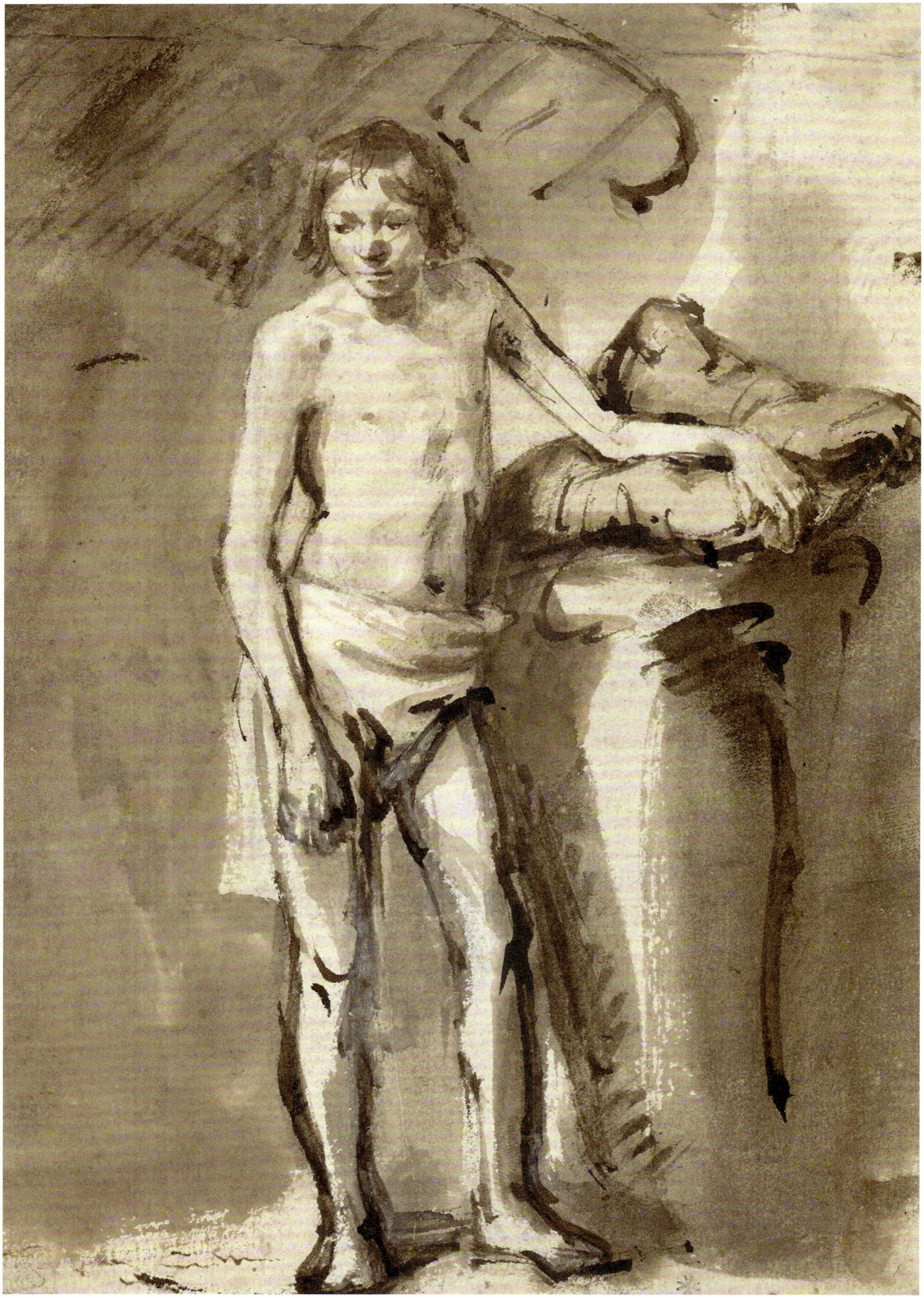

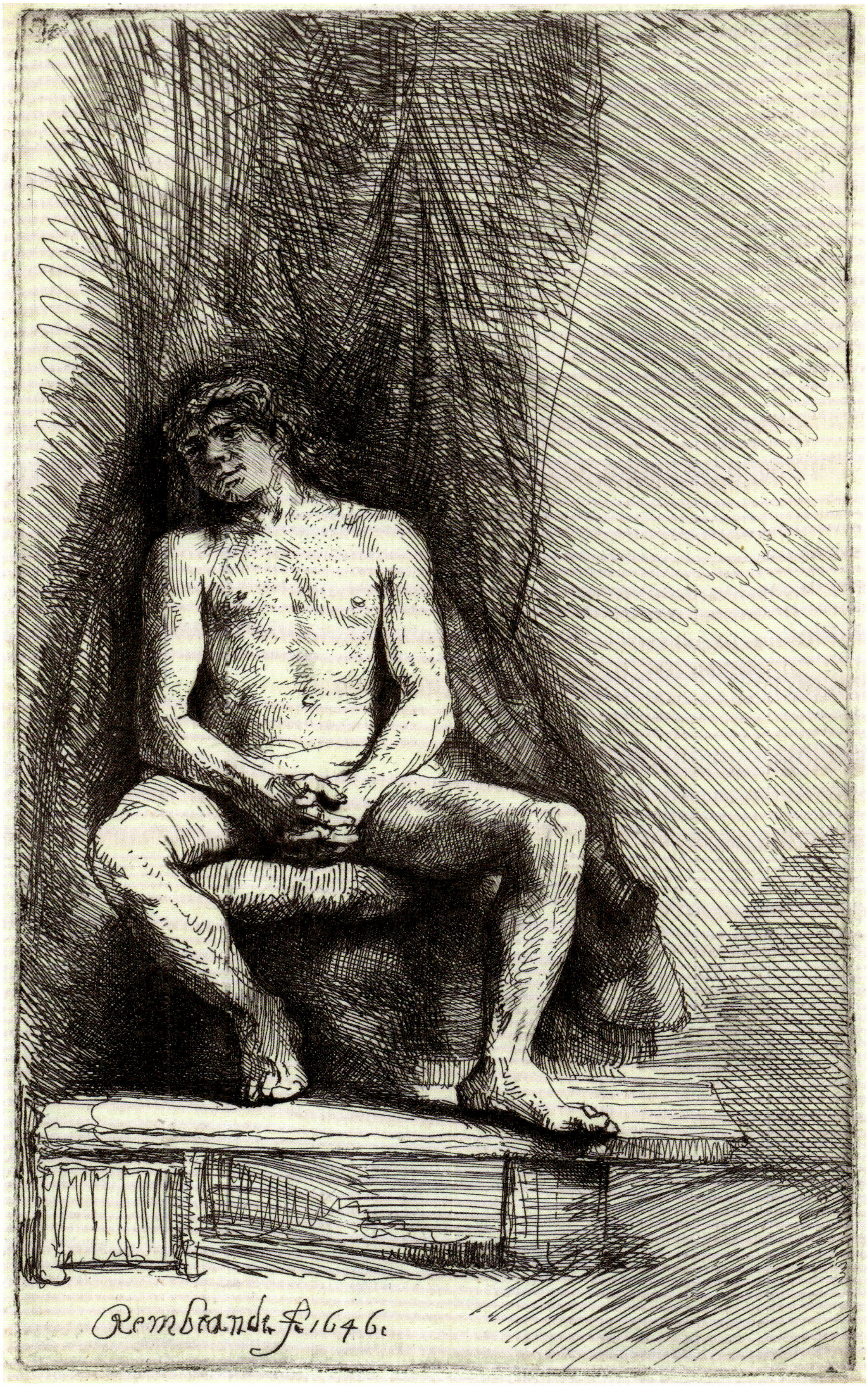

Rembrandt Harmensz. van Rijn
or Pupil
Standing Male Nude, ca. 1646
The ALBERTINA Museum, Vienna

Rembrandt Harmensz. van Rijn
Seated Male Nude, 1646
The ALBERTINA Museum, Vienna

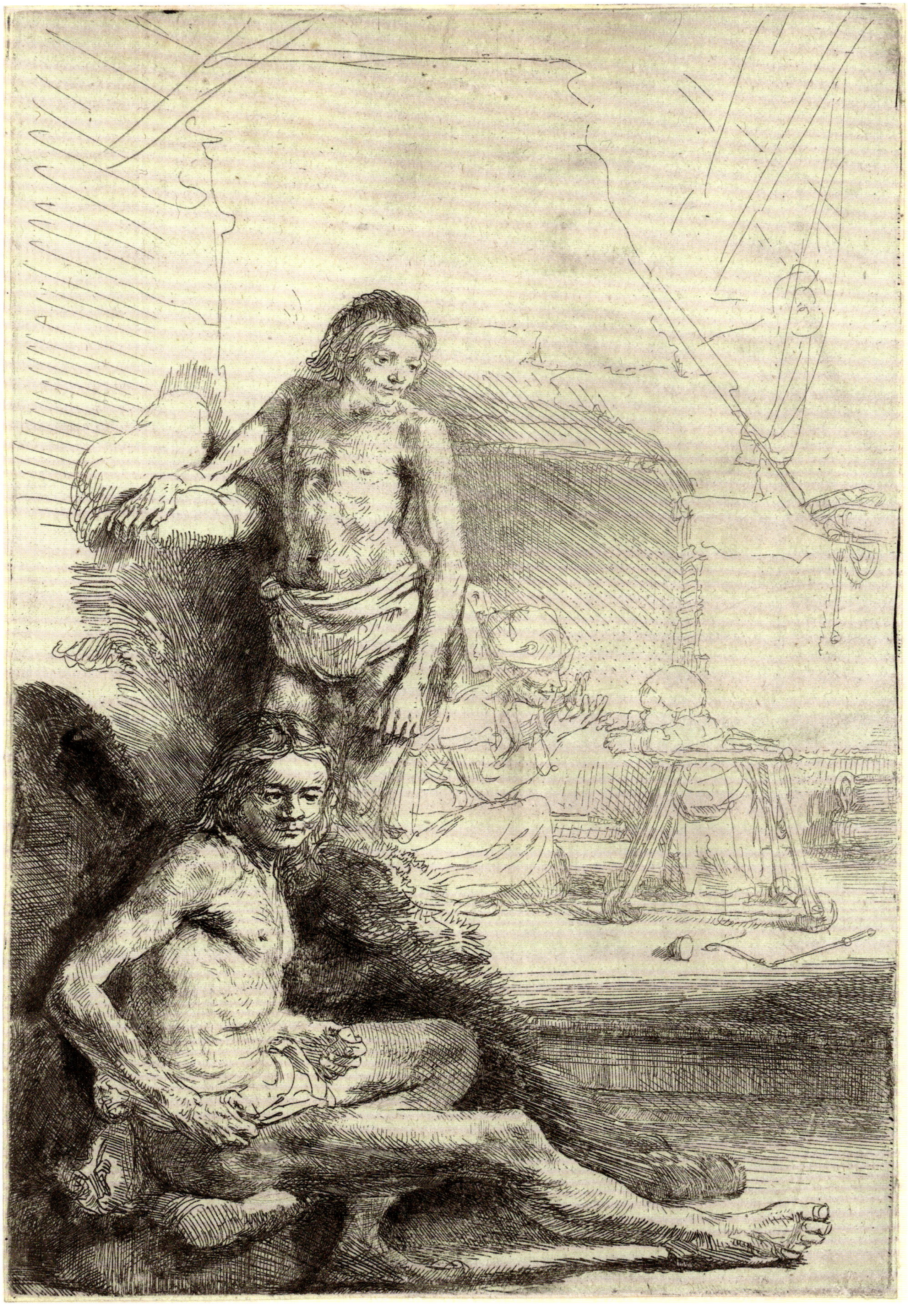

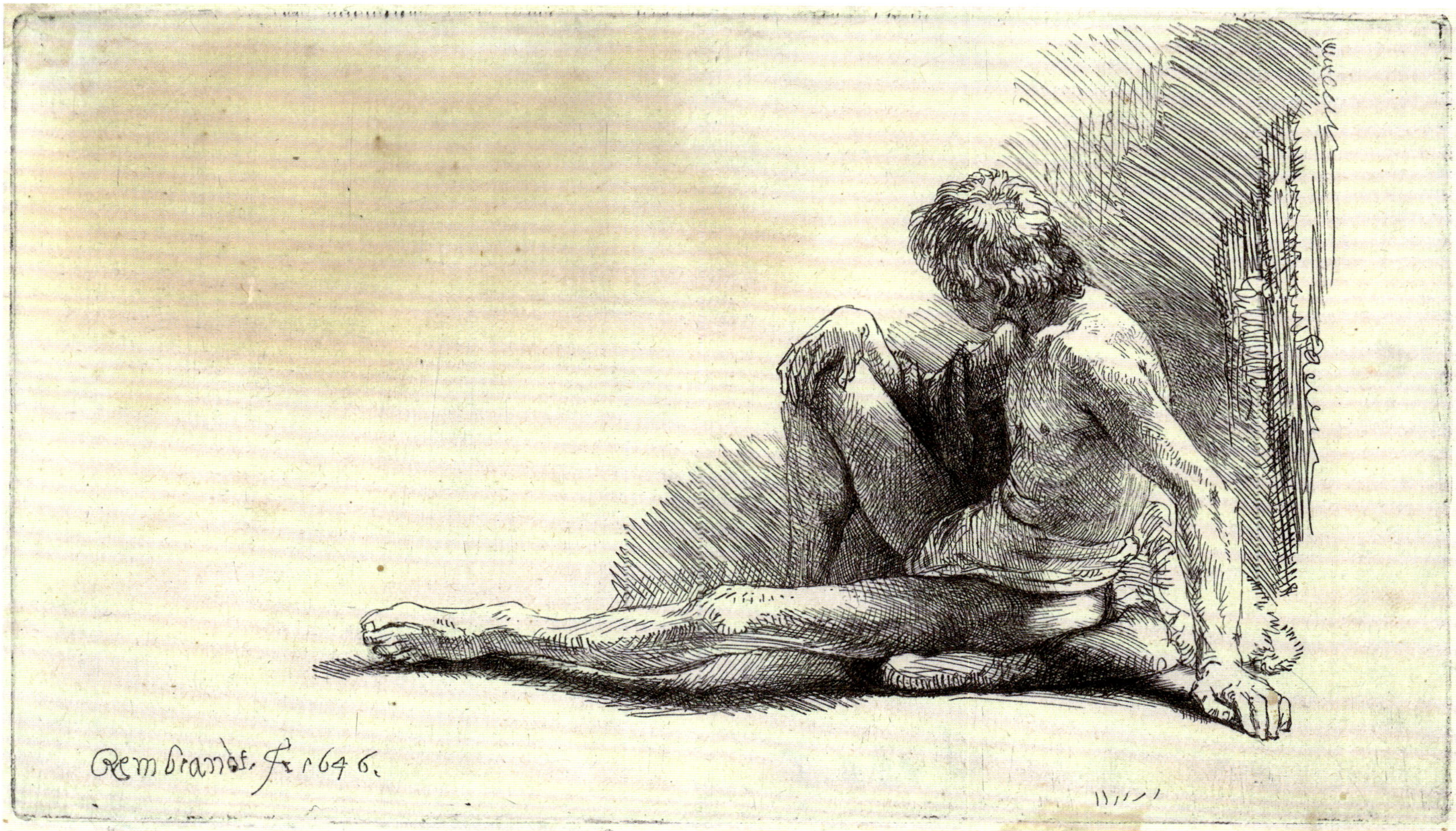

Rembrandt Harmensz. van Rijn
Seated and Standing Male Nudes
(Het Rolwagentje), ca. 1646
The ALBERTINA Museum, Vienna

Rembrandt Harmensz. van Rijn
Male Nude Seated on the Ground, 1646
The ALBERTINA Museum, Vienna

Rubens, or Return of Michelangelo

The brothers Agostino and Annibale Carracci, as well as their cousin Ludovico, are among the pioneers of Italian Baroque painting. In the mid-1580s, they founded the Accademia degli Incamminati in Bologna, one of Italy's first private art academies. Its guiding principle was a return to classical ideals of the Renaissance and to nature. The Mannerist style, with its distorted proportions and extravagant twists and turns, was to be cast aside in favor of greater naturalism. Accordingly, studies of the nude and of nature formed an essential part of training and practice at the academy. Agostino's half-length nude on blue paper and Annibale's chalk drawing of a seated man holding a staff were made from live models. They testify to the importance that the Carracci attached to the study of the human body.

From 1597 to 1604, Annibale—assisted in part by Agostino and by his pupil Domenichino—carried out his greatest work, the fresco cycle in the Galleria Farnese of the Palazzo Farnese in Rome. In this, Annibale took as his guide the works of Raphael and Michelangelo, including the latter's *ignudi* in the Sistine Chapel. In Rome, he met the young Peter Paul Rubens, who was greatly impressed by the Carracci. Like many Flemish artists before him, Rubens had traveled to Italy for study. During his eight-year stay, which lasted from 1600 to 1608, he worked for Vincenzo Gonzaga, Duke of Mantua, and traveled to Rome, Florence, Venice, and Genoa, among other places. This gave him ample opportunities to view and copy ancient sculpture and more recent Italian art. In 1608, having received news that his mother's health had deteriorated, he returned to Antwerp. His bustling workshop there soon became the largest and most important in the Southern Netherlands.

Rubens's time in Italy—especially his experience of the art of Michelangelo—had a lasting impact on his work. For example, in the *Study of a Male Nude Leaning Forward*, Rubens's engagement with Michelangelo's ideal of the athletic body is clear in the lifelike depiction of musculature, the attention to anatomical detail, and the expression of tension and movement. The study was preparatory for an apostle in the left foreground of *The Assumption of the Virgin* executed about 1613–1621 (Kunsthistorisches Museum, Vienna). In the painting, this figure, together with other apostles, braces his back against a slab of rock. The nude was drawn after a live model in order to capture as realistically as possible the play of the musculature in the torso and in the separately worked-up right arm.

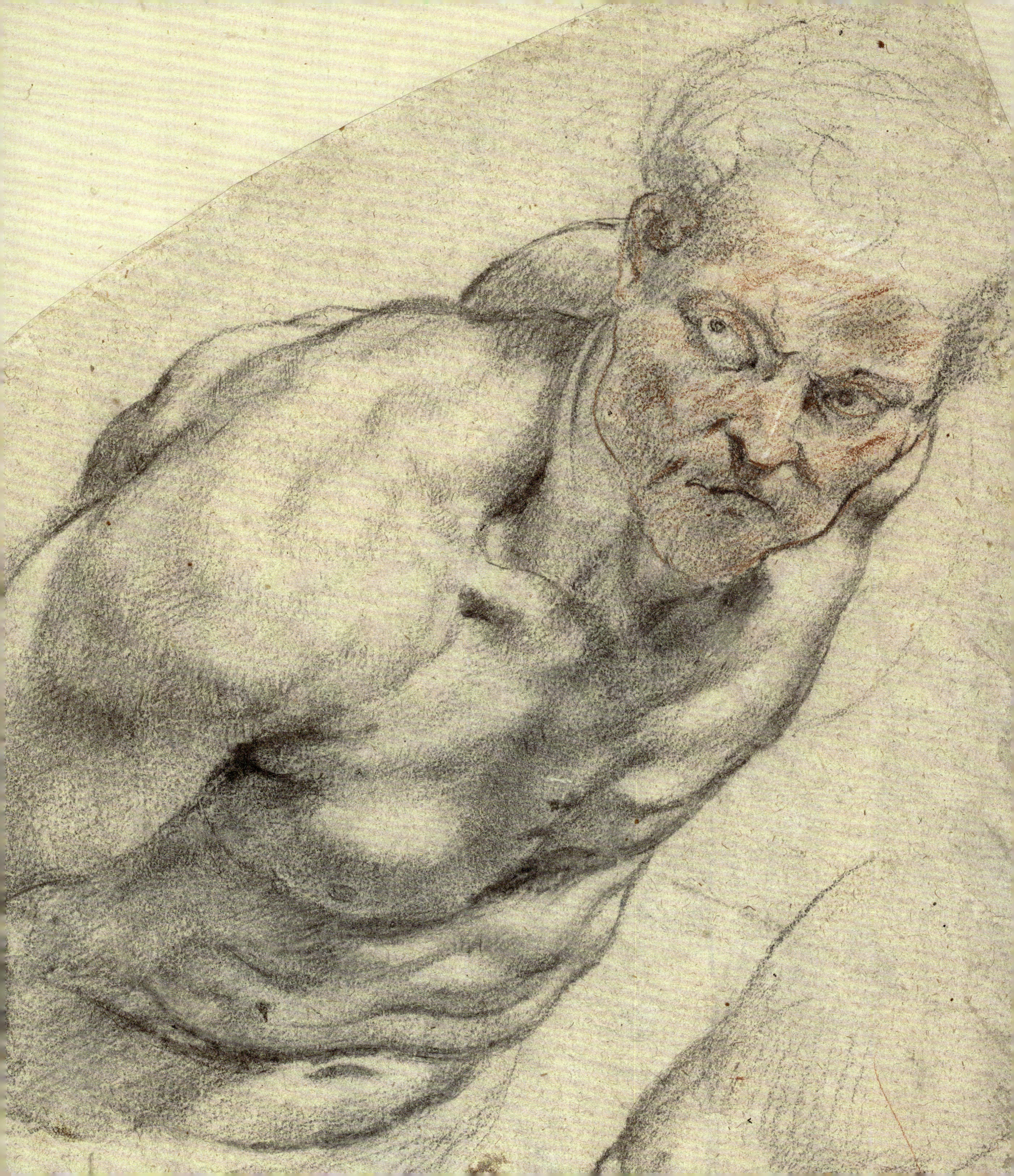

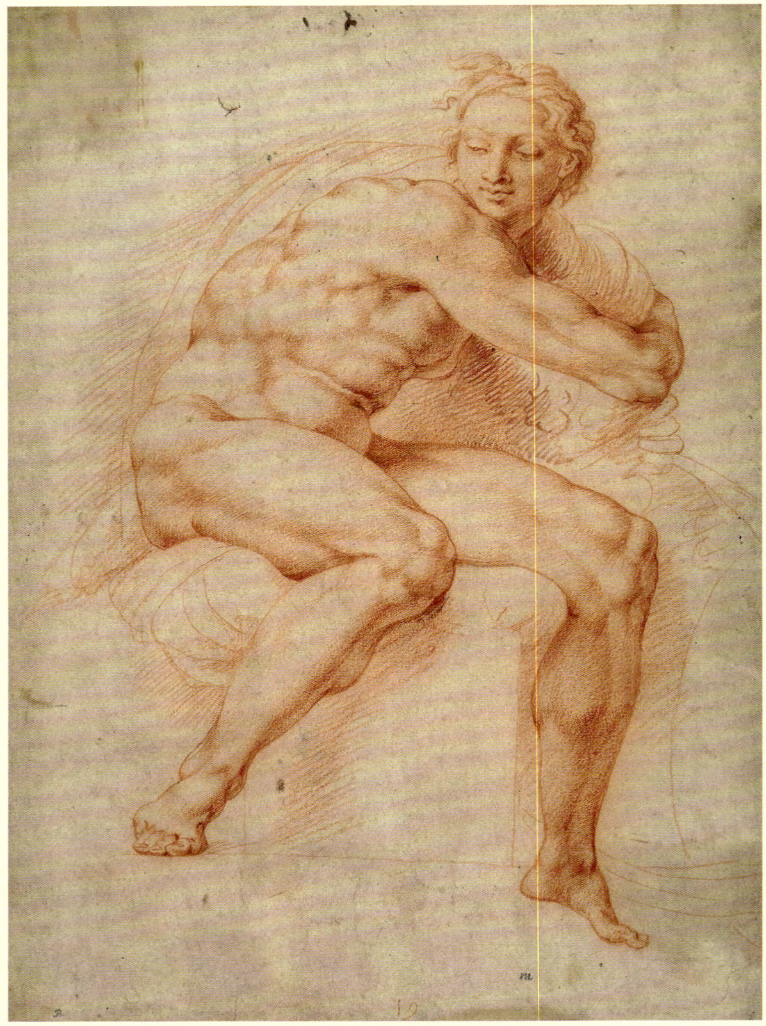

22 Peter Paul Rubens (after Michelangelo), *Ignudo*, 1606
Red chalk, 38.8 × 27.8 cm
British Museum, London

The expressive drawing of a blind man groping his way forward with outstretched arms was a study for the corresponding figure within a group of the blind and sick in *The Miracles of Saint Francis Xavier* (ca. 1617/18; Kunsthistorisches Museum, Vienna). The altarpiece painting had been commissioned by the Jesuit Order in Antwerp, one of Rubens's most important clients. In an earlier oil sketch, the man is shown as old but still able to see, even if poorly, clutching a staff, but in the present drawing and the finished painting he is completely blind. This was a means of demonstrating the effectiveness of the miraculous healings of Saint Francis Xavier in accordance with Counter-Reformation propaganda. Chalk studies of this sort demonstrate the great precision with which Rubens designed individual figures, studying expression, gesture, pose, and musculature down to the smallest detail. Such drawings also served as models for workshop assistants who aided in the execution of his commissions, and Rubens stored them carefully for future reference. The *Study of a Male Nude Falling*, for example, was created for *The Great Last Judgment* (ca. 1617; Alte Pinakothek, Munich) but was also used by Rubens for other works.

The numerous extant copies by Rubens after the Sistine Chapel frescoes bear further witness to his intensive study of Michelangelo (fig. 22). In addition, probably while in Florence or Rome, he acquired several drawings by Michelangelo for his own outstanding art collection, which he later exhibited in his palatial house in Antwerp. Besides drawings, his collection contained paintings, ivory works, engraved gems, and ancient sculptures. The Albertina houses significant parts of Rubens's collection of master drawings, including four of Michelangelo's most beautiful sheets, all drawn on both sides. They bear the inscription "C[oll.] P P Rubens" (inv. no. 116, 118, 120, 123); on the sheet with the *Male Nude Seen from the Rear*, the inscription "Collectione di P P Rubens" was supplemented (inv. no. 123v)—probably by a dealer or later owner—with the comment "impossible de trouver plus beau" (impossible to find anything more beautiful). Rubens also owned a copy after Michelangelo's *The Last Judgment* and Rosso Fiorentino's *Reclining Male Nude*, both then considered to be from the hand of Michelangelo. It is noteworthy that these sheets consist primarily of studies of nudes—the aspect of Michelangelo's work that Rubens particularly admired, collected for study purposes, derived joy from, and was deeply indebted to. In his will, Rubens arranged for his own drawings and his collection to be safeguarded after his death in the hope that a son or son-in-law would also become a painter. When that did not happen, the drawings collection was sold in 1657, seventeen years after Rubens's death, and thus dispersed. It is a fortunate coincidence that Duke Albert of Saxe-Teschen, the founder of the Albertina, was able to reunite in a single collection not only one of the largest assemblages of drawings by Rubens but also parts of the Antwerp artist's own exceptional collection.

EM

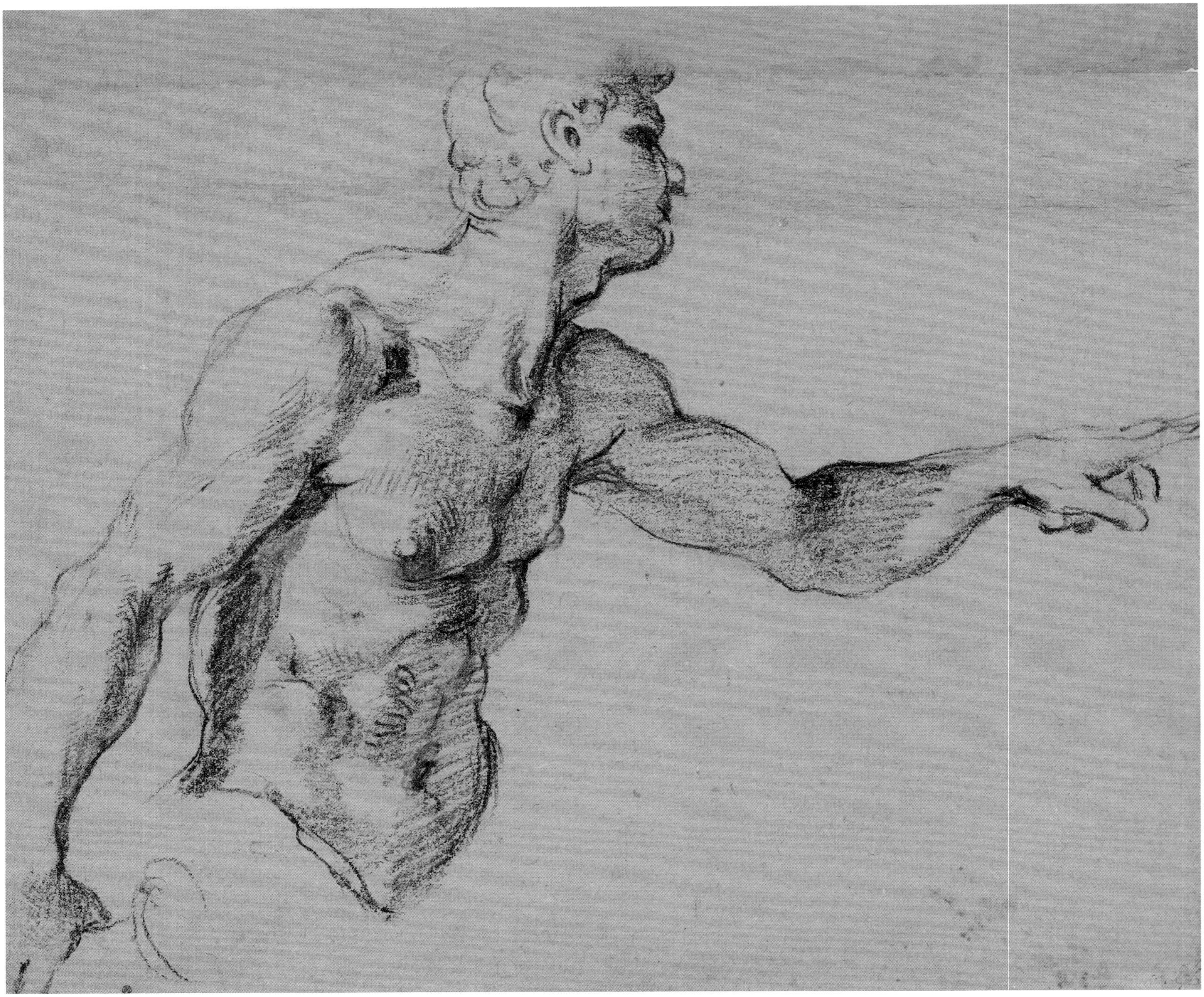

Agostino Carracci
Male Nude Holding a Vessel in Lowered Right Hand, with Left Arm Outstretched, ca. 1600–1602
The ALBERTINA Museum, Vienna

Annibale Carracci
Male Figure, Seated to the Left, Holding a Staff with Both Hands, last third of the 16th century
The ALBERTINA Museum, Vienna

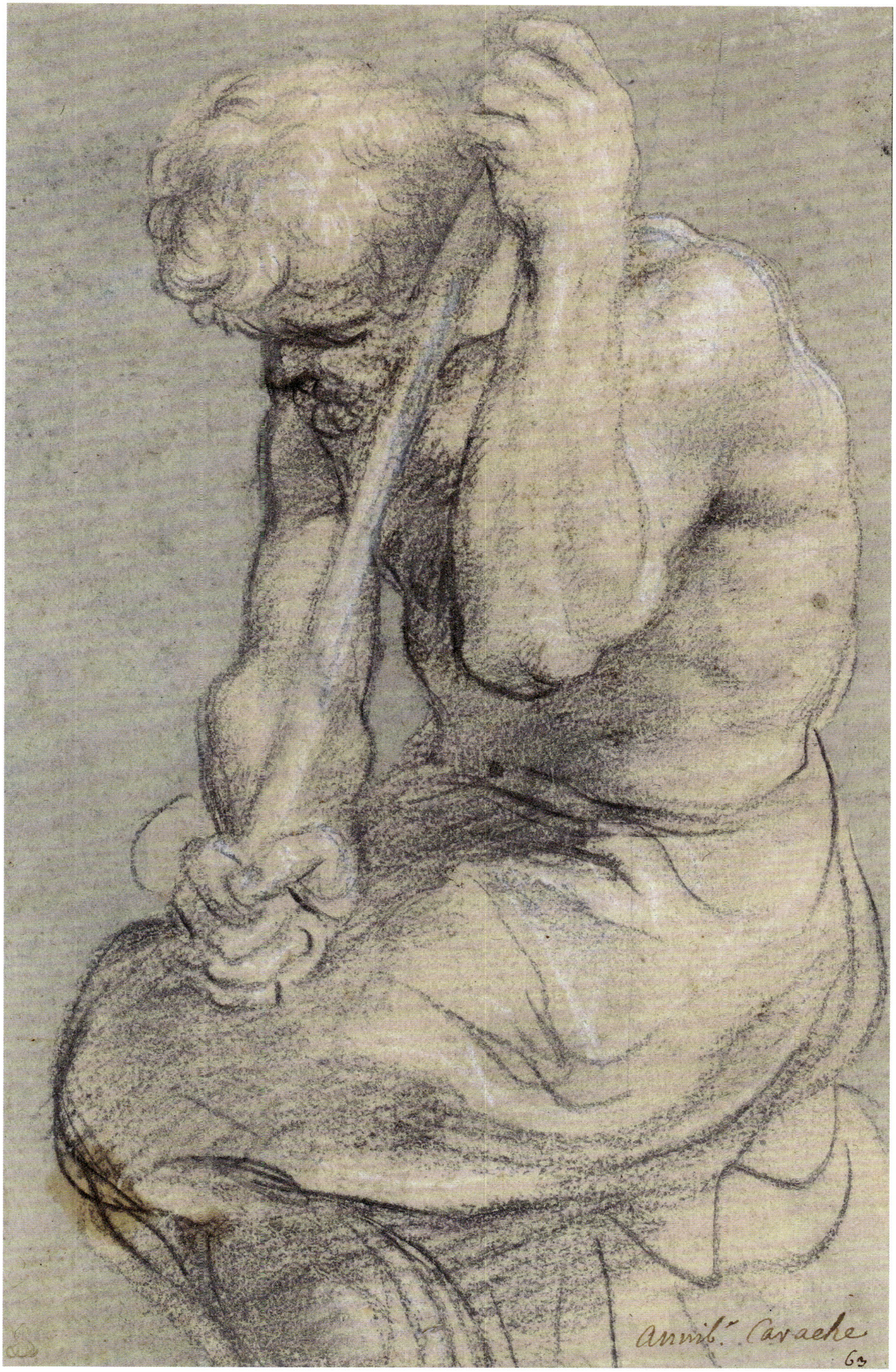

Annib.^e Carache
63

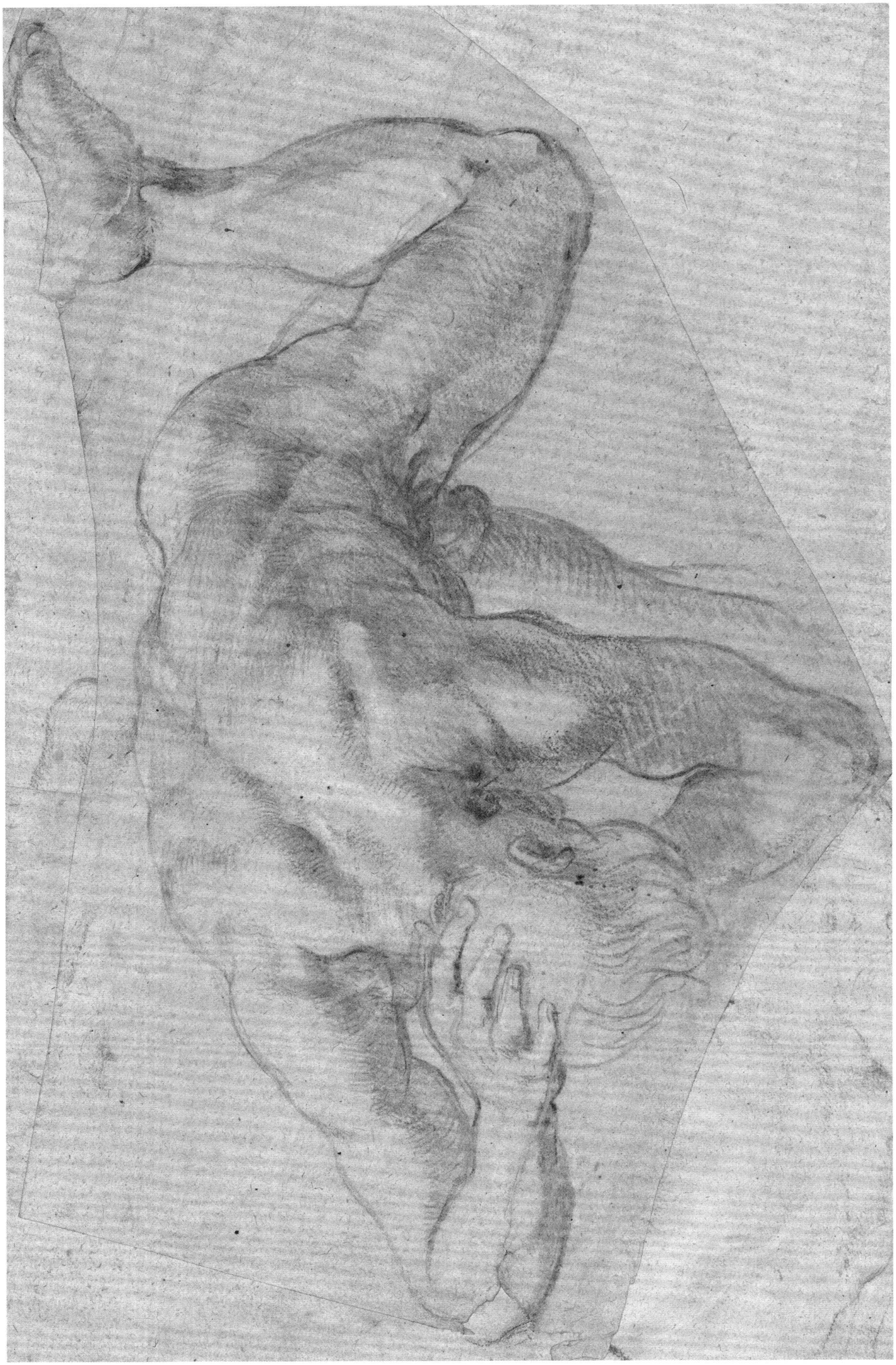

Peter Paul Rubens
Study of a Male Nude Falling,
first third of the 17th century
The ALBERTINA Museum,
Vienna

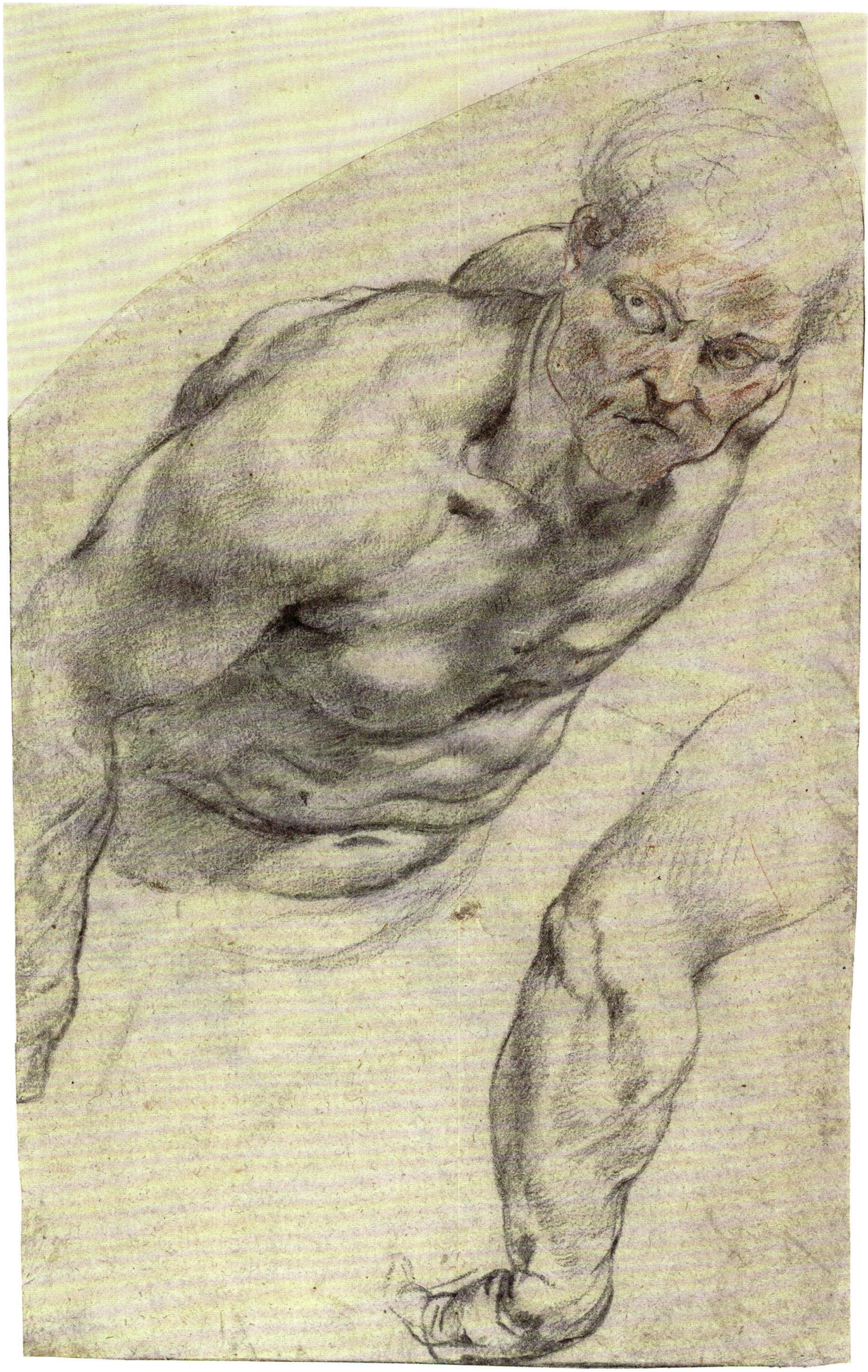

Peter Paul Rubens
Study of a Male Nude Leaning Forward, ca. 1613
The ALBERTINA Museum, Vienna

Peter Paul Rubens
A Blind Man with Arms Outstretched,
ca. 1617/18
The ALBERTINA Museum, Vienna

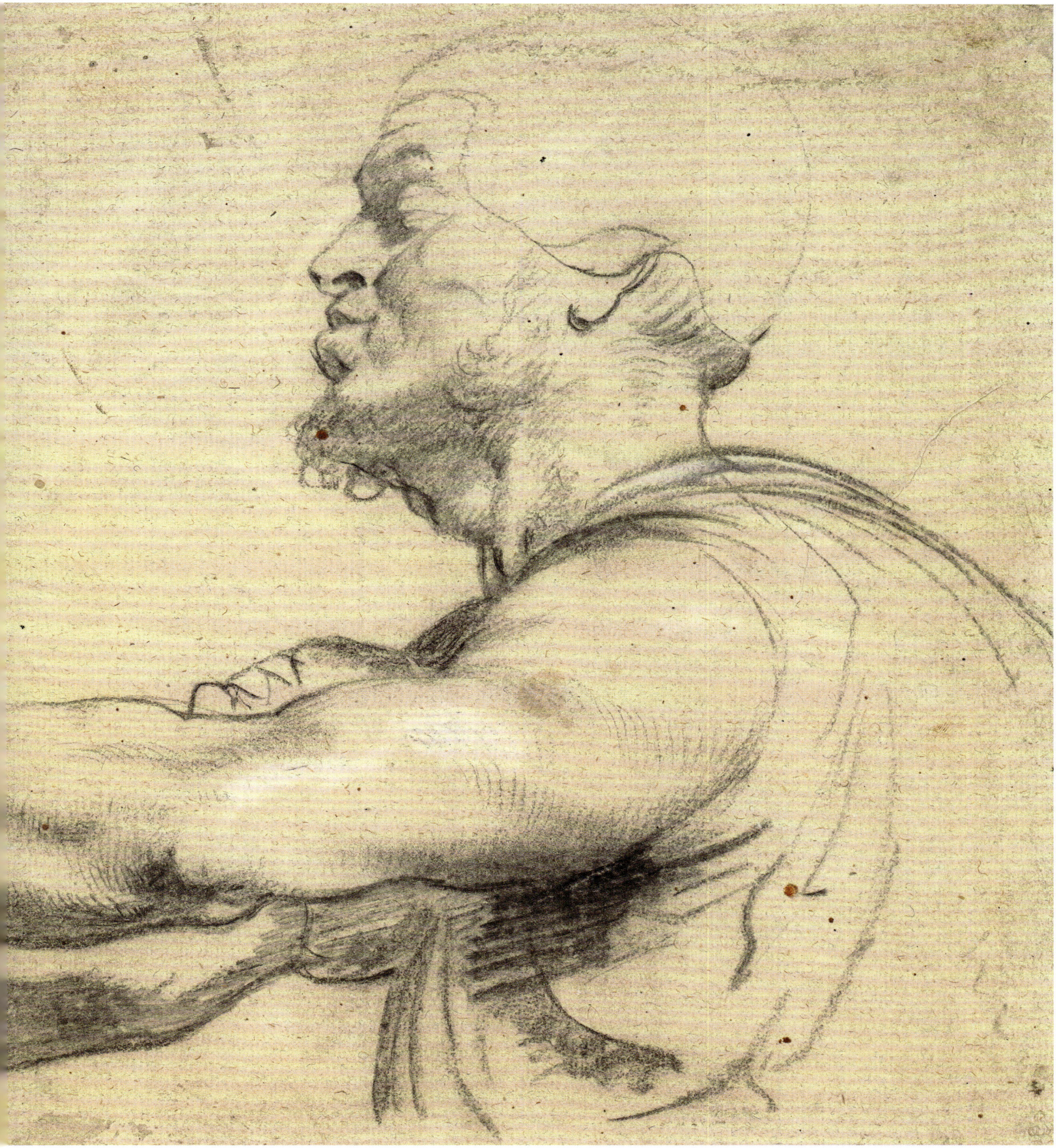

"Michelangesque," or The Canon in Full Bloom

In the eighteenth century, almost two hundred years after Michelangelo's death, the type of athletic, muscular nude devised by him remained the prevailing model for portrayal of the beautiful, idealized male physique. This was reflected in the training at art academies, where students learned drawing after the live model. Life drawing had already been practiced in the seventeenth century at the Carracci school in Bologna, for example, but it truly came into prominence in the art academies of the eighteenth century. Academic activity in Rome had a seminal impact. The city's two leading centers of artistic training were the Accademia di San Luca, founded as early as in the sixteenth century, and the drawing school on the Capitoline Hill known as the Accademia del Nudo (i.e., Academy of the Nude), established in 1754 by Pope Benedict XIV. Instruction at the Accademia del Nudo placed special emphasis on drawing after live models—exclusively male at the time. The nude studies produced in those classes are characterized by great precision in the modeling and articulation of musculature and by an interest in complicated poses and extreme foreshortenings. In this respect, these academic nudes ultimately derive from Michelangelo's anatomical drawings, such as the famous studies for the *Battle of Cascina* and the fresco of the Sistine Chapel ceiling. Even though academic drawing was based directly on the posed model, its fundamental approach to the idealization and staging of the body was a legacy of Michelangelo.

One of the most important academy professors was Anton Raphael Mengs, from Dresden, who taught at both Roman institutions. He became one of the leading Neoclassical artists and worked as court painter to the elector of Saxony and later to the king of Spain. He was an ardent admirer of classical antiquity, a passionate collector of plaster casts of ancient sculpture, and a close friend of the archaeologist and art theorist Johann Joachim Winckelmann, who had a decisive influence on the ideas of Neoclassicism. In agreement with Winckelmann's famed *Gedancken über die Nachahmung der Griechischen Wercke in der Mahlerey und Bildhauer-Kunst* (*Reflections on the Imitation of Greek Works in Painting and Sculpture*), first published in 1755, Mengs regarded ancient Greek sculpture as an ideal to be emulated. Yet his teaching also recognized the importance of studying after the live model. Mengs's own drawings are outstanding examples of the eighteenth-century academic nude. They are characterized by skillful foreshortening and by modeling composed of cross-hatching and white heightening. His interest in the play of muscles under the

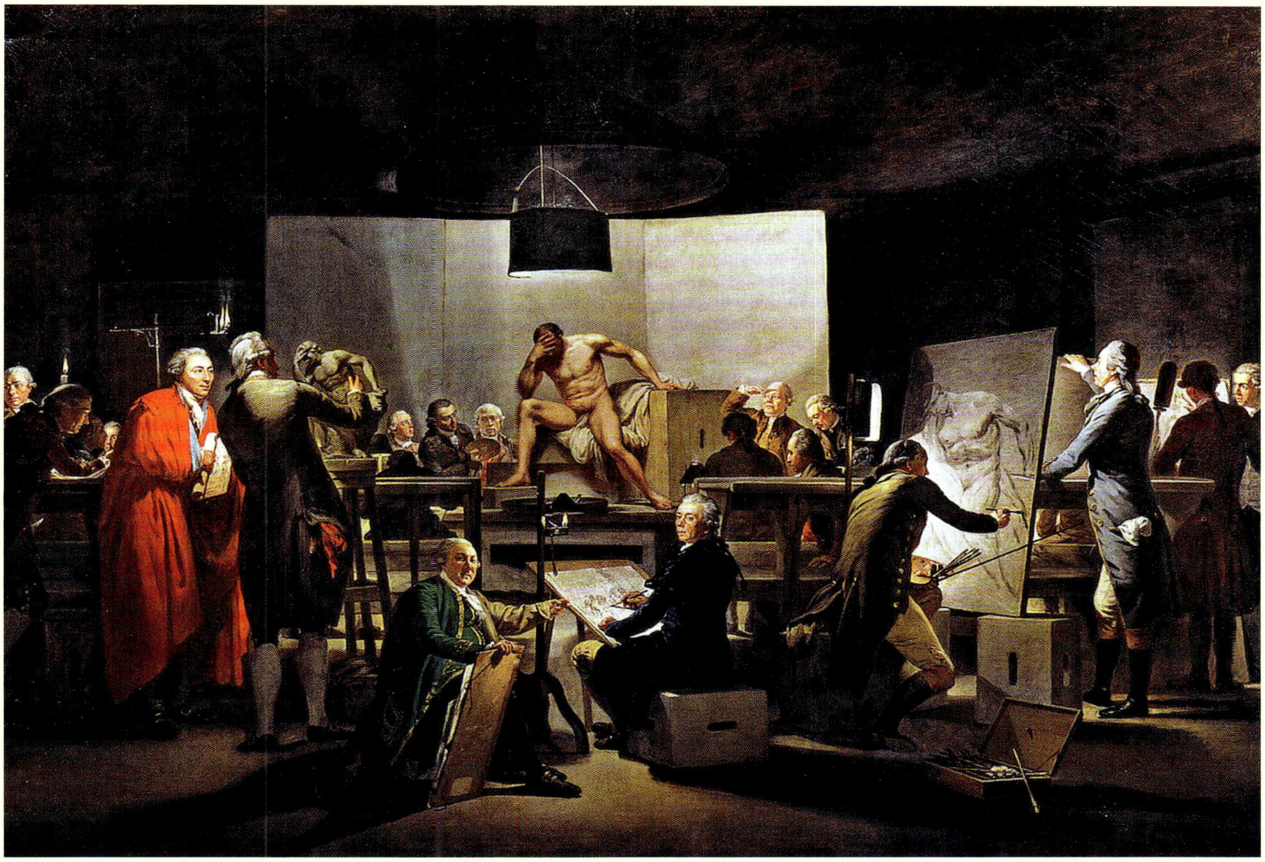

23 Martin Ferdinand Quadal, *Life Class of the Vienna Academy in the St. Anne Building*, 1787
Oil on canvas, 145 × 206.5 cm
Akademie der bildenden Künste, Vienna

skin and in the powerful, athletic ideal of the body was informed primarily by Michelangelo, as well as by Raphael.

Mengs's main rival, Pompeo Girolamo Batoni, also studied drawing after the live model in Rome. A sheet by Batoni from 1765 in the Albertina offers a prime example of the complicated poses that nude models often had to assume. Such twisted and unnatural postures enabled (budding) artists to study the human body from a wide variety of views, and they recall Michelangelo's studies for figures in the Sistine Chapel, such as the Libyan Sibyl or the *ignudi*. These poses helped students to learn the fundamentals of depicting the human physique, lessons they would put to use for large history paintings. The academy professors were responsible for devising a variety of poses for the models. Often the models had to hold difficult positions over long periods of time, a task for which they used aids such as platforms, cushions, or staffs.

In the eighteenth century, the study of the male nude was central to artistic training not only at the academies in Rome but also at the one in Vienna (fig. 23), which had been founded by Peter Strudel in 1692. One of the most noteworthy Viennese representatives of the academic study of the nude is Jacob Matthias Schmutzer. In 1766, with the support of the Dowager Empress, Maria Theresa, he founded the city's Engravers' Academy. As director there, he focused his teaching on drawing the human figure. His approach was deeply influenced by Michelangelo's ideal of the body, as is clear in Schmutzer's drawing *Mercury Putting Argus to Sleep* executed in 1770. This work exemplifies his ability to bring the male nude to paper using masterful gradations of chalk shading. His primary interest lay not in narrating the mythological story but in depicting the nude body in various poses and views. Likewise, a chalk drawing made in 1789 by Johann Peter Pichler, a pupil of Schmutzer, testifies to virtuosic skill in portraying the nude male body. The perfection of Pichler's modeling of the back muscles is reminiscent of Michelangelo's drawings of figures seen from behind, first and foremost those for the *Battle of Cascina*. The idealized nude in the manner of Michelangelo was clearly a touchstone for academicians in Vienna. In a drawing attributed to Joseph Walter, an elderly head is even placed on top of a vigorous, youthful male body as is the case with Michelangelo's *Moses*.

Alongside drawing from the live model, the study of ancient sculpture remained an essential part of artistic training. Along these lines, Mengs's pupil Giovanni Battista Casanova drew the famous marble Wrestlers in the Uffizi of Florence in about 1790. This sculptural group is one of the most important Roman antiquities based on a lost Greek original. It was discovered in Rome near the Porta San Giovanni in 1583 and brought to Florence in 1677. The work was considered an ideal model for young artists learning how accurately to depict the anatomy of the male body in combat, thus also studying complex poses and movement. Drawings created after the Wrestlers are also related to Michelangelo's depictions of men grappling with one another, including sheets that show David's struggle against Goliath from different perspectives.

Drawing the male nude remained a main benchmark of academic art education throughout the eighteenth century. In drawings based on live models, the most important artists of the time, such as Mengs, Batoni, and Schmutzer, brought draftsmanly precision to perfection—in the modeling of muscles, in the play of light and shadow on the skin, and in the correct translation of complex poses onto paper. The figures they created were based on an ideal of the athletic male body that ultimately originated in the art of Michelangelo.

LE

Anton Raphael Mengs
Seated Male Nude, ca. 1760
The ALBERTINA Museum, Vienna

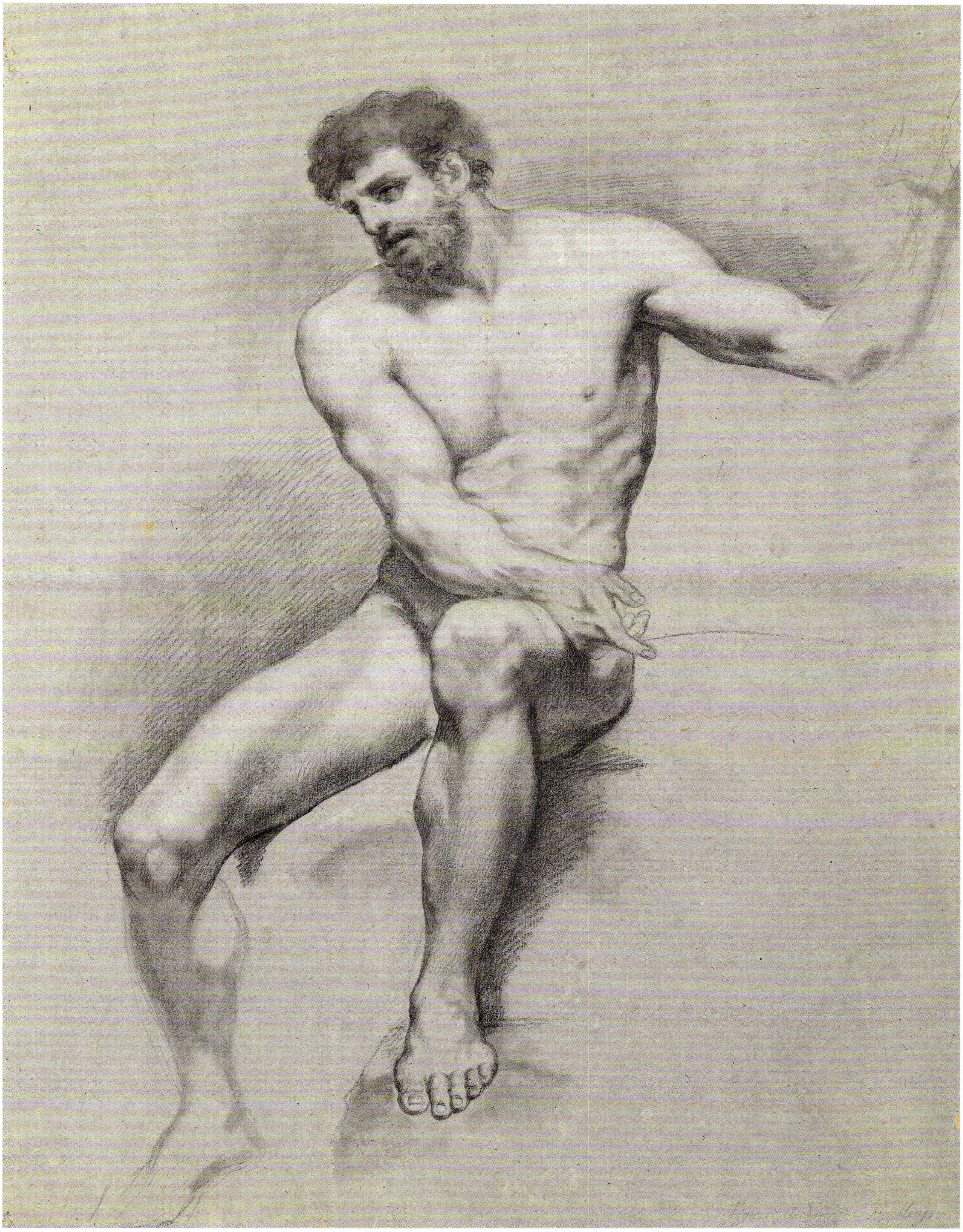

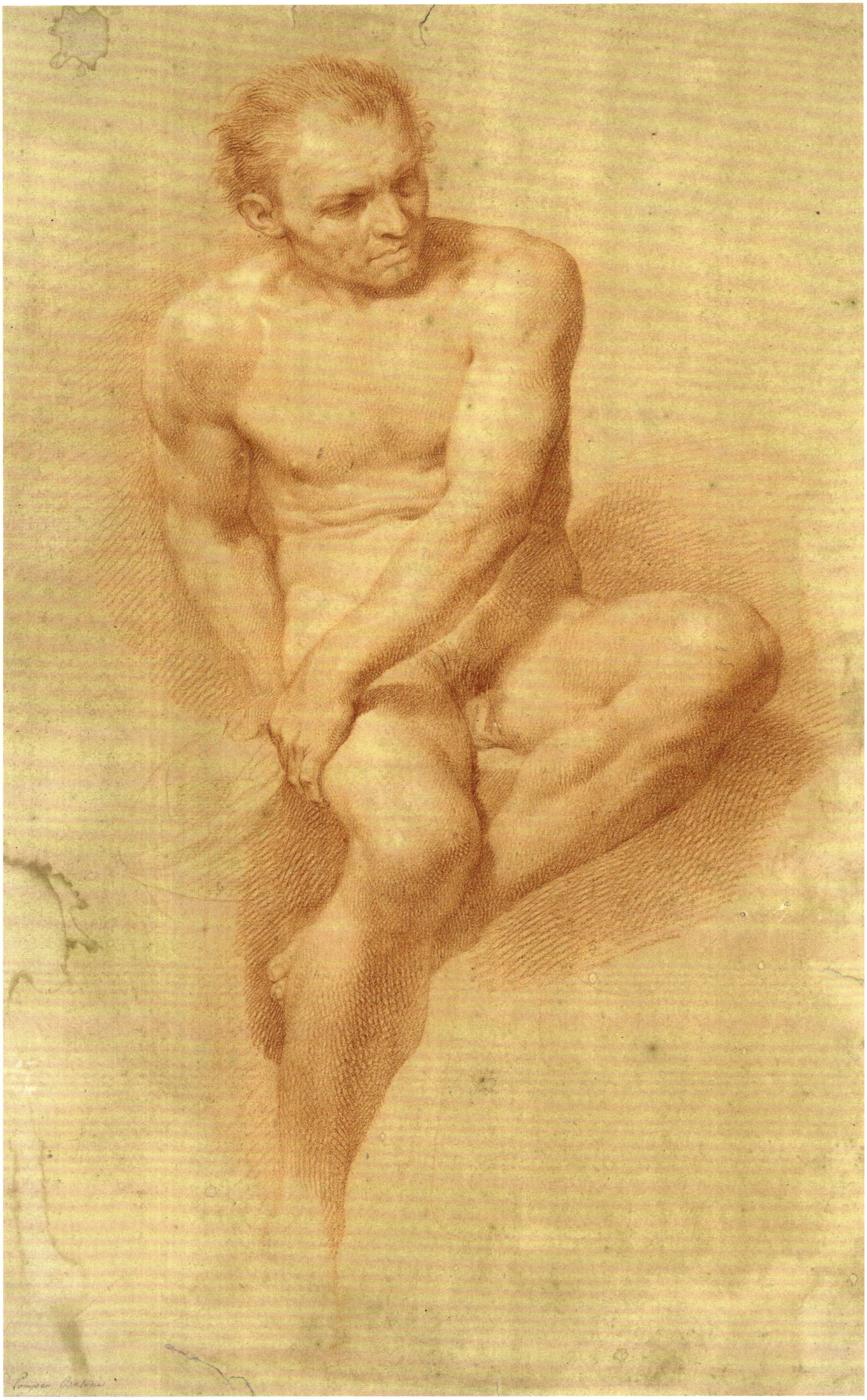

Pompeo Girolamo Batoni
Male Nude Seated on a Block of Stone, 1760s
The ALBERTINA Museum, Vienna

Pompeo Girolamo Batoni
Study of a Nude Youth Seated on Stone Steps, 1765
The ALBERTINA Museum, Vienna

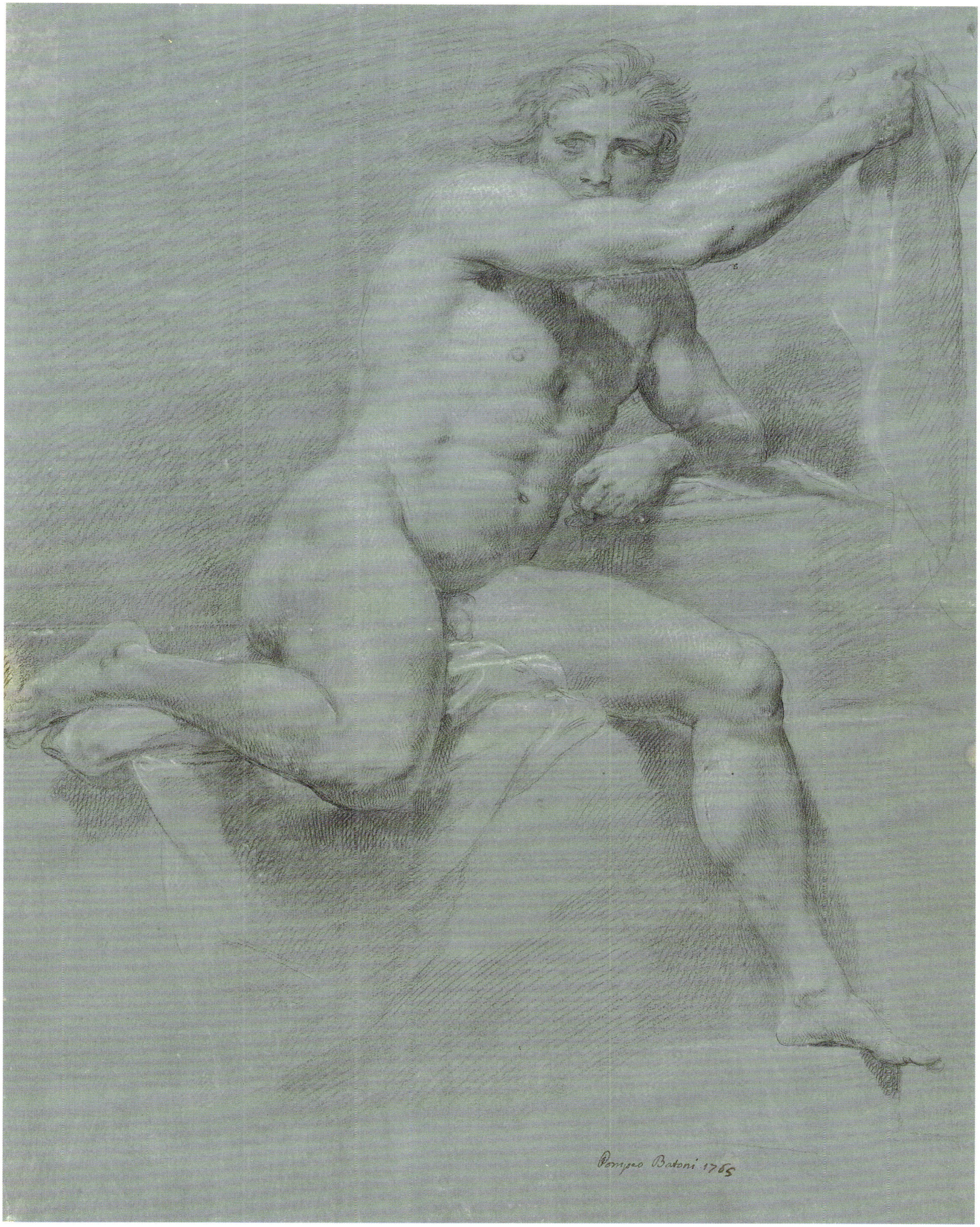
Pompeo Batoni 1765

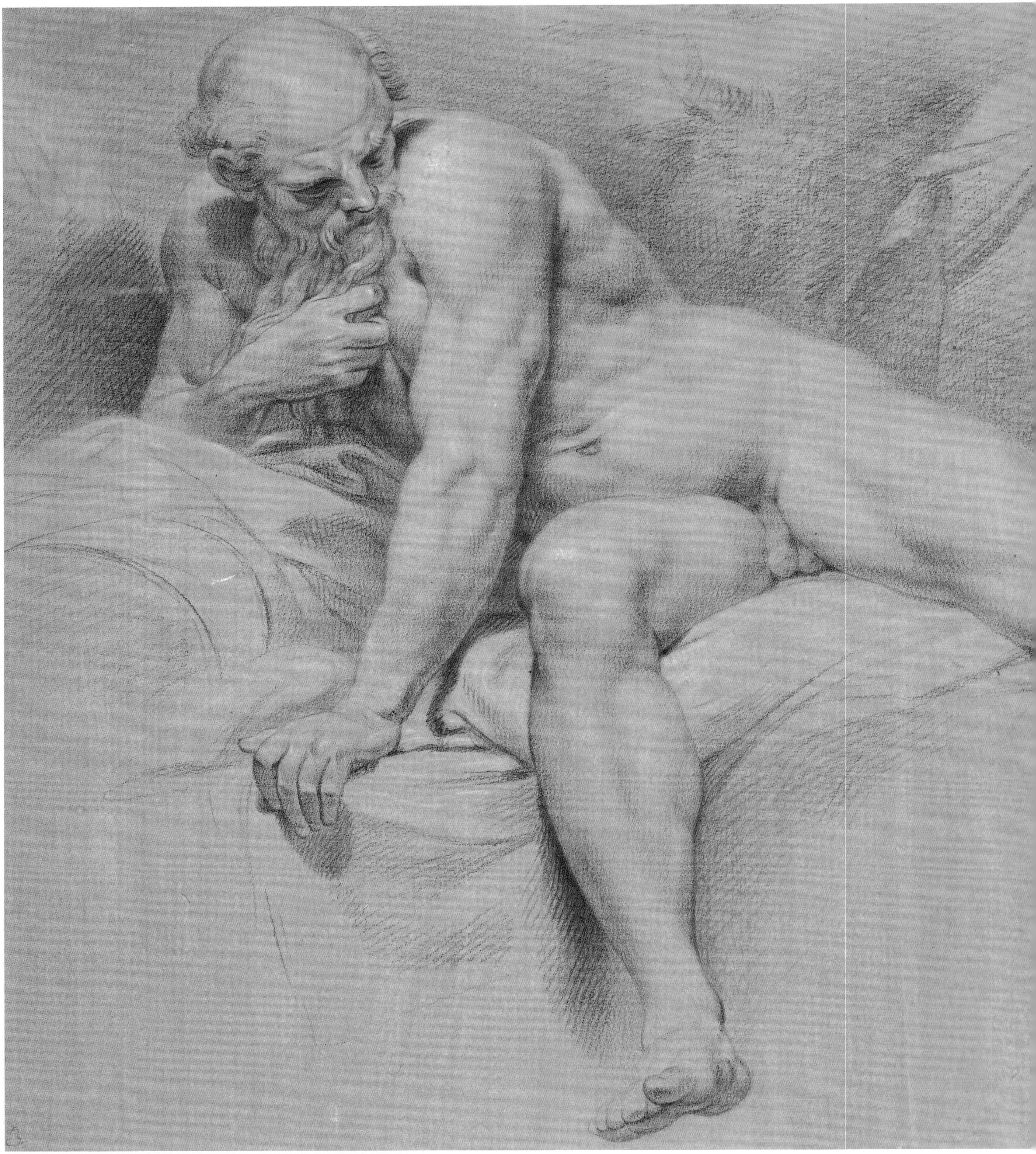

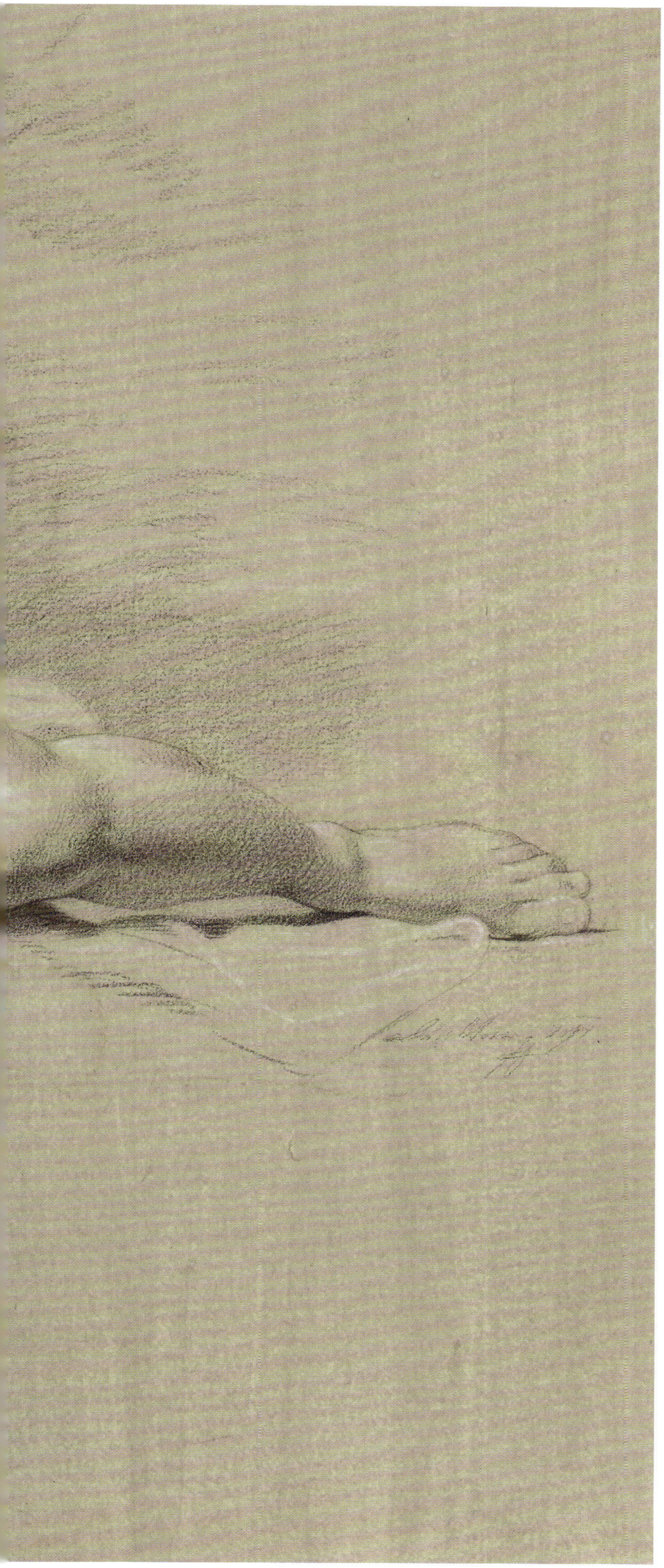

Attributed to Joseph Walter
Elderly Male Nude, ca. 1791–1797
The ALBERTINA Museum, Vienna

The mythological scene *Mercury Putting Argus to Sleep* derives from Ovid's *Metamorphoses* and illustrates an episode from the story of Io. To seduce this priestess of Juno, Jupiter transformed himself into a cloud. Then, in an attempt to conceal his infidelity from Juno, his jealous wife, Jupiter changed Io into a heifer—but Juno was not deceived. She asked for the heifer as a gift and had it guarded by Argus, the hundred-eyed giant who remained vigilant even in sleep. To free Io, Jupiter sent the messenger god Mercury, who lulled Argus to sleep with music from his flute and then slayed him. Jacob Matthias Schmutzer omitted narrative elements from his drawing and instead concentrated on the figures of Mercury and Argus, that is, on the depiction of the nude male body. The motif can be identified thanks to two details of the standing figure that are recognizable as attributes of Mercury: the mouthpiece of a flute, barely visible above his left shoulder and the suggestion of a winged cap through his hair. The artist used fine hatching and white heightening to model the muscles, effectively orchestrating the complex muscular forms of Mercury's back as well as the abdomen of the reclining Argus. Schmutzer, who taught at the Viennese Engravers' Academy, drew both figures from live models. In its quality and refined execution, the sheet is an outstanding example of the eighteenth-century academic nude.

LE

Jacob Matthias Schmutzer
Mercury Putting Argus to Sleep, 1770
The ALBERTINA Museum, Vienna

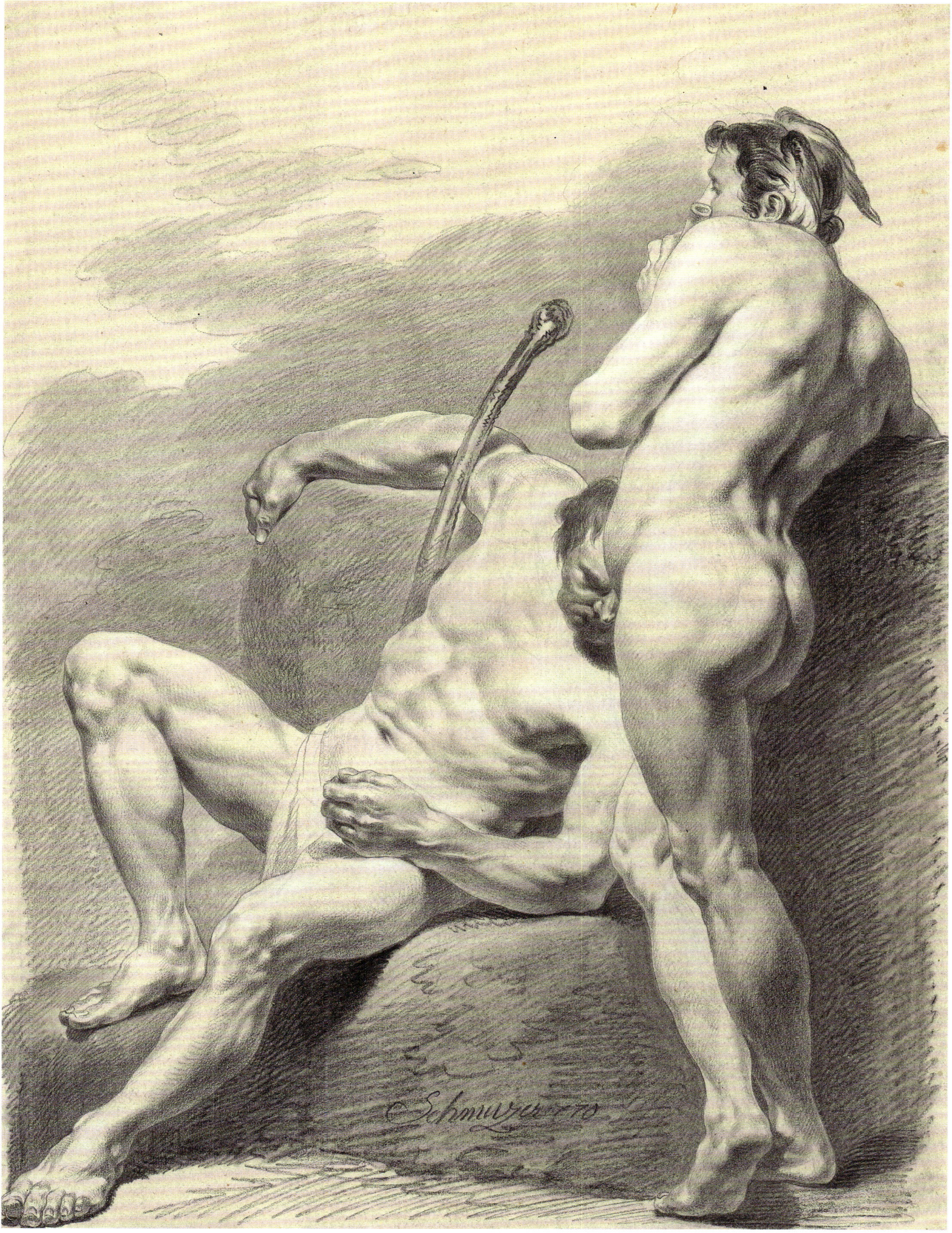

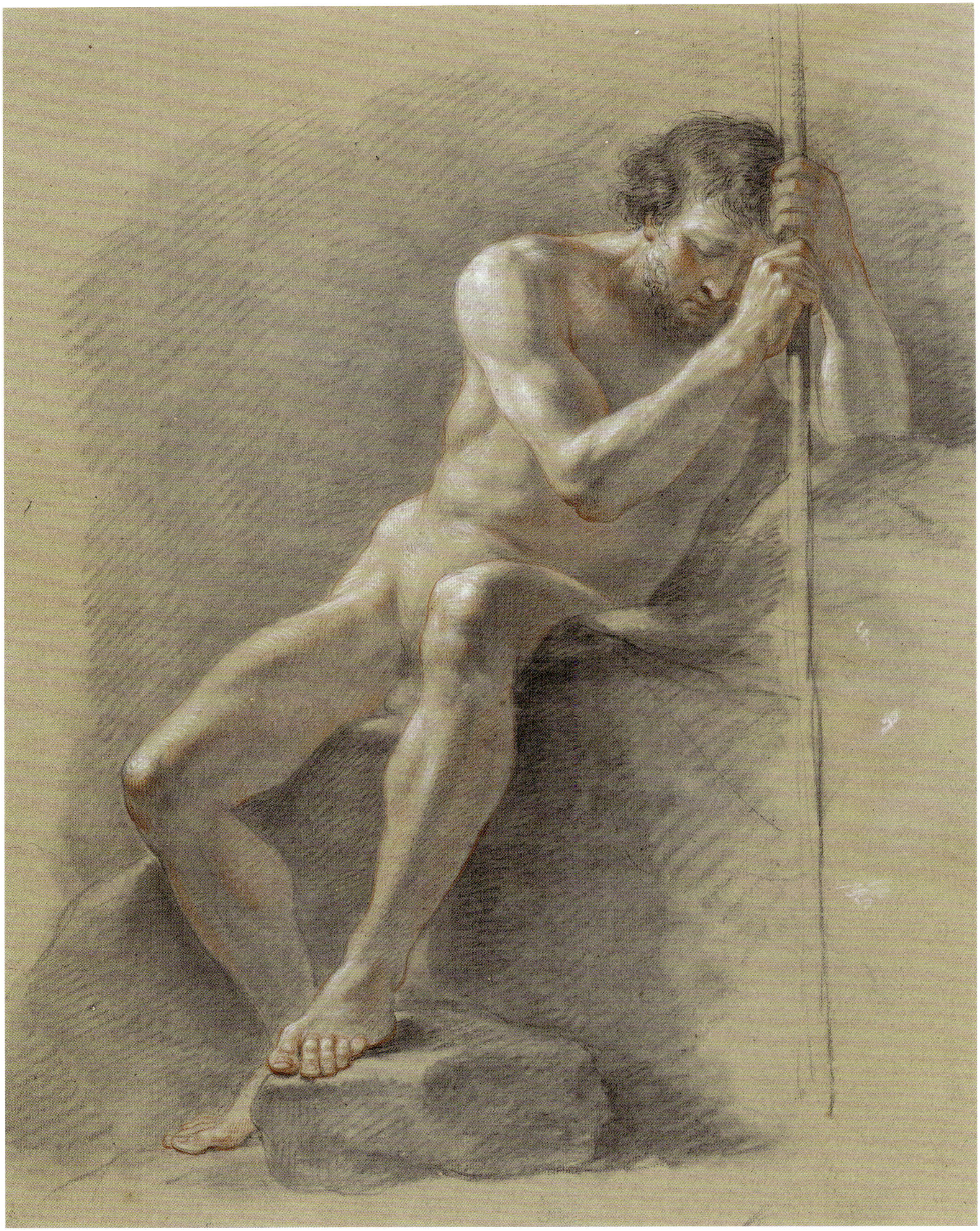

Francesco Bartolozzi
Seated Male Nude Leaning on a Staff, ca. 1760–1764
The ALBERTINA Museum, Vienna

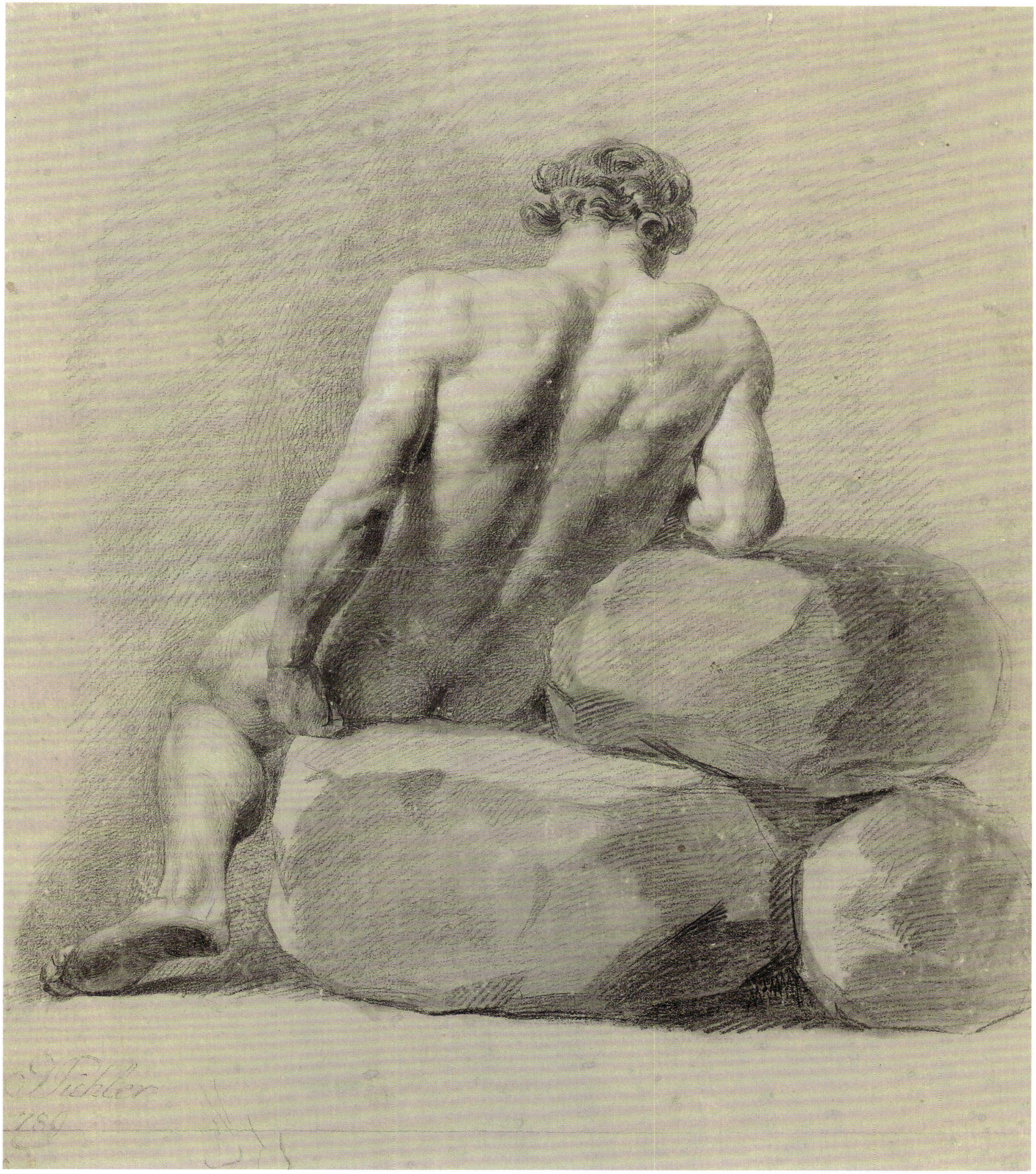

Johann Peter Pichler
Male Nude Seen from the Rear, 1789
The ALBERTINA Museum, Vienna

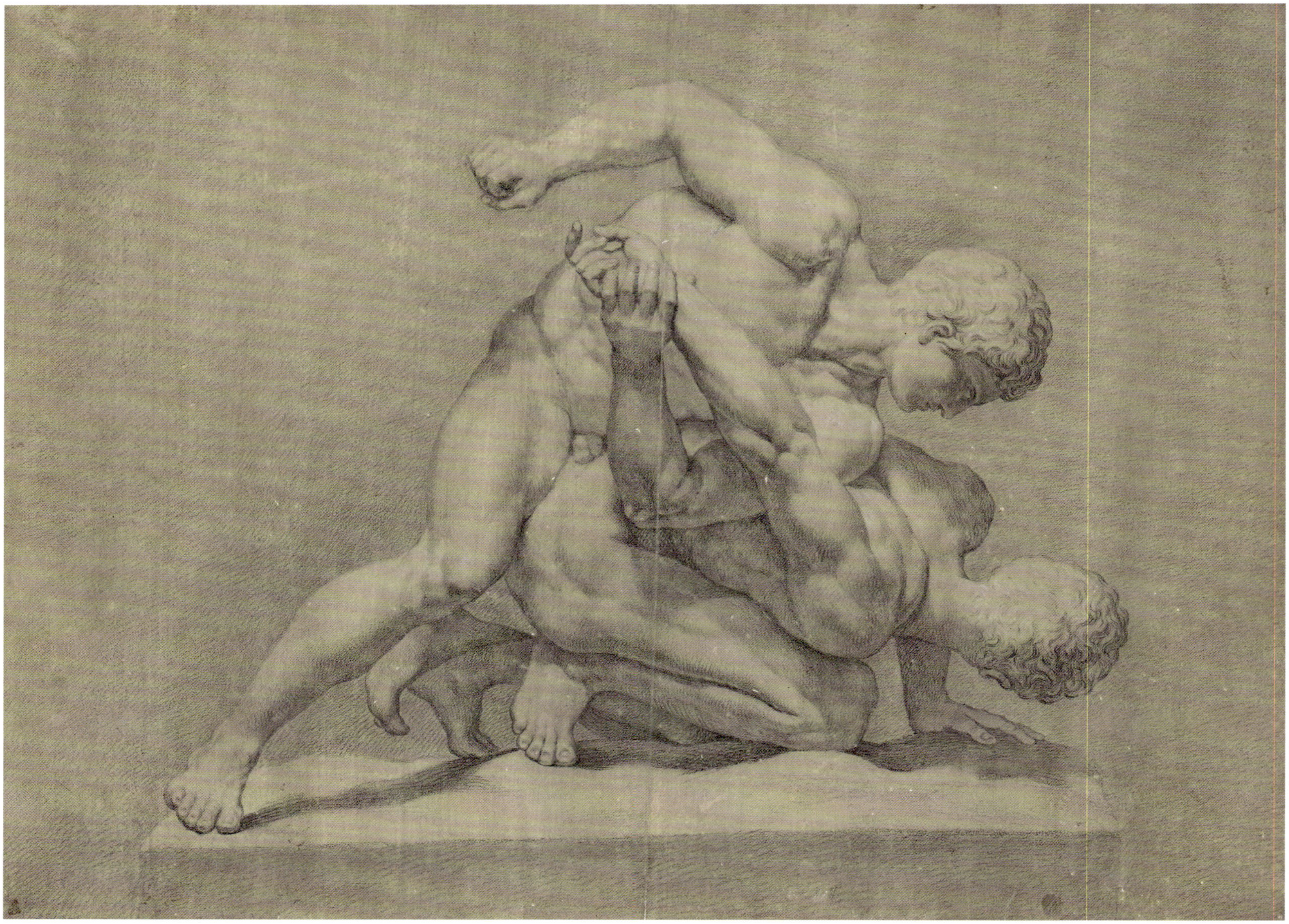

Giovanni Battista Casanova
The Florentine Wrestlers, ca. 1790
The ALBERTINA Museum, Vienna

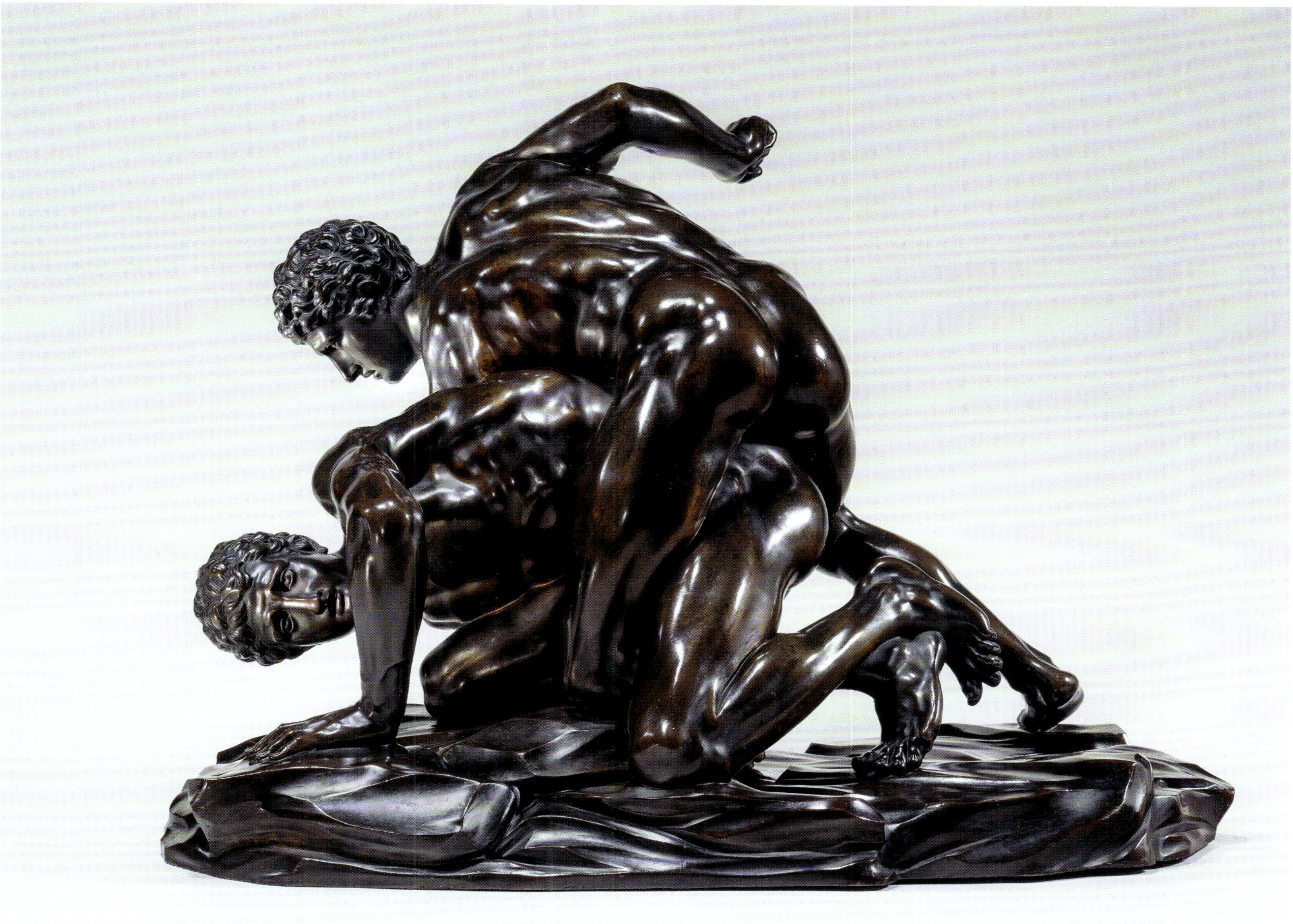

Massimiliano Soldani-Benzi
The Wrestlers, ca. 1710
Bayerisches Nationalmuseum, Munich

The Female, or "The Dark Side of the Moon"

The subliminal positioning of woman alongside the Moon—suggested by the above title—emerges more clearly when we turn our attention back toward the culture of antiquity, with its impressive breadth of astronomical knowledge, a time in which the feminine principle was greatly esteemed: Zeus (known to the Romans as Jupiter) was often inflamed with passion for goddesses and human women alike, and never shied away from undergoing a deceptive transformation in order to achieve a sexual conquest, in the process bestowing a multitude of new divine and semi-divine offspring upon the world. Aphrodite (i.e., Venus), the incarnation of beauty and erotic love, was intensely and universally revered, and was depicted as a flawlessly perfect nude woman (fig. 24). Society afforded at least some women—depending upon region, epoch, and social status, of course—financial independence and high prestige; some, like Cleopatra and Julia Agrippina, were even rulers.

Things changed, however, with the rise of Christianity: the end time was awaited as an imminent event, rendering knowledge of the natural sciences seemingly obsolete. When doomsday failed to arrive, much of this learning was simply lost. Jesus, the only Son of God, was conceived and brought into the world by the Virgin Mary in the absence of any sexual union. The monotheistic structure of belief had no place for the gods and goddesses of the Greco-Roman pantheon. The Church's claims to cultural hegemony meant the downfall of the "idols," which now sank out of sight as cultural debris, whether in their entirety or as fragments. Vanishing from view with them, and from collective consciousness, was Venus—and along with her, the beautiful nude human figure. Collateral damage of a patriarchy in the Near Eastern mold: increasingly, women became invisible—before long, they were indeed the proverbial "far side," or even "dark side" of the Moon.

Only Michelangelo's lifetime saw concerted efforts to reverse these tendencies. At the start of the sixteenth century, Nicolaus Copernicus realized that the Earth was a planet. In 1610, with the *Sidereus Nuncius* (*Sidereal Messenger*), Galileo Galilei extended our knowledge of the Moon, having made detailed observations of its near, "bright side," which perpetually faces Earth, using a telescope based on Dutch models.

Meanwhile, the beautiful female nude had made a comeback in the visual arts. Of course, striving to render the female figure with anatomical correctness should not be confused with opportunities for the societal emancipation of women, to say nothing of their perception as individuals. On the contrary, the more Renaissance and Mannerist artists exploited the visual media in order to liberate the female form from its cloth trappings, the more she would become a surface upon which to project stereotypes: pejorative as well as idealizing—and always, moreover, ensuring a degree of distance.

And now, a long leap forward: Only after World War II did women succeed in eluding the masculine gaze, in perceiving themselves independently at long last. In 1949, in the pioneering study *Le Deuxième Sexe* (*The Second Sex*), Simone de Beauvoir showed that woman's biological sex is only first to be understood within society through its cultural and social framing. The frameworks known as "culture" and "social structure" must be appreciated as having been shaped by men, for men. Meanwhile, women artists began using their own bodies in order to reflect on their own views of themselves and to communicate these perceptions publicly. In Kyoto in 1964, in the performance work *Cut Piece,* Yoko Ono alluded to the traditional exposition of the female body. In 1968, Yoko Ono and John Lennon had themselves photographed together in the nude for the cover of their album *Unfinished Music No. 1: Two Virgins* as exemplary of seizing back control of their own bodies, and hence their persons.

Just a decade earlier, in 1959, the Soviet spacecraft known as *Luna 3* had orbited the Moon for the first time ever, transmitting images of its "dark side" back to Earth. And in 1968, the first humans, American astronauts, saw the Moon from behind for the first time with their own eyes.

MP

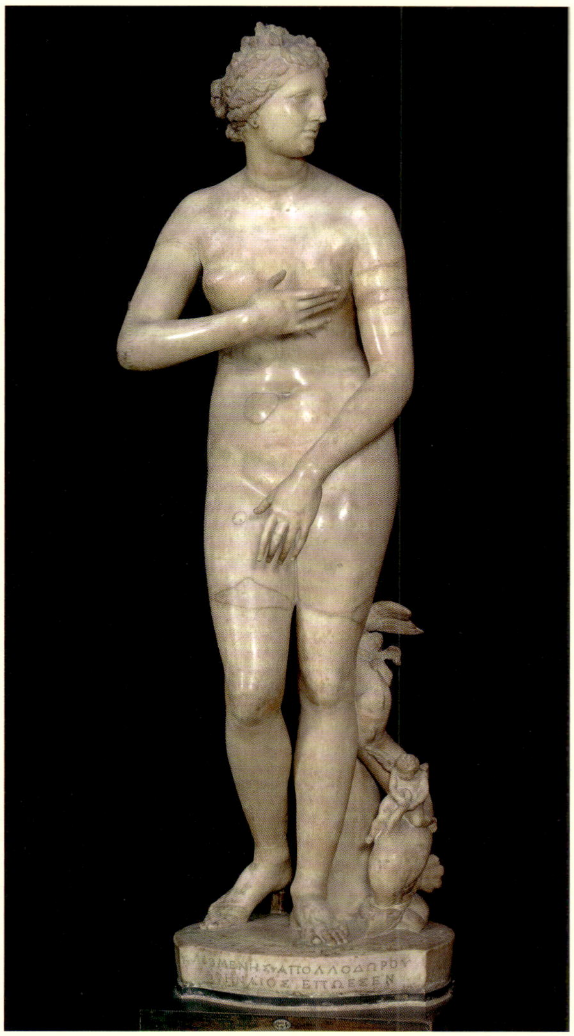

24 Medici Venus, 1st century BC
Roman copy after a Hellenistic recreation of an original by the Greek sculptor Praxiteles, ca. 350–340 BC
Marble, h. 153 cm
Gallerie degli Uffizi, Florence

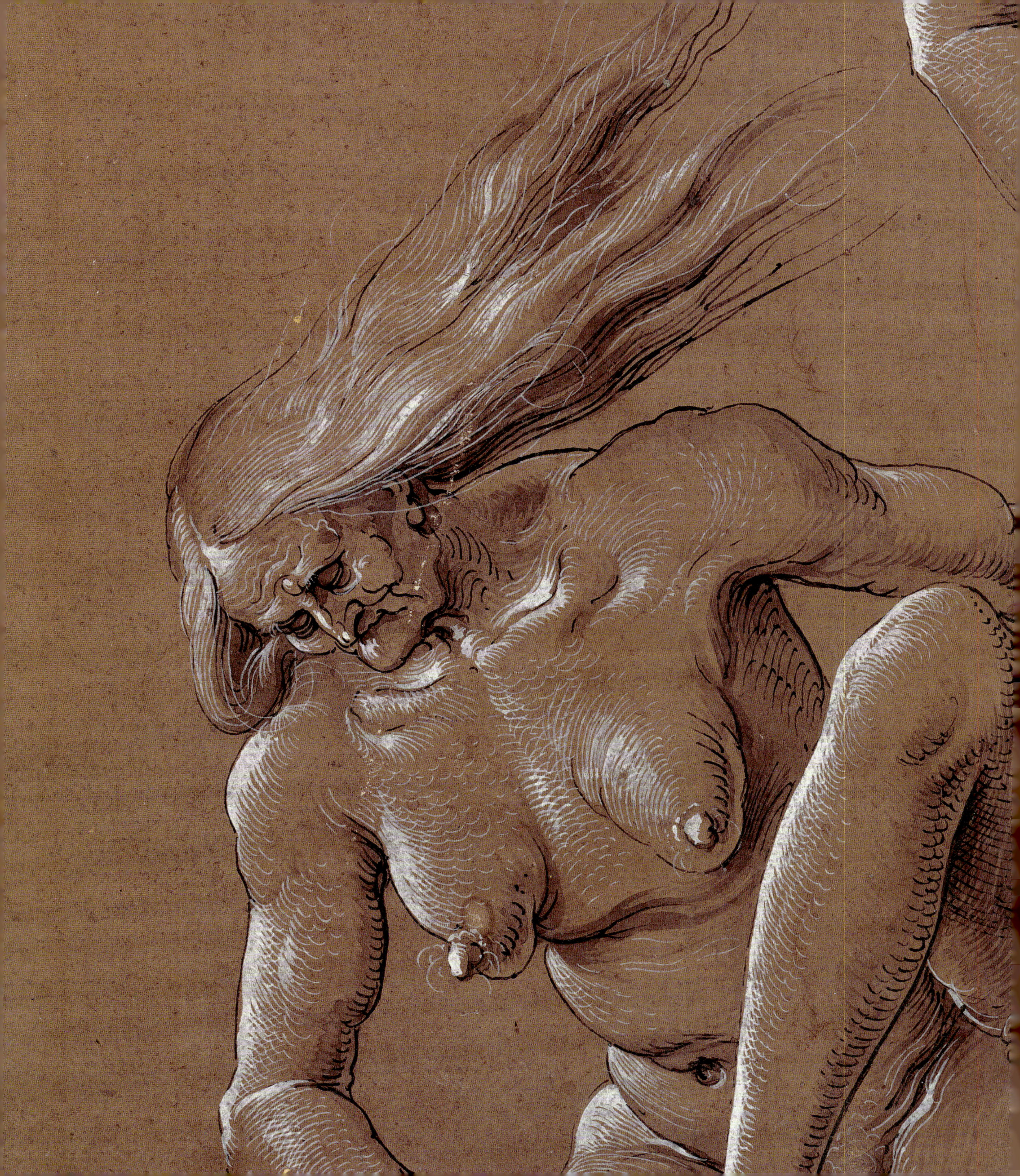

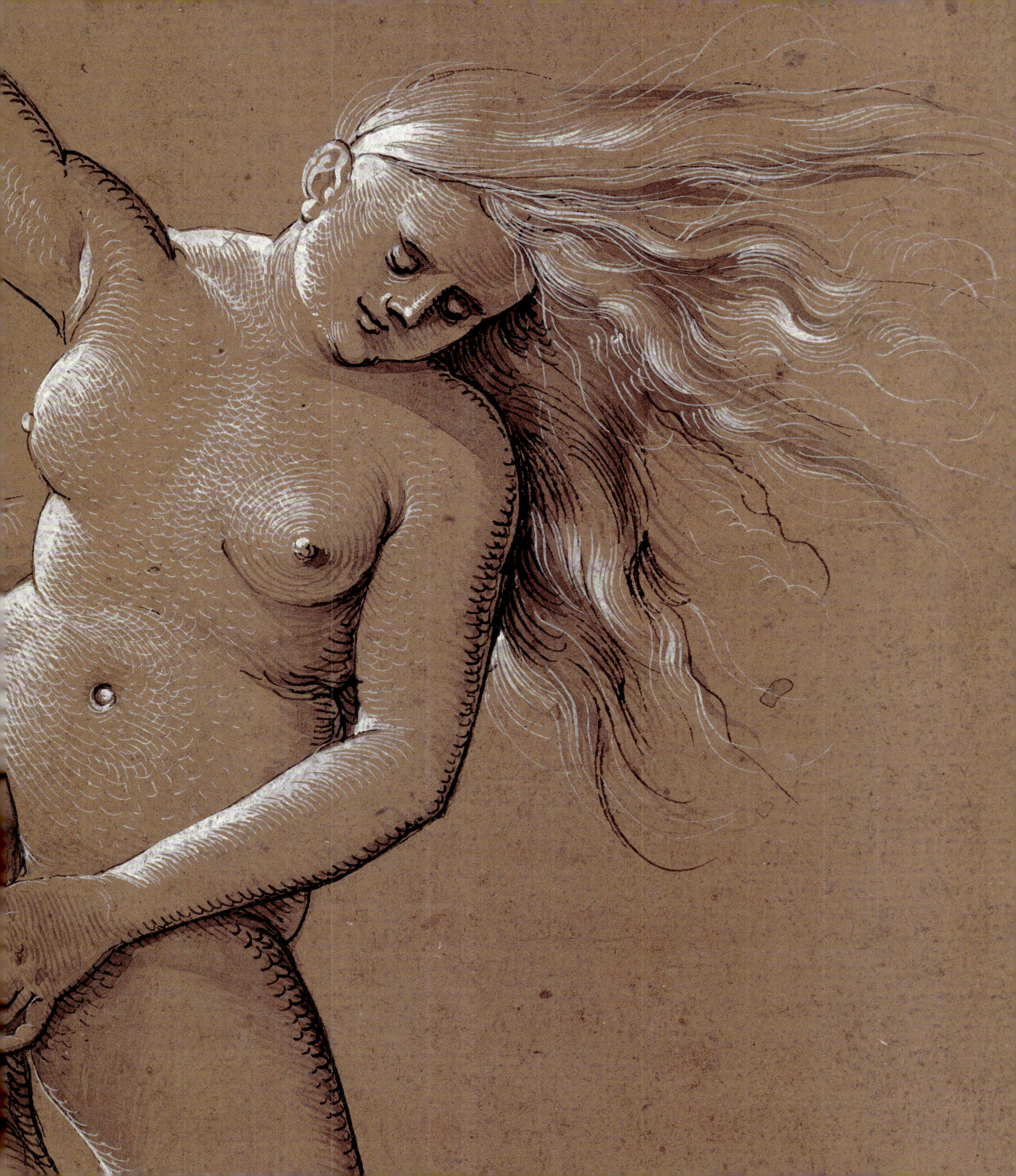

Female Body—
Male Witch Panic

The nineteenth century has bequeathed us an image of the witch as a hideous old woman who lives alone in a desolate cottage in the forest, where she lures children, like poor little Hansel, in order to fatten them up before roasting them as a tasty meal. The shudder of fear evoked by this fairytale is exorcised later when children themselves impersonate the witch; the standard carnival costume consists of a headscarf or pointed hat, ragged clothes, and a broomstick for riding through the air from chimney to chimney.

Recognizing these carnival witches in the beaky nose of a contemporary rubber Halloween mask, we seem to catch a glimpse of the elder sisters of a Hellenistic satyr, whose lascivious and provocative physiognomies vanished from collective memory in late antiquity along with the entire Bacchus cult, only to reappear in the Middle Ages as the grotesque visage of a devil. Tellingly, in *Malleus maleficarum* (*The Hammer of Witches*), first published in Speyer in 1486, Heinrich Kramer, the Alsatian inquisitor, equates satanic demons with Pan, fauns, and satyrs.

The title of Kramer's treatise is already revealing; demons and witches were feared to an equal degree. The latter were regarded as the daughters of human women who had engaged in sexual acts with demons. Such panic around witches and the subsequent witch hunts reached Germany during the second half of the fifteenth century and hence in the cultural milieu of Albrecht Dürer and Hans Baldung, called Grien.

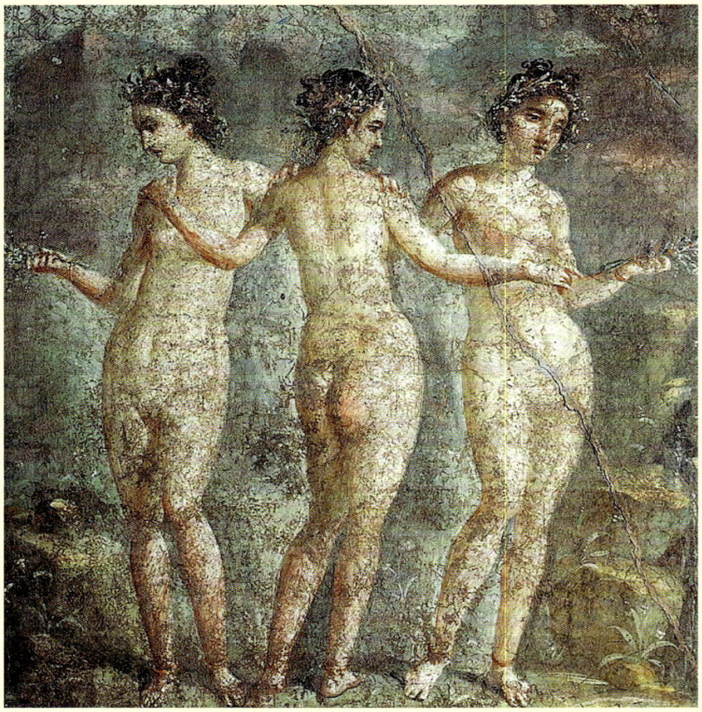

25 *The Three Graces*, 1st century AD
Fresco from Pompeii
Museo Archeologico Nazionale, Naples

Since both artists belonged to Humanist circles, researchers disagree about whether the theme of witchcraft is addressed seriously or, instead, ironically in their works. The fact that, around 1500, witches were also conceived as being young women represents an additional difficulty in interpreting this imagery.

Are the *Four Female Nudes* seen standing close together in Dürer's engraving of 1497 really witches, as Joachim von Sandrart believed in 1675? Coifs, veils, and headscarves identify three of the women as married. The poses adopted by three of them are also suggestive of the Three Graces (fig. 25). The tiered floor facilitates

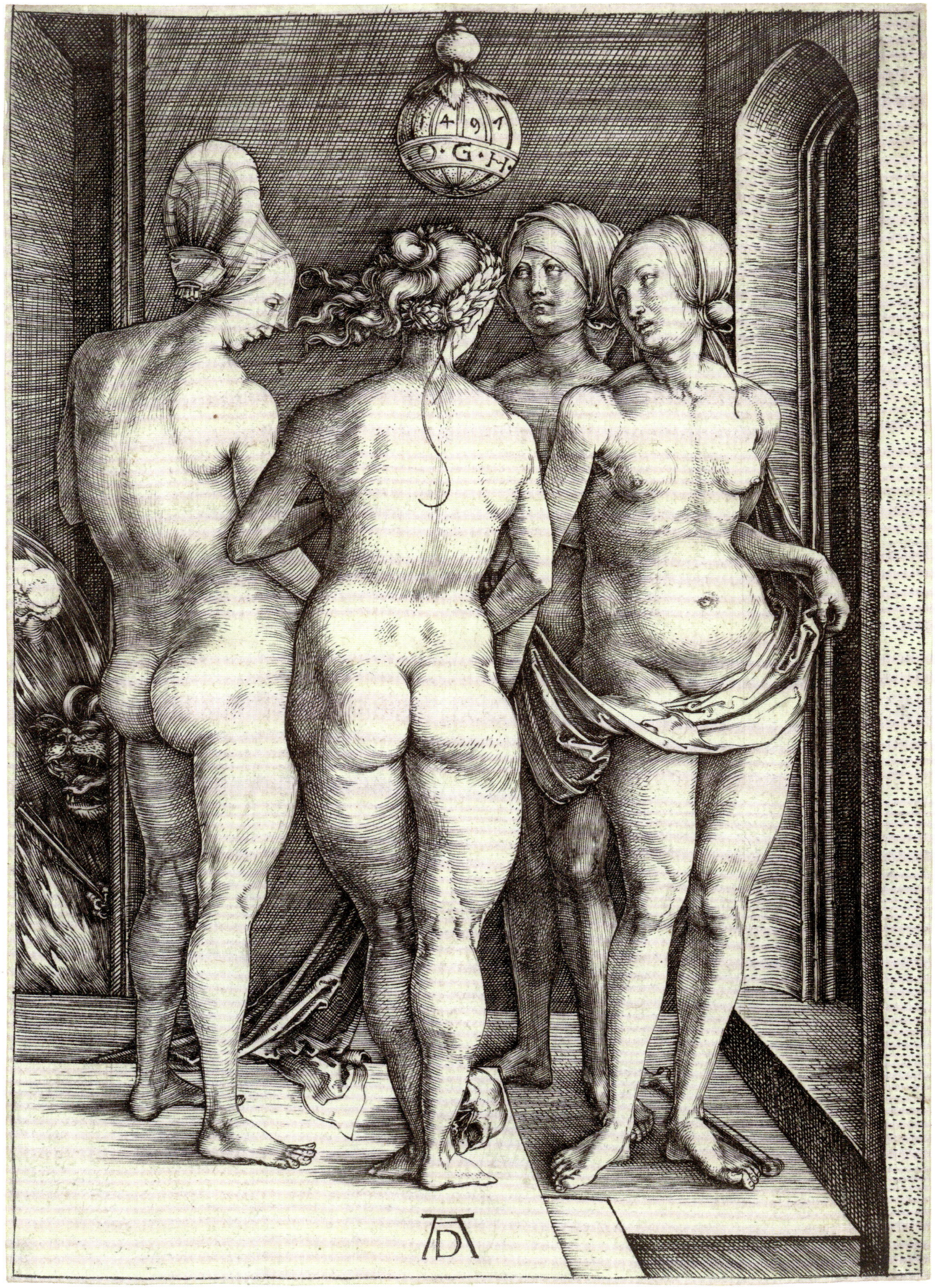

Albrecht Dürer
Four Female Nudes, 1497
The ALBERTINA Museum,
Vienna

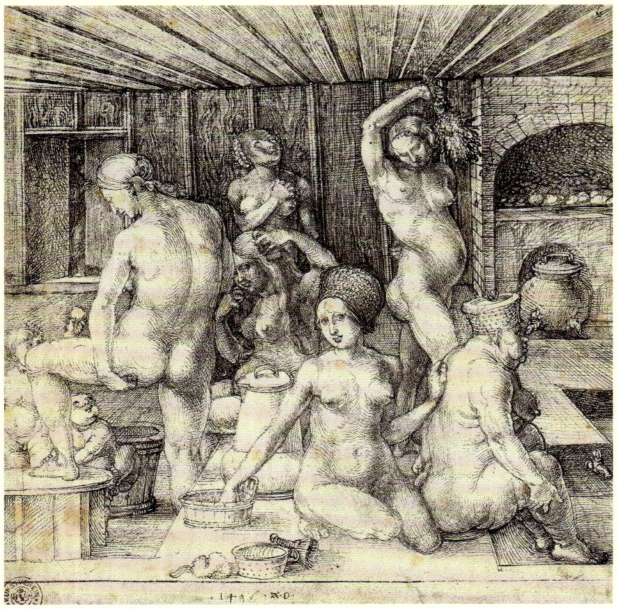

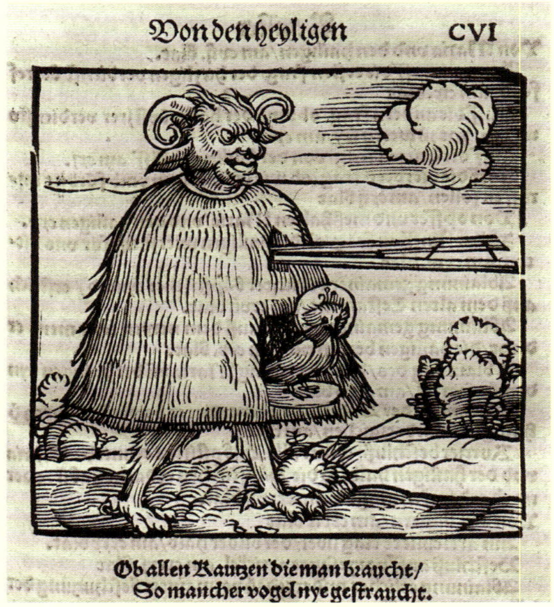

26 Albrecht Dürer, *Women's Bath*, 1496
Pen and black ink, 23.1 × 23 cm
Kunsthalle Bremen

27 Hans Sebald Beham, *The Devil as a Bird-Catcher with a Cloven Stick*
From Johann von Schwarzenberg, *Beschwerung der alten teüfelischen Schlangen mit dem Götlichen wort* (Weighting Down the Old, Devilish Serpents with the Divine Word), Augsburg 1525, Bayerische Staatsbibliothek Munich, fol. Res/4 Polem. 382, fol. CVIr

their isocephalic arrangement (i.e., the placement of heads at the same height) but also suggests the way toward the pool of a bathhouse (fig. 26). Blazing on the far left, in an adjoining room, are the fires of hell. Emerging from the flames is a terrifying demon whose lechery is evidently directed toward the virgin, seen from the rear. The intended wears a laurel wreath in her uncovered hair and hides her breasts and pubic area—just like the antique Venus Pudica (fig. 24). This chaste gesture of modesty is addressed to the demon, who intends to ensnare her with his cloven stick (fig. 27). Wherever the Devil is found, Dürer informs us, Death is not far off, as indicated by the skull seen lying at the women's feet.

Public baths and their proprietors were subject to special scrutiny; according to *Malleus maleficarum*, a woman who ran a bathhouse in Ravensburg was "reduced to ashes" for trying to tempt a pious virgin into having direct contact with the Devil. Dürer's engraving, which is no longer fully decodable today, was addressed to a broad elite with an interest in the topic.

Hans Baldung's chiaroscuro sheets, meanwhile, were private cabinet pieces. His *New Year's Greeting* of 1514 bears a dedication to a canon at Freiburg Minster, with whom he was evidently on friendly terms. Baldung worked on the high altar there from 1512 to 1516. In general, but for clergy in particular, the days around the turn of the year were regarded as extraordinarily dangerous, a time in which witches and demons rampaged wildly. Of the three nude women, one of the younger figures depicted on the sheet is shown kneeling, bent over, in an attempt to see her vulva from below. She is assisted by a muscular hag, perhaps a high sorceress, who presses the first woman downward. A second young woman helps by mounting the kneeling figure. With her right hand, she holds a flaming cauldron aloft while acting as a "mentor" to the kneeling figure, touching her own mons veneris in order to illustrate the awakening and satisfaction of desire's flame. The fact that the gesture of her left hand is comparable to that of the Venus Pudica reveals the discrepancy between appearance and reality. The small plaque set at a right angle with its delicately inscribed signature, almost seems to invite the viewer to kneel down alongside the young women, turning his own head crosswise. This allows him (originally, the cathedral's canon!) to peer between the thighs of the peeping woman, where her "inverted"—and hence, from the perspective of the time, "perverse"—gaze now meets his own.

Baldung's *A Witches' Sabbath II,* dating from the same year, also takes female sexuality as its theme, which more or less automatically converts a woman—again, from the perspective of the time—into a witch or else someone bewitched. Once again, all of the women are nude. The one bathed in the light of the Moon stimulates her vulva—probably using a brush fashioned from the fine witch hair (fig. 28). Another witch, seen dozing off, perhaps having already satisfied herself (according to *Malleus maleficarum,* this involved intercourse with an invisible devil, perhaps taking the form of smoke), holds up a cauldron containing burning oil. On the rising smoke (the echo of lust during sleep?), a young woman, who kneels on the back of a flying cat burns her fingers as she races along, propelled by a toothless hag; the old woman glides silently through the air by means of a two-pronged flying pitchfork. But the young "speeder" cries out! Is she experiencing an orgasm? There are other noises as well. A cat hisses. A ram, straddled witch-style by an infant boy, bleats. Something bubbles in the witch's cauldron; a skull and a half-decomposed arm lie to one side as ingredients (according to *Malleus maleficarum,* the ointment used by witches to fly is prepared from cooking exhumed body parts and dead children; pieces of wood rubbed with this magic brew became apparatuses of flight). Ascending from the fire on the left is a column of smoke into which the witches, the bewitched, and the cat-demon are to be engulfed. Billowing smoke and witch hair already swirl together.

28 Copy after Hans Baldung Grien, *Women's Bath with a Mirror,* ca. 1600 (detail)
Oil on panel, 46.3 × 32.5 cm
Staatliche Kunsthalle Karlsruhe

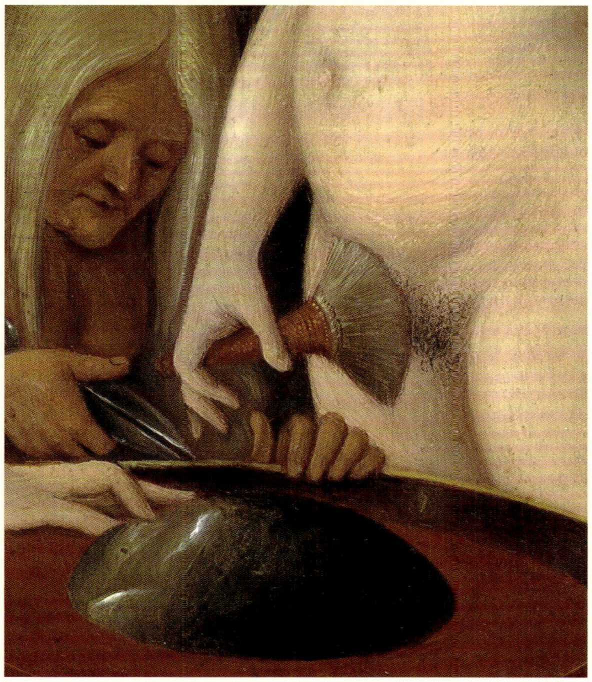

These two sheets visualize what "eyewitnesses" reported—based, of course, on their utter incomprehension of female desire. These images, then, seem to mirror the hidden, "dark side" of the Moon. But the far side of the Moon is not de facto *dark.* Dark were merely the misogynistic fantasies of so-called witnesses whose perceptions were fatally contaminated by a paranoid fear of witches. Even more perfidious: that which was putatively reflected in such imagery served as a sexual stimulus for the beholder—safely ensconced in his righteous indignation!

MP

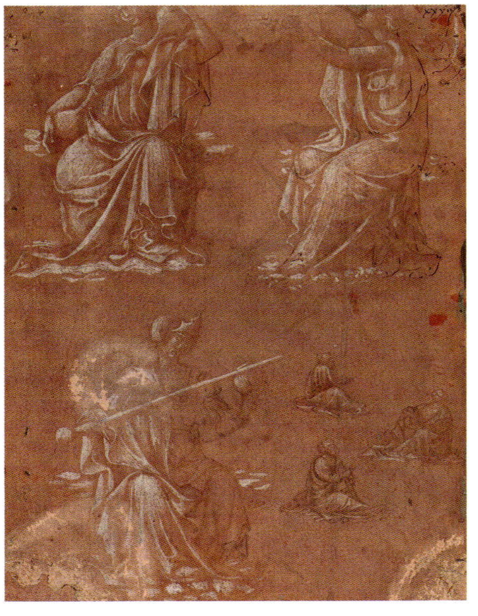

29 Circle of Lorenzo Monaco, *Three Virtues (Temperance, Hope, and Fortitude or Justice)*, ca. 1420
Silverpoint and brush, brown wash, heightened with white, on reddish violet prepared paper, 24.9 × 18.5 cm
The Metropolitan Museum of Art, New York, Robert Lehman Collection

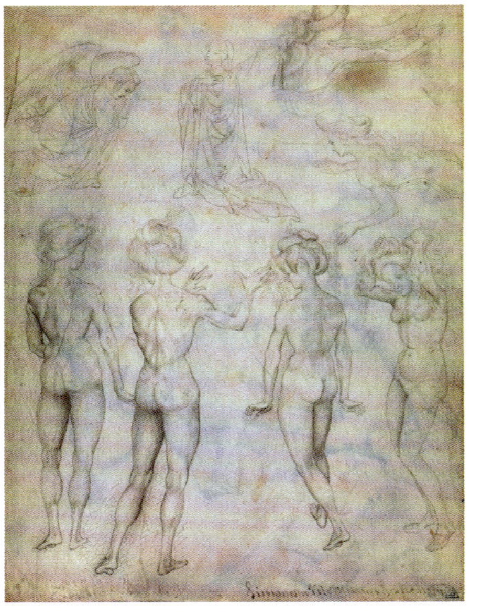

30 Pisanello, *Four Studies of a Female Nude, the Annunciation, and Two Studies of a Woman Swimming*, ca. 1431/32
Pen and ink on parchment, 22.3 × 16.7 cm
Museum Boijmans van Beuningen, Rotterdam

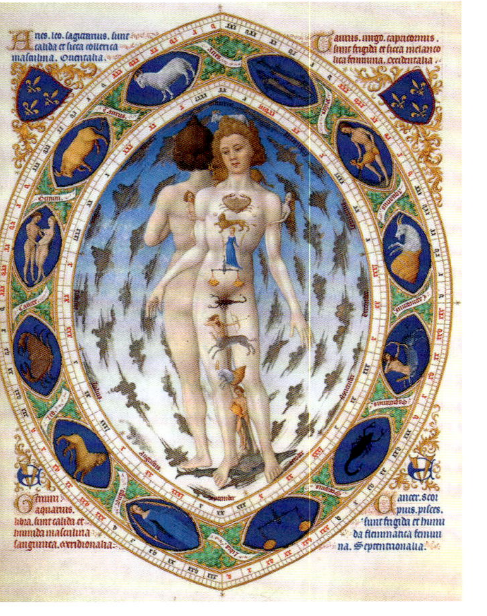

31 Limbourg brothers, *Homo signorum* from *Les Très Riches Heures*, book of hours of the Duke of Berry, 1412–1416
Tempera on vellum, 29.4 × 21.5 cm
Musée Condé, Chantilly

A pen-and-ink drawing by Antonio di Puccio Pisano, called Pisanello, from about 1426, is regarded as the earliest representation of a female nude after antiquity that does not represent either Eve in Paradise or a resurrected corpse on Judgment Day.

Supported on her left arm, her thighs parted slightly in an inviting manner, a young woman reclines "casually" on bedding made of fabric and fur. Her hair has been fashioned in a pompous, turban-like coiffure. Seated at her feet is a rabbit.

Given her nakedness, this woman has been identified as the allegorical personification of *Luxuria*—from a contemporary fifteenth-century perspective, the "vice" of sexual lust. Virtues, meanwhile, were always depicted fully clothed (fig. 29). Since the grammatical gender of these Latin terms is feminine, both virtues and vices were represented as women.

Pisanello approached the task of depicting the nude female form not by copying ancient models, but instead empirically. In the course of his activities at the Gonzaga court in Mantua, he drew the same live model both standing and swimming (fig. 30).

In conceiving his pubescent bodily ideal, Pisanello followed the Limbourg brothers, who may have already used live models for the human couple seen in their zodiac miniature for their book of hours, *Les Très Riches Heures du duc de Berry* (fig. 31).

MP

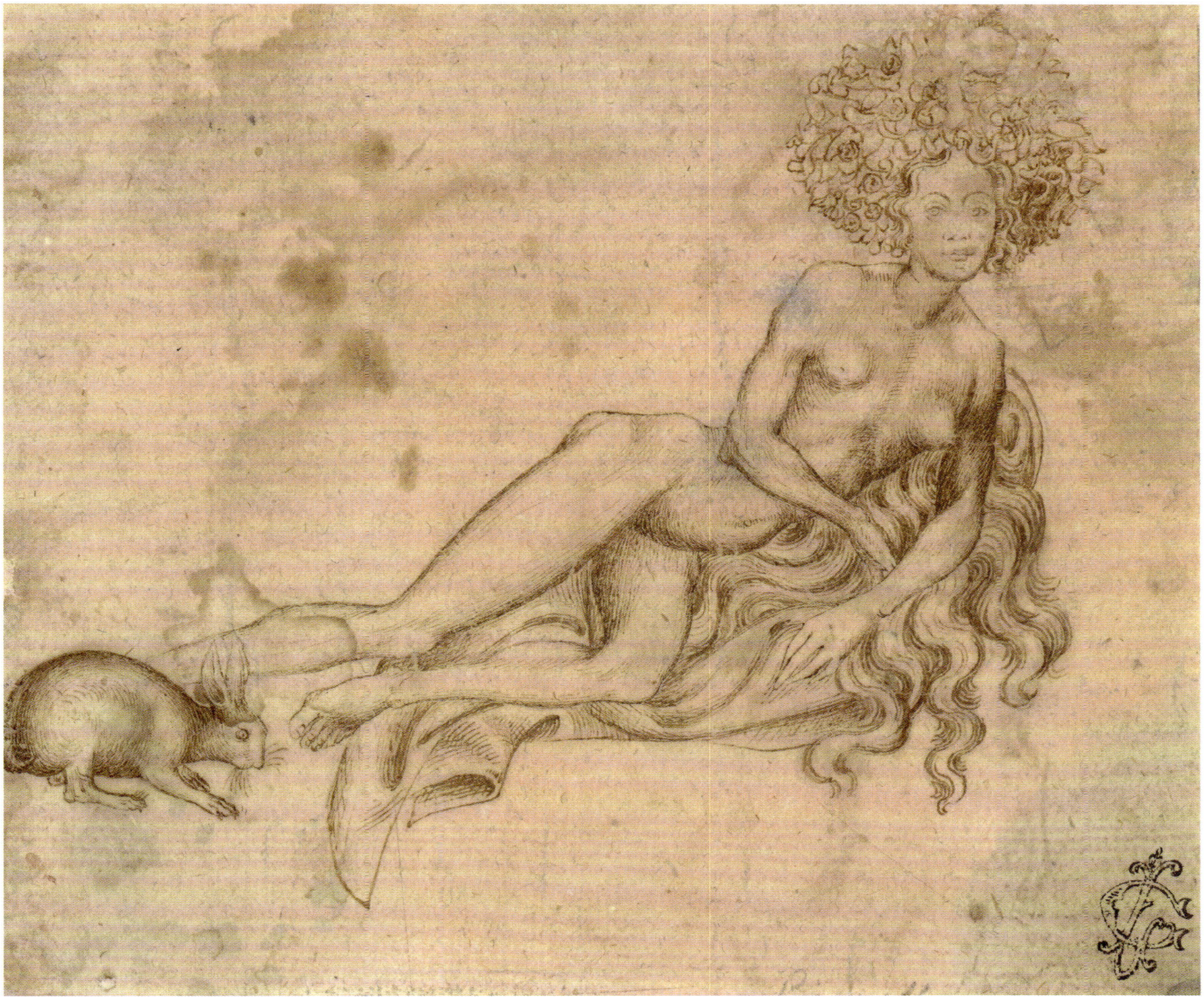

Pisanello
Personification of Lust (Luxuria), ca. 1426
The ALBERTINA Museum, Vienna

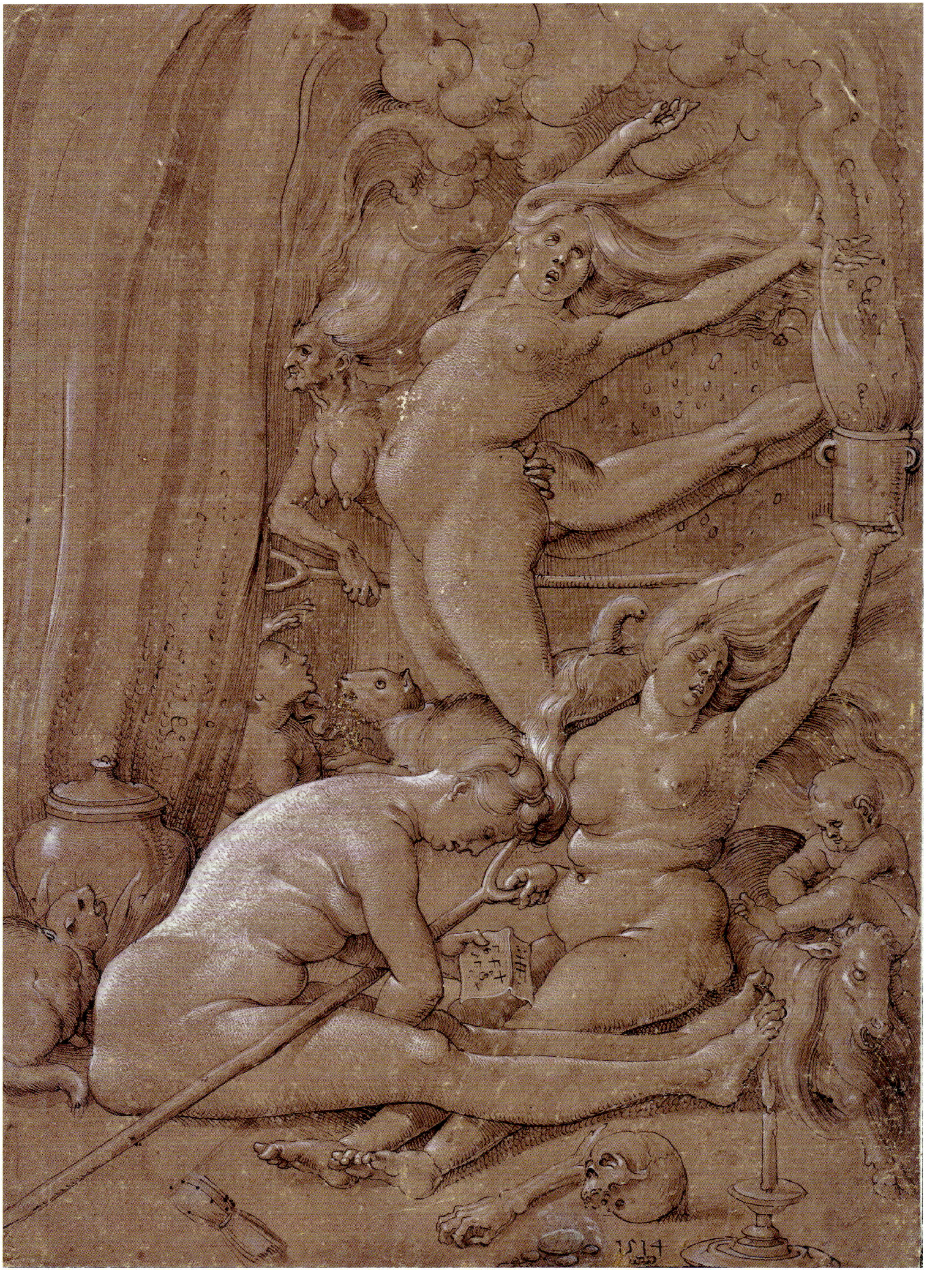

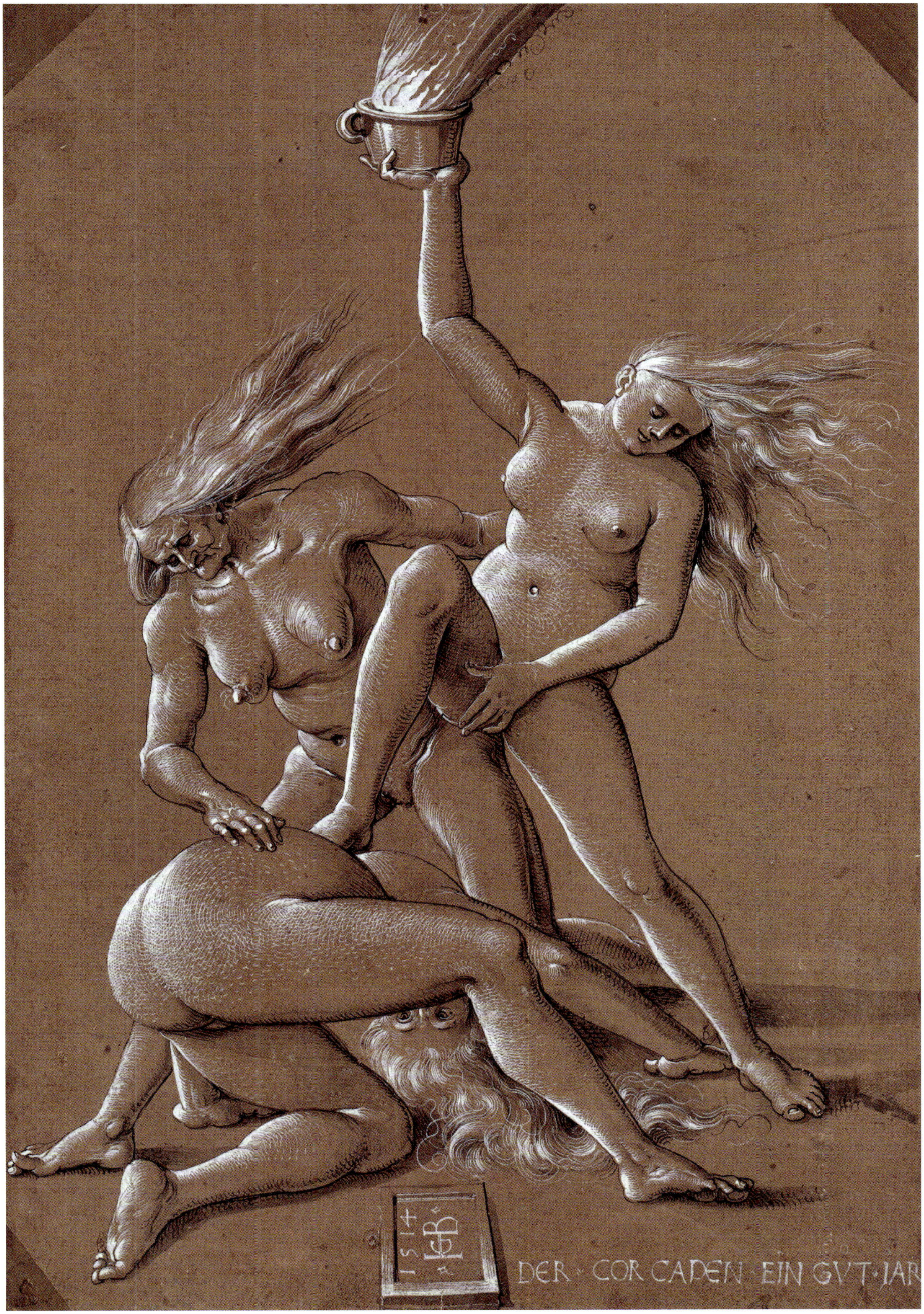

Hans Baldung Grien
A Witches' Sabbath II, 1514
The ALBERTINA Museum, Vienna

Hans Baldung Grien
New Year's Greeting with Three Witches, 1514
The ALBERTINA Museum, Vienna

“. . . must not, will not, cannot . . .”

From the late Gothic period up until Mannerism, the motif of the temptation of the Desert Father Saint Anthony of Egypt (fourth century AD) enjoyed a genuine vogue—north of the Alps, for example, in depictions by Martin Schongauer, Hieronymus Bosch, Matthias Grünewald, and Pieter Bruegel the Elder. People’s own feared sexual drives and the alarming sociocultural developments of the time lent themselves to becoming intertwined with and traced back to the theme of the “temptress”—then identified with demons and witches. Artists were drawn to the oscillation between immanence and appearance, especially since the painterly resources required for their depiction were now available (fig. 32).

The portrait and genre painter Cecil van Haanen (1844–1914), a native of Vienna, who spent the greater part of his life in Venice, addressed this theme in an unusual way. His *The Temptation of Saint Anthony* (who, *nota bene*, wears the Franciscan habit of Saint Anthony of Padua) turns away in revulsion from the lascivious nude who appears to him in front of a crevice in a rock cleft (associative space: female genitalia!), seeking to show him the way out of hermitage and abstinence. He attempts to ward off the temptress using the cross on his rosary. “Apage Satanas!” (“Away with you, Satan!”), you can almost hear him pleading inwardly.

But his aquiline nose, the wild, dark fringes of hair on his forehead (which seem to have escaped his monastic tonsure), along with his pointed cowl, raise the question of whether he is really the exorcist or not Mephistopheles himself in the flesh. The outré self-defense and androgynous elegance of this portmanteau Saint Anthony are reminiscent of the celebrated *Méphistophélès* of Jacques-Louis Gautier (fig. 33). Admittedly, Van Haanen’s study of the head in the Leopold Museum in Vienna suggests that he ultimately sought to strike a far less sarcastic note than his charcoal drawing and the parallels to the French symbolist sculpture might suggest.

Cecil van Haanen
The Temptation of Saint Anthony, 1872
The ALBERTINA Museum, Vienna

32 Matthias Grünewald, *The Temptation of Saint Anthony*, 1512–1516
Interior panel of the inner right wing of the Isenheim Altarpiece
Oil and tempera on panel, 265 × 139 cm
Musée Unterlinden, Colmar

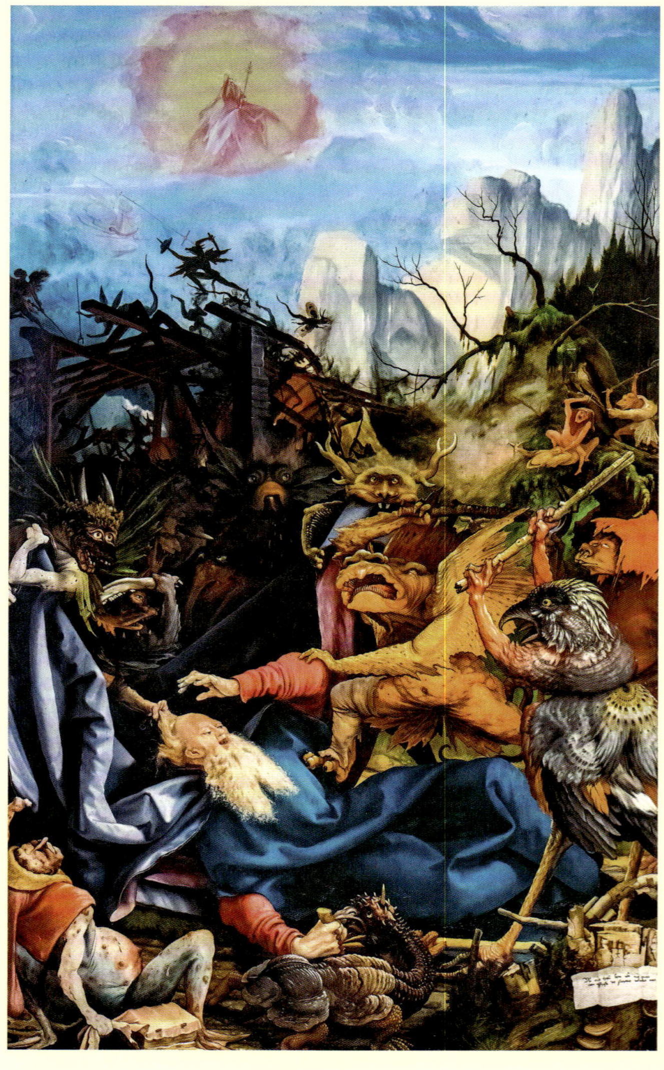

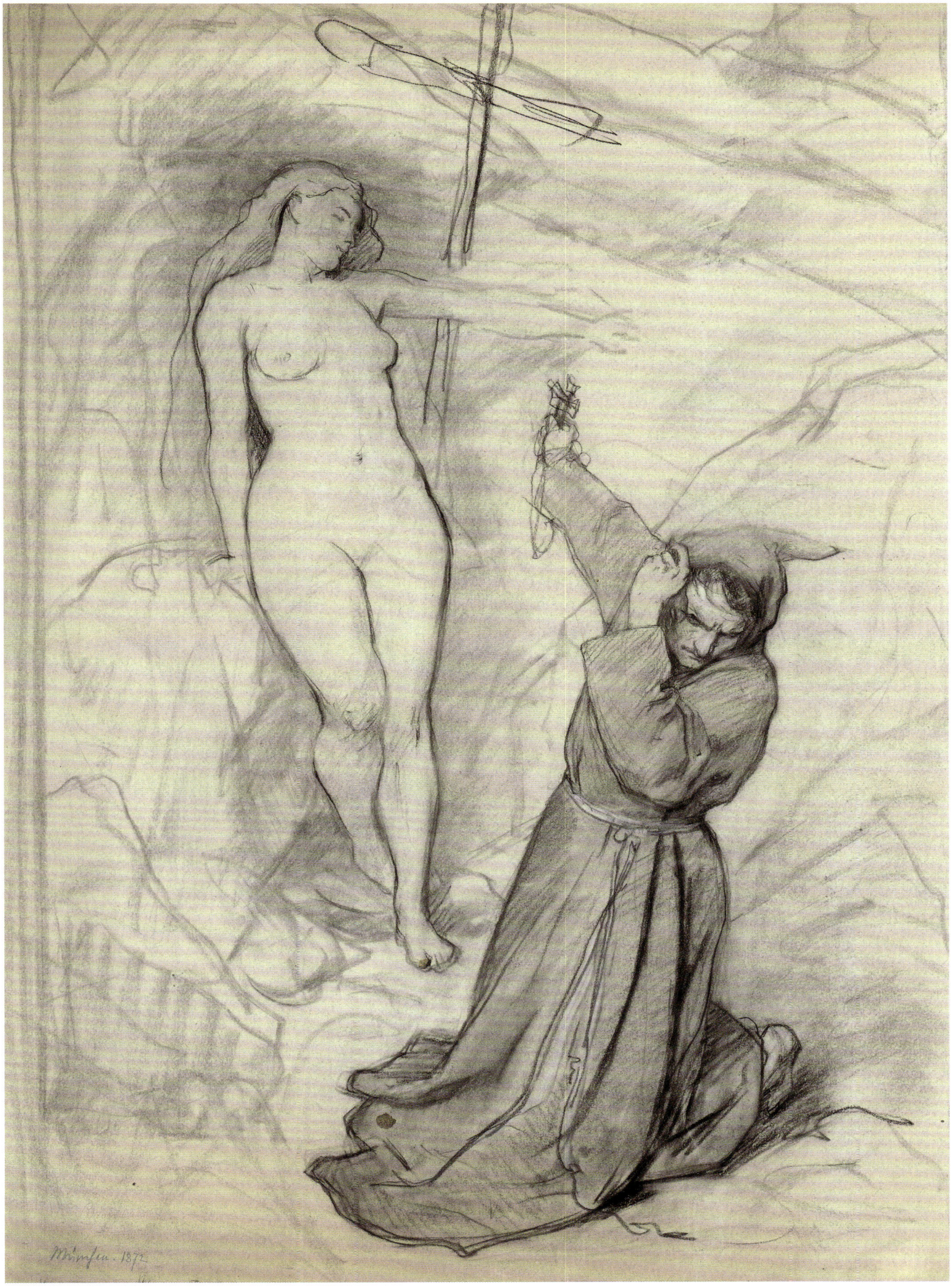
München. 1872

The Hebrew Bible describes how the so-called "Egyptian" Joseph (Jacob's son sold into slavery by his jealous half-brothers) worked in Egypt in the house of Potiphar, a high official appointed by Pharaoh. Potiphar's wife (who remains nameless in the Bible) attempts to seduce the young, handsome Israelite, but the God-fearing Joseph flees. He does so, however, in a state of nakedness—Potiphar's wife having seized his garment. The rejected woman then informs her husband that Joseph had attempted to rape her, and Joseph soon finds himself in prison (Gen. 39: 1–20).

A fixed, easily recognizable iconography for the scene already became established by the early Byzantine era: Potiphar's wife lies or sits on her bed having seized Joseph's robe as he attempts to free himself from her grasp.

In Rembrandt's etching, a curtain, pulled aside, offers the view of a dimly lit bed, where the wanton woman offers her voluptuous body to Joseph without inhibition. Is the upright bedpost an allusion to her unstilled lust? Or is this phallic element of furniture a reflection of the physical effect that her advances have on the object of her desire? In either case, Joseph flees in disgust, but does not get very far—not only because Potiphar's wife holds onto his robe, but also because the brocade bedspread, having twisted itself into a snake, seizes one foot, and the glaring daylight, which enters from the left, seems to secure him to the floorboards with its cast shadows.

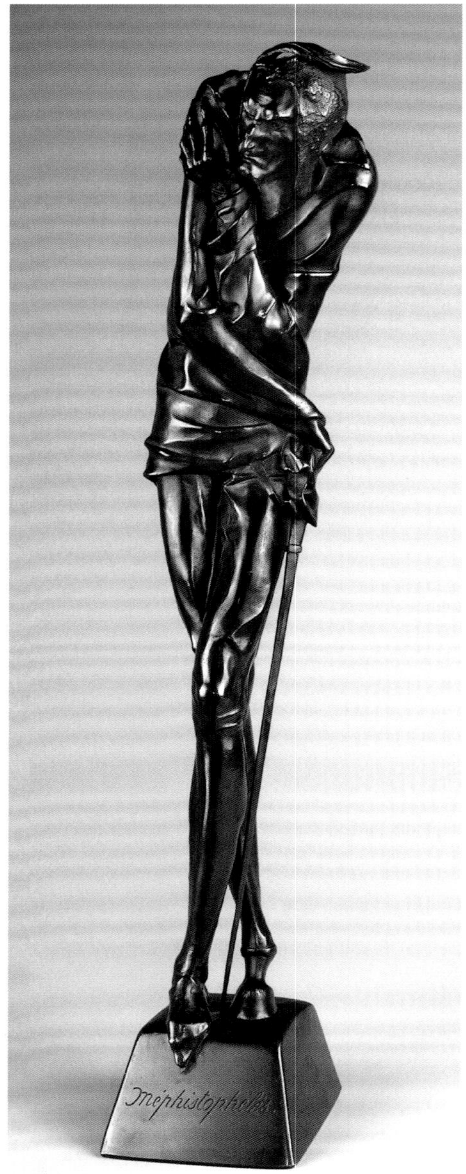

33 Jacques-Louis Gautier, *Méphistophélès*, ca. 1855
Patinated bronze, 64.6 × 19.5 cm
Montreal Museum of Fine Arts, Purchase, the Museum Campaign 1988–1993 Fund

Meanwhile, with the French artist Charles André van Loo everything is grand theater. Potiphar's house is a veritable palace, and his wife is young, slender, and beautiful—her exposed breasts the only enticement. Here as well, the rebuffing Joseph is held firmly by the wife. But rather than flee, he stands next to the bed, wringing his hands and pleading with God for fortitude. Poses, gestures, and drapery (from the curtain mounted at some infinite height, to the wife's chemise): everything is arranged for the sake of the beholder. Indeed, everything present in the small-format pen-and-ink and wash drawing could be encountered again in the composition of some monumental altarpiece. In such works, the established society again celebrates its moral and religious superiority, though it had long ago passed to the other side of the proverbial fence.

In 1846, with his twenty-nine-part series, *The Travel Adventures of Monsignore L. Brunner*, August Xaver Karl Pettenkofen (ennobled in 1876 as Ritter von Pettenkofen), guides his viewers headlong into the abyss of (petty) bourgeois desires and their miscarriages. The fictitious protagonist (might his name be an allusion to Pettenkofen's friend and colleague at the academy, Leopold Brunner the Younger?) undertakes a journey—in a fever dream, more than likely. Among other places, he travels to Paris, where, during Holy Mass, he keeps his eye on a mature, well-dressed lady and speaks to her in the street. Soon, we see the two at her home. Legs spread, the full-figured woman stands on her bed, her skirt raised, demanding sexual satisfaction from the man lying below her. With his limp penis, and visibly intimidated, he is unable to deliver. For which reason he is summarily ejected from the house with a great kick. In its basic tenor, Pettenkofen's *Travel Adventures* resemble William Hogarth's cycle *A Rake's Progress* (1733–1735). Stylistically, and with regard to its biting humor, the Viennese artist follows the political caricatures of Honoré Daumier, a style which went viral during the Napoleonic Wars.

The bottom line: Rembrandt's Joseph does not want to; Van Loo's Joseph must not; and Pettenkofen's Monsignore Brunner simply cannot. From our perspective today, the latter figure points up the difficulties encountered by men in the nineteenth century with the incipient financial independence and gradual emancipation of women.

MP

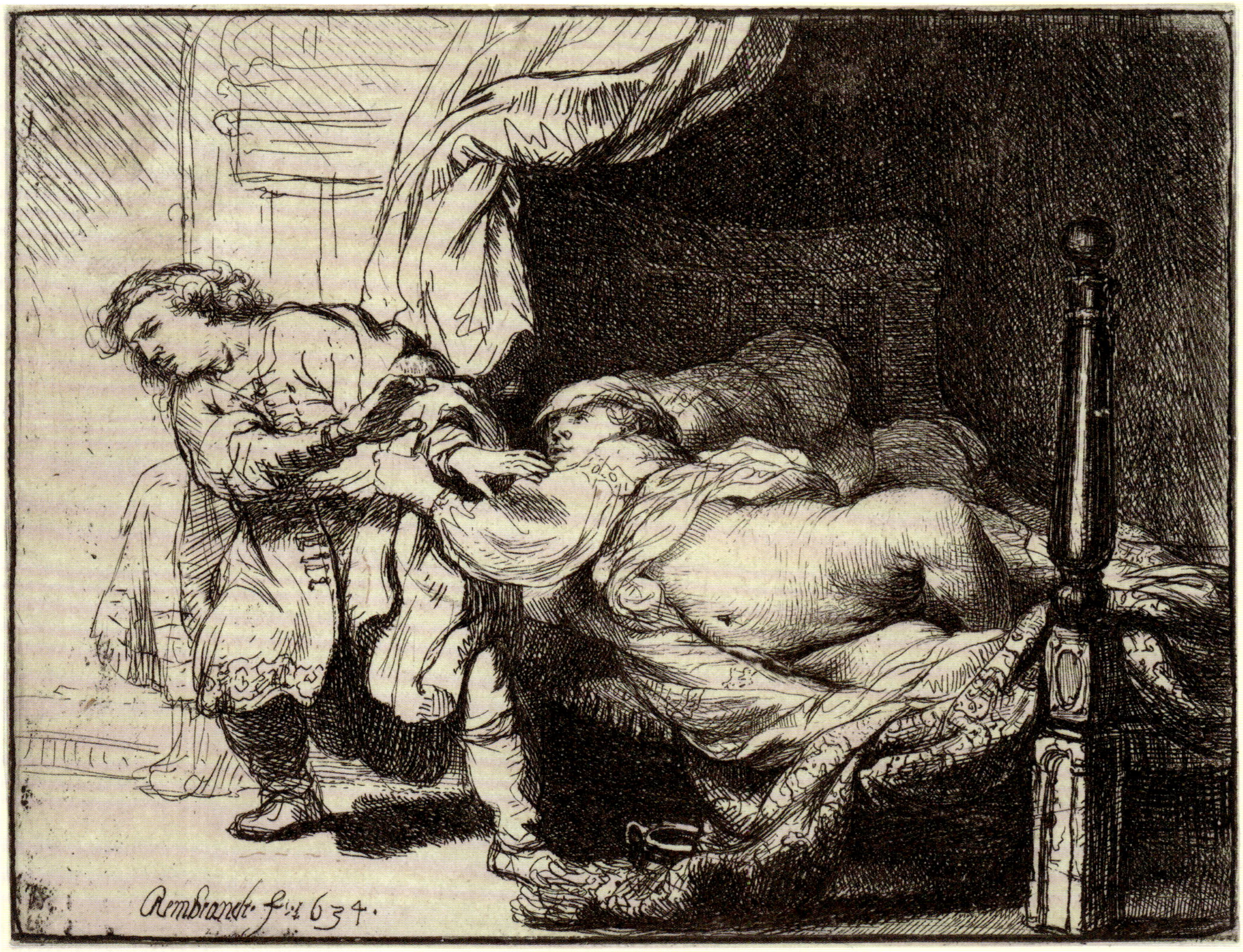

Rembrandt Harmensz. van Rijn
Joseph and Potiphar's Wife, 1634
The ALBERTINA Museum, Vienna

Charles André van Loo
Joseph and Potiphar's Wife,
second third of the 18th century
The ALBERTINA Museum, Vienna

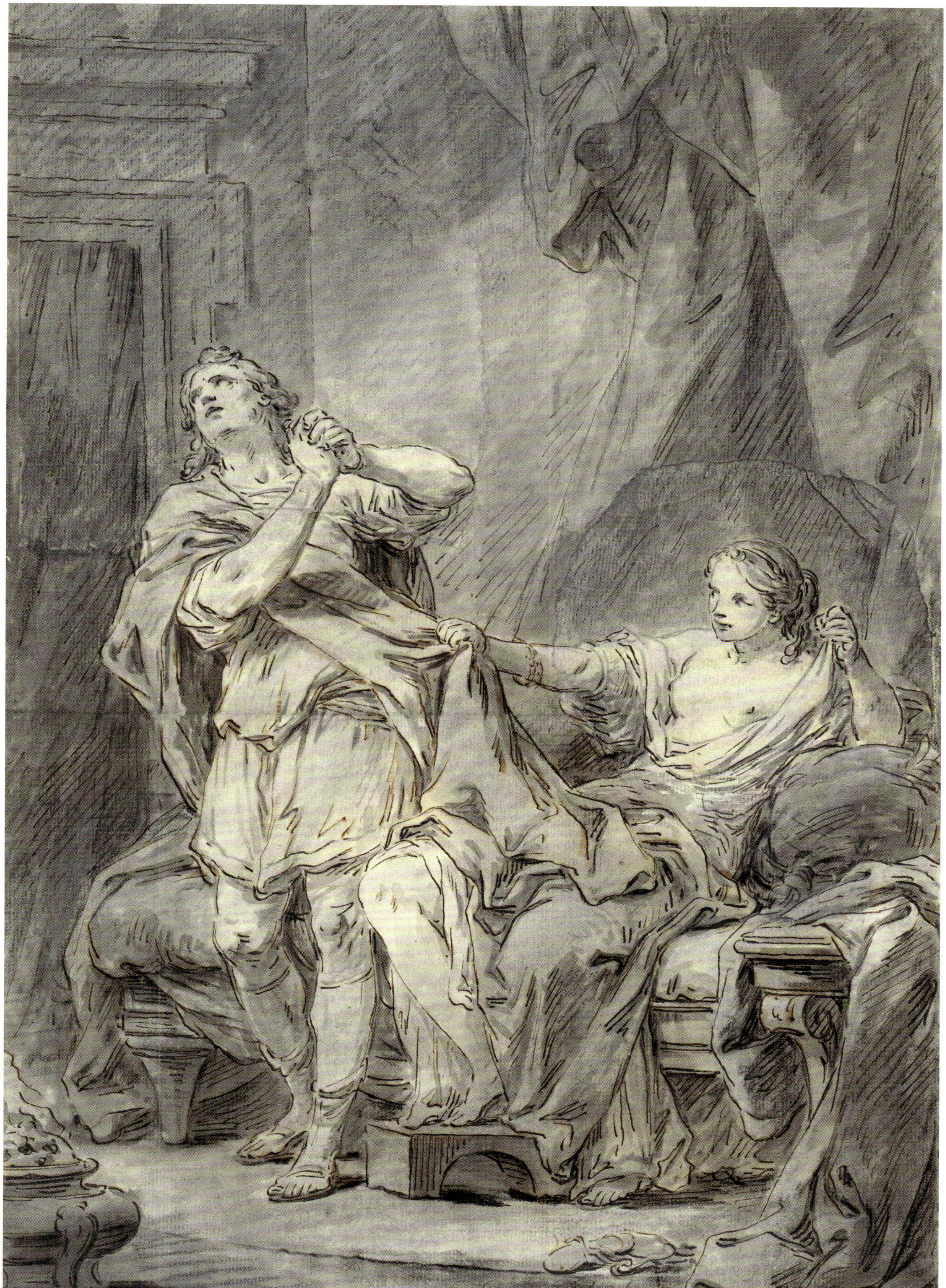

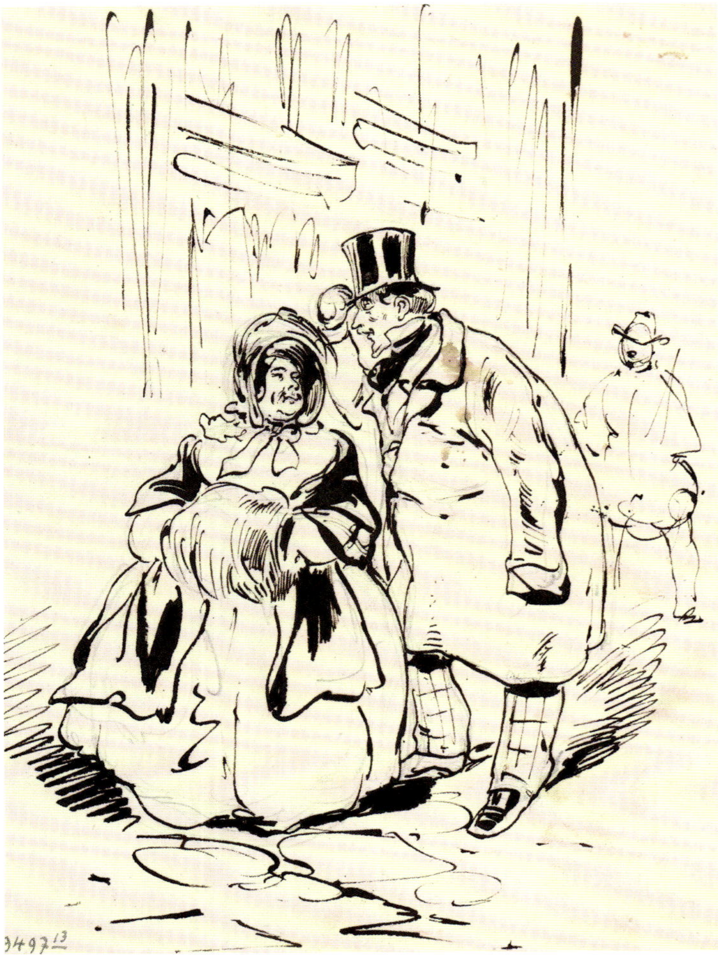

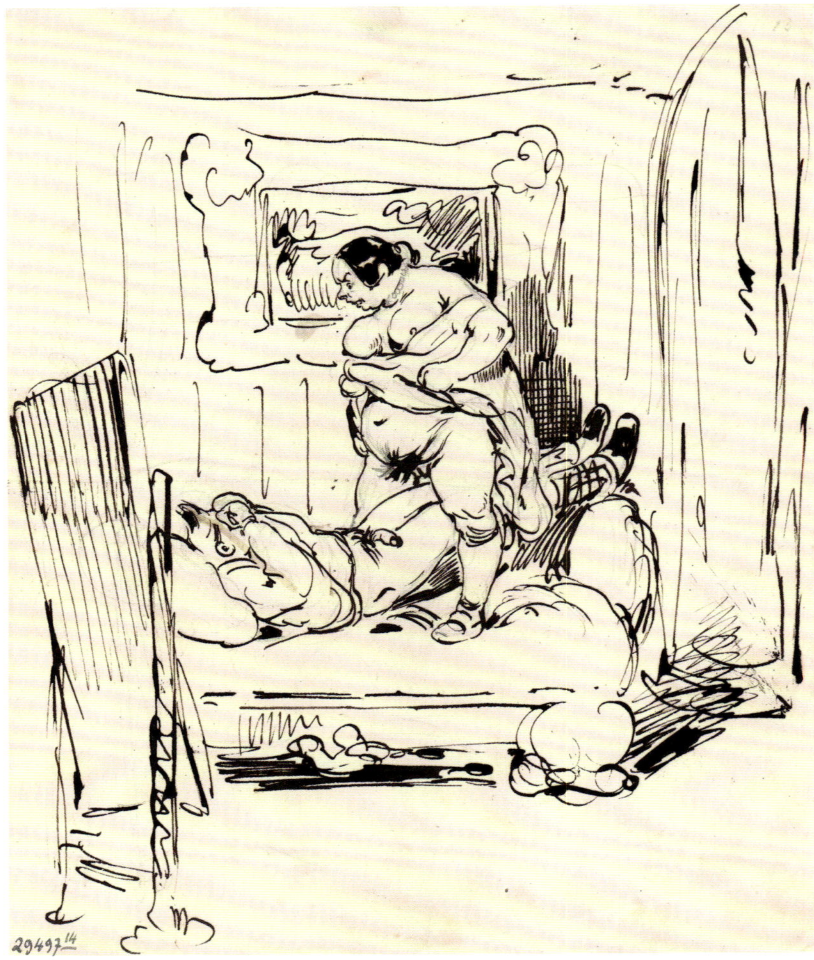

August von Pettenkofen
The Travel Adventures of Monsignore L. Brunner, 1846
Drawings nos. 13–15 from a 29-part series
The ALBERTINA Museum, Vienna

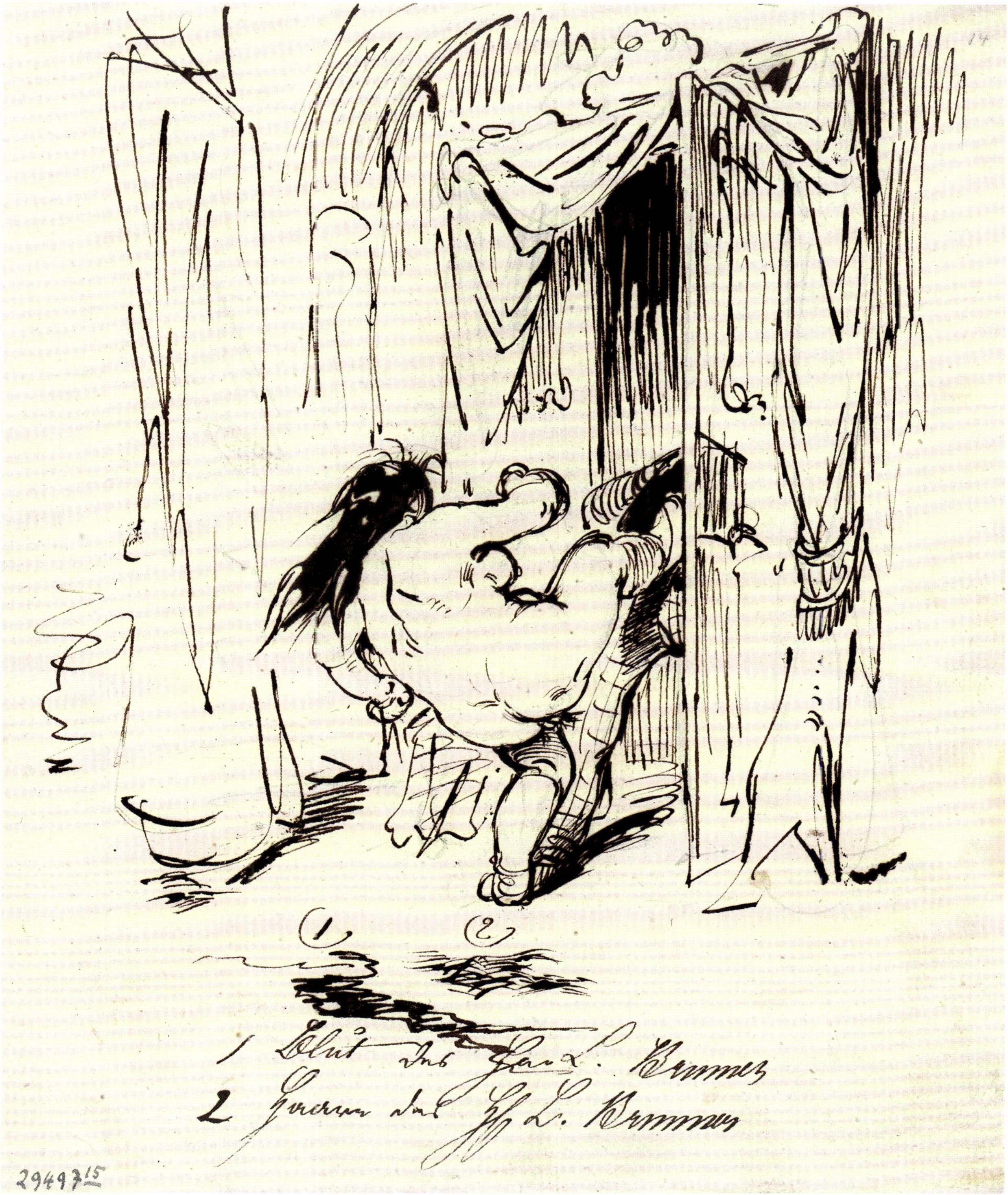

The Rebirth of Venus

In Florence, shortly before 1488, when a thirteen-year-old Michelangelo Buonarroti entered the workshop of the successful Florentine panel and fresco painter Domenico Ghirlandaio as an apprentice, an attempt was made to depict the female nude. Qualifying as a milestone in the history of Western culture was Sandro Botticelli's *The Birth of Venus*, produced around 1485/86 (fig. 34). Standing in a scallop shell and dominating the composition, the nude goddess is wafted toward us by the winds Zephyr and Aura. In a highly suggestive manner, the blown breath of the mild West wind and the morning breeze arriving from the left behind Venus, create an awareness of her unseen rear, of her back and buttocks. In just a moment, before our very eyes, the goddess will step onto the island of Cyprus.

Botticelli's image was based on ancient descriptions of a painted "Ἀναδυομένη" (*Anadyomene*: she rising from the sea) by the Greek artist Apelles (ca. 375/370–late fourth century BC). The pose of the goddess corresponded to that of the so-called Aphrodite of Knidos, from one generation before, the work of the sculptor Praxiteles (ca. 390–ca. 320 BC), produced between 350 and 340 BC for the island city of Kos, although it was actually installed at Knidos. The Aphrodite of Knidos type has been transmitted through numerous Roman copies, among them the Medici Venus (fig. 24) discovered only after Botticelli's death. Admittedly, the Florentine's Venus has a certain affinity with Eve since she completely conceals her mons veneris with lengthy strands of her reddish-blond mane.

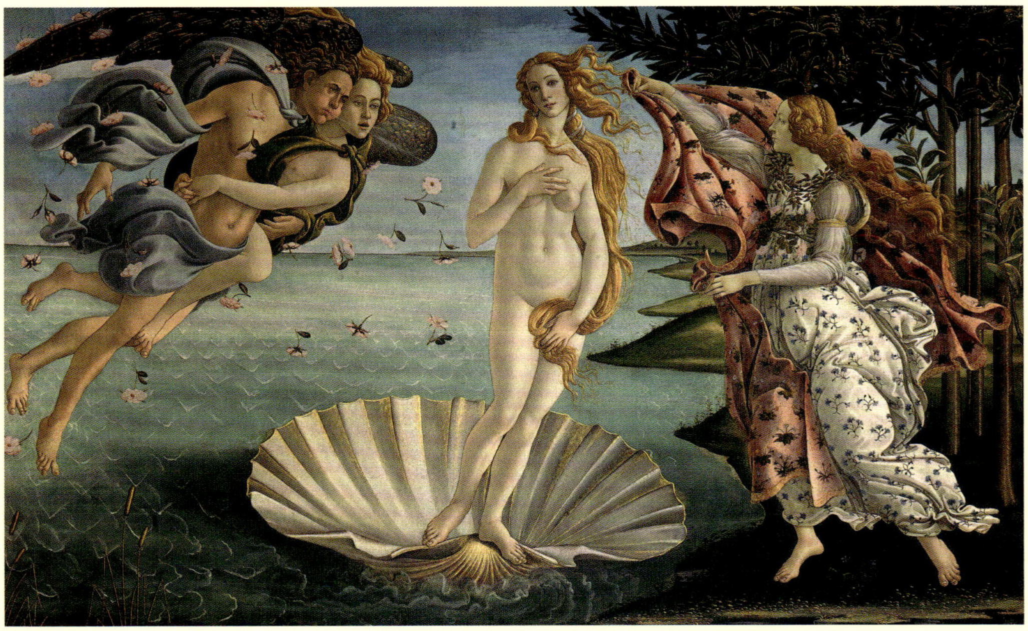

34 Sandro Botticelli, *The Birth of Venus*, 1485/86
Tempera on canvas, 172.5 × 278.5 cm
Gallerie degli Uffizi, Florence

Giovanni Francesco Susini
***Kneeling Woman Bathing*, second quarter of the 17th century**
LIECHTENSTEIN. The Princely Collections, Vaduz–Vienna, Fürstliche Sammlungen Art Service GmbH

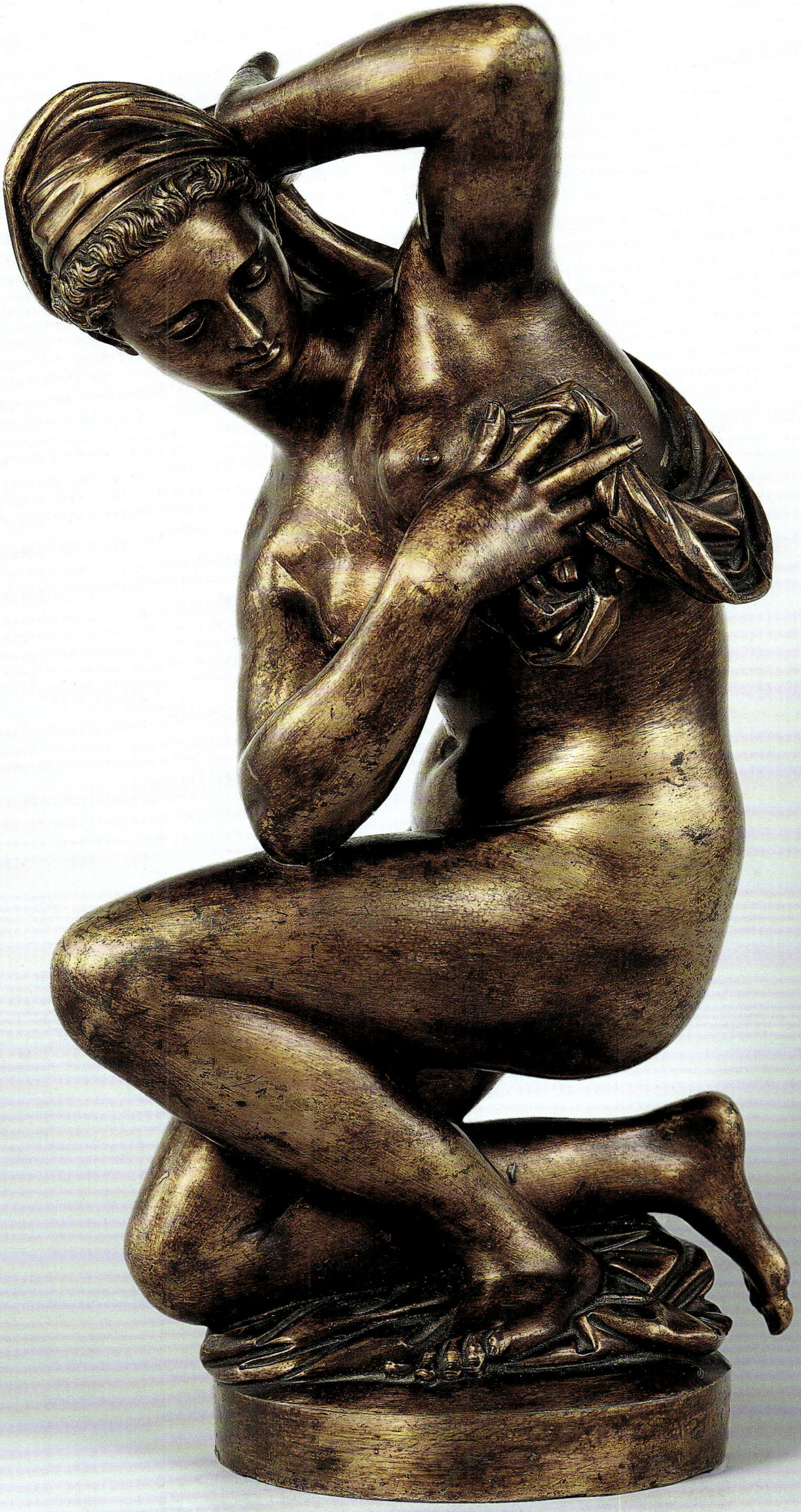

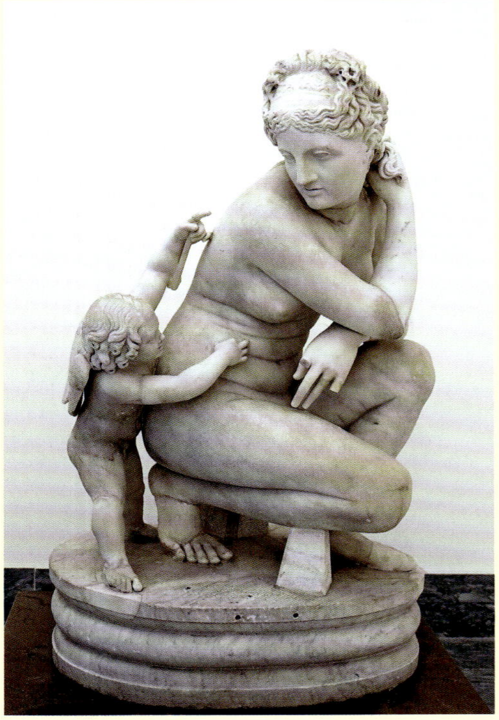

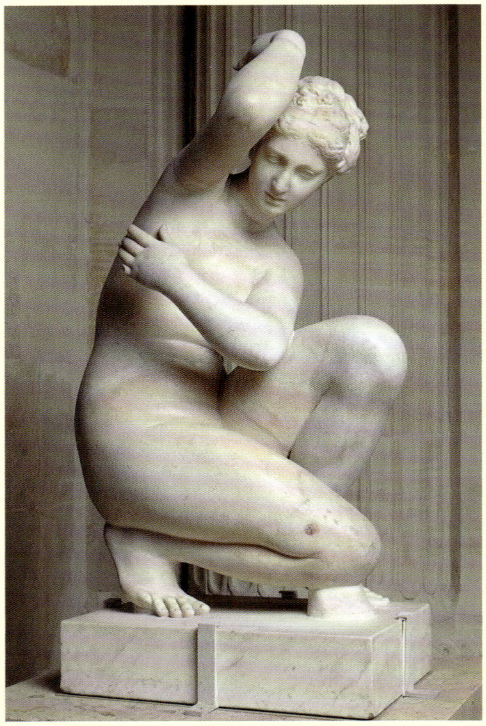

35 Crouching Venus with Cupid,
2nd century AD
Roman copy after a Greek original by the sculptor Doidalses, middle or second half of the 3rd century BC
Marble, h. 122 cm
Museo Archeologico Nazionale, Naples

36 Crouching Venus, Roman Imperial
Roman copy after a Greek original,
275–250 BC
Marble, h. 77 cm
Paris, Musée du Louvre

Eve in Paradise and the female dead arisen on Judgment Day were the only unclothed female figures which the painters and sculptors of the Middle Ages could hardly avoid depicting. Otherwise, female nudity was essentially proscribed in the visual arts. Reemerging across Western civilization through art by means of Botticelli's depiction of *La Nascita* (the birth) was not just female nudity, but also the power of beauty and love, revered during antiquity as the driving force behind all earthly things. Before long, the nude female figure would become the trademark of antiquity reborn: *il Rinascimento.*

Accompanying this rebirth were the excavations that freed numerous antique sculptures—most of them Roman copies of Greek originals—from the cultural debris. Coming to light in this fashion was a second ancient type of the nude Aphrodite/Venus: this one, which shows the goddess crouching during her bath, is regarded as the work of the Hellenistic sculpture Doidalses (figs. 35, 36).

Numerous artists, whether casting or carving statues, or working in materials, such as ivory or precious metals, to create statuettes, had recourse to this Venus type, among them Giambologna and his assistant Giovanni Francesco Susini.

A French Neoclassicist must have sketched his *Vénus accroupie* directly from the marble in the Louvre in Paris. Found on the drawing's frame is the name "Monval" (added later, perhaps?). The figure, which kneels in her bath, is rendered with such accuracy and plasticity that it almost creates the impression of a photograph of a sculpture.

MP

Attributed to Monval
Crouching Venus, ca. 1806–1810
The ALBERTINA Museum, Vienna

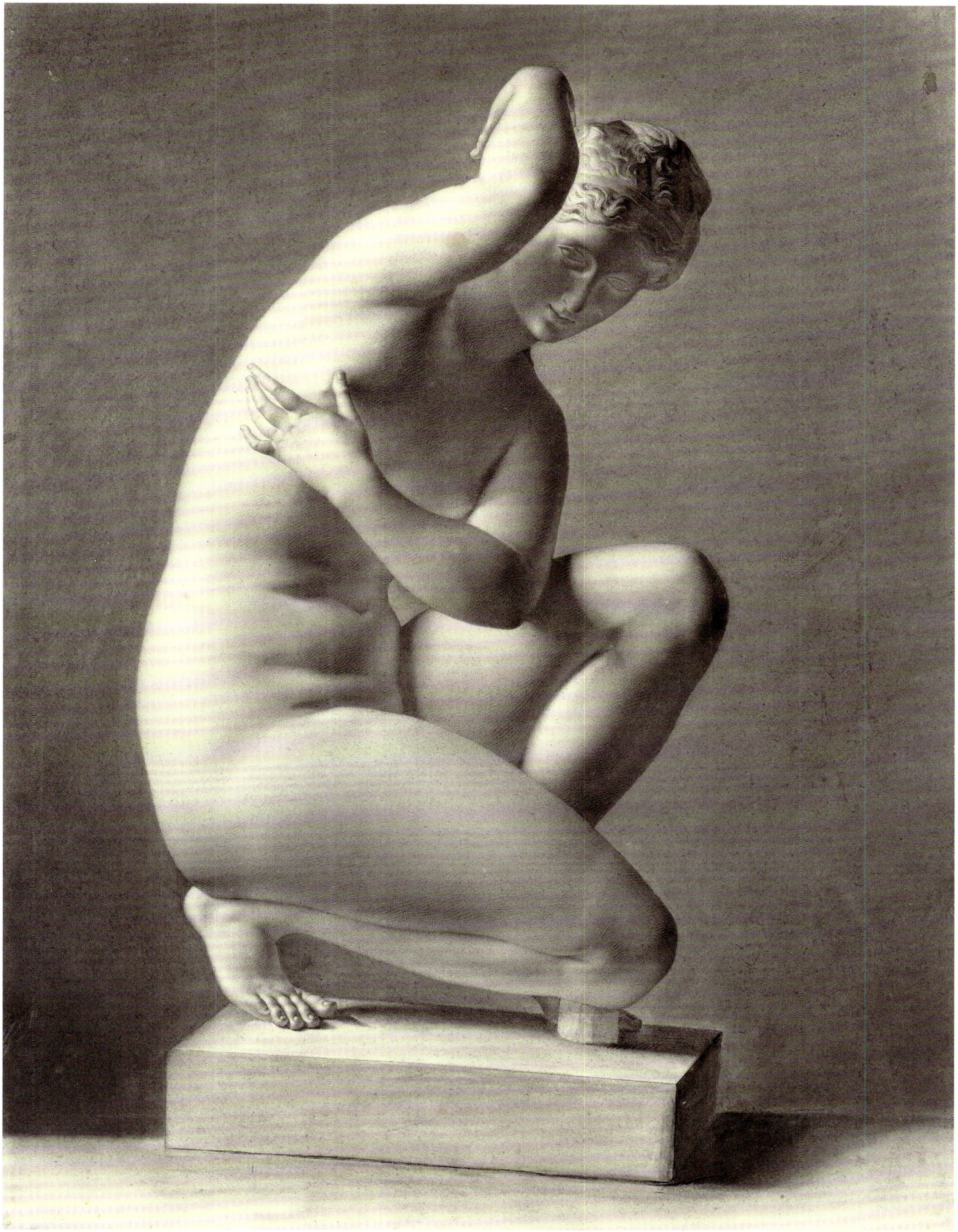

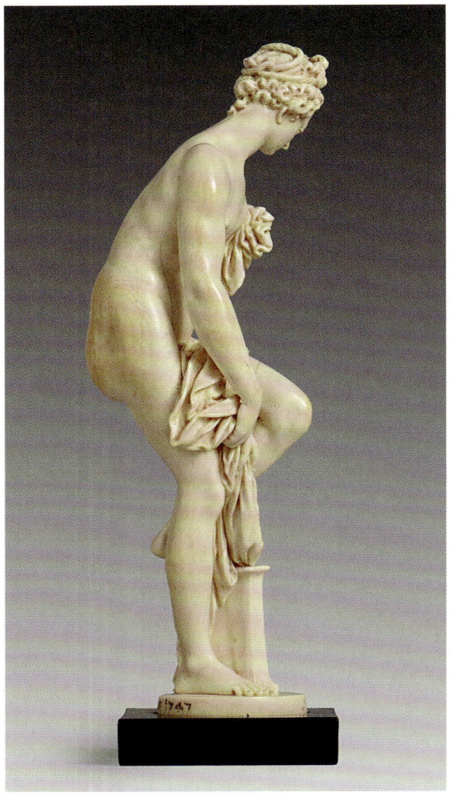

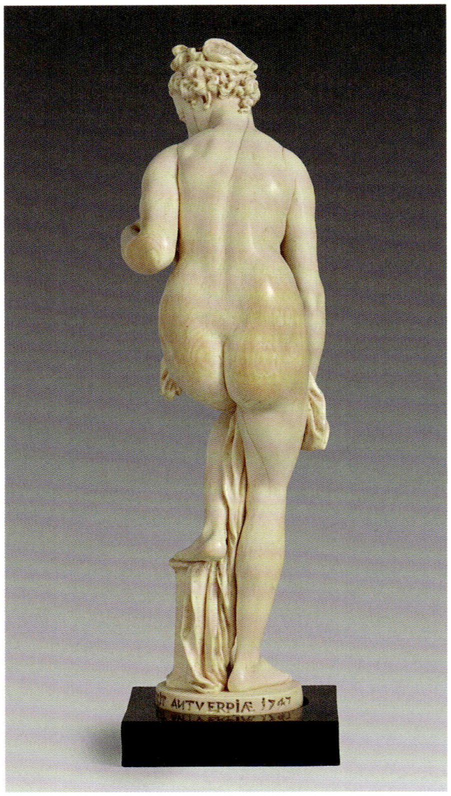

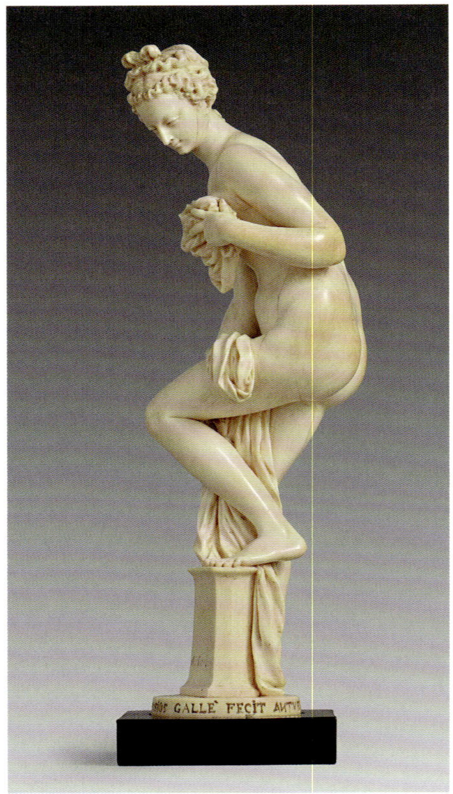

Ambroise Gallé's ivory figure *Venus after the Bath* not only derives from a well-known ancient sculptural type; it is also based, in its motif and composition, on a bronze statuette by Giambologna. The goddess of love delicately places her left foot on a plinth, and the resulting bend in her leg creates a kind of contrapposto. In her right hand, she holds a cloth that drapes gently across her left thigh and, at the same time, conceals her pudenda. With her left hand, she uses a smaller corner of cloth to dry her breast, wet from bathing. The movement in the lower body, generated by the bent knee, contrasts with the opposing motion in the upper body and with the direction of the gaze, which is turned on the left hand. This produces a dynamic rotation within the work. The slender figure twists, snakelike, from base to top, consistent with the principle of the *figura serpentinata*, a sculpture that has no fixed, frontal view and is instead meant to be considered in the round. Gallé's Venus invites endless rediscovery from different angles and points of view, presenting herself with equal beauty on all sides.

LE

Ambroise Gallé
Venus after the Bath, 1747
LIECHTENSTEIN. The Princely Collections, Vaduz–Vienna, Fürstliche Sammlungen
Art Service GmbH

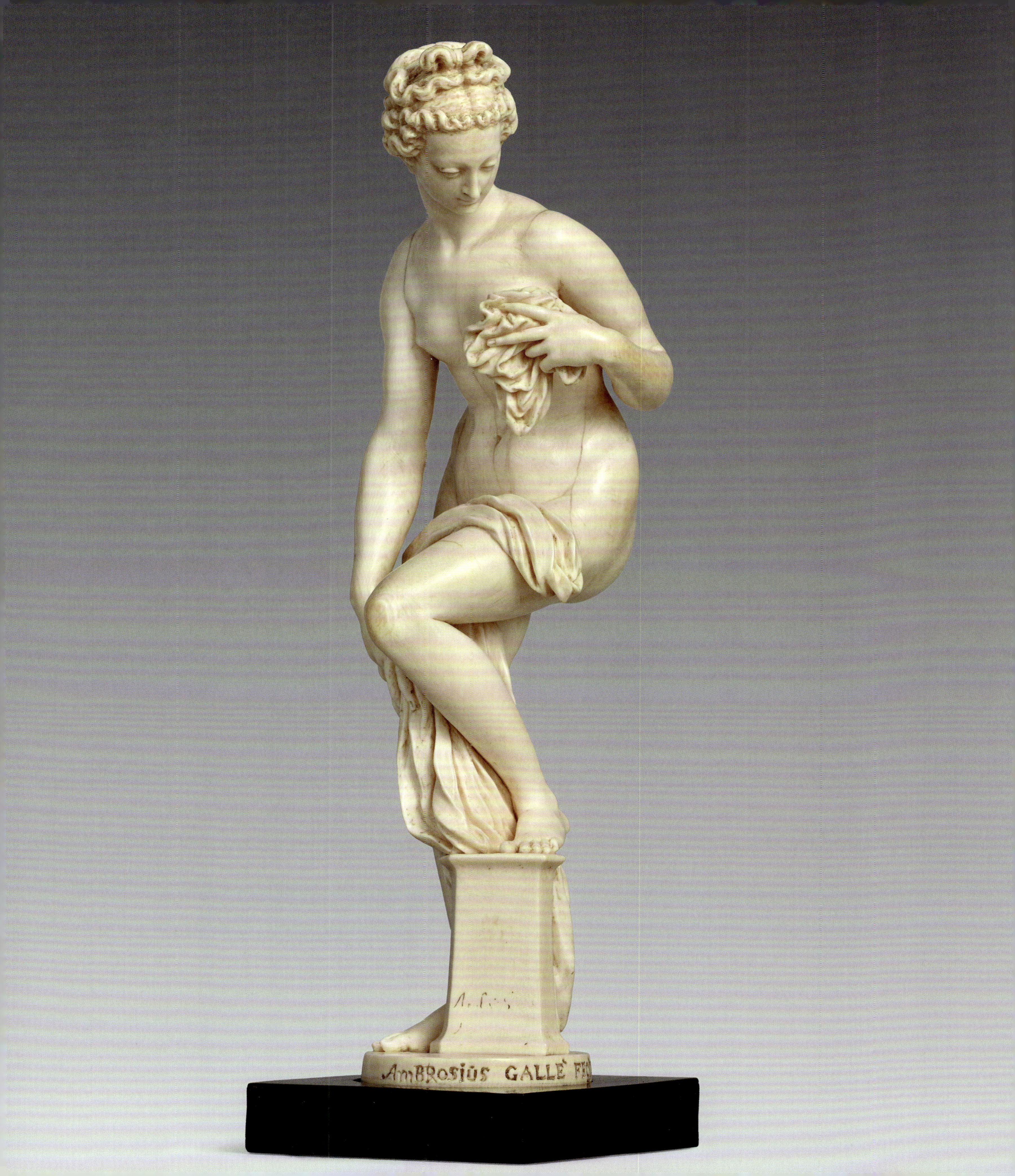
AMBROSIUS GALLÈ FE

For the Fairest of Them All, or The Judgment of Paris

Greek mythology tells how Paris was abandoned in the wilderness after his mother had a premonition in a dream while pregnant and how, as a result, the Trojan prince lived the life of a shepherd. Aware of this, Zeus (the Roman Jupiter) entrusted the royal offspring with a momentous decision.

The Bolognese native Francesco Raibolini, known as Francia—who had studied under Paduan artist Francesco Squarcione, a great lover of antiquity—attempted to simulate a classical relief based on this motif as a trompe l'oeil. In this way, he ventured in the brush drawing to legitimize the nudity of the protagonists, both male and female, which was still a bold act at that time. In fact, Francesco Francia's sheet is not a precise rendering after a Roman work but instead an invention based on two different antique pictorial types: the Judgment of Paris, as depicted on a Roman sarcophagus then housed in the Villa Medici (fig. 37), and the motif of the Three Graces (fig. 25).

Francia shows Paris in three-quarters profile facing right, seated on a large boulder. The prince hesitates in choosing which of the three goddesses is deserving of the golden apple. Hera (Juno), at the far left, is the only clothed figure. Resigned (and probably with a sense of foreboding), the goddess of marriage already turns, preparing to leave. Athena (Minerva), the goddess of wisdom, seen from the rear at the far right, observes the pensive prince. Aphrodite (Venus), who stands closest to Paris, seems somewhat detached from the proceedings but establishes eye contact with the viewer of the work, thereby introducing a second—tropological/moral—level. While Paris weighs his options, the viewer is enjoined to choose between various life paths: between the *vita activa* personified by Juno (a way of life that foregrounds practical activity and political engagement), the *vita contemplativa* (a more introspective form of existence) emblematized by Minerva, and Venus's *vita voluptaria* (the pursuit of pleasure).

37 *The Judgment of Paris*, ca. AD 180–200
Imperial era Roman sarcophagus, front panel
Marble, 90 × 230 cm
Villa Medici, Rome

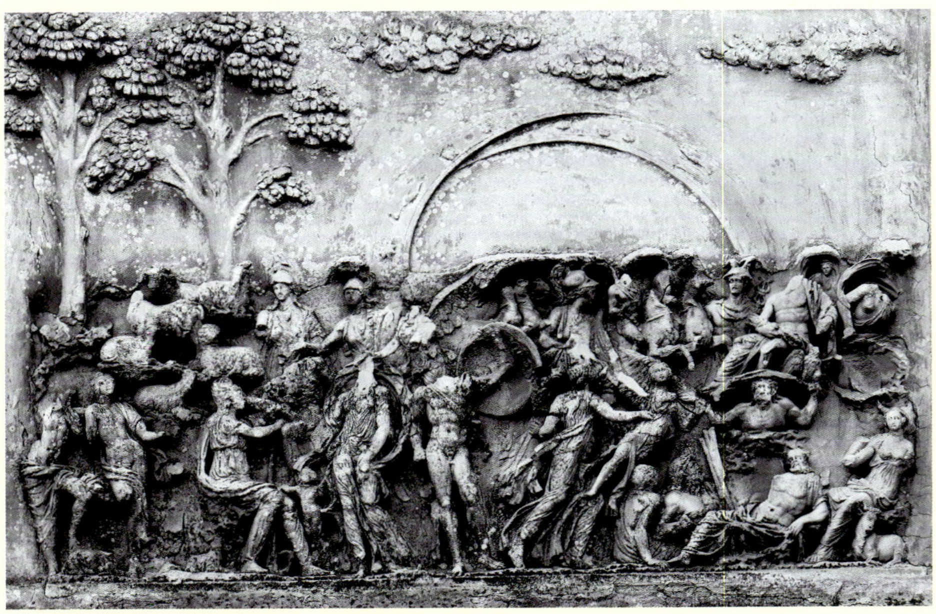

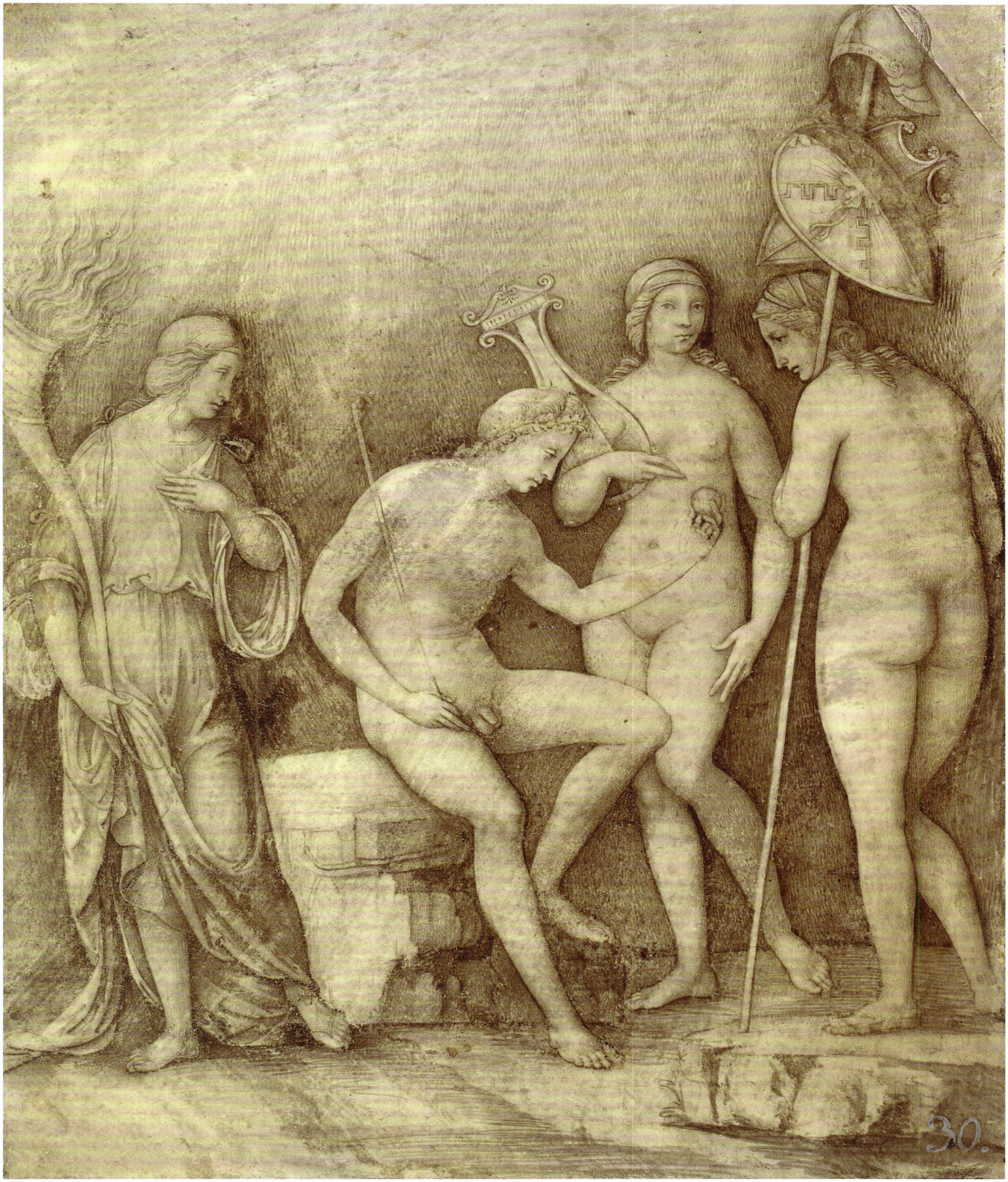

Francesco Francia
The Judgment of Paris, ca. 1505/06
The ALBERTINA Museum, Vienna

As we know, Paris decides in favor of the *vita voluptaria*. In return, Venus has promised him Helen, the most beautiful bride, who is however already married to Menelaus, King of Sparta.

Bestowing the apple concludes the conflict between the three goddesses, but the consequence of Paris's decision is war. Significantly, in Francia's drawing, Minerva has already brought along pieces of armor as *tropaion* (trophies of victory); she will stand on the side of the Greeks.

Hans von Aachen, who was active at the court of the Emperor Rudolf II in Prague beginning in 1596, functioned somewhat as a director. He arranged his scene, based on Raphael's *invenzione* (invention), which survives through Marcantonio Raimondi's engraving (fig. 38), in such a way that invites us to slip into the role of the now clothed Paris, who is seen from the back. Approaching him, and hence the viewer as well, are the three nude goddesses. On the late Mannerist sheet, everything is more sublime than in the world created by Raphael. Winged genii have guided in the small, light-footed rivals. Wafting veils provide covering where necessary. As with Raphael/Raimondi before, there is some uncertainty about whether Cupid is covering or unveiling his mother's genitalia. In either case, the gesture has its effect. In both compositions, she is to be the recipient of the apple awarded by Paris.

The unknown artist who, in the third quarter of the eighteenth century, almost literally repeats a composition by the Italian painter and engraver Sisto Badalocchio, also called Sisto Rosa, has used red chalk in order to endow the flesh tones of the protagonists with a new sensuality. In this pictorial invention, little Cupid, the personification of desire and falling in love, is clearly the real mastermind behind the scenes. He initiates the drama by pulling away the piece of cloth from his mother's mons veneris like a stage curtain, as Paris already initiates the action of handing over the prize, which Venus accepts. An act that leads directly to the tragedy of the Trojan War.

For the Berlin artist George Grosz, the goddesses are whores. Two elderly sex workers are shunned by the petty bourgeois perspective client. With malice, or due to sexual tension, he balls his right hand into a fist as he passes them. With a sense of purpose, he steers toward the youngest one at the top of the page. Whether she is real or merely his imaginary ideal remains unclear.

MP

38 Marcantonio Raimondi (after Raphael), *The Judgment of Paris*, 1513/14
Engraving, 29.4 × 43.7 cm
The ALBERTINA Museum, Vienna

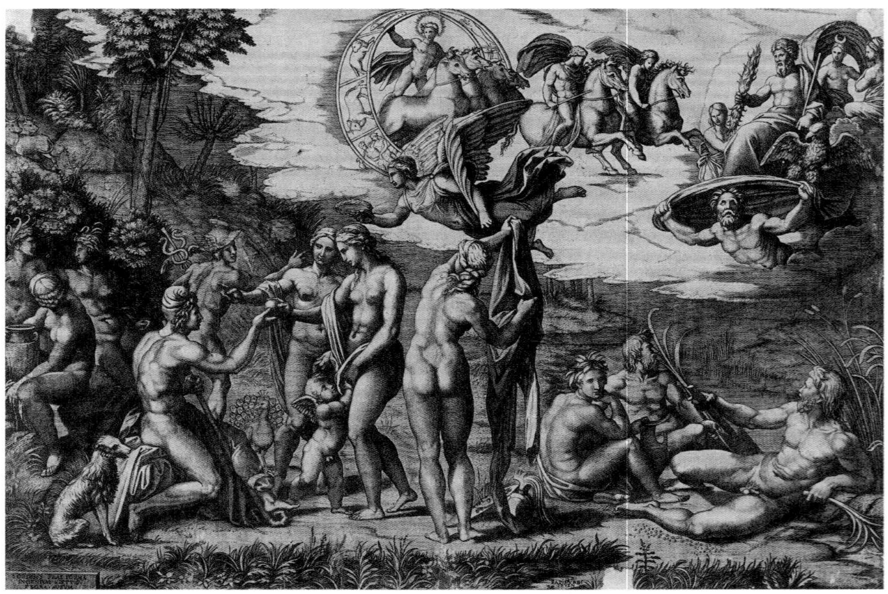

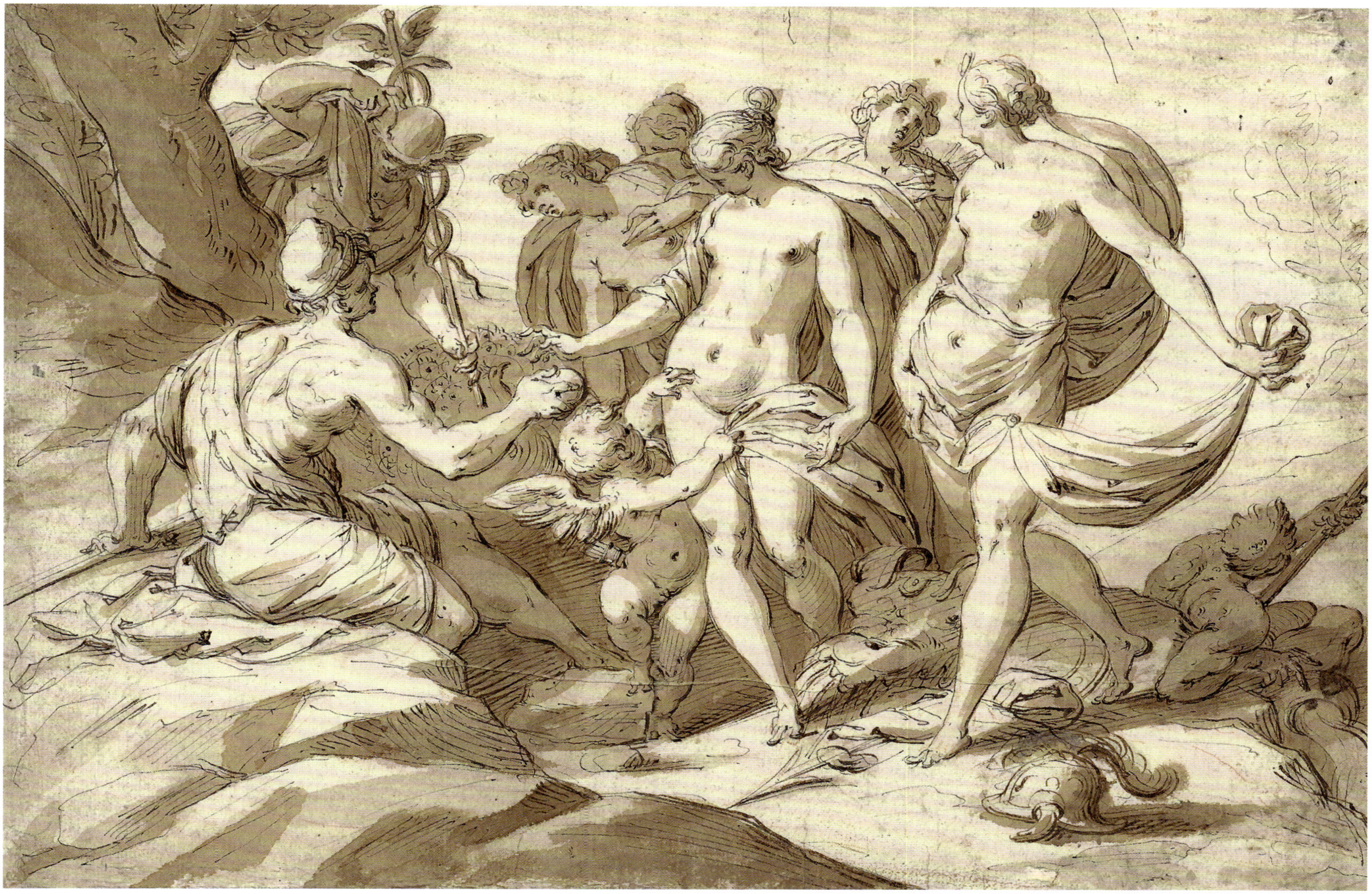

Hans von Aachen
The Judgment of Paris, ca. 1585
The ALBERTINA Museum, Vienna

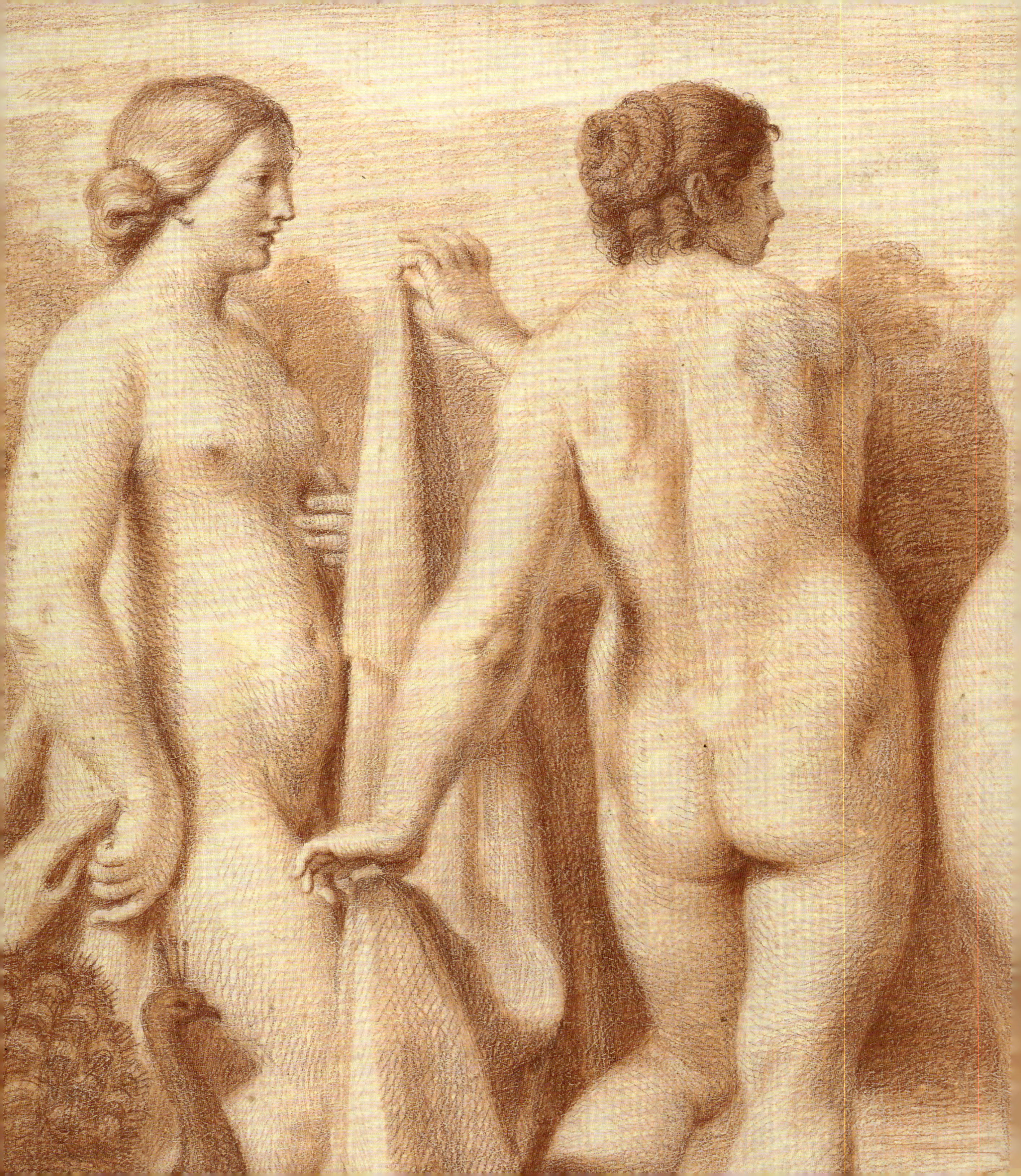

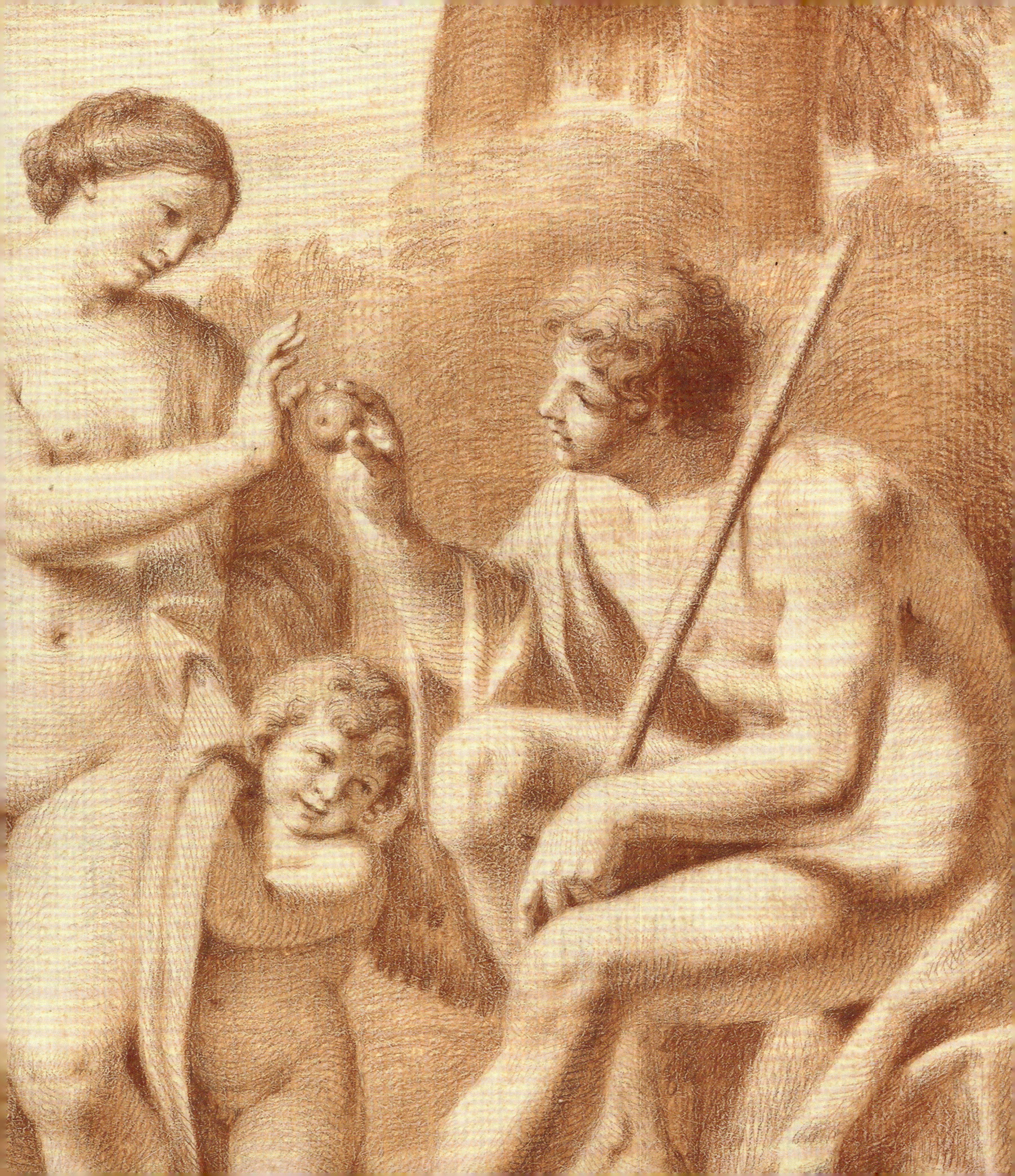

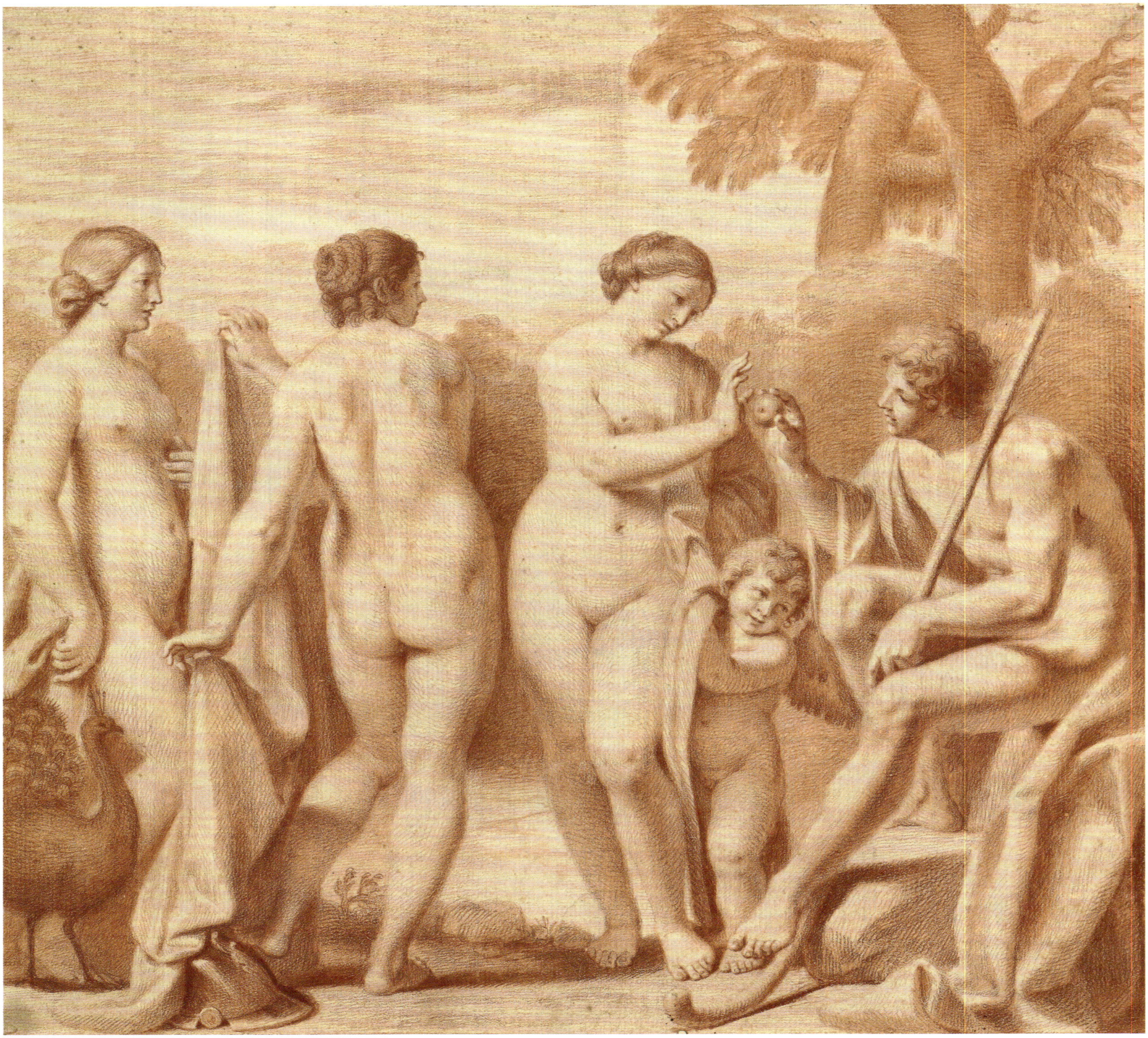

Copy after Sisto Badalocchio
The Judgment of Paris, third quarter of the 18th century
The ALBERTINA Museum, Vienna

George Grosz
Promenade, 1922
The ALBERTINA Museum, Vienna

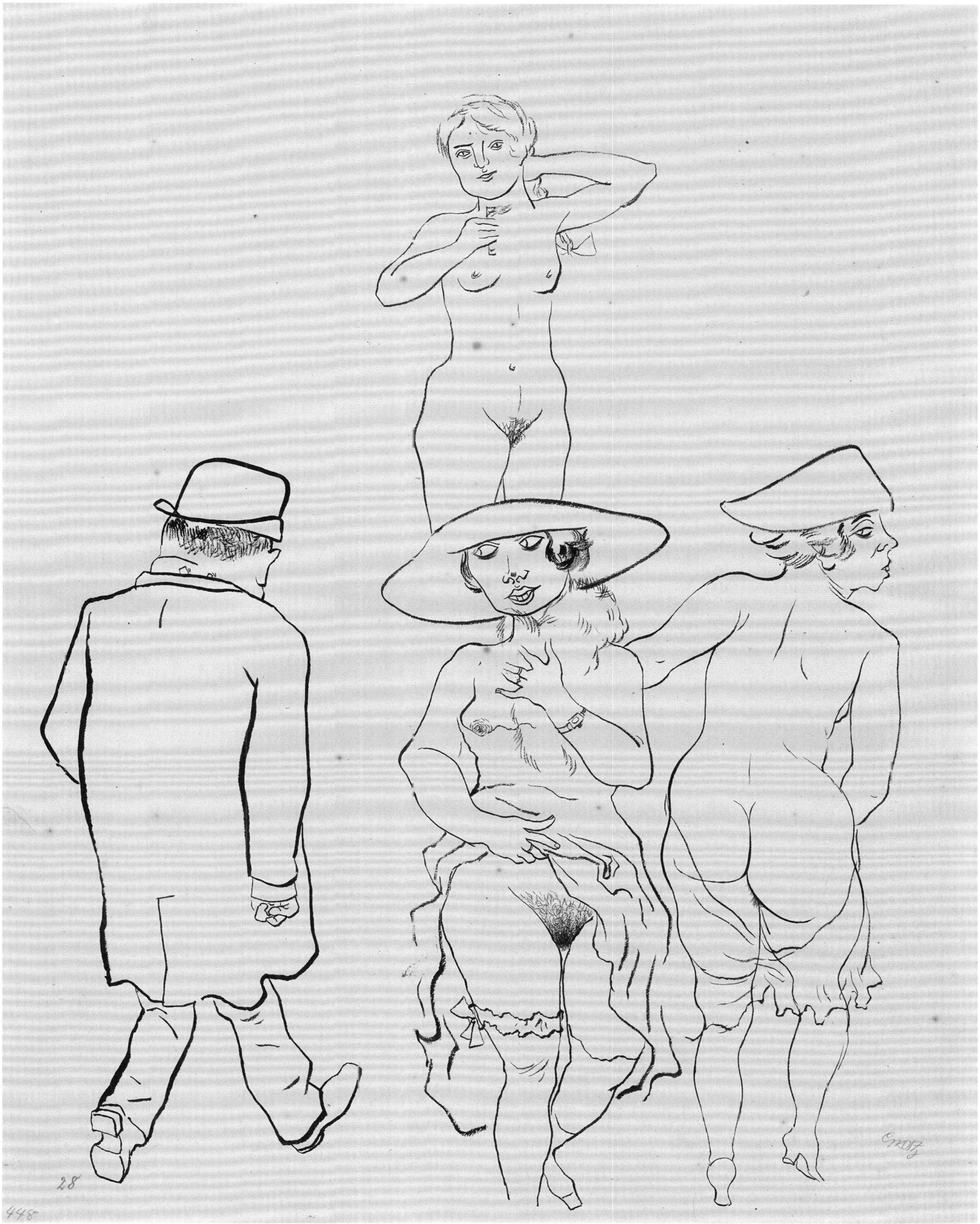
Grosz
28
448

Terra Incognita: Woman, the Unknown Being

Terra incognita (unknown territory) is a Latin expression used by Renaissance cartographers on maps to designate regions that had yet to be reached by European explorers during their expeditions. Coinciding with the great voyages of conquest, Italian, but also French, Dutch, and German artists consolidated the status of the nude female body in their paintings, and in the medium of sculpture as well. Beginning in the fifteenth century, nude live models were used for this purpose (figs. 30, 31). At the same time, the depiction of the female body came to be oriented toward the ideals these artists perceived as having been achieved in the works of antiquity (figs. 24, 35, 36).

From a present-day perspective, the question arises: Should the drawing of women in a state of undress, as seen through the study of the nude female body based on antique prototypes, be equated with a heightened perception of women as individuals? The answer can only be a simple and resounding *no*.

Woman remained "terra incognita," and her nude body continued as the locus for various imputations. If the female body were idealized for the purpose of depicting a goddess, nymph, etc., then this established a proximity to antiquity, not to the model's personality. In equal measure, the defamation of the nude woman as a witch, whore, or temptress insured a sense of distance.

Michelangelo depicted the female nude—*nota bene*: entirely in the medieval tradition—only when it was unavoidable. This meant Eve in Paradise and those resurrected on the Judgment Day; joining them on the Sistine Chapel ceiling were sibyls, and for the Medici tombs, the personifications of *Night* and *Dawn*. The female types employed were, to be sure, based on empirical observation, but this in reference to masculine models. Despite this, or precisely because of it, these works had an impact on subsequent generation of artists. Emerging from this dynamism in the hands of the Mannerists were space-dominating figures, the *figura serpentinata* (serpentine figure), fully on par with any male figures in presence and importance: an artificial figure in the truest sense of the word.

The most radical break with this tradition is found in the art of Rembrandt, who renders the female body with uncompromising naturalism—today, one would say, in the spirit of "body positivity." For the first time, familiarity with the non-ideal soars skyward above the ideality of the unattainable. Here, humanity no longer needs pursue the gods. Now, the Olympians can warm themselves in stuffy parlors and unmade beds with the soft bodies of human women.

Giovanni Battista Piazzetta
Seated Female Nude Seen from the Rear, first half of the 18th century
The ALBERTINA Museum, Vienna

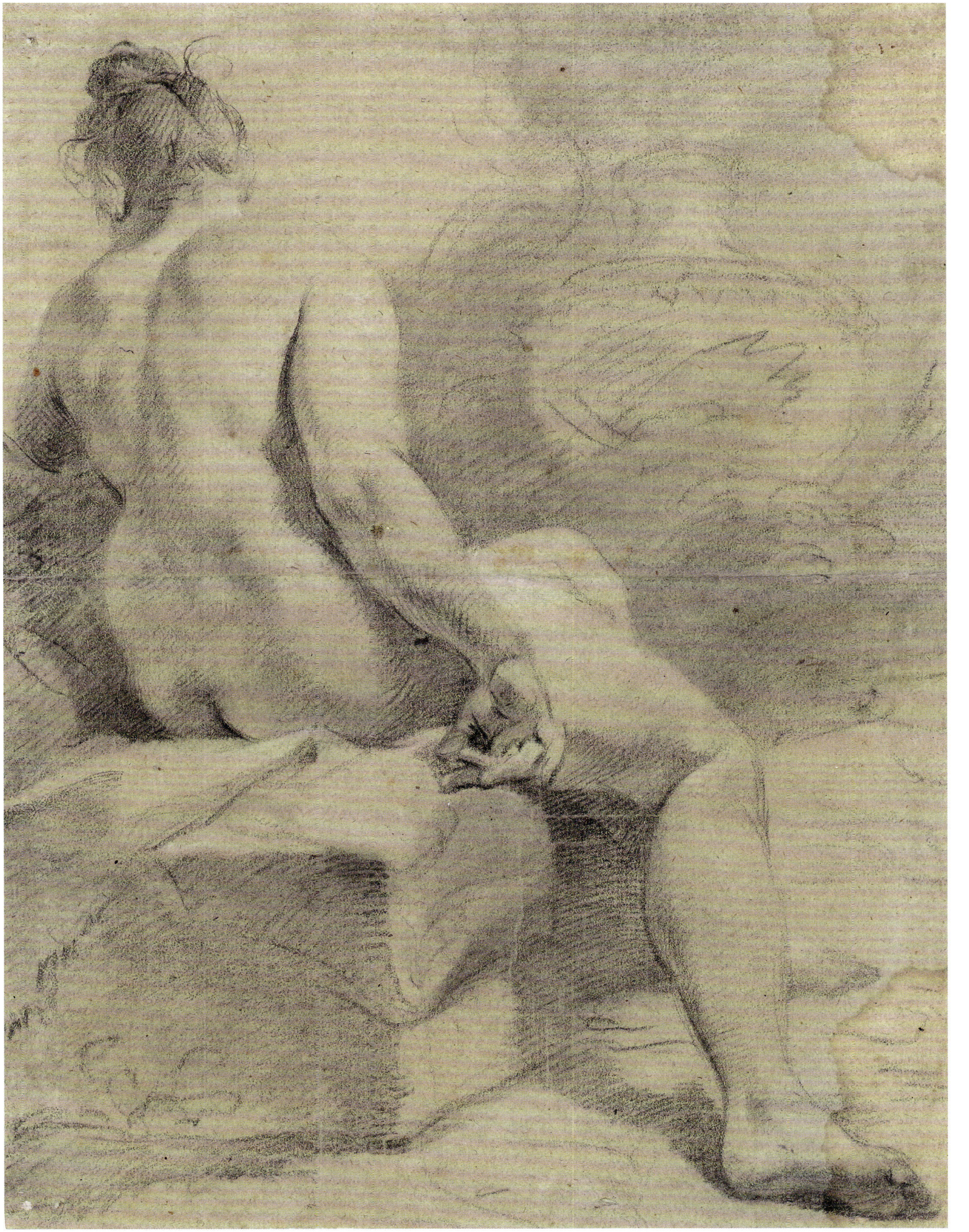

Rembrandt's contemporaries were appalled, and subsequent generations too found this difficult to accept—the Italians in particular. The Venetian Giovanni Battista Piazzetta endowed female figures with a high degree of physical presence, but the model who turns away—at the artist's request, surely—remains intangible as an individual.

The motif of the model who turns away from the artist is indeed particular to the seated female nude. Significantly, the German word for a nude motif (*Akt*) also makes reference to an "action." Since the Renaissance, apprentices and workshop assistants, and later students at art academies, sketched models that seem to be in states of motion. Such works served as preparatory studies for paintings and sculptures with religious, mythological, or historical themes, while also functioning as training exercises for future artistic careers. During the interval when the "acting" models are being sketched, they remain in fixed positions. They strike a pose! And in order to allow those doing the drawing to grasp the organic structure and foreshortening of the model in the best possible way, models were unclothed. And where drawing from the nude still forms part of the art curriculum, the practice continues unaltered up to the present day.

With female models, the primary concern is the body. Artworks document that female models were used in workshops and studios beginning in the fifteenth century. Nude female models, however, were only first used in art academies from the late nineteenth century. A pioneering role was played in 1893 by the Académie Julian in Paris. It was followed by other European art academies, among them the Akademie der bildenden Künste, Vienna's Academy of Fine Arts.

Only later—*nota bene*—were women permitted to enroll in art schools. Once again, it was Paris that led the way, specifically the École des Beaux-Arts in 1897. The art academy in Vienna followed only in 1920, during the First Austrian Republic. Up until that point, the exclusion of female students was justified throughout Europe with the argument that it would be indecent to expose them to the sight of nude male models. It was believed, moreover, that women lacked the requisite creative spirit. And it was male professors, needless to say, who laid down the rules of the game.

Of necessity, ambitious women had recourse to other forms of art training. Deprived of opportunities to study from nude models, but also to acquire knowledge

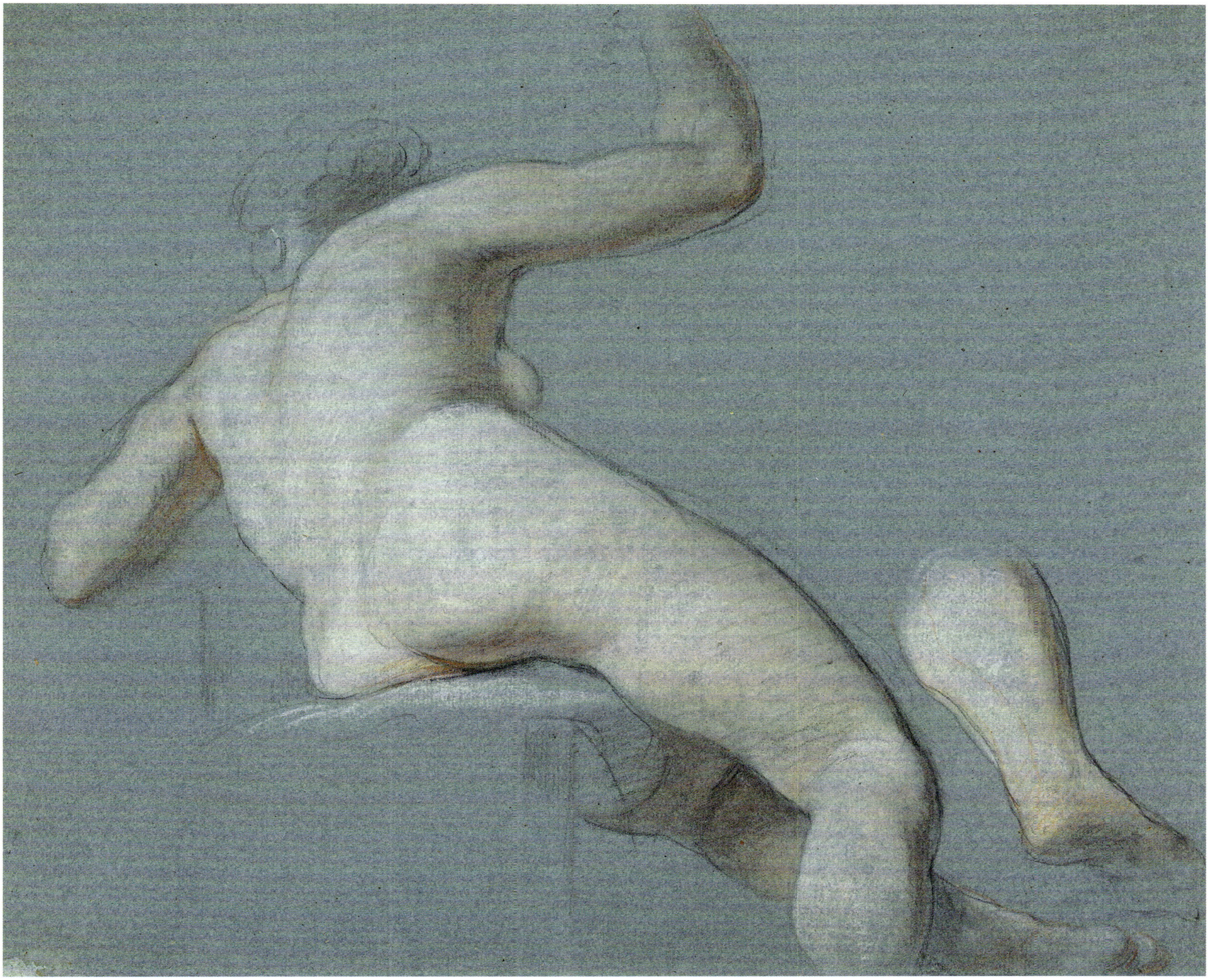

French Artist
Seated Female Nude, second half of the 18th century
The ALBERTINA Museum, Vienna

of perspective drawing as a preparation for the production of history paintings, they concentrated on portraits, floral still lifes, or landscapes.

Among the rare prospects for a woman to receive artistic training was involvement in her own father's workshop. Artemisia Gentileschi (1593–1656 or later), for example, was active at her father's side from a young age. In a number of her paintings depicting women as the victims of male desire (Susanna at her bath) or as Old Testament heroines (Judith, Esther, etc.), she processed the trauma of her own rape at the hands of Agostino Tassi, a colleague of her father's. And when depicting herself as a Christian martyr, for example *Saint Catherine of Alexandria* (1615–1617; National Gallery, London), condemned to be broken on the wheel, she made herself, together with her own suffering, visible in a revolutionary form. Just a few years earlier, in 1612, she had herself endured torture with thumbscrews in the course of the trial against Tassi.

MP

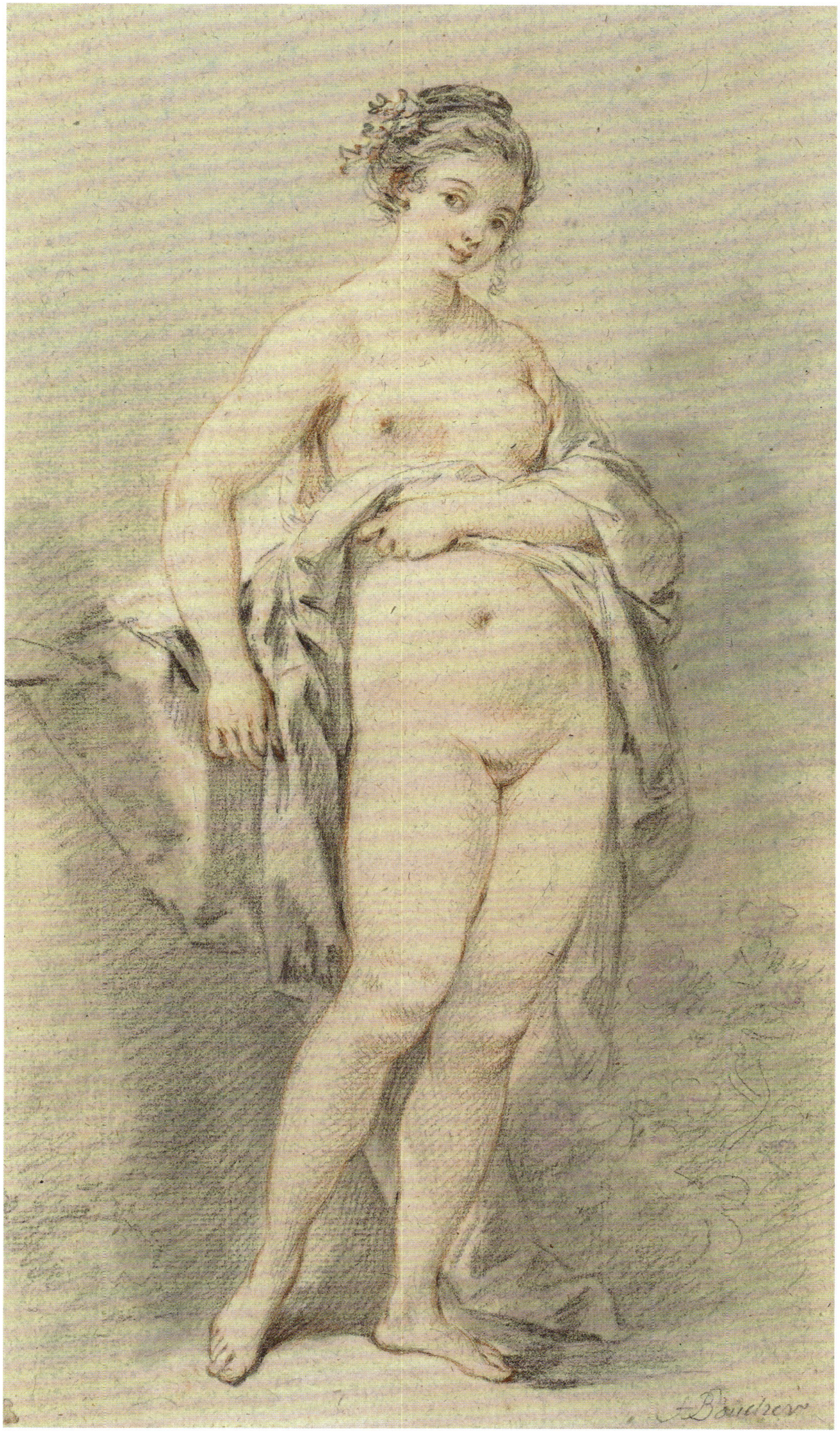

François Boucher
Standing Nude Girl,
second third of the 18th century
The ALBERTINA Museum, Vienna

A subtle play of distance and proximity has been pursued by artists ever since the Renaissance, where the erotic sensations evoked in the viewer seem to cause the distance between *him* and the work of art to vanish. A drawing by Bartholomaeus Spranger shows the goddess of love seated on a dolphin's back, her son, Cupid—the fruit of her relationship with Mars—held loosely in one arm.

Through the use of white chalk, Spranger endows the bodies with sculptural form, the eye of the dolphin with a gleam, and the sea water with its foamy surface. The latter is an allusion to a sobriquet of the goddess, said to have been "born of [sea] foam" (ἀφρογενής: *aphrogenes*). According to legend, the Titan Cronos (the Roman Saturn) castrated the primordial sky god Uranus with a sickle and flung his testicles into the sea. Aphrodite sprang from the foam formed as Uranus's sperm and blood mixed with seawater. As later depicted by Botticelli, Aphrodite/Venus was wafted toward Cyprus by friendly breezes—a scallop half shell serving as her surfboard (fig. 34).

Notwithstanding, in Spranger's drawing, it is a dolphin that carries mother and child toward us. She sits astride the beast in a way that is simultaneously precarious and stable. Venus's center of gravity is found in her pelvis, so that she must only support herself gently on the back of the tame sea monster with her right hand, balancing delicately on its left pectoral fin with the tips of her toes. She has drawn in her legs in a way that exposes her pubic area to view, but it is cast in shadow due to the ink wash applied there.

The sense of immediacy generated by these erotic aspects is directly counteracted stylistically—by the elongation of the figure, the small, girlish breasts, the *sprezzatura* (effortless elegance), as well as the composition's vignette-like cohesion. This ambivalence is characteristic of late Mannerist art, produced in great variety at the Prague court of the Emperor Rudolf II.

MP

Bartholomaeus Spranger
Venus and Cupid on a Dolphin, ca. 1580–1585
The ALBERTINA Museum, Vienna

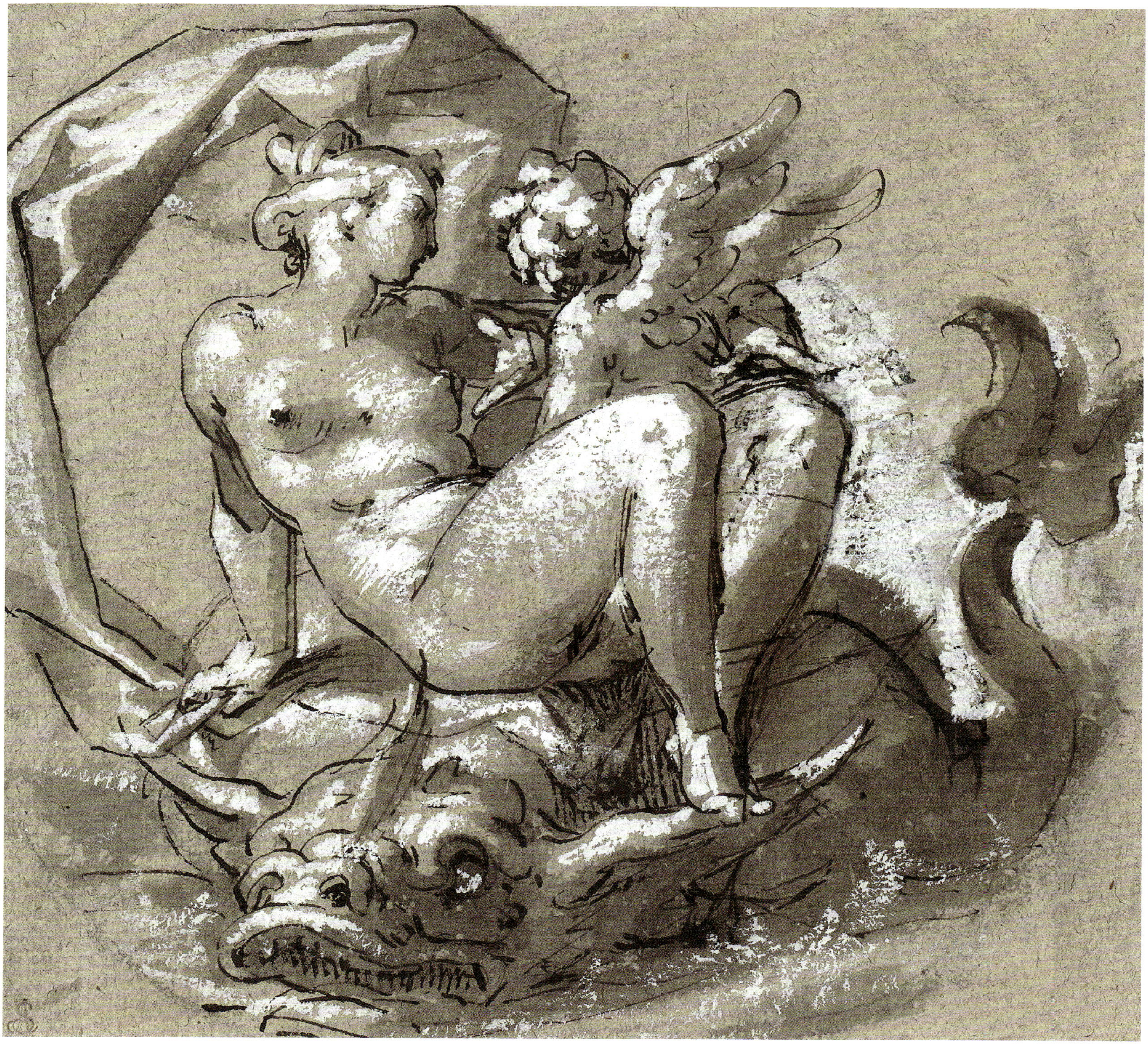

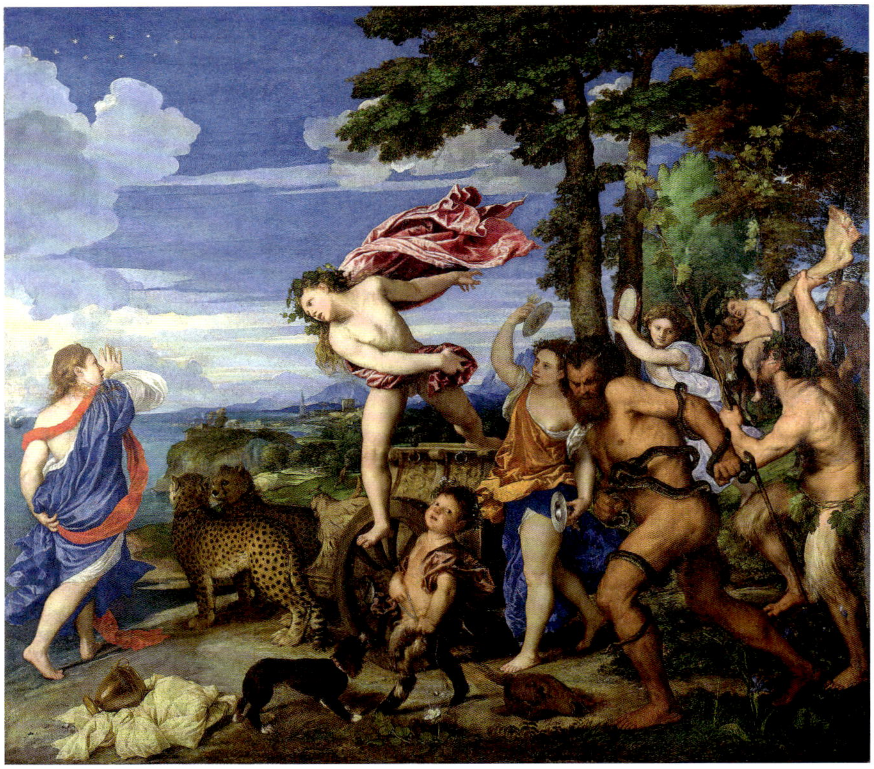

39 Titian, *Bacchus and Ariadne*, 1520–1523
Oil on canvas, 176.5 × 191 cm
National Gallery, London

Thanks to the Venetian artists Giovanni Bellini and Titian, Bacchus (the Greek Dionysus) and his retinue, among them the bacchantes, made a triumphant return in the visual art of the West during the first quarter of the sixteenth century after more than a millennium of exile (fig. 39).

A nude adolescent girl poses for the painter and highly talented decorator Charles-Joseph Natoire in the role of a bacchante with a tambourine. With her, we encounter a new female type, one who strode into view in France before the mid-eighteenth century: a virginal girl with a soft body, the blushing cheeks of a child, hair tied up carelessly with a ribbon. Yet, at the same time, already a woman, who signals with her attitude, gesture, and gaze that she is quite conscience of her allure. A nymphet who has mastered the game of sensual love, right down to the tips of her fingers. A doll, and thanks to her youth, with no memories or morals. This ancestor of Stanley Kubrick's adaptation of Lolita (1962) is no longer preparatory material for a painting that transmits weighty historical or mythological content, but is instead simply what she is: standing, sitting, or draped onto a bed, she is the mistress of the boudoir. Nothing could possibly be further from Michelangelo's superhuman (in Dante's sense) figures, made female through the makeshift attachment of breasts!

Meanwhile, certain mid-eighteenth-century French artists—alongside Charles-Joseph Natoire there was also François Boucher and Jean-Honoré Fragonard—functioned as accomplices in a game of libertinism. Their sketchy delicate strokes, and the sparing use of red chalk heightened with white, transformed blank paper into the skin of pure maidens, preserving a place, once the sheet had attained completion, for the parthenophilic viewer.

MP

Charles-Joseph Natoire
Bacchante with a Tambourine, ca. 1740
The ALBERTINA Museum, Vienna

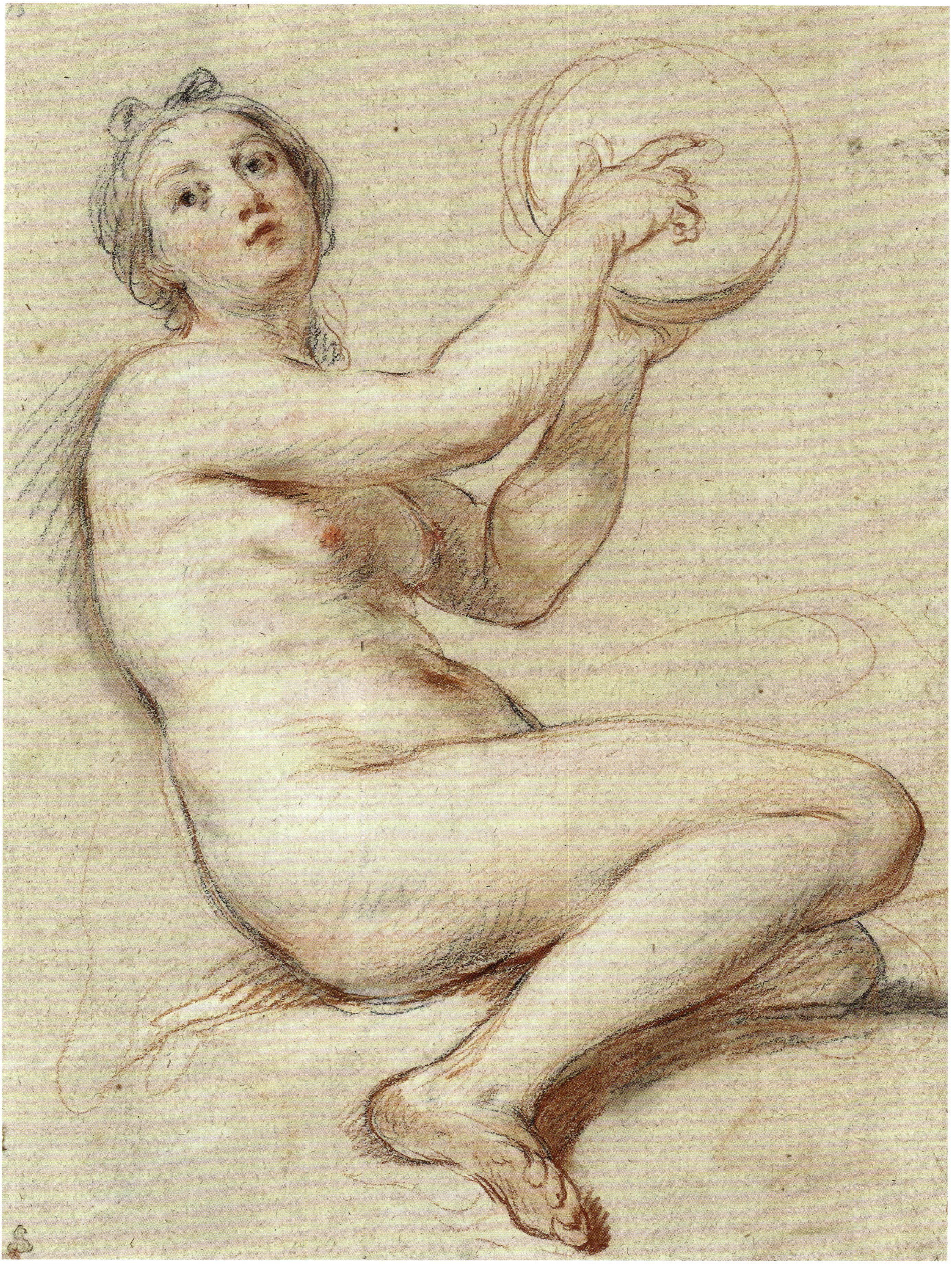

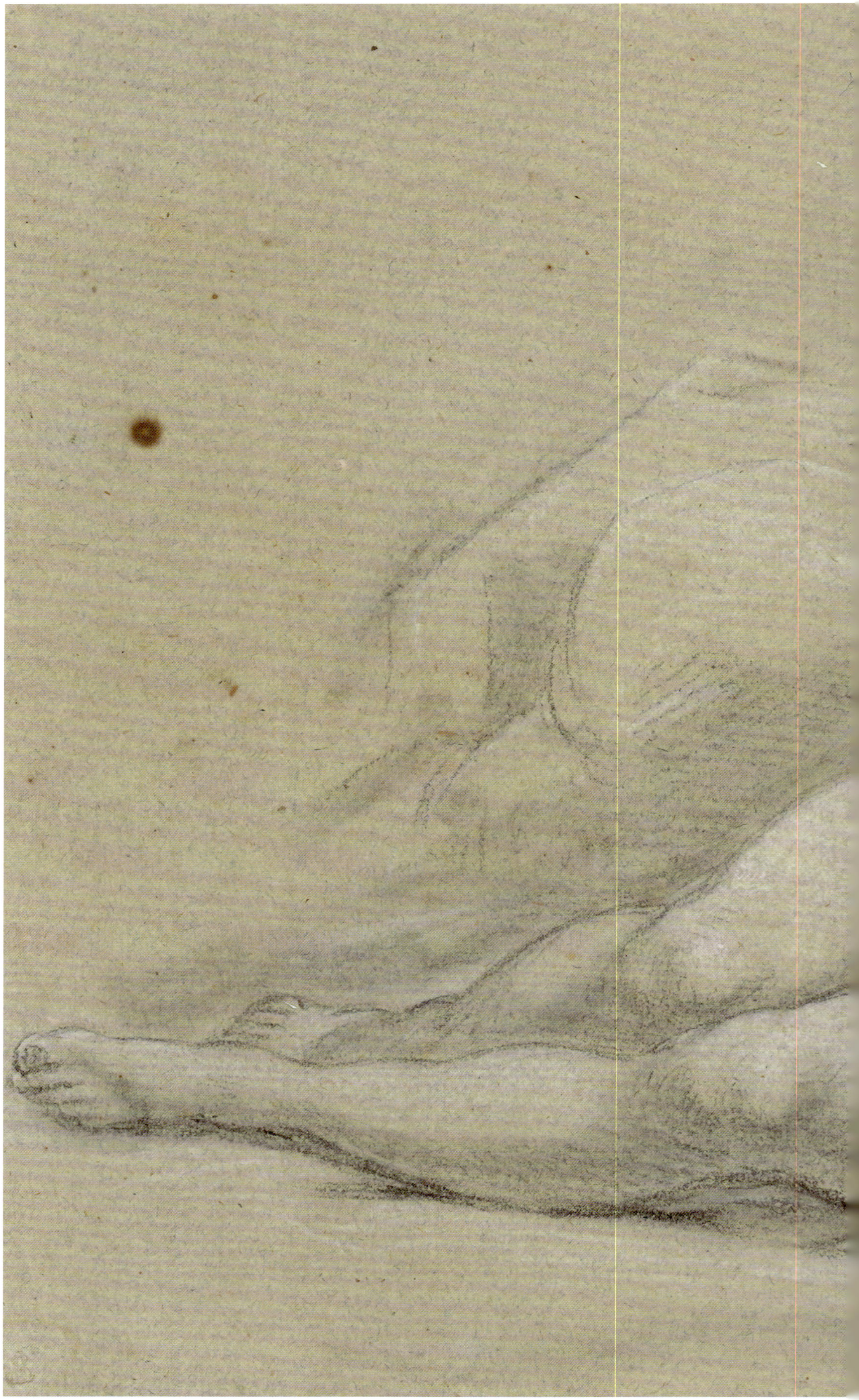

François Boucher
Nude Girl Lying on a Bed,
second third of the 18th century
The ALBERTINA Museum, Vienna

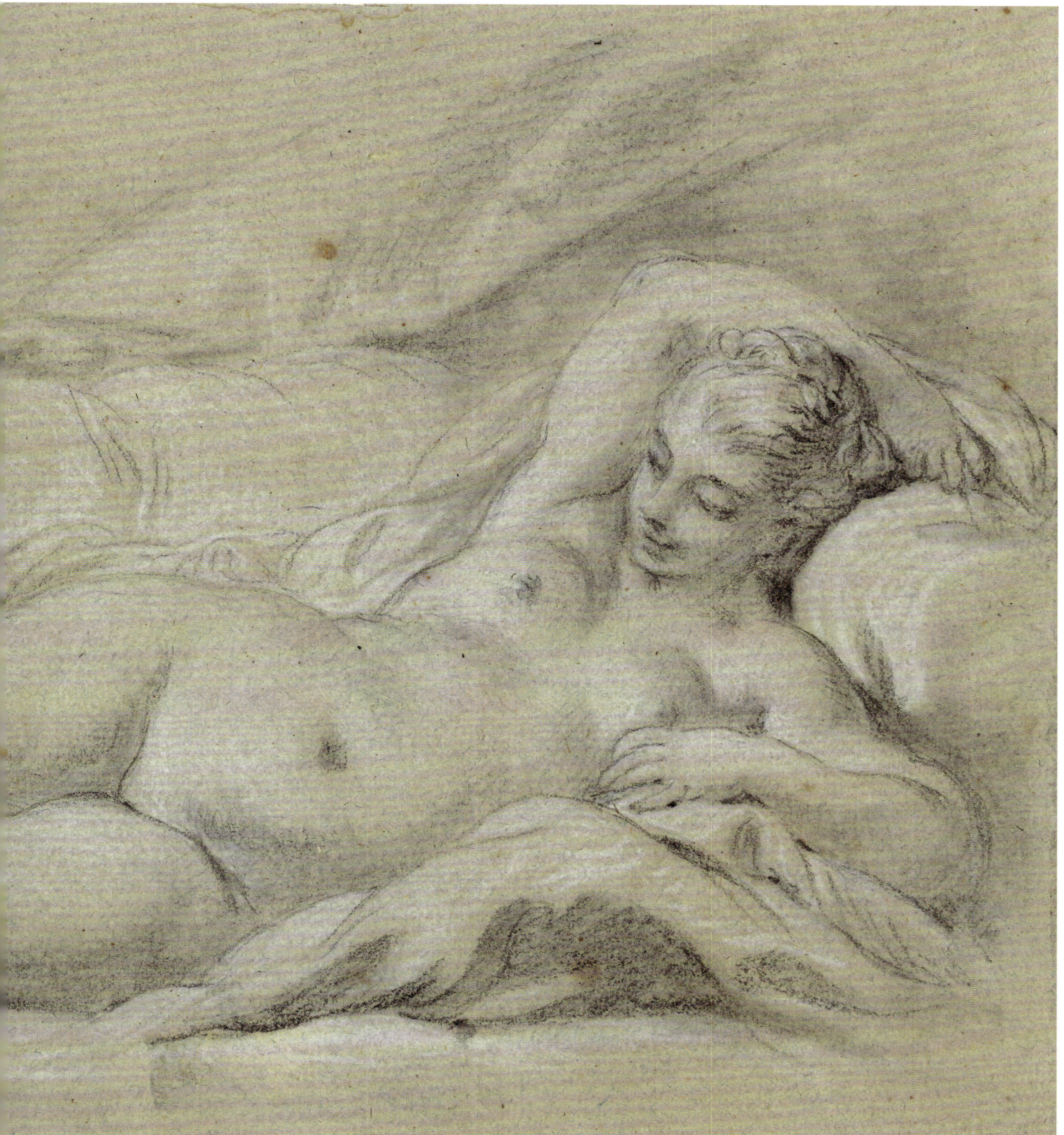

The Cult of Beauty and the Aesthetics of the Ugly

Shock—which is to say, shocking the public—is a modernist strategy. Its origins can be found in the depths of the thoughts underlying the Decadent movement. Or to use a less pejorative term: of Symbolism, a movement that emerged in France during the 1870s to capture all of Europe. It is often overlooked that Austrian artists too, among them Richard Gerstl and Egon Schiele, seven years his junior, also followed this tendency, which rallied poets and painters alike around a call to "épater la bourgeoisie!" (offend the middle classes). In distinctly provocative gestures, Gerstl and Schiele depicted their own bodies, in the process reflecting upon their own highly sensitive personalities.

In ways that go far beyond the reality documented in photographs, Schiele represented himself as an emaciated figure, as oppressed, as tormented, as maltreated, his body, flecked with red, testifying to the same degree of abuse as his face. He depicts himself as a tree that grows crooked, subjected to a perpetual storm, its branches amputated, so that the hair of his head, his genitals, and his torso sprouts directly from the trunk. Or paused in the midst of spastic movements. Or pinned to the surface like a dead butterfly. More logogram than being. The distorted or swollen mouth is that of a boxer after a match. The vacant eyes, however, signal that all of our attempts at empathy will come to naught.

On a metalevel, all of this creates a connection to Michelangelo, who depicts himself as the flayed skin of Bartholomew the Apostle (who was, according to legend, skinned alive) in his *The Last Judgment* of the Sistine Chapel (fig. 40). It is not difficult to relate this act of identification with the hard labor of frescoing the ceiling (1508–1512) and west wall (1536–1541), with the necessity to bargain with theologians concerning iconography, with the battle against accusations of obscenity, and not least of all, with the Sisyphean labor on the tomb of Pope Julius II. While the Medici Pope, Clement VII, and then Paul III, a Farnese, used *The Last Judgment* in the Sistine Chapel to confront the Protestants—who in 1517 had taken up the struggle against the papal "dragon" and the sale of indulgences—with the consequences of their heretical actions, Michelangelo used this crypto-portrait in order to position himself in proximity to Christ.

In Symbolism, meanwhile, the individual confronts the imposition known as "the world" in utter isolation. Gerstl's and Schiele's shrieks may be piercing, but they are audible only in the well-ordered, bright echo chamber erected in Vienna by the

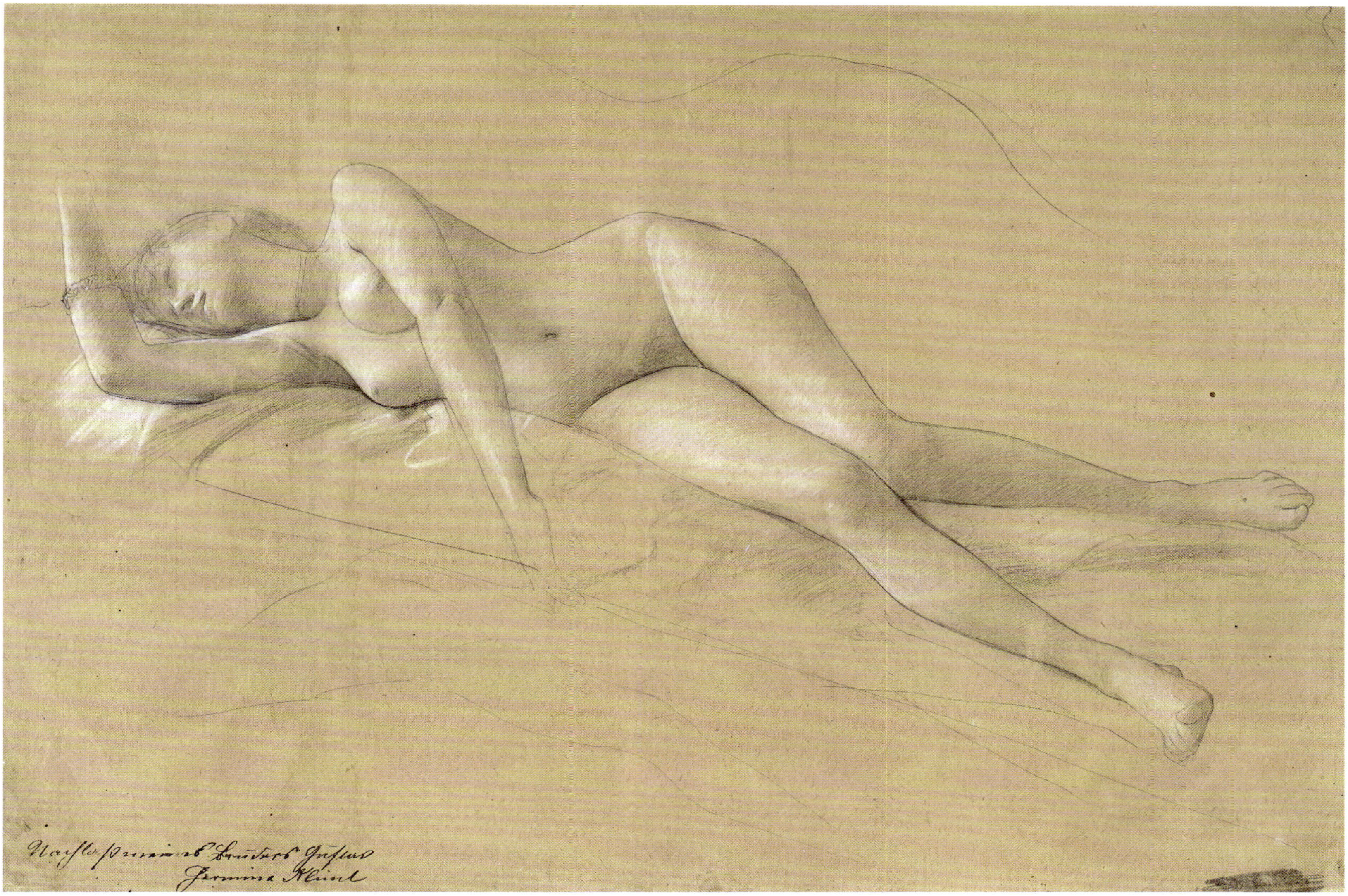

Gustav Klimt
Reclining Maenad (study for *Altar of Dionysus*, Burgtheater, Vienna), 1886/87
The ALBERTINA Museum, Vienna

decorative tendency of Symbolism. The variant known as Viennese *Jugendstil* remained consistently indebted to the Platonic *kalokagathia* ("pulchritudo-bonitas": "the beautiful and the good"). Already in Classical Greece and its Julio-Claudian reception, and again during the Renaissance, as well as in Neoclassicism, the aim was the unity of aesthetic and ethical perfection, which found its purest expression in the idealized human figure—for the womanizer Gustav Klimt, in the nude female body.

When Klimt transformed himself stylistically within the thematic framework of "Symbolism" from an exponent of history painting into a key proponent of the planar art of the Vienna Secession and a master of the beautifully flowing line, he became a kind of Prometheus, who once again, and for the very last time, stole fire of the ideal from the heavens.

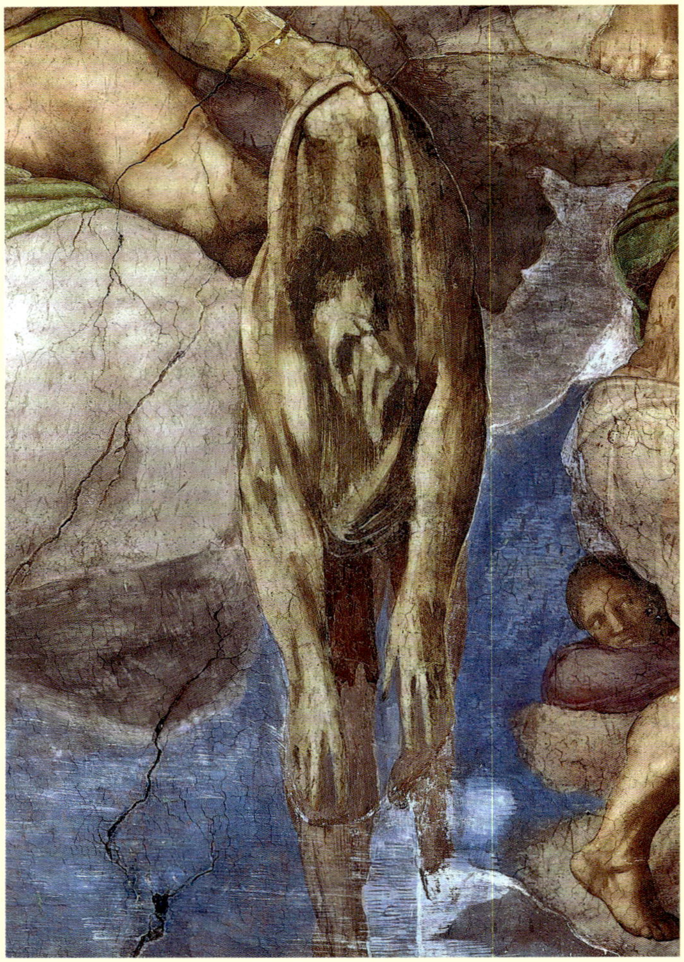

40 Michelangelo, *The Last Judgment*, 1536–1541 (detail)
The flayed skin of St. Bartholomew, crypto-portrait of Michelangelo
Fresco
Sistine Chapel, Vatican, Altar Wall

Despite all of his admiration for his elder colleague, Schiele departed from this decorative variant when he converted his own body into a field for experimentation. Nor did he exclude women from this crisis of the subject. For them as well, decomposition is a constantly lurking danger. In his *Nude Girl with Folded Arms* of 1910, it is the model who must hold herself together to avoid breaking into pieces, as in George Minne's *Kneeling Youth*; but now so radically that the girl's arms appear to be pressed into her emaciated body as if by straitjacket. In another female nude from the same year, the model's left hand lies on her breast as though detached from some corpse.

The sheets from 1914 seems somewhat removed from this scenario of disintegration. Here, the focus lies elsewhere. The reclining woman with spread legs, along with the seated woman with her left elbow resting on her right knee, are among those works by Schiele that cast a radically modern gaze on female sexuality. Here, after centuries of pejorative or idealizing roles and character attributions designed to keep women at a distance, we encounter an unprejudiced view of the nude female form. And she looks back at us with an unflinching gaze. Through this direct eye contact between model and artist (and hence with the viewer of the work as well), two human beings encounter one another as equals, seeing themselves eye-to-eye.

Two beings whose sexuality, with its decisive momentum, holds the subject captive in its proneness to crisis, and at the same time remote from any determinability.

Only a half-century later, after two world wars and immeasurable atrocities, did women succeed in exposing their bodies themselves as the site of centuries of violation (fig. 41). Photography, video, performance art, etc. also allowed them to set aside the medial and iconographic schemata and styles that had been deployed by male artists for centuries, negotiating burning issues with new resources. Accompanying all of this was the need to abandon the mode of frontal communication. Certainly, the discursive space within which the imposition of aesthetic standards (i.e., the classical canon) is to be overcome—just as well as the purely binary gender order and the construct of a colonial divide—is only kept open through tremendous effort and exists under constant threat.

MP

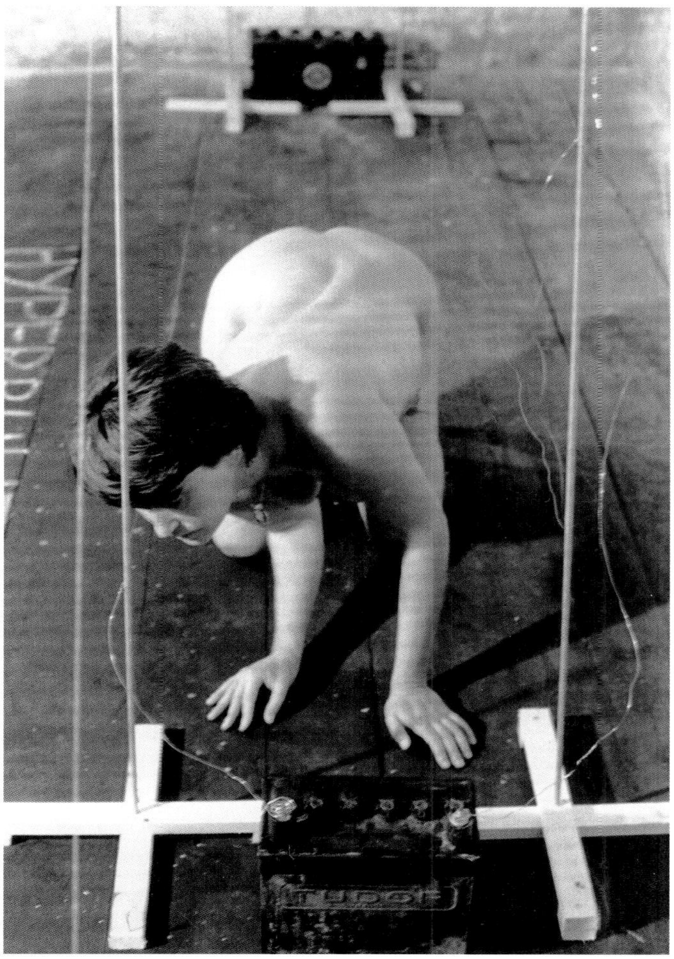

41 VALIE EXPORT, *Hyperbulie*
Body performance, Vienna, 1973

Around 1900, a groundbreaking change occurred in Gustav Klimt's drawing style. In creating studies of the female body and female desire on paper, he was more daring and explicit than he had ever been on canvas. At the same time, he explored the most delicate nuances of emotions and states of mind, seeking their expression through posture and gesture. His depictions of the nude body paved the way for the young Expressionists Egon Schiele and Oskar Kokoschka to produce nudes unburdened by taboo.

The Three Gorgons is part of the *Beethoven Frieze*, a mural measuring 2-by-34 meters originally painted for the Beethoven exhibition held at the Secession Building in 1902. Whereas the Gorgons of Greek mythology are described as frightful winged creatures with snakes for hair, Klimt portrayed them as seductively dangerous *femmes fatales*: with sensually curved bodies, coquettish poses, and hypnotic gazes—provocatively naked, free of any sense of shame.

ED

Study for the Right Figure of "Three Gorgons" in the Beethoven Frieze, 1901
The ALBERTINA Museum, Vienna

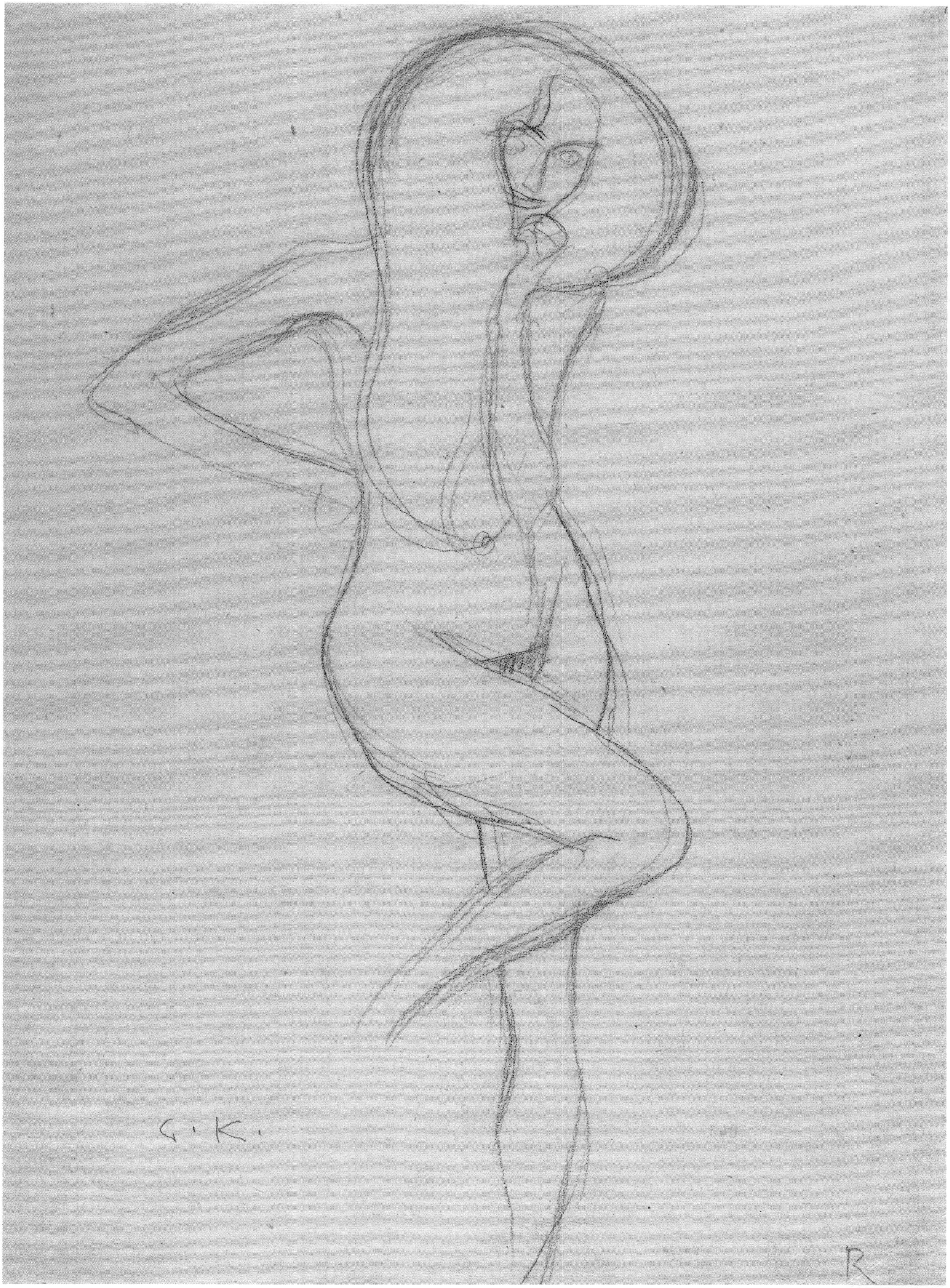

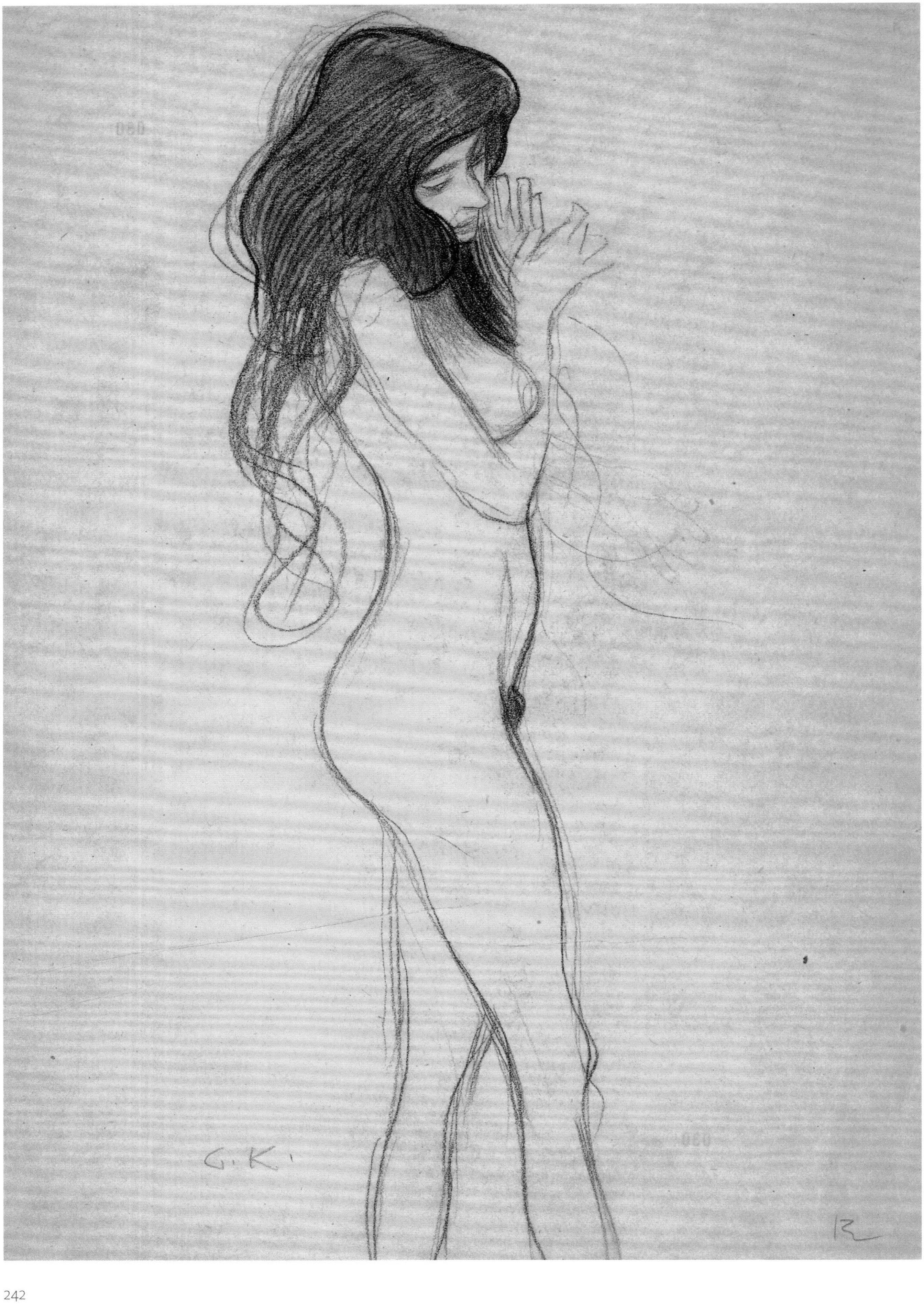

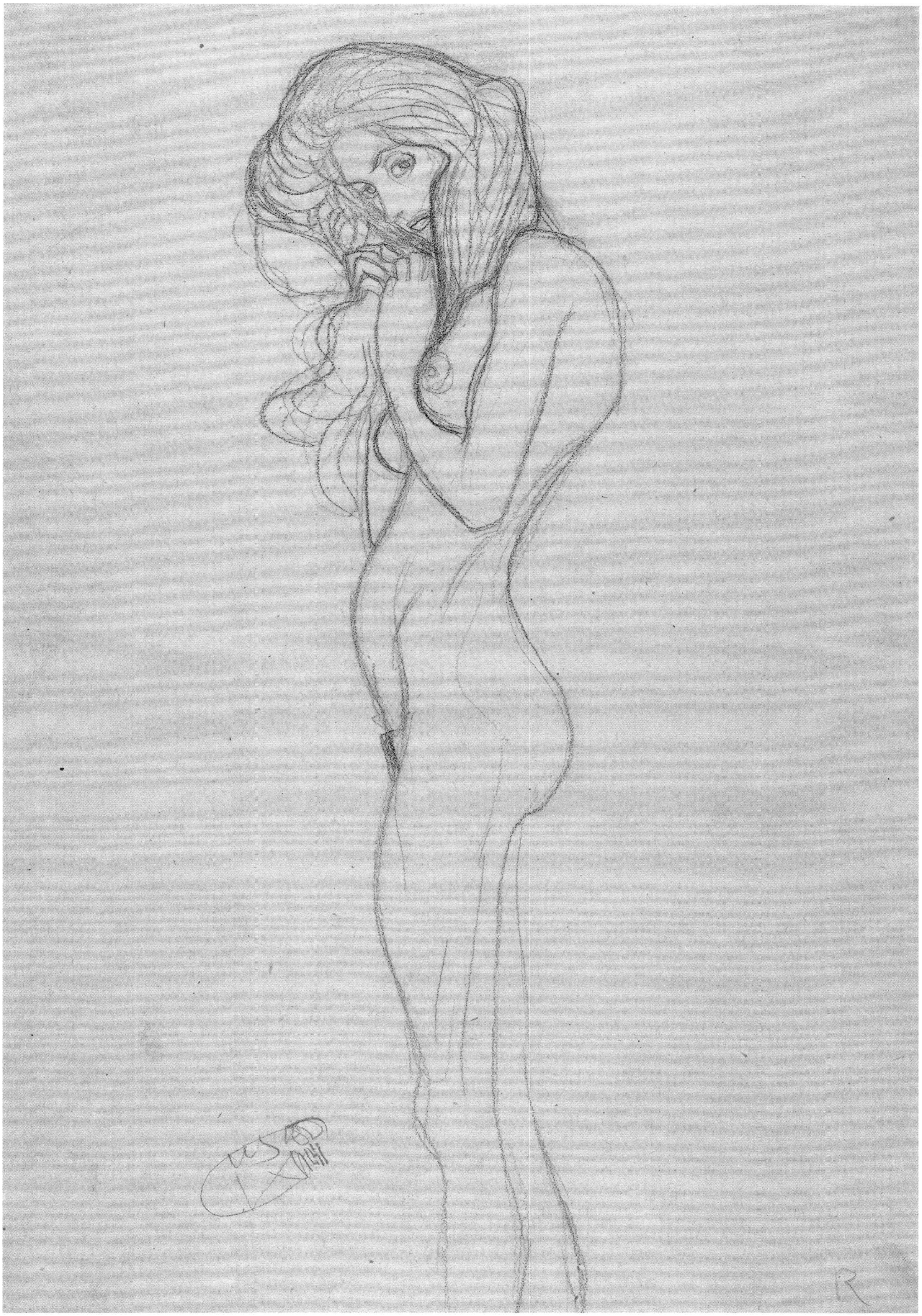

Gustav Klimt
Study for the Left Figure of "Three Gorgons" in the Beethoven Frieze, 1901
The ALBERTINA Museum, Vienna

Gustav Klimt
Study for the Left Figure of "Three Gorgons" in the Beethoven Frieze, 1901
The ALBERTINA Museum, Vienna

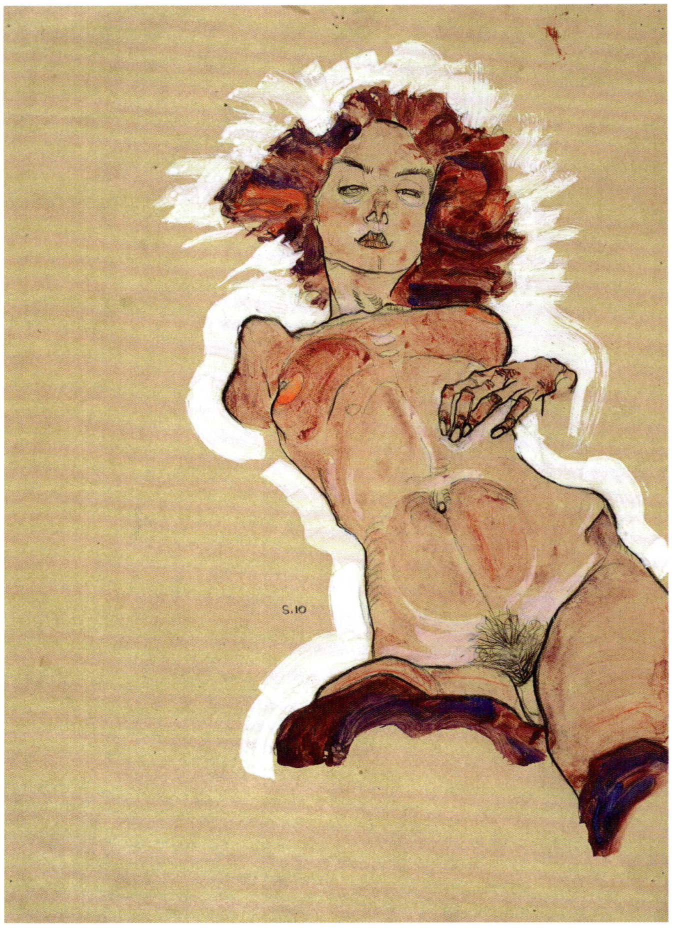

42 Egon Schiele, *Female Nude*, 1910
Pencil, black chalk, watercolor, gouache, heighten with white, 44 × 30.5 cm
The ALBERTINA Museum, Vienna

Although the breakthrough to Expressionism is already discernible in a few drawings dating from 1909, this stylistic development only accelerated dramatically in the spring of 1910. At the start of this year, the nude erupted into Egon Schiele's oeuvre as if overnight, as the most important motif alongside the self-portrait. Even though these first garishly colored female nudes (fig. 42) and the so-called "Red Men" are to be seen as studies related to some external impetus, the inner development of these series is nevertheless evidence of Schiele's own profound interest in the existentialist analysis of the human being thrown back on his or her own resources.

In the most radical female nude of this period, we can still recognize, in the gently undulating contours of the pelvic area, the influence of Klimt's studies for the *Beethoven Frieze*. The angle of view, from below, is doubtless also derived from Klimt. The exaggerations of color, the drastic nakedness of the vulva, the stark fragmentation of the arm stumps, and the tension-filled opposition of concave and convex curves all indicate, however, that this early major work was largely independent of Klimt. For the first time, Schiele anchors the content—namely the exposure of the individual human being—in the form. It is the line which, by activating the negative exterior surface, illuminates the forces acting upon the body, compressing it to a basic minimum and petrifying it.

KAS

Egon Schiele
Nude Girl with Folded Arms, 1910
The ALBERTINA Museum, Vienna

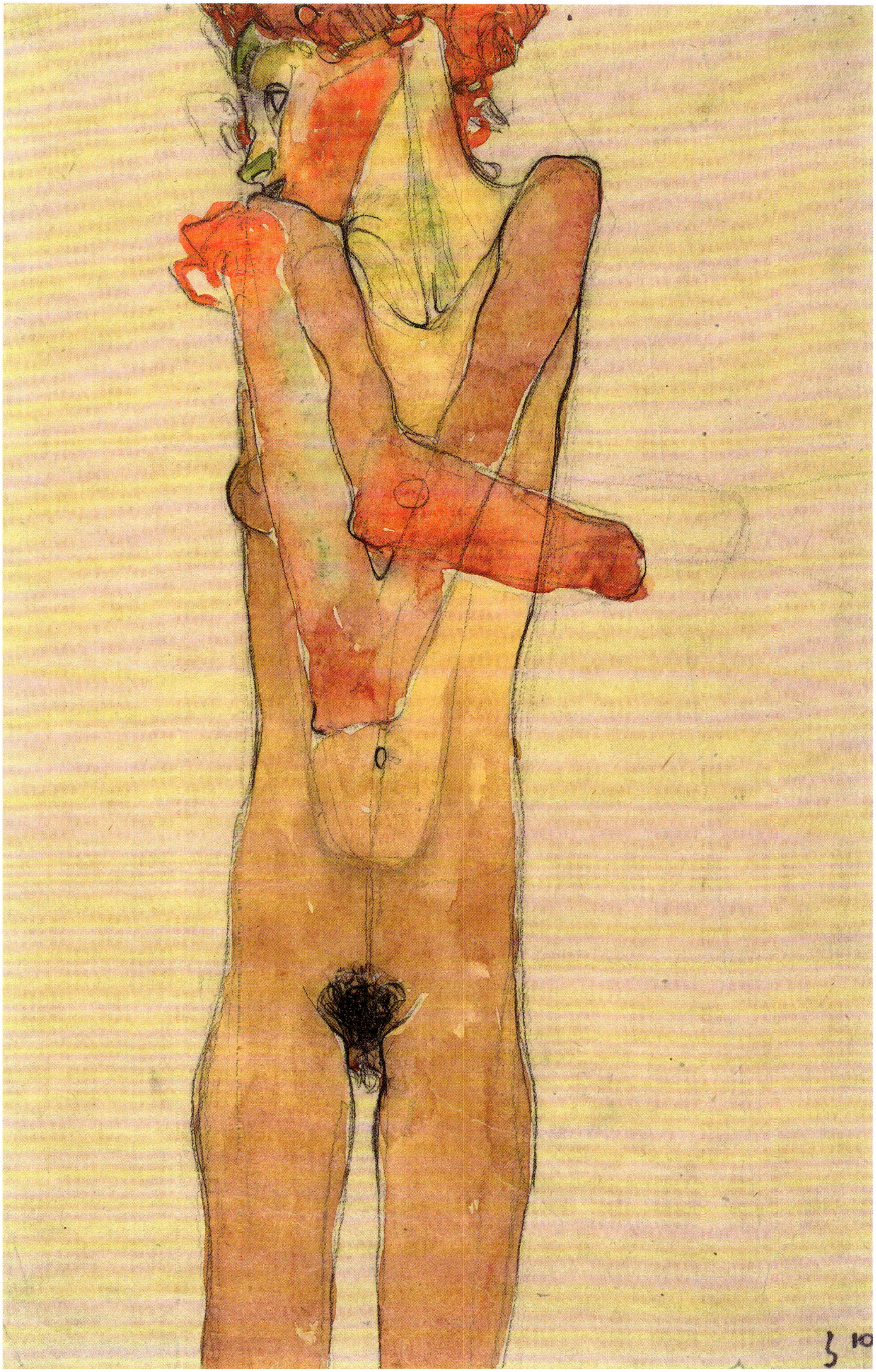

In a series of impressive self-portraits executed towards the end of 1910, Schiele imagined himself as a pathologically emaciated, rickety, consumptive body. Although real-life descriptions of the artist's physiognomy characterize him as a slim ectomorph, in their bony gauntness, these depictions go far beyond any naturalistic reflection of his appearance. The suffering of these ailing bodies is underlined by their wan, bloodshot flesh.

These self-representations are characterized by constraint and constriction. The *Nude Self-Portrait* confronts the viewer with a dismissive expression. The body cuts across the sheet diagonally, unable even to walk upright in its weakness. In the way the body is structured, the depiction contradicts not only every academically sanctioned ideal of an aesthetic physique, the doubting, questioning look in the eyes also contaminates the self-confidence traditionally expected in the art of the male nude. Physically weak, anemic, and lacking in mental strength, the artist stands indecisively in front of the mirror, hoping to see in his exposed body an answer to the question of the psycho-physical basis of his existence.

KAS

Egon Schiele
Nude Self-Portrait, 1910
The ALBERTINA Museum, Vienna

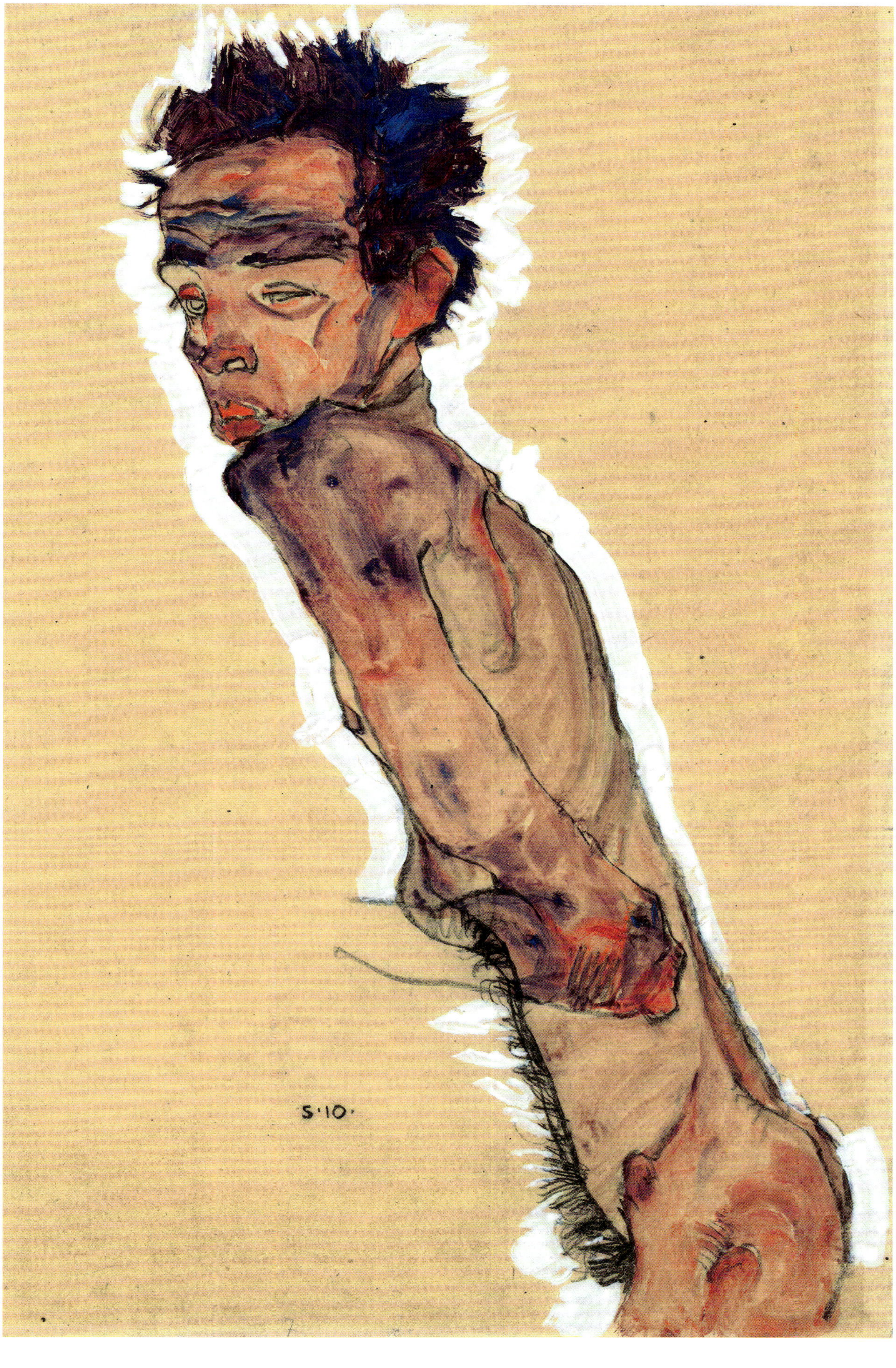
S·10·

In the *Reclining Female Nude with Legs Spread Apart*, only the red lips and the orange areolae stand out from the black of the hair, the cloth, and the stockings. These are joined, as though linked along the axial guideline, by the black pubic hair in the midst of the pale flesh tone. No contemporary saw sexual reality with less prejudice than Schiele. Compositionally, the recumbent body is anchored in the diagonal of the sheet, ensuring its decorative integration into the picture plane. The absence of a spatial context renders the supine position precarious thereby disrupting the voyeuristic fixation on the nude body.

KAS

Egon Schiele
Reclining Female Nude with Legs Spread Apart, 1914
The ALBERTINA Museum, Vienna

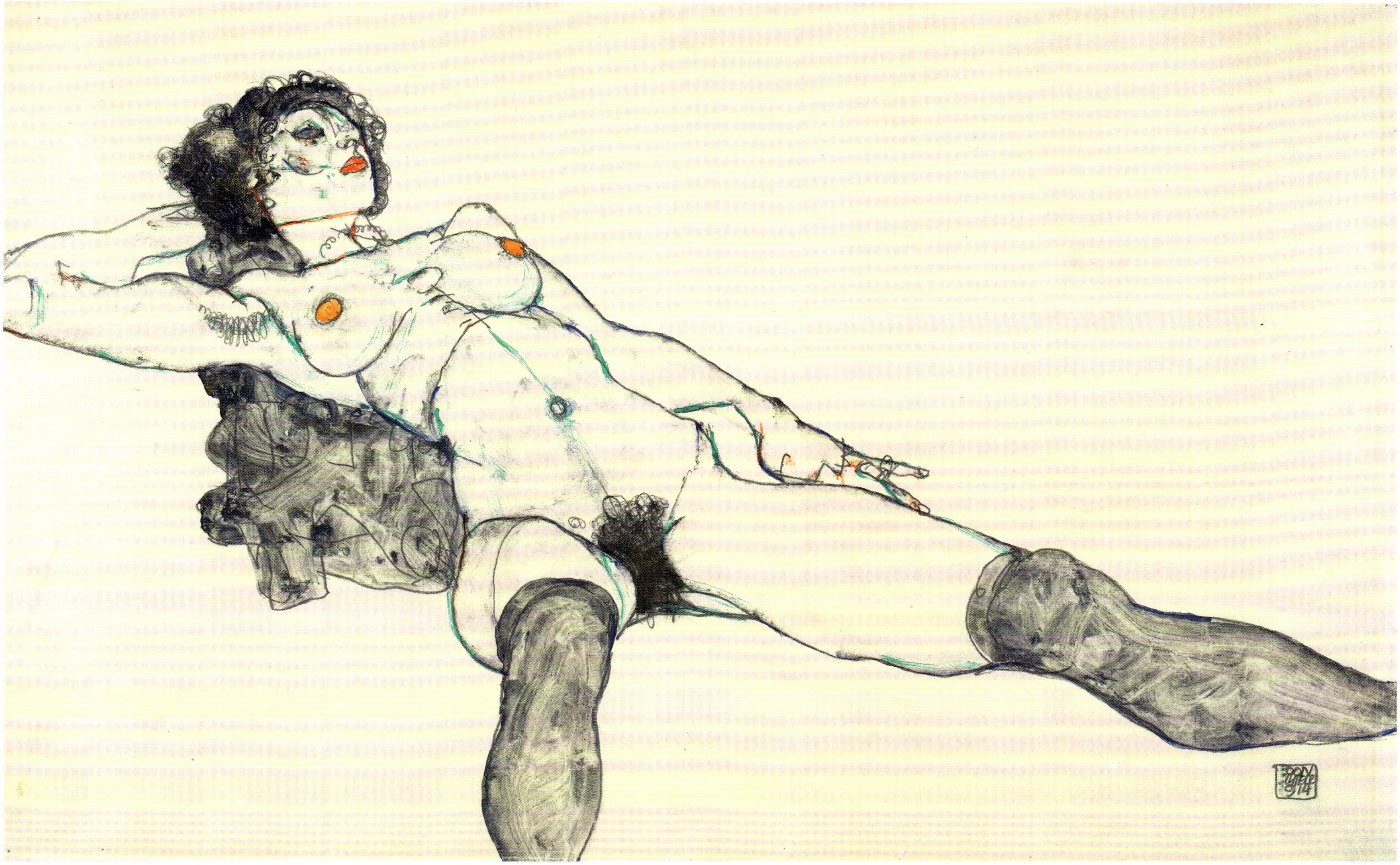

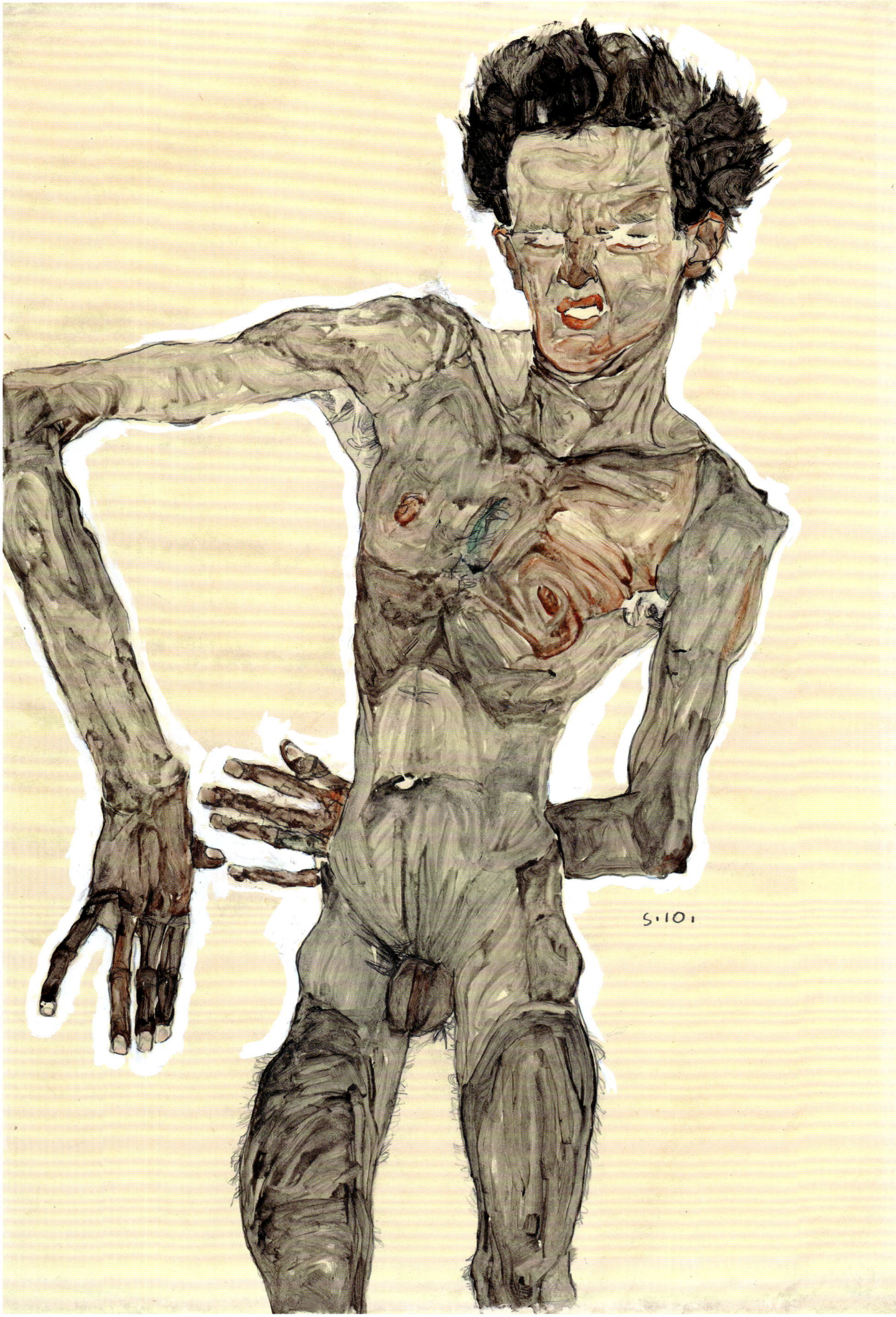
S.10.

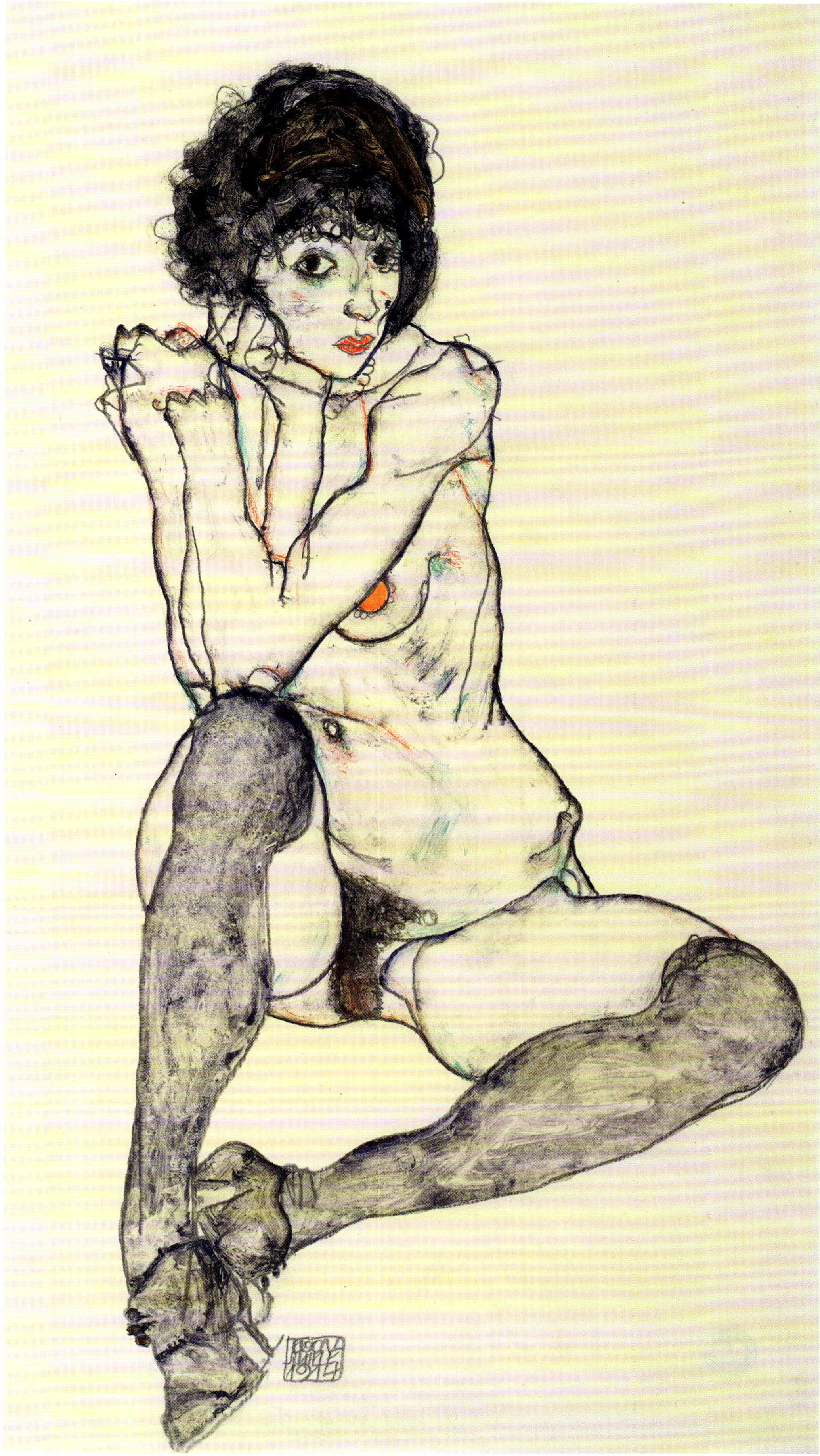

Egon Schiele
Nude Self-Portrait, Grimacing, 1910
The ALBERTINA Museum, Vienna

Egon Schiele
Seated Female Nude Resting on Elbows, 1914
The ALBERTINA Museum, Vienna

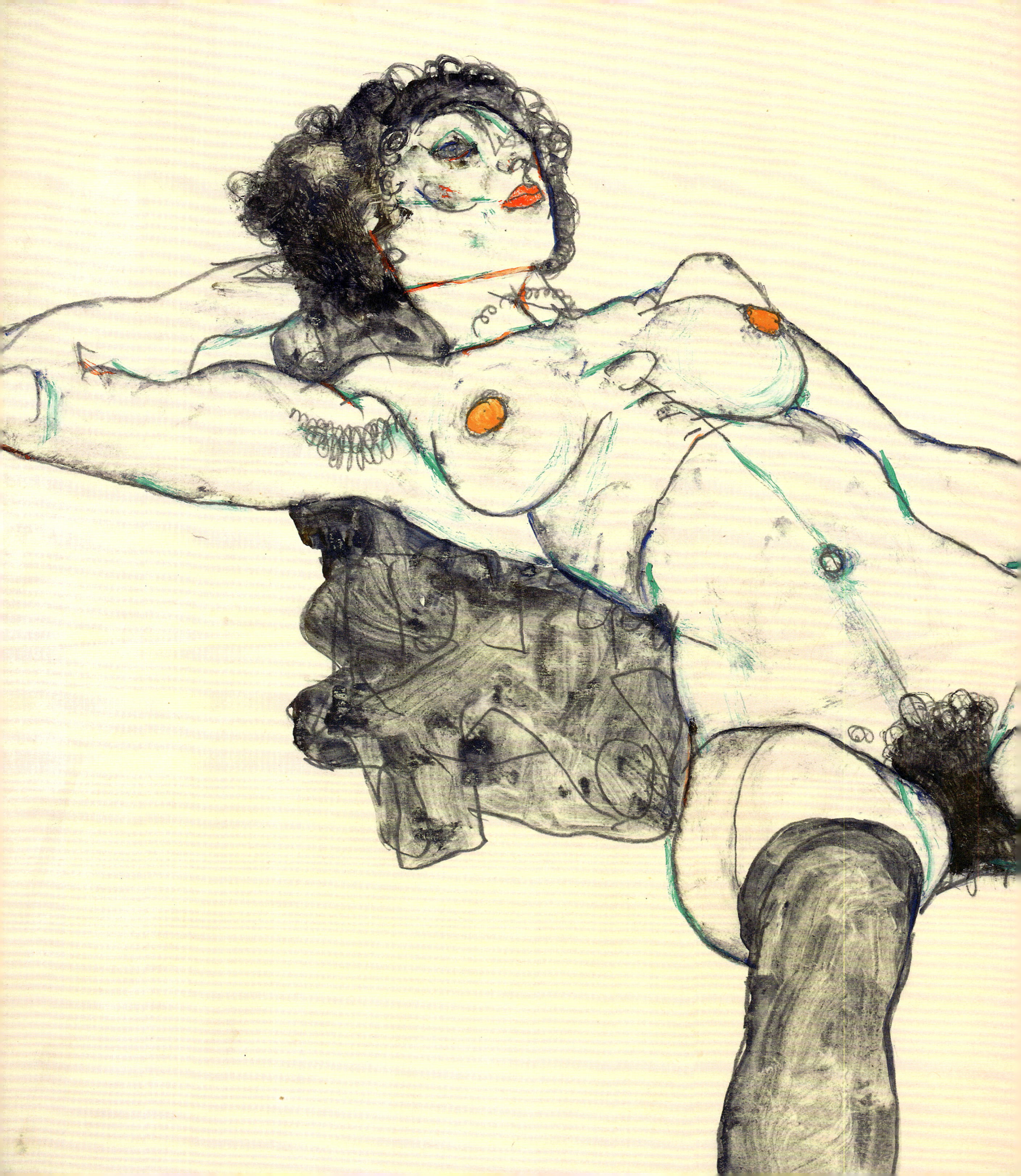

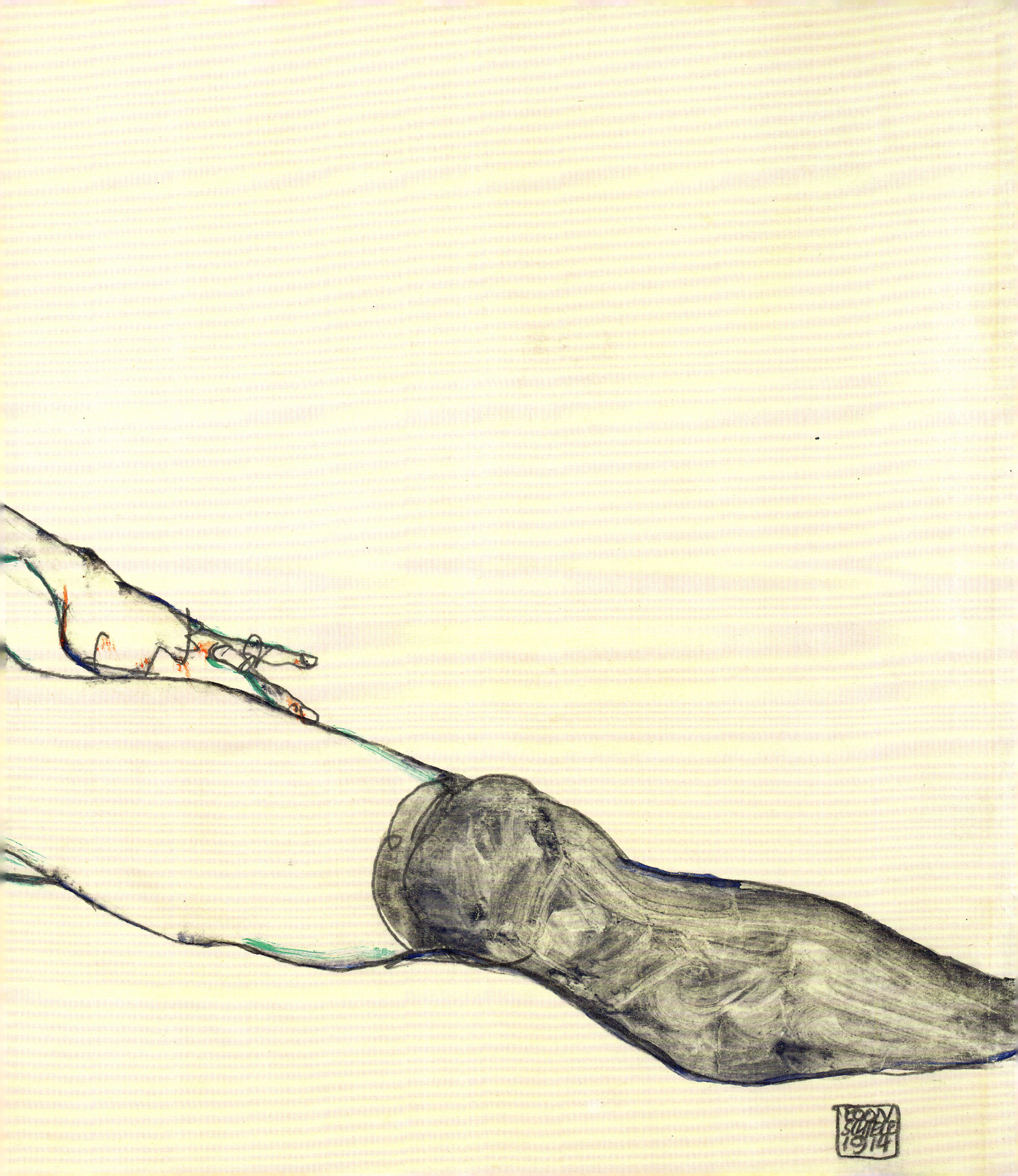
EGON
SCHIELE
1914

List of Works

Hans von Aachen
(Cologne 1552–Prague 1615)

The Judgment of Paris, ca. 1585
Red chalk, pen and brown ink, brown wash
24 × 35.2 cm
The ALBERTINA Museum, Vienna, inv. no. 3292
p. 219

Niccolò dell'Abate
(Modena ca. 1509/1512–Fontainebleau 1571/72)

Jupiter and Cupid, ca. 1560–1570
Pen and brown ink, brown wash, heightened with white
28.1 × 45.4 cm
The ALBERTINA Museum, Vienna, inv. no. 416
pp. 116/117

Copy after Sisto Badalocchio
(Parma 1585–Rome after 1620)

The Judgment of Paris, third quarter of the 18th century
Red chalk
36.6 × 39.7 cm
The ALBERTINA Museum, Vienna, inv. no. 4635
p. 222

Hans Baldung Grien
(Schwäbisch Gmünd ca. 1484/85–Strasbourg 1545)

New Year's Greeting with Three Witches, 1514
Pen and black ink, gray wash, heightened with white, on brown prepared paper
30.9 × 21 cm
The ALBERTINA Museum, Vienna, inv. no. 3220
p. 201

A Witches' Sabbath II, 1514
Pen and brush and black ink, heightened with white, on red-brown prepared paper
28.8 × 20.5 cm
The ALBERTINA Museum, Vienna, inv. no. 3221
p. 200

Baccio Bandinelli
(Florence 1488 or 1493–Florence 1560)

Seated Male Nude with Right Leg Raised to the Left, 1520–1525
Red chalk
34.5 × 24.4 cm
The ALBERTINA Museum, Vienna, inv. no. 255
p. 107

The Creation of Adam, 1545–1548
Pen and brown ink
40.7 × 28.9 cm
The ALBERTINA Museum, Vienna, inv. no. 17673
p. 109

Francesco Bartolozzi
(Florence 1728–Lisbon 1815)

Seated Male Nude Leaning on a Staff, ca. 1760–1764
Black and red chalk, heightened with white, on brownish paper
54.8 × 42.2 cm
The ALBERTINA Museum, Vienna, inv. no. 14306
p. 186

Pompeo Girolamo Batoni
(Lucca 1708–Rome 1787)

Male Nude Seated on a Block of Stone, 1760s
Red chalk, heightened with white, on yellow paper
48 × 28.6 cm
The ALBERTINA Museum, Vienna, inv. no. 1345
p. 180

Study of a Nude Youth Seated on Stone Steps, 1765
Black chalk, heightened with white, on blue prepared paper
50.7 × 38.8 cm
The ALBERTINA Museum, Vienna, inv. no. 14295
p. 181

Domenico Beccafumi
(Monteaperti ca. 1486–Siena 1551)

Reclining Male Nude in a Landscape, ca. 1540–1544
Black chalk, pen and brown ink, brown wash, heightened with white, on brown paper
22.1 × 43.1 cm
The ALBERTINA Museum, Vienna, inv. no. 276
pp. 102/103

Seated Nude Youth with a Stone Tablet and Two Putti, ca. 1544/45
Pen and brown ink, over preliminary drawing in black chalk
33.4 × 22.8 cm
The ALBERTINA Museum, Vienna, inv. no. 277
p. 105

Abraham Bloemaert
(Gorinchem 1564–Utrecht 1651)

Study of a Nude, 1592/93
Pen and black ink, brown wash, heightened with white
31.5 × 19.9 cm
The ALBERTINA Museum, Vienna, inv. no. 8102
p. 122

Bolognese Artist
(after Bartolomeo Passarotti, Bologna 1529–Bologna 1592)

Seated Male Nude in Profile to the Right, ca. 1600
Black chalk, pen and brown ink
37.7 × 32 cm
The ALBERTINA Museum, Vienna, inv. no. 295
p. 115

François Boucher
(Paris 1703–1770 Paris)

Nude Girl Lying on a Bed, second third of the 18th century
Black and white chalk on beige paper
26.7 × 40.7 cm
The ALBERTINA Museum, Vienna, inv. no. 12136
pp. 234/235

Standing Nude Girl, second third of the 18th century
Black, white, and red chalk, pastel
34.7 × 20 cm
The ALBERTINA Museum, Vienna, inv. no. 12133
p. 229

Ugo da Carpi
(Carpi, near Ferrara, ca. 1480–Rome 1532)

Diogenes, ca. 1526/27
Chiaroscuro woodcut from four blocks (green and blue)
47.8 × 34.3 cm
The ALBERTINA Museum, Vienna, inv. no. DG2003/3031
p. 101

Agostino Carracci
(Bologna 1557–Parma 1602)

Male Nude Holding a Vessel in Lowered Right Hand, with Left Arm Outstretched, ca. 1600–1602
Charcoal on blue paper
33.6 × 39.7 cm
The ALBERTINA Museum, Vienna, inv. no. 2174
p. 170

Annibale Carracci
(Bologna 1560–Rome 1609)

Male Figure, Seated to the Left, Holding a Staff with Both Hands, last third of the 16th century
Charcoal, heightened with white, on gray paper
24.4 × 15.5 cm
The ALBERTINA Museum, Vienna, inv. no. 2169
p. 171

Giovanni Battista Casanova
(Venice 1730–Dresden 1795)

The Florentine Wrestlers, ca. 1790
Black and white chalk on brown prepared paper
38.5 × 51.9 cm
The ALBERTINA Museum, Vienna, inv. 1928
p. 188

Albrecht Dürer
(Nuremberg 1471–Nuremberg 1528)

Four Female Nudes, 1497
Engraving
19.2 × 13.5 cm
The ALBERTINA Museum, Vienna, inv. no. DG1930/1415
p. 195

Reclining Female Nude, 1501
Brush and pen and black ink, gray wash, heightened with white, on green prepared paper
16.9 × 21.8 cm
The ALBERTINA Museum, Vienna, inv. no. 3072
pp. 136/137

Adam (construction drawing), 1504
Pen and brown ink
26.2 × 16.6 cm
The ALBERTINA Museum, Vienna, inv. no. 3080r
p. 141

Eve (construction drawing), 1504
Pen and brown ink
26.2 × 16.5 cm
The ALBERTINA Museum, Vienna, inv. no. 3081r
p. 140

Adam and Eve, 1504
Engraving
27 × 21.3 cm
The ALBERTINA Museum, Vienna, inv. no. DG1930/1451
p. 143

Study of Male Proportions in Profile and Front View, ca. 1513
Pen and brown ink
26.8 × 18.3 cm
The ALBERTINA Museum, Vienna, inv. no. 3135r
p. 139

Human Proportion Studies, from *Vier Bücher von menschlicher Proportion* (Four Books on Human Proportions), 1528
Printed book
31.2 × 21 cm
The ALBERTINA Museum, Vienna, inv. no. DG2012/126
pp. 144, 145

Paolo Farinati
(Verona 1524–Verona 1606)

Four Angels Lamenting the Dead Christ, second half of the 16th century
Pen, chalk, wash, heightened with white
44 × 29.2 cm
The ALBERTINA Museum, Vienna, inv. no. 1592
p. 126

Francesco Francia
(Bologna ca. 1447–Bologna 1517)

The Judgment of Paris, ca. 1505/06
Brush on parchment
31 × 25.9 cm
The ALBERTINA Museum, Vienna, inv. no. 4859
p. 217

French Artist
(after Guido Reni, Bologna 1575– Bologna 1642)

Hercules and the Hydra, second third of the 17th century
Red chalk
39.2 × 23.2 cm
The ALBERTINA Museum, Vienna, inv. no. 11592
p. 154

Hercules on the Pyre, second third of the 17th century
Red chalk
39.6 × 23.2 cm
The ALBERTINA Museum, Vienna, inv. no. 11593
p. 155

French Artist

Seated Female Nude, second half of the 18th century
Pastel on blue-green paper
30 × 35.3 cm
The ALBERTINA Museum, Vienna, inv. no. 40068
p. 227

Ambroise Gallé
(Antwerp d. 1755)

Venus after the Bath, 1747
Ivory
31.4 × 10 × 11 cm
LIECHTENSTEIN. The Princely Collections, Vaduz–Vienna, Fürstliche Sammlungen Art Service GmbH, inv. no. SK 1485
pp. 214, 215

Hendrick Goltzius
(Bracht, near Venlo, 1558–Haarlem 1617)

The Great Hercules, 1589
Engraving
56.5 × 40.7 cm
The ALBERTINA Museum, Vienna, inv. no. DG74504
p. 151

Farnese Hercules, ca. 1592
Engraving
41.5 × 29.5 cm
The ALBERTINA Museum, Vienna, inv. no. DG74505
p. 149

George Grosz
(Berlin 1893–Berlin 1959)

Promenade, 1922
Pen and ink
52.8 × 41 cm
The ALBERTINA Museum, Vienna, inv. no. 37530
p. 223

Cecil van Haanen
(Vienna 1844–Vienna 1914)

The Temptation of Saint Anthony, 1872
Charcoal heightened with white
59 × 42.5 cm
The ALBERTINA Museum, Vienna, inv. no. 32362
p. 203

Cornelis Cornelisz. van Haarlem
(Haarlem 1562–Haarlem 1638)

Tityus, 1588
Pen and brown ink, over black chalk, brown wash, heightened with white
36 × 26.8 cm
The ALBERTINA Museum, Vienna, inv. no. 8101
p. 123

Gustav Klimt
(Baumgarten, near Vienna, 1862–Vienna 1918)

Reclining Maenad (study for *Altar of Dionysus*, Burgtheater, Vienna), 1886/87
Black chalk heightened with white
28.7 × 42.5 cm
The ALBERTINA Museum, Vienna, inv. no. 26751
p. 237

Study for the Left Figure of "Three Gorgons" in the Beethoven Frieze, 1901
Black chalk
44.9 × 32 cm
The ALBERTINA Museum, Vienna, inv. no. 39316
p. 242

Study for the Left Figure of "Three Gorgons" in the Beethoven Frieze, 1901
Black chalk
44.5 × 31.9 cm
The ALBERTINA Museum, Vienna, inv. no. 39324
p. 243

Study for the Right Figure of "Three Gorgons" in the Beethoven Frieze, 1901
Black chalk
44.5 × 31.9 cm
The ALBERTINA Museum, Vienna, inv. no. 39317
p. 241

Charles André van Loo
(Nice 1705–Paris 1765)

Joseph and Potiphar's Wife, second third of the 18th century
Pen and black and brown ink, wash, black chalk, heightened with white
44.4 × 31.4 cm
The ALBERTINA Museum, Vienna, inv. no. 12107
p. 207

Anton Raphael Mengs
(Ústí nad Labem 1728–Rome 1779)

Farnese Hercules, early 1740s
Red chalk
35.1 × 20.3 cm
The ALBERTINA Museum, Vienna, inv. no. 4637
p. 153

Seated Male Nude, ca. 1760
Black chalk heightened with white on light grey paper
52.5 × 40 cm
The ALBERTINA Museum, Vienna, inv. no. 14581
p. 179

Michelangelo
(Caprese 1475–Rome 1564)

Three Standing Figures, ca. 1492–1496
Pen and brown inks, brown wash
33 × 20 cm
Private Collection, USA
p. 33

Three Standing Men, ca. 1494–1496
Pen and brown inks
29.2 × 20 cm
The ALBERTINA Museum, Vienna, inv. no. 116r
p. 30

Kneeling Man Seen from the Rear, ca. 1494–1496
Pen and brown ink
29.2 × 20 cm
The ALBERTINA Museum, Vienna, inv. no. 116v
p. 31

Standing Male Nude Seen from the Rear, ca. 1503
Pen and brown ink, over preliminary drawing in black chalk
38.7 × 19.5 cm
The ALBERTINA Museum, Vienna, inv. no. 118r
p. 43

The Virgin with the Child at Her Breast, ca. 1503
Pen and brown ink, over preliminary drawing in black chalk
38.7 × 19.5 cm
The ALBERTINA Museum, Vienna, inv. no. 118v
p. 42

Studies of a Raised Arm with Shoulder Joint, ca. 1504
Pen and brown ink, black chalk
22.6 × 31.5 cm
The ALBERTINA Museum, Vienna, inv. no. 132
pp. 50/51

Studies of Two Male Nudes, One Rushing Forward and One Facing Right, ca. 1504
Pen and brown ink, over preliminary drawing in black chalk
27 × 19.6 cm
The ALBERTINA Museum, Vienna, inv. no. 123r
p. 45

Male Nude Seen from the Rear, ca. 1504
Black chalk heightened with white
19.6 × 27 cm
The ALBERTINA Museum, Vienna, inv. no. 123v
pp. 48/49

Nude Youth, 1508/09
Black chalk over stylus underdrawing
30.8 × 20.6 cm
Paris, Musée du Louvre, Département des Arts graphiques, inv. no. 860 verso
p. 57

Studies for the Libyan Sibyl, ca. 1510/11
Red chalk
28.8 × 21.3 cm
The Metropolitan Museum of Art, New York, Purchase, Joseph Pulitzer Bequest, 1924, inv. no. 24.197.2
p. 63

Study of a Seated Nude Youth and Two Arm Studies, 1511/12
Red chalk, heightened with white, over stylus underdrawing
27.2 × 19.2 cm
The ALBERTINA Museum, Vienna, inv. no. 120r
p. 58

Male Upper Body with Folded Hands and Studies of Hands, 1511/12
Red chalk, traces of white heightening, pen and brown ink
27.2 × 19.2 cm
The ALBERTINA Museum, Vienna, inv. no. 120v
p. 61

Female Nude Seen from the Rear, 1524/25
Black chalk
22.2 × 12.5 cm
Paris, Musée du Louvre, Département des Arts graphiques, inv. no. 725 recto
p. 91

Two Nude Men Wrestling, ca. 1524/25
Red chalk
23.7 × 19.2 cm
Paris, Musée du Louvre, Département des Arts graphiques, inv. no. 709 recto
p. 83

The Lamentation of Christ, ca. 1530–1535
Red chalk over preliminary drawing in black chalk
32 × 24.9 cm
The ALBERTINA Museum, Vienna, inv. no. 102r
p. 79

Pietà, ca. 1530–1536
Red chalk over black chalk and stylus underdrawing
41.1 × 23.4 cm
The ALBERTINA Museum, Vienna, inv. no. 103
p. 81

Study for Seated Female Nudes Seen from the Rear, ca. 1530–1536
Black chalk
17.2 × 19.8 cm
The ALBERTINA Museum, Vienna, inv. no. 4868
p. 93

The Crucified Christ, 1557
Black chalk
24.3 × 13.1 cm
Paris, Musée du Louvre, Département des Arts graphiques, inv. no. 842 recto
p. 97

Copy after Michelangelo

Archers Shooting at a Herm, 1530–1560
Red chalk
23.5 × 34 cm
The ALBERTINA Museum, Vienna, inv. no. 39997
p. 85

Circle of Michelangelo

Study Sheet with a Leg, Skull, and Young Man in Bust-Length, ca. 1525–1540
Red and black chalk
38.2 × 26.6 cm
The ALBERTINA Museum, Vienna, inv. no. 121
p. 89

The Crucified Christ, second third of 16th century
Black chalk
39 × 25.6 cm
The ALBERTINA Museum, Vienna, inv. no. 45355
p. 95

Attributed to Monval
(French, active before 1806–1810)

Crouching Venus, 1806–1810
Black chalk
57 × 42.9 cm
The ALBERTINA Museum, Vienna, inv. no. 15386
p. 213

Jan Harmensz. Muller
(Amsterdam 1571–Amsterdam 1628)

Rape of a Sabine Woman, ca. 1598
Engraving
42.3 × 28 cm
The ALBERTINA Museum, Vienna, inv. no. DG77827
p. 130

Rape of a Sabine Woman, ca. 1598
Engraving
42.3 × 28 cm
The ALBERTINA Museum, Vienna, inv. no. DG77828
p. 131

Charles-Joseph Natoire
(Nîmes 1700–Castel Gandolfo 1777)

Bacchante with a Tambourine, ca. 1740
Black and red chalk, heightened with white gouache, brown wash
28 × 20.5 cm
The ALBERTINA Museum, Vienna, inv. no. 12074
p. 233

Netherlandish Artist

Saint Sebastian, last third of the 16th century
Black chalk, pen and gray ink, heightened with white, on blue-toned paper
46.6 × 24.5 cm
The ALBERTINA Museum, Vienna, inv. no. 2999
p. 121

August von Pettenkofen
(Vienna 1822–Vienna 1889)

The Travel Adventures of Monsignore L. Brunner, 1846
Pen and brown ink, wash, pencil
22 × 17 cm (each)
The ALBERTINA Museum, Vienna, inv. no. 29497/13–15
pp. 208, 209

Giovanni Battista Piazzetta
(Venice 1682–Venice 1754)

Seated Female Nude Seen from the Rear, first half of the 18th century
Black chalk heightened with white on brownish paper
37.5 × 27.7 cm
The ALBERTINA Museum, Vienna, inv. no. 32825
p. 225

Johann Peter Pichler
(Bolzano 1765–Vienna 1807)

Male Nude Seen from the Rear, 1789
Black chalk, wash, heightened with white, on gray paper
49.8 × 42 cm
The ALBERTINA Museum, Vienna, inv. no. 14862
p. 187

Pisanello
(Pisa 1395–Rome or Naples ca. 1455)

Personification of Lust (Luxuria), ca. 1426
Pen and brown ink on reddish prepared paper
12.9 × 15.2 cm
The ALBERTINA Museum, Vienna, inv. no. 24018r
p. 199

Antonio del Pollaiuolo
(Florence ca. 1430–Rome 1498)

Battle of the Nude Men, ca. 1470–1475
Engraving
40.2 × 59.5 cm
The ALBERTINA Museum, Vienna, inv. no. DG1935/964
p. 24

Copy after Antonio del Pollaiuolo

Hercules Combating the Giants, ca. 1470–1475
Engraving
36.8 × 55.5 cm
The ALBERTINA Museum, Vienna, inv. no. DG1935/965
p. 25

Raphael
(Urbino 1483–Rome 1520)

Nude Youth Hanging from a Wall, 1514
Red chalk over stylus underdrawing, gray wash in the background
26.5 × 16.1 cm
The ALBERTINA Museum, Vienna, inv. no. 4882
p. 67

A Young Man Carrying an Old Man, 1514
Red chalk
30 × 17.3 cm
The ALBERTINA Museum, Vienna, inv. no. 4881
p. 66

Studies of Nudes, 1515
Red chalk, metalpoint
40.3 × 28.3 cm
Inscription at center-right in pen and brown ink by the hand of Albrecht Dürer: "1515 / Raffahell de Urbin der so hoch peim / popst geacht ist gewest hat der hat / dyse nackette bild gemacht vnd hat / sy dem albrecht dürer gen nornberg / gechickt Im sein hand zw weisen" (1515. Raphael of Urbino, who has been held in high esteem by the Pope, drew these nude figures, and sent them to Albrecht Dürer, of Nuremburg, to show him his hand)
The ALBERTINA Museum, Vienna, inv. no. 17575
p. 71

Apostle Group, 1518–1520
Red chalk over stylus underdrawing and preliminary drawing in black chalk
32.3 × 27.2 cm
The ALBERTINA Museum, Vienna, inv. no. 4880
p. 75

Rembrandt Harmensz. van Rijn
(Leiden 1606–Amsterdam 1669)

Diana at the Bath, ca. 1631
Etching
18 × 16.4 cm
The ALBERTINA Museum, Vienna, inv. no. DG1926/347
p. 161

Seated Female Nude (Naked Woman Seated on a Mound), ca. 1631
Etching, engraving
17.7 × 16 cm
The ALBERTINA Museum, Vienna, inv. no. DG1926/341
p. 160

Joseph and Potiphar's Wife, 1634
Etching
9.2 × 11.5 cm
The ALBERTINA Museum, Vienna, inv. no. DG1926/65
p. 206

Adam and Eve (The Fall of Man), 1638
Etching
16.2 × 11.5 cm
The ALBERTINA Museum, Vienna, inv. no. DG1926/38
p. 159

Male Nude Seated on the Ground, 1646
Etching, engraving
9.7 × 16.8 cm
The ALBERTINA Museum, Vienna, inv. no. DG1926/332
p. 165

Seated Male Nude, 1646
Etching
16.4 × 9.6 cm
The ALBERTINA Museum, Vienna, inv. no. DG1926/330
p. 163

Seated and Standing Male Nudes (Het Rolwagentje), ca. 1646
Etching with retouched with brush and gray ink
19.4 × 12.8 cm
The ALBERTINA Museum, Vienna, inv. no. DG1926/333
p. 164

Rembrandt Harmensz. van Rijn or Pupil

Standing Male Nude, ca. 1646
Pen and brown ink, wash, white gouache
19.9 × 13.7 cm
The ALBERTINA Museum, Vienna, inv. no. 8827
p. 162

Cristofano Robetta
(Florence 1462–n.p. 1535)

Hercules and Antaeus, ca. 1500–1520
Engraving
25.5 × 19.5 cm
The ALBERTINA Museum, Vienna, inv. no. DG1935/460
p. 27

Rosso Fiorentino
(Florence 1494–Paris 1540)

Reclining Male Nude, 1527/28
Pen and brown ink
22.2 × 38.3 cm
The ALBERTINA Museum, Vienna, inv. no. 104
p. 77

Peter Paul Rubens
(Siegen 1577–Antwerp 1640)

Study of a Male Nude Leaning Forward, ca. 1613
Black and red chalk heightened with white
40.1 × 24.7 cm
The ALBERTINA Museum, Vienna, inv. no. 8300r
p. 173

A Blind Man with Arms Outstretched, ca. 1617/18
Black chalk heightened with white
28.3 × 42 cm
The ALBERTINA Museum, Vienna, inv. no. 17641
pp. 174/175

Study of a Male Nude Falling, first third of the 17th century
35 × 48.1 cm
The ALBERTINA Museum, Vienna, inv. no. 8303
p. 172

Copy after Peter Paul Rubens

Farnese Hercules, second third of the 17th century
Black chalk heightened with white on gray-brown paper
41.1 × 25.7 cm
The ALBERTINA Museum, Vienna, inv. no. 13296
p. 152

Francesco Salviati (Francesco de' Rossi)
(Florence 1510–Rome 1563)

Apollo Standing on the Dragon Python, ca. 1543–1548
Black chalk
44.3 × 25.7 cm
The ALBERTINA Museum, Vienna, inv. no. 487
p. 111

Egon Schiele
(Tulln 1890–Vienna 1918)

Nude Girl with Folded Arms, 1910
Black chalk, watercolor, on brown paper
44.6 × 27.8 cm
The ALBERTINA Museum, Vienna, inv. no. 30772
p. 245

Nude Self-Portrait, 1910
Black chalk, watercolor, gouache, heighten with white, on brown paper
45 × 31.8 cm
The ALBERTINA Museum, Vienna, inv. no. 23599
p. 247

Nude Self-Portrait, Grimacing, 1910
Pencil, charcoal, gouache, heighten with white, on wrapping paper
55.8 × 36.7 cm
The ALBERTINA Museum, Vienna, inv. no. 30766
p. 250

Reclining Female Nude with Legs Spread Apart, 1914
Pencil and gouache on Japan paper
31.2 × 48 cm
The ALBERTINA Museum, Vienna, inv. no. 26667
p. 249

Seated Female Nude Resting on Elbows, 1914
Pencil and gouache on Japan paper
48 × 32 cm
The ALBERTINA Museum, Vienna, inv. no. 31632
p. 251

Jacob Matthias Schmutzer
(Vienna 1733–Vienna 1811)

Mercury Putting Argus to Sleep, 1770
Black and white chalk
60.9 × 45.4 cm
The ALBERTINA Museum, Vienna, inv. 14913
p. 185

Massimiliano Soldani-Benzi
(Montevarchi 1656–Montevarchi 1740)

Dancing Faun, 1695–1697
Bronze, red-brown lacquer patina
139 × 80 × 50 cm
LIECHTENSTEIN. The Princely Collections, Vaduz–Vienna, Fürstliche Sammlungen Art Service GmbH, inv. no. SK 541
p. 37

Bacchus, 1695–1703
Bronze
198 × 76 × 73 cm
LIECHTENSTEIN. The Princely Collections, Vaduz–Vienna, Fürstliche Sammlungen Art Service GmbH, inv. no. SK 573
p. 35

The Wrestlers, ca. 1710
Bronze
W. 54.2 cm
Bayerisches Nationalmuseum, Munich, inv. no. 11/106
p. 189

Bartholomaeus Spranger
(Antwerp 1546–Prague 1611)

Venus and Cupid on a Dolphin, ca. 1580–1585
Pen and black-brown ink over charcoal or black chalk, brown wash, heightened with white
18.8 × 20.1 cm
The ALBERTINA Museum, Vienna, inv. no. 7994
p. 231

Attributed to Antonio Susini
(Florence 1558–Florence 1624)

Rape of a Sabine Woman, ca. 1600
Bronze, reddish gold lacquer patina
58 × 24 × 23 cm
LIECHTENSTEIN. The Princely Collections, Vaduz–Vienna, Fürstliche Sammlungen Art Service GmbH, inv. no. SK 115
p. 129

Giovanni Francesco Susini
(Florence 1585–Florence 1653)

Farnese Hercules, second quarter of the 17th century
Bronze, reddish gold lacquer patina
41.9 × 18 × 17 cm
LIECHTENSTEIN. The Princely Collections, Vaduz–Vienna, Fürstliche Sammlungen Art Service GmbH, inv. no. SK 556
p. 147

Kneeling Woman Bathing, second quarter of the 17th century
Bronze, golden brown lacquer patina
25.9 × 11 × 14 cm
LIECHTENSTEIN. The Princely Collections, Vaduz–Vienna, Fürstliche Sammlungen Art Service GmbH, inv. no. SK 569
p. 211

Laocoön, second quarter of the 17th century
Bronze
54 × 44 × 21 cm
LIECHTENSTEIN. The Princely Collections, Vaduz–Vienna, Fürstliche Sammlungen Art Service GmbH, inv. no. SK 526
p. 53

Jacopo Tintoretto
(Venice ca. 1518/19–Venice 1594)

Study of a Male Nude, ca. 1590
Charcoal
32.8 x 22.7 cm
The ALBERTINA Museum, Vienna, inv. 24475
p. 119

Daniele da Volterra
(Volterra 1509–Rome 1566)

Aeneas with a Boy, ca. 1555/56
Black chalk
52.2 × 35 cm
The ALBERTINA Museum, Vienna, inv. no. 497
p. 113

Adriaen de Vries
(The Hague ca. 1556–Prague 1626)

Christ at the Column, ca. 1613–1615
Bronze
86.5 × 19.2 × 21.4 cm
Kunsthistorisches Museum, Vienna, Kunstkammer, inv. no. KK 8908
p. 127

Attributed to Joseph Walter
(Vienna, active ca. 1790)

Elderly Male Nude, ca. 1791–1797
Black chalk, heightened with white, on brown-gray paper
36.9 × 49.4 cm
The ALBERTINA Museum, Vienna, inv. no. 6733
pp. 182/183

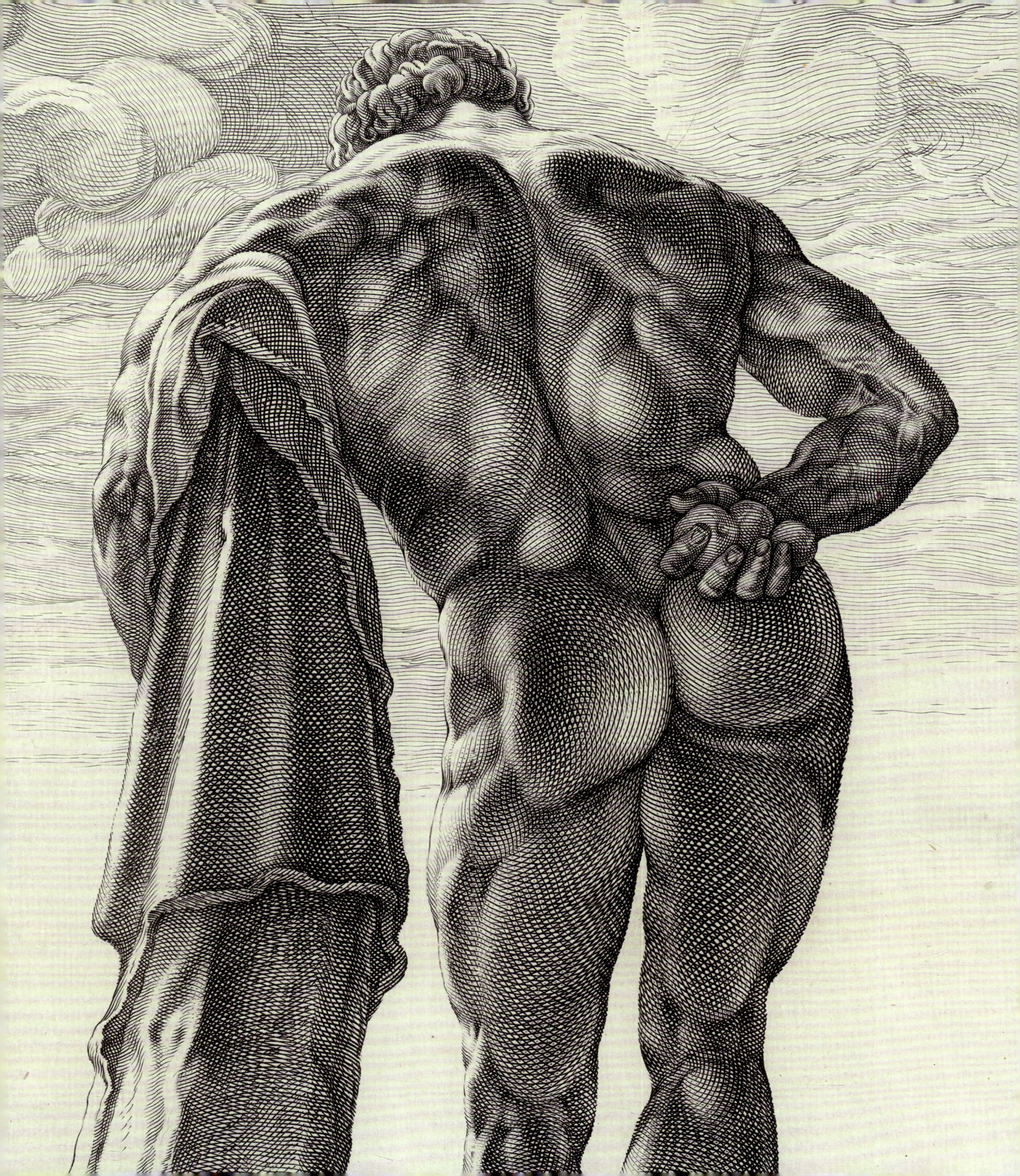

Selected Bibliography

Publications (by author)

Acidini Luchinat, Cristina. *Michelangelo pittore*. Milan: Federico Motta, 2007.

Armstrong Andersen, Lilian. "Copies of Pollaiuolo's *Battling Nudes*." *Art Quarterly* 31, no. 2 (Summer 1968): 154–167.

Bambach, Carmen C. "A Note on Michelangelo's Cartoon for the Sistine Ceiling: Haman." *Art Bulletin* 65, no. 4 (December 1983): 661–665.

Barolsky, Paul. *Daniele da Volterra: A Catalogue Raisonné*. New York: Garland, 1979.

Baumgart, Fritz. "Contributi a Michelangelo: I. Daniele da Volterra e Michelangelo." *Bollettino d'Arte* 28 (1934): 344–353.

Benesch, Otto, ed. *Beschreibender Katalog der Handzeichnungen in der Albertina: Die Zeichnungen der niederländischen Schulen des XV. und XVI. Jahrhunderts*. 2 vols. Vienna: Anton Schroll, 1928.

Berenson, Bernard. *The Drawings of the Florentine Painters*. Amplified edition. 3 vols. Chicago: University of Chicago Press, 1938.

Birke, Veronika, and Janine Kertész. *Die italienischen Zeichnungen der Albertina: Generalverzeichnis*. 4 vols. Vienna: Böhlau, 1992–1997.

Bonnet, Anne-Marie. *"Akt" bei Dürer*. Cologne: Walther König, 2001.

Burke, Jill. "The Body in Artistic Theory and Practice." In *The Renaissance Nude*, edited by Thomas Kren with Jill Burke and Stephen J. Campbell, 183–199. Exh. cat. J. Paul Getty Museum, Los Angeles, 2018/19; Royal Academy of Arts, London, 2019. Los Angeles: J. Paul Getty Museum, 2018.

Christie's. *Michelangelo's First Nude: A Drawing Rediscovered*. Sale cat. Christie's Paris, May 18, 2022.

Ciardi, Roberto Paolo, and Benedetta Moreschini, *Daniele Ricciarelli: Da Volterra a Roma*, Rome: CIRF, 2004.

Clément, Charles. *Michelangelo, Lionardo da Vinci and Raphael, with a Preliminary Chapter on Art in Italy before the Sixteenth Century*. Translated by Louisa Corkran. 2nd edition. London: Seeley, 1890.

Condivi, Ascanio. *Vita di Michelagnolo Buonarroti raccolta per Ascanio Condivi da la Ripa Transone*. Rome, 1553. Published in English as *The Life of Michelangelo*. Translated by Alice Sedwick Wohl. Edited by Hellmut Wohl. Oxford: Phaidon, 1976.

Dürer, Albrecht. *Vier Bücher von menschlicher Proportion*. Nuremberg, 1528. Published in contemporary German, with commentary by Berthold Hinz. Berlin: Akademie Verlag, 2011.

Dunkelman, Martha. "Michelangelo's Earliest Drawing Style." *Drawing* 1, no. 6 (March–April 1980): 121–127.

Dussler, Luitpold. *Die Zeichnungen des Michelangelo: Kritischer Katalog*, Berlin: Gebr. Mann, 1959.

Echinger-Maurach, Claudia. *Michelangelos Grabmal für Papst Julius II.* Munich: Hirmer, 2009.

Echinger-Maurach, Claudia, Achim Gnann, and Joachim Poeschke, eds. *Michelangelo als Zeichner: Akten des Internationalen Kolloquiums Wien, Albertina-Museum, 19.–20. November 2010*. Münster: Rhema, 2013, 201–236.

Echinger-Maurach, Claudia with Maria Forcellino. *Michelangelo's Tomb for Julius II: Genesis and Genius*. Los Angeles: J. Paul Getty Museum, 2014.

Ettlinger, Leopold D. "Hercules Florentinus." *Mitteilungen des Kunsthistorischen Institutes in Florenz* 16, no. 2 (1972): 119–142.

Faber, Friedrich, and Johann Andreas Romberg, *Conversations-Lexicon für Bildende Kunst*, vol. 4. Leipzig: Renger'sche Buchhandlung, 1848. S.v. "Faun."

Fend, Mechthild, and Marianne Koos, eds. *Männlichkeit im Blick. Visuelle Inszenierungen in der Kunst seit der frühen Neuzeit*. Cologne: Böhlau, 2004.

Fogelman, Peggy, Peter Fusco, and Marietta Cambareri. *Italian and Spanish Sculpture: Catalogue of the J. Paul Getty Collection*. Los Angeles: J. Paul Getty Museum, 2002.

Frey, Carl, ed. *Die Dichtungen des Michelagniolo Buonarroti*. Berlin: G. Grote'sche Verlagsbuchhandlung, 1897. Reprinted in an edition by Herman-Walther Frey. Berlin: Walter de Gruyter, 1964.

Fusco, Laurie Smith. "The Nude as Protagonist: Pollaiuolo's Figural Style Explicated by Leonardo's Study of Static Anatomy, Movement, and Functional Anatomy." PhD dissertation, New York University, 1978.

Gilbert, Creighton. "Michelangelo's Drawings after Masaccio's Sagra." *Gazette des Beaux-Arts*, 6th series, 34 (December 1948): 389–404.

Gnann, Achim. *Parmigianino: Die Zeichnungen*. 2 vols. Petersberg: Michael Imhof, 2007.

Goldscheider, Ludwig. *Michelangelo Drawings*. London: Phaidon, 1951. 2nd edition. London: Phaidon, 1966.

Hartt, Frederick. *The Drawings of Michelangelo*. London: Thames and Hudson, 1971.

Hatfield, Rab. *The Wealth of Michelangelo*. Rome: Edizioni di storia e letteratura, 2002.

Haussherr, Reiner. *Michelangelos Kruzifixus für Vittoria Colonna: Bemerkungen zu Ikonographie und theologischer Deutung*. Opladen: Westdeutscher Verlag, 1971.

Hirst, Michael. *Sebastiano del Piombo*. Oxford: Clarendon, 1981.

Hirst, Michael. "I disegni di Michelangelo per la Battaglia di Cascina (ca. 1504)." In *Tecnica e stile: esempi di pittura murale del Rinascimento italiano*, vol. 1, edited by Eve Borsook and Fiorella Superbi Gioffredi, 43–58. 2 vols. Cinisello Balsamo: Silvana, 1986.

Hirst, Michael. *Michelangelo and His Drawings*. New Haven, CT: Yale University Press, 1988.

Houbraken, Arnold. *De Groote Schouburgh der Nederlantsche Konstschilders en Schilderessen*. 3 vols. Amsterdam, 1718–1721. Published in English as *Houbraken Translated: Arnold Houbraken's Great Theatre of the Netherlandish Painters and Paintresses*. Translated by Hendrik J. Horn and Rieke van Leeuwen. The Hague: RKD, 2021, https://houbraken-translated.rkdstudies.nl/.

Joannides, Paul. "Michelangelo's Lost Hercules." *Burlington Magazine* 119, no. 893 (August 1977): 550, 552–555.

Joannides, Paul. "Daniele da Volterra's *Dido*." *Burlington Magazine* 135, no. 1089 (December 1993): 818–819.

Joannides, Paul. "Francesco Salviati et Michel-Ange." In *Francesco Salviati (1510–1563) ou la Bella Maniera*, edited by Catherine Monbeig Goguel, 53–55. Exh. cat. Villa Medici, Rome, 1998; Musée du Louvre, Paris, 1998. Paris: Réunion des Musées Nationaux, 1998.

Joannides, Paul. *Michel-Ange, élèves et copistes*. Musée du Louvre, département des arts graphiques, Inventaire général des dessins italiens, vol. 6. Paris: Réunion des Musées Nationaux, 2003.

Knab, Eckhart, Erwin Mitsch, and Konrad Oberhuber with Sylvia Ferino Pagden. *Raphael: Die Zeichnungen*. Stuttgart: Urachhaus. 1983.

Knofler, Monika. "Das Zeichnen nach dem Modell – Kontinuum und Bedeutungswandel." In Monika Knofler and Peter Weiermair, *Das Bild des Körpers in der Kunst des 17. bis 20. Jahrhunderts: Zeichnungen aus dem Kupferstichkabinett der Akademie der bildenden Künste Wien*, 10–21. Exh. cat. Rupertinum, Salzburg, 2000; Palazzo Margherita, Modena, 2001. Zürich: Oehrli, 2000.

Köhler, Wilhelm. "Michelangelos Schlachtkarton." *Kunstgeschichtliches Jahrbuch der KK Zentral-Kommission für Erforschung und Erhaltung der Kunst- und Historischen Denkmale* 1 (1907): 115–172.

Kramer, Heinrich [Henricus Institoris]. *Malleus maleficarum*. Speyer 1486. Published in English as *The Hammer of Witches: A Complete Translation of the Malleus maleficarum*. Translated by Christopher S. Mackay. Cambridge: Cambridge University Press, 2009.

Laurenza, Domenico. *Art and Anatomy in Renaissance Italy: Images from a Scientific Revolution*. New York: The Metropolitan Museum of Art, 2012. Reprint of *The Metropolitan Museum of Art Bulletin* (Winter 2012).

Mancinelli, Fabrizio. "La progettazione della volta della Cappella Sistina di Michelangelo." In *Michelangelo Drawings*, edited by Craig Hugh Smyth, 43–55. Studies in the History of Art, vol. 33; Center for Advanced Study in the Visual Arts Symposium Papers, vol. 17. Washington, DC: National Gallery of Art 1992.

Mancinelli, Fabrizio. "Il ponteggio di Michelangelo per la Cappella Sistina e i problemi cronologici della volta." In *Michelangelo, la Cappella Sistina: documentazione e interpretazioni*, vol. 3, edited by Kathleen Weil-Garris Brandt, 43–49. Atti del convegno internazionale di studi, Roma, marzo 1990. Novara: Istituto geografico de Agostini, 1994.

Van der Meulen, Marjon. *Rubens Copies after the Antique*, 3 vols. Corpus Rubenianum Ludwig Burchard, vol. 23. London: Harvey Miller, 1994/95.

Morozzi, Luisa. "La *Battaglia di Cascina* di Michelangelo: nuova ipotesi sulla data di commissione" *Prospettiva* 53–56 (April 1988–January 1989): 320–324.

Müller-Bechtel, Susanne. *Von allen Seiten anders: Die akademische Aktstudie, 1650–1850*. Berlin: Deutscher Kunstverlag, 2018.

Natali, Antonio. *Rosso Fiorentino: Leggiadra maniera e terribilità di cose stravaganti*. Milan: Silvana, 2006.

Nims, John Frederick, trans. *The Complete Poems of Michelangelo*. Chicago: University of Chicago Press, 1998.

Oberhuber, Konrad. "Raphael und Michelangelo." In *Michelangelo*, 156–164. Vol. 2 of *Stil und Überlieferung in der Kunst des Abendlandes, Akten des 21. Internationalen Kongresses für Kunstgeschichte in Bonn 1964*. Berlin: Gebr. Mann, 1967.

Owens, Yvonne. *Abject Eroticism in Northern Renaissance Art: The Witches and Femmes Fatales of Hans Baldung Grien*. London: Bloomsbury, 2022.

Panofsky, Erwin. *Studies in Iconology: Humanistic Themes in the Art of the Renaissance*. Oxford: Oxford University Press, 1939. Republished by New York: Routledge, 2018.

Poeschke, Joachim. *Michelangelo und seine Zeit*. Vol. 2 of *Die Skulptur der Renaissance in Italien*. Munich: Hirmer, 1992.

Redig de Campos, Deoclecio. "Il Crocifisso di Michelangelo per Vittoria Colonna." In *Michelangelo e Dante*, 133–142. Exh. cat. Casa di Dante in Abruzzo, Castello Gizzi, Torre de' Passeri, 1995. Milan: Electa, 1995.

Rinaldi, Furio. "Looking at Masaccio: A Rediscovered Drawing by the Young Michelangelo." *Burlington Magazine* 164, no. 1431 (June 2022): 536–545.

Schoen, Christian. *Albrecht Dürer: Adam und Eva; Die Gemälde, ihre Geschichte und Rezeption bei Lucas Cranach d. Ä. und Hans Baldung Grien*. Berlin: Reimer, 2001.

Schröder, Klaus Albrecht, ed. *The Great Masters of the Albertina*. Petersberg: Michael Imhof, 2008.

Sickel, Lothar. "Jacopo Rocchetti alias Giacomo Rocca: Ein Protagonist der frühen Sammlungsgeschichte von Michelangelos Zeichnungen." In *Michelangelo als Zeichner, Akten des Internationalen Kolloquiums Wien, Albertina, 19.–20. November 2020*, edited by Claudia Echinger-Maurach, Achim Gnann, and Joachim Poeschke, 3–96. Münster: Rhema 2013.

Sluijter, Erik Jan. *Rembrandt and the Female Nude*. Amsterdam: Amsterdam University Press, 2006.

Swoboda, Gudrun. "Baccio Bandinelli (1494–1560). Die Zeichnungen der Albertina." Diplomarbeit, Universität Wien, 1994.

Thode, Henry. *Michelangelo: Kritische Untersuchungen über seine Werke*. 3 vols. Berlin: G. Grote'sche Verlagsbuchhandlung, 1908–1913.

Thode, Henry. *Der Künstler und seine Werke*. Vol. 3.2 of *Michelangelo und das Ende der Renaissance*. Berlin: G. Grote'sche Verlagsbuchhandlung, 1912.

Thöny, Sabrina. "Das Zeichnen nach dem lebenden Modell an den Akademien." In *Zeichenunterricht: Von der Künstlerausbildung zur ästhetischen Erziehung seit 1500*, edited by Graphische Sammlung ETH Zürich, Michael Matile, 94–105. Petersberg: Michael Imhof, 2017.

de Tolnay, Charles. *Michelangelo*. 5 vols. Princeton: Princeton University Press, 1943–1960.

de Tolnay, Charles. *Corpus dei disegni di Michelangelo*. 4 vols. Novara: Istituto geografico de Agostini, 1975–1980.

Vasari, Giorgio. *Le Vite de' più eccellenti pittori, scultori et architettori [. . .]*. 2 vols. Florence, 1550. Revised, enlarged edition, 3 vols. Florence, 1568. Annotated edition by Gaetano Milanesi. 9 vols. Florence: G. C. Sansoni, 1878–1885. Published in English as *Lives of the Most Eminent Painters, Sculptors and Architects*. Translated by Gaston du C. de Vere. 10 vols. London: Macmillan; Medici Society, 1912–1915. Republished in 3 vols. by London: Everyman's Library, 1996.

Voss, Hermann. "Ein wiedergefundenes Bild des Daniele da Volterra." *Kunstchronik und Kunstmarkt* 34 (1922/23): 375–378.

Weißmann, Carina A. E. *Die Bronzen des Massimiliano Soldani Benzi (1656–1740): Repräsentationsstrategien des europäischen Adels um 1700*. Doctoral dissertation, Universität Wien, 2017. Berlin: De Gruyter, 2022.

Wilde, Johannes. "Cartonetti by Michelangelo." *Burlington Magazine* 101, no. 680 (November 1959): 370–380.

Wilde, Johannes. *Michelangelo. Six Lectures*. Oxford: Clarendon, 1978.

Wölfflin, Heinrich. *Die Jugendwerke des Michelangelo*. Munich: Theodor Ackermann, 1891.

Wood, Jeremy. *Copies and Adaptations from Renaissance and Later Artists: Italian Masters, III. Artists working in Central Italy and France*. Corpus Rubenianum Ludwig Burchard vol. 26. London: Harvey Miller, 2011.

Zaidenberg, Beatrice. "Das idealisierte und erinnerte Modell." In *Zeichenunterricht: Von der Künstlerausbildung zur ästhetischen Erziehung seit 1500*, edited by Graphische Sammlung ETH Zürich, Michael Matile, 106–109. Petersberg: Michael Imhof, 2017.

Zöllner, Frank, Christof Thoenes, and Thomas Pöpper, *Michelangelo, 1475–1564: Complete Works*. Cologne: Taschen, 2007.

Exhibition Catalogues (chronological)

Drawings by Michelangelo in the Collection of Her Majesty the Queen at Windsor Castle, The Ashmolean Museum, The British Museum and Other English Collections, introduction by John A. Gere. Department of Prints and Drawings, British Museum, London, 1975.

Italienische Zeichnungen der Renaissance zum 500. Geburtsjahr Michelangelos, edited by Walter Koschatzky. Graphische Sammlung Albertina, Vienna, 1975.

Mitsch, Erwin. *Die Rubenszeichnungen in der Albertina: Zum 400. Geburtstag*. Graphische Sammlung Albertina, Vienna, 1977.

Carroll, Eugene A. *Rosso Fiorentino: Drawings, Prints, and Decorative Arts*. National Gallery of Art, Washington, DC, 1987/88.

Hirst, Michael. *Michelangelo Draftsman*. National Gallery of Art, Washington DC, 1988; Musée du Louvre, Paris, 1989.

Rembrandt: The Master and His Workshop. 2 vols. Kupferstichkabinett SMPK, Altes Museum, Berlin, 1991; Rijksmuseum, Amsterdam, 1991/92; National Gallery, London, 1992. Vol. 2, *Drawings & Etchings*, by Holm Bevers, Peter Schatborn, and Barbara Welzel. New Haven, CT: Yale University Press, 1992.

Die Beredsamkeit des Leibes: Zur Körpersprache in der Kunst, edited by Ilsebill Barta Fliedl and Christoph Geissmar. Graphische Sammlung Albertina, Vienna, 1992.

Griswold, William M., and Linda Wolk-Simon, *Sixteenth-Century Italian Drawings in New York Collections*. The Metropolitan Museum of Art, New York, 1994.

Joannides, Paul. *Michelangelo and His Influence: Drawings from Windsor Castle*. National Gallery of Art, Washington, DC, 1996/97; Kimbell Art Museum, Fort Worth, 1997; Art Institute of Chicago, 1997; Fitzwilliam Museum, Cambridge, 1997; The Queen's Gallery, London, 1998.

Vittoria Colonna: Dichterin und Muse Michelangelos, edited by Sylvia Ferino-Pagden. Kunsthistorisches Museum, Vienna, 1997.

Zeichnungen aus der Toskana: Das Zeitalter Michelangelos, edited by Ernst-Gerhard Güse and Alexander Perrig. Saarland-Museum, Saarbrücken, 1997.

Giovinezza di Michelangelo, edited by Kathleen Weil-Garris Brandt. Palazzo Vecchio and Casa Buonarroti, Florence, 1999/2000.

Gnann, Achim. *Roma e lo stile classico di Raffaello*, edited by Konrad Oberhuber. Palazzo Te, Mantua, 1999; Graphische Sammlung Albertina, Vienna, 1999. German edition, *Raphael und der klassische Stil, 1515–1527*.

Vignau-Wilberg, Thea. *Rembrandt auf Papier: Werk und Wirkung/Rembrandt and his Followers: Drawings from Munich*. Staatliche Graphische Sammlung München, Alte Pinakothek, Munich, 2001/02; Museum Het Rembrandthuis, Amsterdam, 2002.

Peter Paul Rubens, edited by Klaus Albrecht Schröder and Heinz Widauer. Albertina, Vienna, 2004.

Rembrandt, edited by Klaus Albrecht Schröder. Albertina, Vienna, 2004.

Scaillieréz, Cécile. *Rosso: Le Christ mort*. Musée du Louvre, Paris, 2004/05.

Gnann, Achim. *The Era of Michelangelo: Masterpieces from the Albertina*, edited by Klaus Albrecht Schröder. Peggy Guggenheim Collection, Venice, 2004; Albertina, Vienna, 2004; Guggenheim Museum, Bilbao, 2004/05.

Egon Schiele, edited by Klaus Albrecht Schröder. Albertina, Vienna, 2005/06.

Chapman, Hugh. *Michelangelo Drawings: Closer to the Master*. Teylers Museum, Haarlem, 2005/06; British Museum, London, 2006.

Witches' Lust and the Fall of Man: The Strange Fantasies of Hans Baldung Grien, edited by Bodo Brinkmann. Städel Museum, Frankfurt am Main, 2007.

Sebastiano del Piombo, 1485–1547: Raffaels Grazie – Michelangelos Furor, edited by Bernd Wolfgang Lindemann and Claudio Strinati. Museo Nazionale del Palazzo di Venezia, Rome, 2008; Staatliche Museen zu Berlin, Gemäldegalerie, 2008.

From Raphael to Carracci: The Art of Papal Rome, edited by David Franklin. National Gallery of Canada, Ottawa, 2009.

Sonnabend, Martin. *Michelangelo: Zeichnungen und Zuschreibungen/Drawings and Attributions*. Städel Museum, Frankfurt am Main, 2009.

Michelangelo: Public and Private; Drawings for the Sistine Chapel and Other Treasures from the Casa Buonarroti, edited by Susanne Kotz. Seattle Art Museum, 2009/10.

Michelangelo: The Drawings of a Genius, edited by Achim Gnann. Albertina, Vienna, 2010/11.

Bosch, Bruegel, Rubens, Rembrandt: Masterpieces of the Albertina, edited by Christof Metzger and Klaus Albrecht Schröder. Albertina, Vienna, 2013.

Chiaroscuro: Renaissance Woodcuts from the Collections of Georg Baselitz and the Albertina, Vienna, edited by Achim Gnann. Albertina, Vienna, 2013/14; Royal Academy of Arts, London, 2014.

Heikamp, Detlef, and Beatrice Paolozzi Strozzi. *Baccio Bandinelli: Scultore e Maestro (1493–1560)*. Museo Nazionale del Bargello, Florence, 2014.

Pontormo and Rosso Fiorentino: Diverging Paths of Mannerism, edited by Carlo Falciani and Antonio Natali. Palazzo Strozzi, Florence, 2014.

Alberti, Alessia, Alessandro Rovetta, and Claudio Salsi. *D'Après Michelangelo*. Castello Sforzesco, Milan, 2015/16.

Rembrandt's Naked Truth: Drawing Nude Models in the Golden Age, edited by Judith Noorman and David de Witt. Museum Het Rembrandthuis, Amsterdam, 2016.

Bambach, Carmen C. *Michelangelo: Divine Draftsman and Designer*. The Metropolitan Museum of Art, New York, 2017/18.

Raphael, edited by Achim Gnann. Albertina, Vienna, 2017/18.

Hans Baldung Grien: heilig | unheilig, edited by Holger Jacob-Friesen. Staatliche Kunsthalle Karlsruhe, 2019/20.

Triumph of the Body: Michelangelo and Sixteenth-Century Italian Draughtsmanship, edited by Zoltán Kárpáti. Szépművészeti Múzeum, Budapest, 2019.

Treves, Letizia. *Artemisia*. National Gallery, London, 2020.

Gegossen für die Ewigkeit: Die Bronzen der Fürsten von Liechtenstein, edited by Johann Kräftner. Palais Liechtenstein, Vienna-Rossau, 2023.

Picture Credits

Unless otherwise stated below: The ALBERTINA Museum, Vienna (photos: Daniel Antalfi, Ana Paula Franco, and Paul Landl).

p. 32: NMUIM / Alamy Stock Photo; p. 33: Private Collection, USA; pp. 34, 80, 98, 110: 2023 © Photo Scala, Florence – courtesy of the Ministero Beni e Att. Culturali e del Turismo; pp. 35, 37, 53, 129, 147, 211, 214, 215: © LIECHTENSTEIN. The Princely Collections, Vaduz–Vienna, Fürstliche Sammlungen Art Service GmbH; p. 39: By kind permission of the Earl of Leicester and the Trustees of the Holkham Estate / Bridgeman Images; p. 44: Don Mennig / Alamy Stock Photo; pp. 54/55: MB_Photo / Alamy Stock Photo; p. 56: EmmePi Images / Alamy Stock Photo (detail); pp. 57, 83: Photo © RMN-Grand Palais (musée du Louvre) / Thierry Le Mage; p. 59: Peter Barritt / Alamy Stock Photo (detail); p. 60: Photo © Musée du Louvre, Dist. RMN-Grand Palais / Raphaël Chipault; p. 62: Heritage Image Partnership Ltd. / Alamy Stock Photo; pp. 63, 198, fig. 29: © bpk / The Metropolitan Museum of Art; p. 68: public domain sourced / access rights from Mango Art / Alamy Stock Photo; p. 70: ART Collection / Alamy Stock Photo; p. 74: incamerastock / Alamy Stock Photo; p. 76: Lanmas / Alamy Stock Photo; p. 78: The Morgan Library & Museum, New York. I, 47. Purchased by Pierpont Morgan (1837–1913) in 1909; pp. 90, 216: Alinari Archives, Florence; p. 92: Wojciech Stróżyk / Alamy Stock Photo; p. 112: Carmen C. Bambach, *Michelangelo: Divine Draftsman and Designer* (New York: Metropolitan Museum of Art, 2017), 238; p. 127: KHM-Museumsverband; p. 146: adam eastland / Alamy Stock Photo; p. 157: Wolfgang Fuhrmannek, Hessisches Landesmuseum Darmstadt; p. 168: © The Trustees of the British Museum; p. 177: ART Collection / Alamy Stock Photo; p. 189: Bayerisches Nationalmuseum, Munich, Photo: Bastian Krack; pp. 191, 210: Gabinetto Fotografico delle Gallerie degli Uffizi; p. 194: Art Collection 2 / Alamy Stock Photo; p. 196, fig. 26: Artefact / Alamy Stock Photo; p. 196, fig. 27: Bayerische Staatsbibliothek Munich; p. 197: Staatliche Kunsthalle Karlsruhe; p. 198, fig. 30: Archivart / Alamy Stock Photo; p. 198, fig. 31: Pictorial Press Ltd. / Alamy Stock Photo; p. 202: imageBROKER.com GmbH & Co. KG / Alamy Stock Photo; p. 204: The Montreal Museum of Fine Arts, Christine Guest; p. 212, fig. 35: FOST / Alamy Stock Photo; p. 212, fig. 36: Photo © RMN-Grand Palais (musée du Louvre) / Hervé Lewandowski; p. 232: incamerastock / Alamy Stock Photo; p. 238: Album / Alamy Stock Photo; p. 239: Ulrich Ghezzi.

Full- and Double-Page Spreads

p. 7:	Detail from p. 33
p. 8:	Detail from p. 81
p. 11:	Detail from p. 43
p. 12:	Detail from p. 83
p. 17:	Detail from p. 58
pp. 20/21:	Detail from pp. 48/49
p. 23:	Detail from p. 24
p. 29:	Detail from p. 30
pp. 40/41:	Detail from p. 39, fig. 3
pp. 46/47:	Detail from p. 45
pp. 54/55:	Michelangelo, ceiling fresco of the Sistine Chapel, 1508–1512 (detail)
p. 65:	Detail from p. 66
pp. 72/73:	Detail from p. 71
pp. 86/87:	Detail from p. 85
p. 99:	Detail from p. 101
p. 125:	Detail from p. 127
pp. 132/133:	Detail from p. 131
p. 135:	Albrecht Dürer, *Human Proportion Studies*, from *Vier Bücher von menschlicher Proportion*, Nuremberg 1528
p. 167:	Detail from p. 173
pp. 192/193:	Detail from p. 201
pp. 220/221:	Detail from p. 222
pp. 252/253:	Detail from p. 249
p. 259:	Detail from p. 149

This catalogue has been published on the occasion of the exhibition

Michelangelo and Beyond

The ALBERTINA Museum, Vienna
September 15, 2023 – January 14, 2024

Annual partner of the ALBERTINA Museum — Bank Austria, Member of UniCredit

Partner of the ALBERTINA Museum — BMW

Sponsor of the exhibition — Raiffeisen Bank International

Exhibition

Director General
Klaus Albrecht Schröder

Curatorial Team
Achim Gnann, Constanze Johanna Malissa, Eva Michel, Martina Pippal, Klaus Albrecht Schröder

Curatorial Assistant
Lydia Eder

Exhibition Management
Barbara Buchbauer and Elisabeth Wolfik

Conservation Supervision
Eva Glück (Head of Department), Karine Bovagnet, Magdalena Duftner, Klaus Mohideen-Rubitzko, Alexandra Moser, Ida Rupp, Julia Wikarski

Framing and Mounting
Ines Aßmann, Armin Solderer, Andrew Draper, Viktor Moisejev, Gregor Kaufmann

Catalogue

Edited by
Eva Michel and Klaus Albrecht Schröder

Managing Editor
Lydia Eder

Authors
Elisabeth Dutz (ED)
Lydia Eder (LE)
Achim Gnann (AG)
Constanze Johanna Malissa (CJM)
Eva Michel (EM)
Martina Pippal (MP)
Klaus Albrecht Schröder (KAS)

Project Direction
Sandra Maria Rust

Editorial Direction, Prestel
Markus Eisen

Copy Editor
José Enrique Macián

Translations into English
Joshua Waterman (Preface and texts by ED, LE, AG, EM)
Ian Pepper (Texts by CJM, MP)
Michael Scuffil (Other texts by KAS)

Design
Klaus E. Göltz

Production
Cilly Klotz

Prepress
Reproline mediateam GmbH & Co. KG, Unterföhring

Typeface | Paper
Albertina, Myriad | Gardamatt ultra 150 g/m^2

Printing and Binding
L.E.G.O. Spa, Vicenza

Printed in Italy

Penguin Random House Verlagsgruppe
FSC® N001967

A CIP catalogue record for this book is available from the British Library.
Library of Congress Control Number: 2023943745

The Deutsche Nationalbibliothek lists this publication in the Deutsche Nationalbibliografie; detailed bibliographic data is available online at http://www.dnb.de.

ISBN 978-3-7913-7716-2 (English trade edition)
ISBN 978-3-7913-9116-8 (English museum edition)
ISBN 978-3-7913-7715-5 (German trade edition)
ISBN 978-3-7913-9115-1 (German museum edition)

www.prestel.com
www.albertina.at

Front Cover:
Michelangelo, *Studies for the Libyan Sibyl*, ca. 1510/11
The Metropolitan Museum of Art, New York, Purchase, Joseph Pulitzer Bequest, 1924 (detail, p. 63)

Back Cover:
Michelangelo, *Male Nude Seen from the Rear*, ca. 1504
The ALBERTINA Museum, Vienna (detail, pp. 48/49)

Frontispiece :
Copy after Michelangelo, *Archers Shooting at a Herm*, 1530–1560
The ALBERTINA Museum, Vienna (detail, p. 85)